The Relational Leader

Educational Leadership: Innovative, Critical, and Interdisciplinary Perspectives

Series Editors: *Jeffrey S. Brooks, Alan J. Daly, Yi-Hwa Liou, Chen Schechter and Victoria Showunmi*

The Educational Leadership series provides a forum for books that push the conceptual boundaries of educational leadership and that introduce novel perspectives with the promise of improving, challenging, and reconceptualizing the field of study and informing practice. Books in the series take a global, interdisciplinary focus and cover educational phases ranging from early years to higher education. They aspire to be field-leading innovations that advance new theories, topics, and methodologies. The series will be of interest to those working across disciplines such as educational leadership, school leadership, teacher education, sociology, anthropology, economics, psychology, political science, philosophy, and public policy.

Also available in the series:
Educational Leadership and Critical Theory: What Can School Leaders Learn from the Critical Theorists, edited by Charles L. Lowery, Chetanath Gautam, Robert White and Michael E. Hess

Forthcoming in the series:
Women Navigating Educational Research, Jana L. Carlisle

The Relational Leader

Catalizing Social Networks for Educational Change

Edited by Yi-Hwa Liou and Alan J Daly

BLOOMSBURY ACADEMIC
LONDON • NEW YORK • OXFORD • NEW DELHI • SYDNEY

BLOOMSBURY ACADEMIC
Bloomsbury Publishing Plc, 50 Bedford Square, London, WC1B 3DP, UK
Bloomsbury Publishing Inc, 1385 Broadway, New York, NY 10018, USA
Bloomsbury Publishing Ireland, 29 Earlsfort Terrace, Dublin 2, D02 AY28, Ireland

BLOOMSBURY, BLOOMSBURY ACADEMIC and the Diana logo are
trademarks of Bloomsbury Publishing Plc

First published in Great Britain 2024
Paperback edition published 2025

Copyright © Yi-Hwa Liou and Alan J Daly, 2024

Yi-Hwa Liou and Alan J Daly have asserted their right under the Copyright,
Designs and Patents Act, 1988, to be identified as Editors of this work.

Series design by Tjaša Krivec
Cover image © Niday Picture Library / Alamy Stock Photo

All rights reserved. No part of this publication may be: i) reproduced or transmitted in any form, electronic or mechanical, including photocopying, recording or by means of any information storage or retrieval system without prior permission in writing from the publishers; or ii) used or reproduced in any way for the training, development or operation of artificial intelligence (AI) technologies, including generative AI technologies. The rights holders expressly reserve this publication from the text and data mining exception as per Article 4(3) of the Digital Single Market Directive (EU) 2019/790.

Bloomsbury Publishing Plc does not have any control over, or responsibility for, any third-party websites referred to or in this book. All internet addresses given in this book were correct at the time of going to press. The author and publisher regret any inconvenience caused if addresses have changed or sites have ceased to exist, but can accept no responsibility for any such changes.

A catalogue record for this book is available from the British Library.

A catalog record for this book is available from the Library of Congress.

ISBN: HB: 978-1-3503-3642-1
PB: 978-1-3503-3646-9
ePDF: 978-1-3503-3643-8
eBook: 978-1-3503-3644-5

Series: Educational Leadership: Innovative, Critical, and Interdisciplinary Perspectives

Typeset by Integra Software Services Pvt. Ltd.

For product safety related questions contact productsafety@bloomsbury.com.

To find out more about our authors and books visit www.bloomsbury.com
and sign up for our newsletters.

Contents

List of Figures	vii
List of Tables	ix
List of Contributors	x
Series Editors' Foreword *Jeffrey S. Brooks, Chen Schechter, Alan J. Daly, Victoria Showunmi, and Yi-Hwa Liou*	xvi
Prologue: Growing Social Roots *Alan J. Daly and Yi-Hwa Liou*	xix

Part 1 Introduction: The Relational Leader

1	The Relational Leader: Mapping the Landscape of Leadership and Change through Social Networks *Yi-Hwa Liou and Alan J. Daly*	2
2	Organizational Advancement by Learning Together: Leadership for Professional Learning *Kenneth Leithwood*	16

Part 2 Students, Leadership, and Networks

3	Leading toward Relational Inclusivity for Students Identified as Having Special Educational Needs and Disabilities *Christoforos Mamas and David Trautman*	34
4	The Impact of Support Networks on the Education and Development of Pre-Service Teachers *Chloe Eddy and Christopher Downey*	50
5	Strong Ties and Social Boundaries: Social Networks and Program Influence on Pre-Service Teachers' Social Justice Teacher Identities *Peter Bjorklund Jr.*	73

Part 3 School-Wide Networks

6	Teachers' Interactions about Multilingual Learner Instruction: Considerations for Elementary School Leaders in the United States *Megan Hopkins, Lisa Matsukata, and Tracy M. Sweet*	96
7	Teacher Collaboration in Times of Change—Enhancing Existing Research in Norway through A Social Network Analysis Perspective *Esther T. Canrinus and Jo Inge Johansen Frøytlog*	115

8 Structures That Support Leader Development and School Improvement: Insights from Mixed Method Research *Darren Bryant and Allen Walker* 127

Part 4 System-Wide Leadership Networks

9 Competition to Cross-School Collaboration: A Social Network Perspective of Local System Leadership in England *Sotiria Kanavidou and Christopher Downey* 150
10 In Pursuit of Community of Learning: Investigating a Cross-School Leadership Team *Joelle Rodway, Rachel Cann, and Claire Sinnema* 172
11 The Role of Relationships: Illustrating System-Wide Disruption on Leadership Networks *David Trautman, Anita Caduff, and Alan J. Daly* 193
12 Knowledge Brokers as Informal Leaders in a Multi-District Learning Network *Joelle Rodway, Yi-Hwa Liou, Alan J. Daly, Mica Pollock, and Susan Yonezawa* 209

Part 5 Educational Leadership beyond Traditional Boundaries

13 An Investigation of the Northeast Big Data Innovation Hub through Social Network Analysis *René Bastón, Catherine Cramer, Alan J. Daly, Florence D. Hudson, Yi-Hwa Liou, Kathryn Naum, Wren Thompson, Laycca Umer, and Stephen Uzzo* 230
14 Bridging the Divide—How Principals Can Broker Information and Resources between Off- and Online Spaces *Martin Rehm, Alan J. Daly, Peter Bjorklund Jr., Yi-Hwa Liou, and Miguel del Fresno* 253

Part 6 Conclusion

15 New Directions and Next Steps for Social Network Research and Design of Teachers' Professional Development: Building Critical Network Literacy *Kira J. Baker-Doyle* 271
16 Where Are We Headed? A Relationally Focused Agenda for Research and Practice in Leadership *Yi-Hwa Liou and Alan J. Daly* 280

Index 299

Figures

1	A mycorrhizal network of the fungi Rhizopogon Spp. Genets and Douglas-fir Trees in a multi-aged old-Growth forest	xx
3.1	An example of a friendship network map	42
4.1	Simple mean line graph demonstrating the mean trajectory over time	60
4.2	Latent growth curve model of observation scores (Ob) and perceived self-efficacy (Dev) with standardized coefficients (model 1)	62
4.3	Latent growth curve model of observation scores (Ob) and perceived self-efficacy (Dev) with network intentionality at time 1 as a predictor, and showing standardized coefficients	63
6.1	Multilingual learner instructional advice or information networks, by school	109
8.1	Cascade design of educational infrastructure (adapted from Bryant & Walker, 2022)	136
8.2	Middle leaders advise networks for teaching and learning and capacity building	136
9.1	Network visualizations for three professional relations	159
10.1	Example of extracting an ego network from a larger network	175
10.2	Collaboration patterns within the Pohutukawa CoL and among CoL leadership team members	178
10.3	Collaboration ego networks for Pohutukawa CoL leadership team	181
11.1	Ego network "research evidence" of area superintendents over time	200
11.2	Area network "research evidence" over time	202
12.1	Conceptual Framework: Direct versus Indirect Knowledge Brokering	214
12.2	Network maps for advice and materials relations at time 1 and time 2 sized by indegree or betweenness	218
12.3	Relationship between indegree centrality (direct brokering) and betweenness centrality (indirect brokering)	220
13.1	Pre-existing collaboration networks (binary)	236
13.2	Collaboration networks	237
13.3	Go-to organization/s networks (binary)	239
13.4	Advice networks	240

13.5	Strategic planning networks (binary)	241
14.1	Sociograms: Bridging the divide between offline and online	260
14.2	Exemplary user combining online and offline Networks	261
14.3	Most commonly used (a) hashtags and (b) domains (Wordcloud)	262

Tables

4.1	A crosstabulation of the sample of pre-service teachers showing demographic characteristics of the participants	57
4.2	Model fit indices for null LGM for observation scores and development scores (perceived self-efficacy) over time	61
4.3	Predictive variables and their respective fit indices and regression weights to the slopes and intercepts of observation scores and self-efficacy	65
5.1	Sample demographics	78
5.2	Interview participants	81
5.3	Hierarchical OLS regression on teaching for social justice beliefs	83
6.1	Demographics of schools in the study sample	100
6.2	Hierarchical latent space models with regression coefficient estimates and intervals, showing results for the ESL teacher variable only	105
6.3	Hierarchical latent space models with regression coefficient estimates and intervals, showing results for the teacher trust variable only	108
8.1	Sample interview questions by topic	132
8.2	Leadership practices and distribution of interactions among leaders and teachers	134
9.1	Cohesion measures for the professional learning network	158
9.2	E-I index for the learning and teaching, professional development and use of data professional networks based on the participants' school/site	160
9.3	E-I index for the learning and teaching, professional development and use of data professional networks based on the participants' role	161
9.4	Regression analysis	162
9.A	Factor loading of the competition scale	166
10.1	Cohesion measures for school and CoL collaboration networks	179
12.1	Cohesion measures for advice and materials networks	217
13.1	Scale-level descriptive statistics of perceived innovative climate scale	234

Contributors

Yi-Hwa Liou, Ph.D., is Professor in the Department of Educational Management at the National Taipei University of Education, Taiwan. Her research primarily focuses on leadership and development, organizational change, professional and networked learning communities, with a particular methodological emphasis on social network analysis. She has been working with international research teams and scholars on multiple (inter)national research projects around the evolution of organizational networks and systems change and is committed to using network analysis to support organizations' strategic planning and development.

Alan J. Daly, Ph.D., is Professor and Director of the Joint Educational Leadership doctoral program at the University of California, San Diego, USA. His research and teaching are influenced by his sixteen years of public school experience in a variety of instructional and leadership roles. Professor Daly's research primarily focuses on the role of leadership, social networks, educational policy, and organizational theory. He draws on his methodological expertise in social network analysis in his work and has a book on the topic published by Harvard Press entitled, *Social Network Theory and Educational Change* and several other books on leadership and systems.

Kira Baker-Doyle, Ph.D., is Associate Director of Curriculum Instruction and the Director of the Center for Literacy at the University of Illinois at Chicago, USA. Dr. Baker-Doyle is the author of three books and over twenty-five peer-reviewed studies on teacher's social networks and professional learning. Her forthcoming book, *No Educator is An Island: Fostering Humanizing Professional Development through Critical Network Literacy*, is due to be published in Spring 2023 through Harvard Education Press.

René Bastón is Vice President of Strategic Alliances at Team8's Digital Health Foundry where he develops and executes strategies for foundry and portfolio company growth via strategic alliances; cultivates the Team8 Digital Health Ecosystem; and is a startup Ideation Team member. He is the co-founder of three startups and a national Lean Startup instructor for the U.S. National Science Foundation (NSF). His most recent role prior to Team8, was as the founding Executive Director of the Northeast Big Data Innovation Hub at Columbia University. René earned both his Master's in Biomedical Informatics and his B.A. from Columbia University, USA.

Peter Bjorklund Jr., Ph.D., is Postdoctoral Researcher in the Education Studies Department and Lecturer in Human Developmental Sciences at University of California San Diego, USA. His research focuses on social networks, trust, sense of belonging, and identity in K-16 educational contexts. Prior to completing his Ph.D. at UC San Diego he was a high school social studies teacher.

Darren Bryant is Professor of Education Policy at the School of Education, Curtin University in Western Australia. He was Associate Director of the Asia Pacific Centre for Leadership and Change (2014–2023) and Head of the Department of Education Policy and Leadership (2016–2023) at The Education University of Hong Kong, Hong Kong. He serves as Associate Editor of the International Journal of Educational Management. Previously, Darren worked as a middle leader, Curriculum Coordinator, and teacher in Hong Kong, China, and Canada. His research primarily focuses on leader development, middle leadership, and educational leaders' work in policy enactment.

Anita Caduff is a Ph.D. candidate in Education Studies at the University of California San Diego, USA. Her research interests include social network analysis and social capital, educational change, teacher and school leader social networks, cross-national research, newcomer and immigrant-origin students, multicultural and inclusive classrooms and schools, and parental engagement.

Rachel Cann is a Ph.D. candidate at the University of Auckland, New Zealand. Her Master's thesis investigated the actions that educational leaders can take to help enhance teacher well-being. Her doctoral studies explore the individual, relational, and organizational influences on educator well-being, drawing on positive psychology and social network theory. Building upon findings from initial empirical work, she is developing and implementing a social network intervention to improve educator well-being. Previously, Rachel was a head of science in an Auckland secondary school; she has also led cross-curricular teams of teachers for project-based learning, pastoral care, and teaching as inquiry.

Esther T. Canrinus is Professor at the Department of Education, University of Agder, Norway. Her research focuses on the coherence and quality of teacher education, teachers' professional development, and their professional identity. Collaboration, both national and international, characterizes her work. She is, furthermore, interested in teachers' social networks, classroom behavior, and teachers' and students' motivation.

Catherine B. Cramer is Assistant Director of the EarthCube Office at the San Diego Supercomputer Center, USA. She is also Director of the Woods Hole Institute, 501(c)3 nonprofit that brings leaders, thinkers, and doers together to converge new ideas for solutions to some of our biggest problems. She works at the intersection of data-driven science and learning, specifically as it pertains to the understanding of complexity and its application to data and network sciences, with a focus on underrepresented communities. She serves on the Boards of the Network Science Society and the Children's School of Science.

Christopher Downey is Professor of Education and Associate Dean Education for the Faculty of Social Sciences at the University of Southampton, UK. In his early career

Chris worked as a science teacher in high schools and gained experience of middle and senior leadership, and school-centered approaches to initial teacher education. His current research interests include the study of relational networks in a range of educational contexts including teachers and leaders in various settings engaged in educational improvement, students in pre-service teacher education and most recently students on programs of study involving complex transitions such as periods of professional placement.

Chloe Eddy is Doctoral Researcher at the Southampton Education School, University of Southampton, UK. Chloe's doctoral research aims to explore the way autism is diagnosed. Other notable research interests include social network analysis and advanced quantitative research methods. Chloe is also co-founder of the Partnership for Educational Reform, a student-run partnership that aims to address equity, diversity and inclusion in Education.

Miguel del Fresno, Ph.D., is Associate Professor at the Universidad Nacional de Educacion a Distancia, Spain, and teaches in the Masters of Communication program at Universidad de Navarra (UN), UPV (Bilbao), UCM (Madrid), and University of Sevilla in Spain, as well as a visiting professor at University of the Republic of Uruguay (Montevideo) and visiting researcher at the U.C. Berkley and U.C. San Diego. Miguel earned an MBA and an Executive Masters in e-Business from IE Business School, Madrid, Spain.

Jo Inge Johansen Frøytlog is Associate Professor of pedagogy at the Department of Educational Science, University of South-Eastern Norway, Norway. His main academic interests are teaching and learning through dialogue, educational uses of digital technology, mixed methods, and social network analysis.

Megan Hopkins is Associate Professor in the Department of Education Studies at the University of California, San Diego, USA. Her research examines whether and how state and local policies and practices enable or constrain equity for multilingual students in K–12 public schools.

Florence D. Hudson is Executive Director for the NSF Northeast Big Data Innovation Hub at Columbia University in New York City, USA, Principal Investigator for the COVID Information Commons, Founder of the National Student Data Corps, Founder and CEO of FDHint, LLC, an advanced technology and diversity & inclusion consulting firm, a former IBM Vice President and Chief Technology Officer, and NASA scientist. She is a published Springer editor and author for their women in engineering and science series. She earned her Mechanical and Aerospace Engineering degree from Princeton University, and executive education diplomas from Harvard Business School and Columbia University.

Sotiria Kanavidou is Ph.D. candidate at the School of Education, University of Southampton, UK. After receiving her BA in Early Childhood Education from the

Aristotle University of Thessaloniki, she worked as a pre-school teacher in various settings. In 2019, Sotiria received an M.Sc. from the University of Southampton and later she decided to continue her studies at a doctoral level. Her current research interests include the development of inter-school collaborative relations over time and the potential of school networks in promoting improvement and change, with a particular focus on Social Network Analysis and social network interventions.

Kenneth Leithwood, Emeritus Professor, University of Toronto, Canada, Honorary Professor, University College London, UK, and University of Nottingham, UK. Professor Leithwood's extensive research and writing is about school leadership, educational policy, and organizational change. Among his most recent books are *Leadership Development on a Large Scale: Lessons for Long-term Success* (2018, Corwin), *How School Leaders Contribute to Student Success* (2017, Springer), and *Linking Leadership to Student Learning (Jossey Bass)*. A bibliometric analysis published in 2019 found Professor Leithwood to be the most frequently cited, highest impact educational leadership researcher in the world.

Christoforos Mamas, Ph.D., is Assistant Professor in Transforming Special Education at the University of California, San Diego, USA. His research at the Department of Education Studies primarily examines the social participation and inclusion of students with disabilities in general education settings. Methodologically, Dr. Mamas applies social network analysis methods and perspectives as well as mixed methods approaches. His research is driven by a commitment toward bridging the gap between research and practice. One of the main contributions of his work is the development of a social network analysis toolkit to enable educators and school leaders to create more socially responsive and inclusive K-12 classrooms and school communities.

Lisa Matsukata is a Ph.D. student in Education Studies at the University of California, San Diego, USA. Her research interests involve language education policy, program evaluation, and multilingual students' identity development and sense of belonging in schools.

Kathryn Naum, PMP is Project Manager at the University of Illinois Urbana-Champaign, USA, where their work focuses on creating meaningful community engagement and communications strategy for scientific research communities. They hold a degree in sustainable development from Columbia University.

Mica Pollock, an anthropologist, is Professor of Education Studies and Director of the Center for Research on Educational Equity, Assessment, and Teaching Excellence (CREATE) at the University of California, San Diego, USA. Pollock's work emphasizes educators' crucial role in daily efforts for antiracism and equity and pinpoints the key role of communications in educators' work. Pollock's work at CREATE explores with colleagues how networks of partners can pursue collective equity efforts—and leverage an entire university to create K-12 local opportunities to learn.

Martin Rehm earned his Ph.D. at Maastricht University, the Netherlands. He is currently a postdoctoral scholar at the University of Regensburg, Germany. He is also the Chief Data Wrangler at the SOSNetLab, a joint project financed by the Bill & Melinda Gates Foundation. His research interests include informal learning in social media, social opportunity spaces and applying mixed-methods to assess the educational value of social media. His recent work includes contributions to the American Journal of Education, Teachers College Record and PlosOne.

Joelle Rodway is Assistant Professor in Educational Leadership Studies in the Faculty of Education at Memorial University, Canada. Her work queries how the relational patterns among and between education stakeholders both facilitate and constrain school improvement processes with specific interests in knowledge brokerage and professional learning. Currently, she is working with colleagues across Canada to develop a network of education researchers whose focus is on examining the ways in which professional learning (often unintentionally) reproduces privilege in ways that impede equitable education for all. Joelle is a former secondary school teacher who is passionate about connecting research and practice.

Claire Sinnema is Associate Professor at the Faculty of Education and Social Work, The University of Auckland, New Zealand. Her research focuses on educational improvement, and deals with the improvement of teaching and learning across five main strands—curriculum, networks, educational leadership, practitioner inquiry, and standards—fields that each influence (albeit in different ways) the nature of student experience in schooling, and the quality of outcomes for diverse learners. Her research is concerned with understanding how teachers and educational leaders, including system leaders, can improve their practice. It is also concerned with the role of policy in such improvement.

Tracy M. Sweet is Associate Professor in the Measurement, Statistics, and Evaluation Program at the University of Maryland, USA, and serves as the associate director of the Maryland Longitudinal Data System Center Research Branch. Her research focuses on statistical methodology for educational and social science applications, in particular social network analysis and machine learning.

Wren Thompson is a behavioral researcher, earning a Master's Degree in Museology and Evaluation at the University of Washington, USA. She combines approaches from wildlife biology, museum evaluation, learning science, and accessibility principles to understand informal learning environments. Wren's work covers a wide range of subjects from the prevalence of a novel avian distraction display to how art museums' gallery environments create or disrupt audiences' senses of belonging. Her recent work drives toward the creation of environments where all learners are supported in playful exploration and low-stakes failure, where their unique perspectives and expertise are valued as integral to the experience.

David Trautman is a Ph.D. student at the University of California, San Diego, USA in the Department of Education Studies. He is a former California public school teacher and administrator whose research focus revolves around equity and school district reform, with a particular emphasis on leadership. In addition to his scholarly work, Dave remains active in practitioner spaces as a consultant and coach with teacher leaders and aspiring administrators.

Laycca Umer is Manager of the Research, Exhibits, and Programs division at the New York Hall of Science, USA. Her work focuses on developing inclusive and equitable learning opportunities for diverse populations and leading research to inform the development of innovative learning tools. Her research interests include the intersection of technology and equity in STEM learning, and the changing perception of the role and utility of cultural institutions in broader society. She has a B.S. in Childhood Education and Psychology and a M.S. in TESOL from CUNY City College.

Stephen Miles Uzzo is Chief Technology Officer for the National Museum of Mathematics in New York City, USA, where he leads transformational efforts to deepen engagement in mathematical ideas through advanced technology. Dr. Uzzo's research interests also include the coupling of complex human and natural systems, evolution and scaling of complex networks, equity and artificial intelligence, and the effect of climate change on vulnerable coastal communities. He holds a terminal degree in network theory and environmental studies from Union Institute and serves on a number of institutional and advisory boards related to his interests.

Allan Walker is Research Chair Professor of International Education Leadership and Co-Director of the Asia Pacific Centre for Leadership and Change at The Education University of Hong Kong, Hong Kong. He was Dean of the Faculty of Education and Human Development from 2013 to 2020. He has experience as a teacher, principal, professor, and dean and has worked in universities in Australia, Singapore, and Hong Kong, where he spent the last twenty-five years. His research and writing focus on school leadership in East and Southeast Asia. Allan's most recent book is *Deciphering School Leadership in China: Conceptualisation, Context, and Complexities*.

Susan Yonezawa is Project Research Scientist at the University of California, San Diego, USA, and Associate Director of the Center for Research on Educational Equity, Assessment and Teaching Excellence (CREATE). Her work focuses on educational equity and access for underrepresented, low-income, students of color. She has published 25+ peer-reviewed journals and invited chapters documenting how K12 students interpret, understand, and access formal and informal educational opportunities, particularly in STEM. Yonezawa has received support from the National Science Foundation, Office of Naval Research, University of California, Price Philanthropies, Gates, Carnegie, and Spencer Foundations, and the US Departments of Defense & Education.

Series Editors' Foreword

Jeffrey S. Brooks[1]
Chen Schechter[2]
Alan J. Daly[3]
Victoria Showunmi[4]
Yi-Hwa Liou[5]

The history of thought and practice in educational leadership can be conceived as a punctuated equilibrium (English, 2008). The arc of the field's history is a steady evolution of traditional ideas centered around management, administration, efficiency, rational decision-making, authority, and power (Beck & Murphy, 1993). Heavily influenced by business administration and management literature, the field is also shaped by sociology, anthropology, economics, psychology, political science, philosophy, and public policy. As an applied field, scholarship in educational leadership shapes—and is shaped by—developments in schools, universities, policy making processes, and in other formal and informal education settings (Brooks & Miles, 2006). This has meant that there is space in the field for both highly theoretical work and research grounded in a specific context. Of course, quite a lot of scholarship in the field seeks these aims at the same time as a way of generating relevant knowledge *in situ* while also advancing thought and practice throughout the world (Gunter, 2016).

Occasionally, ideas are introduced that compel scholars and practitioners to reconsider the foundations of "what they know" and adopt new ways of thinking about and practicing their work. Among intellectual movements that upset educational leadership's orthodoxy were postmodernism, critical theory, feminist theories, social justice, culturally relevant school leadership, distributed leadership, and more purposeful studies of the relationship between leadership and learning (Brooks & Normore, 2017). Each of these domains of inquiry produced novel perspectives on educational leadership (to be sure there are others—we do not pretend this is an exhaustive list) that inform contemporary conceptual and empirical research. Additionally, each of these intellectual movements initiated a paradigmatic shift in the way people engage in the practice of educational leadership, think about their work, and conduct themselves as leaders and followers in formal and informal education settings.

For all this innovation, the arc toward improvement has been slow, and often the emphasis on the traditional has subdued the exploration of the radical. This book series seeks to establish a space for research that (a) explores promising concepts at the edges of the field, (b) encourages the publication of new ideas, and (c) critiques contemporary assumptions about educational leadership. Our hope is that the series may play some role in prompting future conceptual and empirical revolutions that will move the field forward via emergent scientific and artistic revolutions.

New perspectives are emerging from across the field and other disciplines that have great potential to influence (and be influenced by) educational leadership scholarship and practice. Among these are exciting developments related to sustainability and climate change, social networking, religion and spirituality, immigration and globalization, student-centered leadership, and innovative contributions to traditional topics such as community-school relations, gender, race, ethnicity, sexuality, diversity, intercultural/cross-cultural studies, globalization, early childhood and adult education, student voice, and activism. To be sure, there are others. While it is easy to point to individual articles or small groups of scholars working in these areas, there is no clear publication outlet for deeper, focused, and nuanced works that explore and challenge such ideas in the detail afforded by a full-length book or highly focused edited volume. Reaching out beyond the field of educational leadership, there are developments in sociology, anthropology, political science, policy studies, psychology, curriculum studies, brain-based research, environmental science, creativity studies, medicine, law, and other fields that have yet to be deeply explored or understood in terms of their possible applicability to educational leadership. We see the series as a place where such disciplines, ideas, and lines of inquiry can come into dialogue and create innovation. We see this book series as a forum for interdisciplinary, innovative, creative, and indeed controversial work.

In addition to providing a forum for such exciting ideas, we aim for this series to also include a diversity of authors and contexts under-represented in many extant book series. This means diversity of author, geographical context, and perspective. As this is a series of research books, we anticipate the primary audience being academics, but we also anticipate that the topics will be of interest to practicing school leaders, teachers, policymakers, and scholars working across disciplines such as educational leadership, school leadership, teacher education, sociology, anthropology, economics, psychology, political science, philosophy, and public policy. We invite you to join us in the conversation to share your work and your insights as we explore and extend the field of educational leadership.

Notes

1   Curtin University School of Education, Australia.
2   Bar-Ilan University, Israel.
3   University of California, San Diego, USA.
4   UCL Institute of Education, England.
5   National Taipei University of Education, Taiwan.

References

Beck, L. G., & Murphy, J. (1993). *Understanding the principalship: Metaphorical themes, 1920s–1990s*. New York: Teachers College Press.

Brooks, J. S., & Miles, M. T. (2006). From scientific management to social justice … and back again? Pedagogical shifts in educational leadership. *International Electronic Journal for Leadership in Learning, 4*(1), 2–15.

Brooks, J. S., & Normore, A. H. (2010). Educational leadership and globalization: Literacy for a glocal perspective. *Educational Policy, 24*(1), 52–82. doi:10.1177/0895904809354070

Brooks, J. S., & Normore, A. H. (2017). *Foundations of educational leadership: Developing excellent and equitable schools*. Routledge: New York.

English, F. W. (2008). *Anatomy of professional practice: Promising research perspectives on educational leadership*. Lanham, MD: Rowman & Littlefield Education.

Gunter, H. (2016). *An intellectual history of school leadership practice and research*. London: Bloomsbury.

Jackson, L. L., Lopoukhine, N., & Hillyard, D. (1995). Ecological restoration: A definition and comments. *Restoration Ecology, 3*(2), 71–5.

Kensler, L. A. W., & Uline, C. L. (2017). *Leadership for green schools: Sustainability for our children, our communities, and our planet*. New York: Routledge, Taylor & Francis Group.

Kensler, L. A. W., & Uline, C. L. (2019). Educational restoration: A foundational model inspired by ecological restoration. *International Journal of Educational Management, 33*(6), 1198–1218. doi:10.1108/ijem-03-2018-0095

Senge, P. M., Cambron-McCabe, N., Lucas, T., Smith, B., & Dutton, J. (2012). *Schools that learn (updated and revised): A fifth discipline fieldbook for educators, parents, and everyone who cares about education*. Crown Business.

Stafford-Smith, M., Griggs, D., Gaffney, O., Ullah, F., Reyers, B., Kanie, N., & O'Connell, D. (2017). Integration: The key to implementing the sustainable development goals. *Sustain Sci, 12*(6), 911–19. doi:10.1007/s11625-016-0383-3

Prologue: Growing Social Roots

The cover of our book is from a painting by Vincent Van Gogh done in 1888 entitled, the Sower at Sunset. Van Gogh turned to the theme of the "Sower" on numerous occasions as he was drawn to imagery around agrarian life and connection to the natural world. It is in many ways this connection to the natural world that underscores the core messages of connection and relationships in this book. These foundational ideas remind us of some research around the *Wood Wide Web* (otherwise known by its less fun name, Mycorrhizal Network).

In an excellent article written by Kevin Beiler and colleagues (2010)[1] indicated that there was a network of connections among and between trees in every section of a forest (shown below). The researchers found that within the forest roots crisscross and overlap as might have been expected. However, the scholars also found that the roots of these trees are connected to one another through fungi attached to the roots. These fungi essentially act as a link between the root systems of different types of tress and are "brokers" connecting otherwise disconnected trees and ultimately creating an interdependent system (shown below).

This graph represents an interconnected and interdependent network between trees at the root level. The fungi, in their brokerage capacity, support trees to essentially share resources such as sugar, nitrogen, and phosphorus between and among themselves. Interestingly, this network of connections also provides for a type of early warning system. If one tree is under attack from a beetle or pest that tree can actually "warn" other trees (both of the same species and other species of trees) to raise a defensive response to ward off the upcoming siege. Even more remarkable, a dying tree may send its resources out to the larger community of trees for the collective benefit of the wood wide web. For example, seedlings that may be in a shady location in the wood and require a supplement of energy resources may receive those resources from other healthier trees.

The notion that trees themselves are surviving and thriving based on a network of connections is a powerful and potentially instructive perspective for the emphasis of our book the larger effort of understanding social systems. The *Wood Wide Web* as research and as an idea. The forest grows and continues to thrive based on a set of resource exchanges, but without the individual trees themselves adding to the larger network there can be no exchange. This suggests that relational leaders have to consider the network and the individual to understand and support educational systems.

This book and the work of relational leadership is about growing and nurturing the social roots in order for systems to grow and thrive. We hope you enjoy the book and take the lessons from the natural and social world to heart in the work of relational leadership.

Alan J. Daly and Yi-Hwa Liou

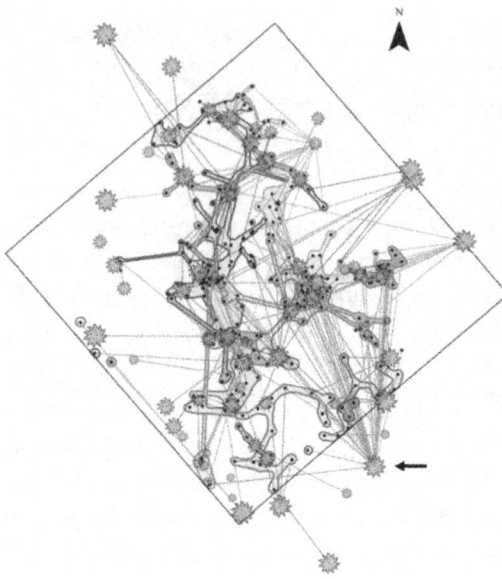

Figure 1 A mycorrhizal network of the fungi Rhizopogon Spp. Genets and Douglas-fir Trees in a multi-aged old-growth forest.

Note

1   Beiler, K. J., Durall, D. M., Simard, S. W., Maxwell, S. A., & Kretzer, A. M. (2010), Architecture of the wood-wide web: *Rhizopogon* spp. genets link multiple Douglas-fir cohorts. *New Phytologist*, 185(2), 543–53. https://doi.org/10.1111/j.1469-8137.2009.03069.x

Part 1

Introduction: The Relational Leader

The Relational Leader: Mapping the Landscape of Leadership and Change through Social Networks

Yi-Hwa Liou and Alan J. Daly

Introduction

Despite decades of attention, research, and reform efforts, rising social and educational inequality at a global scale has become a major fault line of our time. This is not to undermine the strides made; however, as a global educational community that is deeply committed to sustaining social good for educational improvement, we have a long distance to travel in providing quality and equitable education. Perhaps one key driver of the rise in social inequality in recent decades is that many educational systems—and, in fact, individual educators, schools, and districts—operate as independent units. As such, they may continue to create and replicate separate and unequal opportunities for learners and communities.

As our society has become increasingly interconnected and interdependent, many decisions, actions, and inactions are mutually influential and consequential to individual and collective outcomes. This network-driven society directly affects education, demanding its radical transformation if we want to cultivate future-ready citizens. Such a transformation requires systems change as well as leadership that enables that change. Failure to attend to the interdependent and interconnected nature of educational systems may inhibit our collective ability to address pressing issues that have, for far too long, plagued educational organizations across the globe.

This book is grounded in the idea that educational entities are ecological systems embedded in a larger network of social systems where interdependent subsystems and agents (organizations and individuals) connect and evolve in concert to create conditions that can result in diverse and equitable learning opportunities (Alfadala et al., 2021; Hannon et al., 2019; Shaked & Schechter, 2020). Of central importance are network relationships that facilitate change efforts and the kind of leadership that enables such change across educational systems. While this view places educational ecosystems at the top of the global agenda for sustainable lifelong learning, most reform and leadership efforts have not kept up with our fast-changing global society, which has become increasingly complex, connected, and intertwined. It is this concern that motivated us to develop this book. A decade ago, we had the opportunity to witness and document several relation-based change efforts to address educational issues related to learning, leadership, and reform (Daly, 2010). Now, with another decade of advanced work in this space, we have had the privilege of collecting the set of studies in this edited volume. This work allows us to continue to forge knowledge that not only helps address equity issues but also informs practices in educational change and leadership.

Our argument for focusing on networks in educational change and leadership is grounded in the idea that the work of change is a people endeavor—one that is highly relational and involves leadership efforts. As such, we foreground the role of relationships and leaders through and with networks in the deep work of educational change (Baker-Doyle, 2017; Daly, 2010; Daly & Russell, 2022; Finnigan et al., 2018; Greany & Kamp, 2022; Leithwood, 2019; Pitts & Spillane, 2009; Supovitz et al., 2019). This scholarship, coupled with an intuitive sense that relationships are central to change, brings important attention to connections between relational networks, leadership, and change efforts. This book attends to these aspects of change and continued pressing concerns in research and practice from a social network perspective. The perspective is best suited for guiding the ecology of educational research, practices, and policies, as it takes into consideration the interdependent and interconnected nature of the social world in which we live, work, and learn.

Empirical and Practical Inquiries and Observations

In moving forward with this social endeavor, if research and ultimately practice are to help improve systems and outcomes for equity and excellence, the research and practice communities of educational change and leadership must address the following fundamental questions: How do we define educational leaders in the educational change equation? What are the roles of educational leaders in the educational change equation in our interconnected world? How can educational organizations leverage networks to create the conditions for the equitable learning systems that are necessary for the overall well-being of students, teachers, and their organizations? How do networks provide an opportunity to challenge the social status quo in education? In what ways can individual leaders in a networked social system develop and exert social network literacy to inform and improve the efficacy of change efforts? The chapters in this volume respond to these essential questions.

The book is built upon four important observations from existing research and practice. First, the relationship between educational leadership and systems improvement is exceedingly complex, dynamic, and socially driven, and thus requires attention to multiple aspects of systems change. For any change to happen, it must be enacted by people who are embedded or work in social structures of relationships that facilitate or constrain the diffusion of practices. In this regard, the key determinant of how change takes effect, diffuses, and is sustained resides in the patterns of relationships that may support or constrain individual and collective actions (Balkundi & Kilduff, 2006; Lin, 2009). This is the social and relational element we refer to in this book; it is the interactivity between and among individuals, groups, and organizational entities (Liou & Daly, 2021, 2022). This is a key component in facilitating learning during change processes for sustainable improvement (Daly et al., 2020; Shirrell & Spillane, 2020). Yet existing research that links leadership and reform from this socio-relational perspective is limited and often pays minimal attention to key aspects of organizational behaviors, such as intra-/inter-personal, intra-/inter-organizational, and between people, policy, and/or organizations (Greany & Kamp, 2022; Kilduff & Krackhardt, 2008; Russell et al., 2015).

Second, in recent years we have seen rapidly growing interest in using networks as a promising lens through which to consider how social systems work. What remains unaddressed in education and leadership, however, is how the field defines and uses the concept in research and practice. We have seen some scholars interchangeably use the terms *communities* (Lieberman, 2000; Stoll, 2010), *learning circles* (Fahmi Dajani & Yousef, 2014; Tripp, 2004), *networked PLCs* (Jackson & Temperley, 2006; Katz & Earl, 2010), and *(professional) learning networks* (Azorín et al., 2020) to describe phenomena related to group work or collective professional practices. And some use the term *networks* from a structuralist perspective to investigate structural effects on individual or organizational outcomes or behaviors (Hinds et al., 2000; Penuel et al., 2009; Tortoriello & Krackhardt, 2017; Wullschleger et al., 2023). As a growing number of scholars and practitioners use the term *network*, there is a need to better understand the space and perhaps offer some coherence to the term. Thus, in this volume, as we explore each study, we discuss what we mean by *social networks* in different educational settings across several countries and levels of educational systems as well as how leadership is shaped and understood.

Third, the fact that we live in a social world—and as such are deeply affected by others, sometimes in ways in which we are unaware—suggests the underlying influence of social embeddedness on our work and life. Research suggests that our happiness, health, weight, voting behavior, and even wealth are influenced by the social networks in which we are embedded, and yet our fluency around social networks is limited (Organisation for Economic Co-operation and Development, 2020; Thomas & Gupta, 2021; Webster et al., 2021). This further suggests a need to develop the social network literacy of individuals. Those who are network literate are more likely to be intentional about shaping their social networks and to use networks to achieve purposive outcomes; as such, organizational systems would benefit from the intentional design and practice of social network literacy (Baker-Doyle, 2023; Pegrum, 2010). As learning and leading for equity are interactive, social, and context-specific (Brooks & Normore, 2010; Brown & Shaked, 2018; Shaked & Schechter, 2020; Showunmi & Kaparou, 2017), and at their best create change in the learners, leaders, and systems in which they do their work, attending to the social network literacy of educational leaders is imperative as they go about creating socially embedded and equitable learning ecosystems (Walcutt & Schatz, 2019).

Fourth, while nearly all research on educational leadership links to these basic notions to some extent, education social network scholarship has not been fully realized globally. This is due in part to a limited focus on social networks (Daly, 2012; Henrick et al., 2017), the scarcity of (longitudinal) network data, and the frequent failure to articulate how given research findings connect to local practices (Coburn & Penuel, 2016; Coburn et al., 2021; Peurach et al., 2022). In addressing this gap, the chapters in this book draw on findings from a variety of empirical studies conducted in different educational settings across several countries and propose a series of implications related to leadership practice and change that can be applied in many more settings that the few countries showcased on this volume.

Within the text we include studies from England, Japan, New Zealand, Norway, and the United States of America (US) to provide various perspectives and approaches to change practices that are network oriented. While each of these countries has its unique cultural, social, economic, and political contexts that shape its educational systems, practices, and policies, their effort in foregrounding relational aspect of reform is noteworthy. As is evidenced in education policy developments: for instance, the "Community of Learning" policy of 2016 in New Zealand, self-improving school-led system blueprint of 2014 in England, and the Norwegian competence development model for schools (Government of Norway, 2017). Similarly, recent reforms in Japan have aimed at promoting internationalization in education through International Baccalaureate programs and introducing new curricula and teaching methods to enhance innovation, creativity, and collaboration. In the United States, there are ongoing emphases on equity, inclusion, diversity in education, as well as efforts to promote systemic reform and social and emotional learning. While the selection of study contexts is certainly not exhaustive, we believe that it offers nuanced insights in different contexts related to the socio-relational aspect of change. The collection may also enrich the discussion around common themes, challenges, and opportunities that transcend national boundaries. We are hopeful the book is a starting place for a much wider global discussion in these spaces.

Many pieces of research and resulting practice suggest the growing importance of the socio-relational space in leadership and change. Our hope is that this knowledge can be translated into languages that practitioners not only understand, but also carry out through network-based leadership practices that are focused on systemic change in educational settings and research.

Relational Leadership

From the outset, we are not advocating for a particular style of educational leadership. Rather, we seek to strengthen our understanding of the nature of leadership and of being in leadership through a social network approach. In 2022, we published an article in the 4th edition of the *International Encyclopedia of Education* (Tierney et al., 2022). There, we discussed in detail the type of leadership that takes a network approach to systems change (Liou & Daly, 2022). In the current text, we draw on some of the discussion in that article to present what we mean by *relational leadership*.

In a nutshell, relational leadership presents itself in the socio-relational space as a way of being influential in a social system. The level of influence is predominately determined by individuals' relational connectivity with others within a given social or organizational system. Their connectivity can facilitate or hinder the flow of resources—information, idea, knowledge, materials, and so on—that can be used for achieving individual or collective purposes. This socio-relational aspect of leadership shifts our attention from individual, trait-based leadership to sets of relationships that surround a leader and shape that leader's role.

Relationships in the form of social interactions serve as a medium through which leadership is exerted. In this sense, leadership occurs through interaction and can flow between the agent and subject of influence. This means that the influence of leadership is not necessarily unidirectional. In a school organization, for example, a teacher who serves as a resource hub—that is, they are frequently sought out for advice or information—tends to have a high degree of connections. They tend to possess an advantage point to filter, broker, or disseminate resources to or among those to whom they have a direct or indirect tie. At the same time, they are exposed to the idea or information shared by their subject of influence through exchanges or interactions. This suggests that leadership is reciprocal and a relational phenomenon. Leaders and their constituent parts are both important components of understanding leadership influence. As such, leaders in educational systems can be defined as those individuals in networks of relational ties who possess a certain degree of social influence over the practice of others toward a purpose.

This view of leaders pertains not only to those in formal positions with designated leadership titles but also to those who play informal leadership roles as determined by their relational ties (Balkundi & Kilduff, 2006; Penuel et al., 2010). The social and relational role of both types of leaders—formal and informal—is not mutually exclusive. A formal leader can also play an important informal leadership role, and vice versa. Importantly, the notion of leadership roles (formal and informal) also applies to the study of inter-organizational networks (e.g., cross-school, cross-sector collaboration) because leadership and organizational change are human endeavors that involve the social and relational work of individuals representing their organizations. Keep this in mind later as we introduce some of the chapters that examine networks beyond the school level.

Through a socio-relational lens, *relational leadership* points toward the essential nature inherent in leaders' day-to-day practices. These practices involve social activities; building relationships or (un)maintenance; distributing, accessing, or mobilizing resources; and exerting network influences at different levels of educational systems toward an outcome or purpose. These practices are essentially a relational way of being in leadership and making change. Social networks provide a tool, data, a method, a perspective, and an approach that can help the field understand the relational nature of leadership and change.

Ultimately, we are social beings living in a social world. That sociability does not stop outside the schoolhouse door or when we are in physical isolation. In fact, the work of social networks is consequential for outcomes at the individual, dyadic, group, and organizational-system level. Social systems together with social network theory and analysis offer a useful and complimentary framework for understanding and exploring the influence of social infrastructure on efforts toward change at different levels. Taken together, we argue, leading and learning are interactive, socio-relational, and at their best create changes in learners, leaders, and the systems in which they do their work. That leadership is not confined to certain roles in educational organizations; rather, it flows through networks of roles that comprise organizations' social systems.

In this regard, leadership is a systems quality that is embedded within networks of social systems and shaped by social processes. It is this social and relational nature of leadership that drives the work of change in education.

Overview of the Book

With these gaps, research inquiries, and concepts in mind, this book is intended to inspire, support, and push practitioners and researchers as they go about making educational change and exerting leadership in schools, districts, and broader systems. In the chapters that follow, we present a broad agenda for research on educational change and leadership that we hope can galvanize and create synergies with the efforts of practitioners and many research investigators. Following an introductory part, four individual parts contain studies that are connected by theme and within particular educational systems. These chapters are followed by a conclusion part where we summarize the key ideas and new learnings in the book and offer suggestions for next steps.

Introductory Chapters

In this introductory chapter, we have provided a rationale for the need to attend to leadership and educational change from a social network perspective. This discussion foregrounds the role of relationships in a broad sphere of educational ecosystems and systems change while discussing the social and relational aspects of leadership that are necessary to bring about change.

In Chapter 2, Leithwood provides a more in-depth introduction to leadership, with a particular focus on professional learning through the kind of organizational designs that facilitate it. Leithwood both guides and pushes the field of educational leadership to reorient leadership practices from a collective learning perspective. The intention of this unique and important piece is to provide clear but non linear steps and guidelines for leaders to practice their own work for individual and collective learning and development. It represents an increasing area of interest for social network scholars who intend to explore the relationship between leadership, learning, and organizational change. Together, the two introductory chapters set up the core parts of the text.

Part 2: Students, Leadership, and Networks

Part 2 focuses on networks of student learners. As leadership can be manifested in classrooms among and between students, the second part describes student-learner networks that cover a range of cohorts, including K–12 students and pre-service teachers in teacher preparation programs. The authors in this part address critical research gaps in special and inclusive education and in teacher education by attending to the social and relational aspects of learning. In particular, they draw on social network concepts and analysis to explore peer social support networks among the target learners and to examine how these networks play a role in understanding classroom inclusivity, personal growth and performance, peer influence, and professional identity. In addition, the pieces extend the current empirical research by providing different kinds of network analysis that attend to network effects at the individual, dyadic, and whole-network levels.

In Chapter 3, Mamas and Trautman introduce a novel way of measuring the degree of inclusivity in a classroom by using a social network analysis toolkit to examine students' social support networks (e.g., friendship). They posit that relational inclusivity is seen as equity and can be measured through peer networks. Further, they offer specific guidelines for how school leaders can use the toolkit and its results to inform the creation of culturally responsive and inclusive learning environments. Particular attention is paid to the social embeddedness of students with special educational needs and disabilities within their classroom networks as an effort to discuss equity and inclusion in education as well as school leadership for equitable learning.

Chapters 4 and 5 introduce another set of important but underexplored student networks in teacher education—that is, cohorts of pre-service teachers. Chapter 4, presented by Eddy and Downey, examines pre-service teachers in England, looking at their peer support networks over a one-year training program and the extent to which these networks are associated with the development of self-efficacy and instructional performance. A significant contribution of this work is the longitudinal examination of actor-level network connectivity (e.g., outdegree) and the consideration of critical factors (i.e., perceived support-seeking and peer trust) to which those developments are attributed over time.

The study presented by Bjorklund in Chapter 5 investigates networks of close relationships among two cohorts of pre-service teachers in the US context. Special attention is paid to examining how pre-service teachers shape their social justice identities as they engage in close relationships with peers in their preparation program. This is one of few studies to utilize a mixed-methods approach in exploring pre-service teachers' networks, learning contexts, and identities. Another unique and important contribution of this piece is the use of an actor-level, ethno-racial E-I (External-Internal) index to measure the degree of in-group or out-group cohesion as a way to represent pre-service teachers' inclinations to interact with individuals from similar or different ethno-racially identified groups. Together with Chapter 4, this chapter provides important implications for designing social infrastructure in teacher education programs that enables individuals' leadership agency to impact their identify, efficacy, and overall development.

As a group, the three chapters in Part 2 point to the influence of peer networks on access to social support. They also suggest that peer social support is consequential to better outcomes, such as more equitable and inclusive learning environments, enhanced self-efficacy and teaching performance, and stronger professional identities.

Part 3: School-wide Networks

The third part turns our attention from student learners' social networks to the networks of in-service teachers and administrators at the school level in multiple contexts.

Networks of educators have gained much attention in the research in the last ten years; however, in some contexts (e.g., Norway, Taiwan), they remain understudied. The chapters in Part 3 represent some of the latest work in this area. They introduce several forms of school networks—including grade-level teams, teams of teacher leaders and middle leaders, and an ego network of school principals and their administrative teams. The pieces focus on networks of formal school leaders (principals, team lead, administrators) as well as informal school leaders (key players in social networks). They discuss how networks help us understand the social terrain of these leaders and how networks can inform decisions and practices in relation to professional learning and development, reform implementation, and school improvement.

In Chapter 6, Hopkins, Matsukata, and Sweet examine factors that explain teachers' advice—and information-seeking relationships around teaching and student learning across eight elementary schools in two US school districts. Their focus on all teaching staff within these schools provides a holistic understanding of school-wide improvement efforts with respect to how teachers interact with their colleagues to shape their instructional practices to support multilingual learners. Attention to multilingual learners' learning in the formation of relational ties is very much needed in research and practice, and this piece is one of the mixed-methods studies in this collection. Beyond its substantive contributions, a unique and important feature is the use of hierarchical latent space models to analyze multischool network data. This work is particularly useful as a way to suggest an alternative, novel way of conducting network analysis.

Teacher collaboration is widely studied across many international contexts, though little is known in the Norwegian context. Canrinus and Frøytlog address this gap in Chapter 7 as they introduce how teacher collaboration is orchestrated under Norway's recent national curriculum policy framework and how social networks can be used to understand teacher teams and collaboration. They describe an important factor in the Norwegian school context—the role of the school principal, who is in charge of how "common time" is organized for teacher teams. This policy and school context has striking implications for evolving network structures among teachers as they are encouraged to work in teams. The authors also review several recent, more general studies on teacher collaboration conducted in Norway to show the research efforts, gaps, and focus in this area. They then provide directions for future research from a network perspective. This chapter is the first attempt to utilize social network concepts and perspectives to disentangle complex professional behaviors of teachers in Norway as they work in teams to implement a national curriculum reform.

The mixed-methods study presented by Bryant and Walker in Chapter 8 was conducted in Japan. Again, we have little knowledge regarding the use of social networks in exploring school leadership and improvement in this context. Bryant and Walker examine the role of school principal leadership in the development of middle leaders (e.g., subject-area or program coordinators) in one Japanese international school that offers International Baccalaureate programs. The chapter focuses on the design of social infrastructure and how it may influence the network configurations of middle leaders as they engage in professional conversations with their teacher colleagues and in efforts to promote school improvement initiatives.

The authors present an infrastructure design model (the cascade model) to explain an interconnected but tiered approach to structuring professional learning. The focus of middle leaders and infrastructure design provides a unique and important—albeit overlooked—perspective on leadership capacity building for professional learning.

The collection of studies in Part 3 continues to push the field to attend to some overlooked areas of school-wide reform (e.g., instructional practice of multilingual learners, the social terrain of teacher teams and middle leaders) as we continue to formulate leadership practice. The part explores how leadership may be configured and distributed across formal and informal leadership roles and the relationship of leadership to change.

Part 4: System-wide Leadership Networks

From a global viewpoint, the intersection between networks and leadership within a larger school community (e.g., a school district, a cross-school learning network, a community of learning) is relatively understudied. The chapters in Part 4 thoughtfully address this gap by presenting recent research from England, New Zealand, and the United States. The authors explore multiple forms of school community systems and examine networks of collaborative relationships among formal and informal leaders as they work jointly for a common purpose.

In Chapter 9, Kanavidou and Downey investigate multischool collaboration networks among school leaders within a formal professional learning system in England that is working toward capacity building for improvement and development of system leadership. They present structural properties of three types of collaboration networks—around learning and teaching, use of data, and professional development— and reveal factors associated with the degree of collaborative ties. They find that of these factors, a sense of competition between schools enhances leaders' intention to collaborate with other schools, formulating a unique phenomenon they call *co-opetition*. In addition, like the authors of Chapter 8, these authors reveal the important but understudied role of middle leaders in brokering connectivity for collaboration and cohesion across a school system.

Chapter 10, by Rodway, Cann, and Sinnema, moves the policy context from England to New Zealand. These authors present a multischool network formed under the Community of Learning (CoL) policy context. A CoL is typically composed of schools from primary to secondary levels, and the CoL policy promotes cross-school collaboration. Focusing on the role of cross-school and within-school leaders in facilitating collaboration, the authors reveal several structural properties of the network and network positions of these leaders in bridging ties for collaboration. This is one of the few studies that present the ego networks of a leadership team within its larger CoL network. Moreover, the study further disentangles collaboration relationships by looking at ties that connect members from different schools as well as ties that only involve leadership team members. It offers a unique perspective on the very current topic of interschool collaboration through an in-depth and multiangle understanding of what is often treated as a monolithic concept of collaboration.

In Chapter 11, Trautman, Caduff, and Daly situate the social system in one large urban school district in the United States. They investigate a longitudinal set of network data from a districtwide leadership team as the district undergoes organizational restructuring and churn. The authors focus on the relationship between leaders that involves the adoption of new ideas based on research evidence/results as a way to understand knowledge communities that are crucial to organizational change. Specifically, they present four case studies to illuminate the relationships between network interactions around research evidence use and the level of leadership churn—in this case, superintendent mobility. The study provides a unique lens through which to understand some of the untapped areas that help explain change in network structures during leadership churn and organizational restructuring.

Chapter 12, by Rodway, Liou, Daly, Pollock, and Yonezawa, moves beyond a single district or interschool system to investigate the interdistrict social system of two US school districts that have feeder relationships with each other. Scholarship that uses a social network approach to examine the pattern of feeder relationships between and across entire districts remains limited. The authors examine a longitudinal set of network data to investigate an interdistrict network of mathematics teaching professionals as they seek advice or exchange materials with one another. One of the important contributions of this work is the emphasis on knowledge brokers in bridging relational resources that are critical to sustaining feeder relationships. The findings shed new light on how relational infrastructure can be designed to facilitate an interdistrict learning ecosystem for professional learning and development.

The studies in Part 4 continue to push the field to think systematically about leadership and change and to address aspects that remain understudied. Underlying each of these studies is the idea of leadership influence beyond school boundaries and across the larger system in which schools reside. Many of these chapters underscore the importance of social networks in understanding the level and pattern of systems cohesion and how leadership plays a role in supporting or constraining it.

Part 5: Educational Leadership beyond Traditional Boundaries

While the previous parts focus on leadership and change within a finite boundary of an organizational system (a cohort, school, district, or community of schools), Part 5 extends the understanding of leadership and its effect on cohesion within a system that is open and extends beyond these conventional boundaries. These studies bring several new approaches to the exploration of educational leadership and change.

Chapter 13, by Bastón, Cramer, Daly, Hudson, Liou, Naum, Thompson, Umer, and Uzzo, situates educational leadership in the context of a STEM ecosystem that comprises hundreds of cross-sector organizations within which clusters of educational institutions are embedded and work together to form alliances or establish strategic collaborations for STEM reform. This area of cross-sector, inter-organizational networks in educational leadership is unique and understudied. The authors map out a set of STEM networks in an effort to identify strengths and weaknesses of such an ecosystem in support of leadership development at the systems level. Creating and sustaining interdependent systems of meaningful collaboration within the larger STEM ecosystem is one of the important implications of this work.

In Chapter 14, Rehm, Daly, Bjorklund, Liou, and del Fresno recognize the increasingly important influence of virtual communities (e.g., social media) on leaders' decision-making, professional development, and practices. They do so by examining the interplay between educational leaders' virtual footprints on Twitter and their face-to-face interactions at work. The authors take both the online and offline social networks of leaders into account to capture a more complete picture of their social terrain. Their study reveals a certain degree of overlap between leaders' online and offline networks, key influencers who bridge the resources (information) between the two spheres, and the type of information and resources being accessed and shared within these social spaces. In addition to these substantive contributions, this is one of first attempts to utilize a novel set of network data and analysis to study the social and relational side of educational leadership.

The studies in Part 5 introduce new perspectives on leadership (practice) and systems change. They shed new light on the social side of leadership by extending the scope of investigation to include a broader social ecosystem that can be interorganizational, virtual, and boundaryless. This macro view on leadership and change supplements the equally important micro perspective on individual traits and agency that shape their leadership.

Conclusion

The conclusion part synthesizes concepts and lessons learned in previous parts around social networks, educational leadership, and change. The part presents a new agenda for research around the social and relational side of educational leadership for change, including frameworks that delineate individual social network literacy and leadership for learning and systems change. The intention of this section is to encompass, as much as possible, the depth and range of work around educational leadership while establishing connections between leadership, networks, and systems improvement and keeping a focus on issues of equity.

In Chapter 15, Baker-Doyle presents a framework of critical network literacy that educational leaders can adopt to promote learning and development at the individual and organizational levels. This novel framework posits that organizational systems will benefit from reformers and change-makers who engage with critical perspectives to develop network literacy as they co-construct knowledge and expertise together and intentionally design conditions or infrastructures that can lead to better outcomes of learning systems. This piece provides guidance and a push for those who aspire to make systems change for improvement.

The book concludes with Chapter 16 by Liou and Daly. Inspired and informed by the work presented in each chapter, this summary discusses major learnings and considers promising future directions for scholarship and practice. The core intent of this book overall is to reinforce the influential role of relationships in bringing about change in education toward more equitable outcomes. It also intends to bring awareness of social networks and action for change as a way to support an increasingly interconnected world. The collection of studies from multiple international contexts and settings provides a richer understanding of our complex social world, thus offering important insights and opportunities for developing local and global practices designed for educational change.

References

Alfadala, A., Morel, R. P., & Spillane, J. P. (2021). Multilevel distributed leadership: From why to how. In Netolicky, D. M. (Ed.), *Future alternatives for educational leadership* (pp. 79–92). Routledge.

Azorín, C., Harris, A., & Jones, M. (2020). Taking a distributed perspective on leading professional learning networks. *School Leadership & Management, 40*(2–3), 111–27. https://doi.org/10.1080/13632434.2019.1647418

Baker-Doyle, K. J. (2017). *Transformative teachers: Teacher leadership and learning in a connected world*. Harvard Education Press.

Baker-Doyle, K. J. (2023). *Critical network literacy: Humanizing professional development for educators*. Harvard Education Press.

Balkundi, P., & Kilduff, M. (2006). The ties that lead: A social network approach to leadership. *The Leadership Quarterly, 17*(4), 419–39. https://psycnet.apa.org/doi/10.1016/j.leaqua.2006.01.001

Brooks, J. S., & Normore, A. H. (2010). Educational leadership and globalization: Literacy for a glocal perspective. *Educational Policy, 24*(1), 52–82. https://doi.org/10.1177/0895904809354070

Brown, K. M., & Shaked, H. (2018). *Preparing future leaders for social justice: Bridging theory and practice through a transformative andragogy*. Rowman & Littlefield.

Coburn, C. E., & Penuel, W. R. (2016). Research–practice partnerships in education: Outcomes, dynamics, and open questions. *Educational Researcher, 45*(1), 48–54. https://doi.org/10.3102/0013189X16631750

Coburn, C. E., Penuel, W. R., & Farrell, C. C. (2021). Fostering educational improvement with research–practice partnerships. *Phi Delta Kappan, 102*(7), 14–19. https://doi.org/10.1177/00317217211007332

Daly, A. J. (Ed.). (2010). *Social network theory and educational change*. Harvard Education Press.

Daly, A. J. (2012). Data, dyads, and dissemination: Exploring data use and social networks in educational improvement. *Teachers College Record, 114*(11), 1–38.

Daly, A. J., & Russell, J. L. (2022). Designs, tools, and methods of improvement research in education. In Peurach, D. J., Russell, J. L., Cohen-Vogel, L. & Penuel, W. R. (Eds.), *The foundational handbook on improvement research in education* (pp. 375–81). Roman & Littlefield.

Daly, A. J., Liou, Y.-H., & Der-Martirosian, C. (2020). A capital idea: Exploring the relationship between human and social capital and student achievement in schools. *Journal of Professional Capital and Community, 6*(1), 7–28. https://doi.org/10.1108/JPCC-10-2020-0082

Fahmi Dajani, M., & Yousef, M. (2014). Learning circles: Promoting collaborative learning culture for teacher professional development. *Arab World English Journal, 5*(3), 142–53.

Finnigan, K. S., Luengo-Aravena, D. E., & Garrison, K. M. (2018). Social network analysis methods in educational policy research. In Lochmiller, C. (Ed.), *Complementary* research methods for educational leadership and policy studies (pp. 231–52). Palgrave Macmillan.

Government of Norway (2017). *Desire to learn—early intervention and quality in schools*. White Paper no. 21, Government of Norway.

Greany, T., & Kamp, A. (2022). *Leading educational networks: Theory, policy and practice*. Bloomsbury.

Hannon, V., Thomas, L., Ward, S., & Beresford, T. (2019). *Local learning ecosystems: Emerging models*. World Innovation Summit for Education.

Henrick, E. C., Cobb, P., Penuel, W. R., Jackson, K., & Clark, T. (2017). *Assessing research—practice partnerships: Five dimensions of effectiveness*. William T. Grant Foundation.

Hinds, P. J., Carley, K. M., Krackhardt, D., & Wholey, D. (2000). Choosing work group members: Balancing similarity, competence, and familiarity. *Organizational Behavior and Human Decision Processes, 81*(2), 226–51. https://psycnet.apa.org/doi/10.1006/obhd.1999.2875

Jackson, D., & Temperley, J. (2006). *From professional learning community to networked learning community*. National College for School Leadership.

Katz, S., & Earl, L. (2010). Learning about networked learning communities. *School Effectiveness and School Improvement, 21*(1), 27–51. https://doi.org/10.1080/09243450903569718

Kilduff, M., & Krackhardt, D. (2008). *Interpersonal networks in organizations: Cognition, personality, dynamics, and culture*. Cambridge University Press.

Leithwood, K. (2019). Characteristics of effective leadership networks: A replication and extension. *School Leadership & Management, 39*(2), 175–97. https://doi.org/10.1080/13632434.2018.1470503

Lieberman, A. (2000). Networks as learning communities: Shaping the future of teacher development. *Journal of Teacher Education, 51*(3), 221–7. https://doi.org/10.1177/0022487100051003010

Lin, N. (2009). *Social capital: A theory of social structure and action* (8th ed.). Cambridge University Press.

Liou, Y.-H., & Daly, A. J. (2021). Obstacles and opportunities for networked practice: A social network analysis of an inter-organizational STEM ecosystem. *Journal of Educational Administration, 59*(1), 94–115. https://doi.org/10.1108/JEA-02-2020-0041

Liou, Y.-H., & Daly, A. J. (2022). Networked systems leadership: The potential of social network theory and analysis. In Tierney, R., Rizvi, F., & Ercikan, K. (Eds.), *International encyclopedia of education* (4th ed.). Elsevier.

Organisation for Economic Co-operation and Development. (2020). *How's life? 2020: Measuring well-being*. OECD Publishing. https://www.oecd.org/wise/how-s-life-23089679.htm

Pegrum, M. (2010). "I link, therefore I am": Network literacy as a core digital literacy. *E-learning and Digital Media, 7*(4), 346–54. https://doi.org/10.2304/elea.2010.7.4.346

Penuel, W. R., Riel, M., Krause, A., & Frank, K. A. (2009). Analyzing teachers' professional interactions in a school as social capital: A social network approach. *Teachers College Record, 111*(1), 124–63. https://doi.org/10.1177/016146810911100102

Penuel, W. R., Riel, M., Joshi, A., Pearlman, L., Kim, C. M., & Frank, K. A. (2010). The alignment of the informal and formal organizational supports for reform: Implications for improving teaching in schools. *Educational Administration Quarterly, 46*(1), 57–95. https://doi.org/10.1177/1094670509353180

Peurach, D. J., Russell, J. L., Cohen-Vogel, L., & Penuel, W. R. (2022). *The foundational handbook on improvement research in education*. Roman & Littlefield.

Pitts, V. M., & Spillane, J. P. (2009). Using social network methods to study school leadership. *International Journal of Research & Method in Education, 32*(2), 185–207. https://doi.org/10.1080/17437270902946660

Russell, J. L., Meredith, J., Childs, J., Stein, M. K., & Prine, D. W. (2015). Designing interorganizational networks to implement education reform: An analysis of state race to the top applications. *Educational Evaluation and Policy Analysis, 37*(1), 92–112.

Shaked, H., & Schechter, C. (2020). Systems thinking leadership: New explorations for school improvement. *Management in Education, 34*(3), 107–14. https://doi.org/10.1177/0892020620907327

Shirrell, M., & Spillane, J. P. (2020). Opening the door: Physical infrastructure, school leaders' work-related social interactions, and sustainable educational improvement. *Teaching and Teacher Education, 88*, 102846. https://doi.org/10.1016/j.tate.2019.05.012

Showunmi, V., & Kaparou, M. (2017). The challenge of leadership: Ethnicity and gender among school leaders in England, Malaysia and Pakistan. In Miller, P. (Ed.), *Cultures of educational leadership* (pp. 95–119). Palgrave Macmillan.

Stoll, L. (2010). Connecting learning communities: Capacity building for systemic change. In Hargreaves, A., Lieberman, A., Fullan, M. & Hopkins, D. (Eds.), *Second international handbook of educational change* (pp. 469–84). Springer.

Supovitz, J. A., D'Auria, J., & Spillane, J. P. (2019). *Meaningful and Sustainable School Improvement with Distributed Leadership*. CPRE Research Reports. https://files.eric.ed.gov/fulltext/ED597840.pdf

Tierney, R., Rizvi, F., & Ercikan, K. (Eds.). (2022). *International encyclopedia of education* (4th ed.). Elsevier.

Thomas, A., & Gupta, V. (2021). Social capital theory, social exchange theory, social cognitive theory, financial literacy, and the role of knowledge sharing as a moderator in enhancing financial well-being: From bibliometric analysis to a conceptual framework model. *Frontiers in Psychology, 12*, 664638. https://doi.org/10.3389/fpsyg.2021.664638

Tortoriello, M., & Krackhardt, D. (2017). Intra-organizational networks of innovations. *Academy of Management Proceedings, 2017* (1), 13989. http://dx.doi.org/10.5465/AMBPP.2017.13989abstract

Tripp, D. (2004). Teachers' networks: A new approach to the professional development of teachers in Singapore. In Day, C. & Sachs, J. (Eds.), *International handbook on the continuing professional development of teachers* (pp. 191–214). Open University Press.

Walcutt, J. J., & Schatz, S. (Eds.). (2019). *Modernizing learning: Building the future learning ecosystem*. Advanced Distributed Learning Initiative.

Webster, D., Dunne, L., & Hunter, R. (2021). Association between social networks and subjective well-being in adolescents: A systematic review. *Youth & Society, 53*(2), 175–210. https://doi.org/10.1177/0044118X20919589

Wullschleger, A., Vörös, A., Rechsteiner, B., Rickenbacher, A., & Merki, K. M. (2023). Improving teaching, teamwork, and school organization: Collaboration networks in school teams. *Teaching and Teacher Education, 121*, 103909. https://doi.org/10.1016/j.tate.2022.103909

2

Organizational Advancement by Learning Together: Leadership for Professional Learning

Kenneth Leithwood

Increasing numbers of organisational scholars have come to realise that an organisation's learning capability will be the only sustainable competitive advantage in the future.[1]

I first heard the phrase "learning our way forward" from Sir Michael Barber who, at the time, was the first head of the UK government's *Prime Minister's Delivery Unit* under the prime minister of the day, Tony Blair. My colleagues and I had been hired by Barber in the late 1990s to monitor progress and evaluate the effects of England's country-wide Literacy and Numeracy Strategies (e.g., Earl et al, 2003). We all learned a great deal from our experience with that project and with Sir Michael. Primarily, we learned that even the most detailed, sophisticated, and well-funded plans for implementing a large-scale change in education provided not much more that a starting point for what followed. After that starting point, success depended on having ready access to reliable information from those in the proverbial "trenches" about how useful the change was likely to be, what challenges were encountered in moving forward, how the new thing to be implemented needed to be altered if it was to become useful and what all those involved in its implementation needed to learn to succeed. And all of this was a rough approximation to what Barber had in mind when he described his approach to implementing the two Strategies as "learning our way forward."

Leadership for Professional Learning (LPL)

A considerable amount of independent evidence has accumulated by now, largely endorsing Barber's conception of successful educational change as a process of individual and especially collective learning whether the change is across whole systems or limited to a district or a school. This chapter describes how leaders can help their colleagues learn their way forward through two distinct but complementary avenues. One avenue entails designing into their organizations conditions that encourage and reward the largely spontaneous (and often uncodified) acquisition of capacities members need to sustain their organizations through repeated cycles of innovation and change (leader as organizational designer). The second avenue involves engaging individual colleagues in targeted, intentional learning of strategic capacities (leader as tutor and coach). The chapter refers to leaders who enact both of these approaches to fostering the learning of their colleagues as *Leaders of Professional Learning* (LPL).

Two Perspectives on Learning

Learning is an intensely social process whether it occurs, for example, in the isolation of one's own office, or in the middle of a crowded room of colleagues and strangers. Sometimes intentional and sometimes spontaneous, learning depends very much on the nature of those social processes. Contemporary sociocultural conceptions of learning and the processes giving rise to it look quite different depending on the relative weight placed on the *external contexts* in which learning occurs, as compared with the *cognitive processes* involved in a person's learning.

The first and longest section of this chapter, *Learning Through Organizational Design*, argues that by far the largest proportion of what educators learn on the job, sometimes referred to as *workplace learning*, is explained by perspectives on learning which foreground the learner's external contexts especially, for purposes of this chapter, the organizational contexts in which educators work. A synopsis of evidence is provided in this section about the designs of whole districts, schools, networks, and teams which promote the learning of their members.

The second briefer section of the chapter, *Learning Through Targeted, Individual Intervention*, begins by explaining why organizational advancement cannot rely on organizational design alone for enhancing members' learning. Some of the most strategic and complex capacities needed for such advancement require the intentional and targeted learning of individual members. While explanations of such individual learning acknowledge the influence of the learners' social contexts, mostly they foreground the learner's internal cognitive processes; they also distinguish among processes associated with the acquisition of skills, knowledge, and dispositions. Both sections of the chapter include guidelines for those who chose to lead the professional learning of their colleagues.

Organizational Designs that Foster Learning

The perspective on learning germane to organizational designs foregrounds learners' external social contexts. This perspective is elaborated in theories described, for example, as "situated" (Brown, Collins & Duguid, 1989), "informal" (Rogoff et al., 2016), "organizational" (Levitt & March, 1988), and "workplace" (Billett & Choy, 2013) learning. According to these theories, what is learned is strongly influenced by the circumstances in which it is learned, helping to reduce the gap between abstract knowledge and knowledge that can be used in practice. *Informal learning*, as Rogoff and colleagues explain, "is non-didactic, is embedded in meaningful activity, builds on the learner's initiative, interest, or choice ... and does not involve assessment external to the activity." (2016, p. 358). Informal learning is shaped by "authentic activity" and is interactive. A significant portion of the guidance for this form of learning typically comes from others learning in the same context and, together, they "hone their existing knowledge and skills and also innovate, developing new ideas and skills" (Murphy & Knight 2016, p. 360). *Workplace learning* is embedded in the context of unique tasks, cultures, power relationships, and politics, all of which constitute the social processes influencing both individual and collective learning among organizational members. As Fenwick (2013) explains, such learning:

> can involve formal or informal teaching but is practice-based and participative, embedded in action, not centered in an individual's head but distributed among activities, continuous interactions and relationships of people (and tools, texts, architecture, etc.) within a system.
>
> (p. 228)

No matter the label, learning that is prompted and powerfully shaped by external contexts likely accounts for the vast majority of the learning that occurs among organizational members (e.g., Stenmark, 2000). A significant proportion of what is learned is uncodified and tacit and the processes through which such learning occurs is frequently spontaneous. This is the learning of capacities relied on by teachers and school leaders, for example, to "get through the day," to meet the typical expectations of students and families, and to successfully cope with change and innovation in their organizations. A leader who is able to "run a smooth ship"—as the ship is being renovated—has acquired a great deal of her know-how through immersion in the many contexts in which she finds herself. Indeed, learning through immersion in those contexts and "experience" are much the same thing.

This section of the chapter describes the designs of whole districts, schools, networks, and teams that encourage and enable significant learning on the part of their members. Leadership for such learning is conceptualized in this section as any actions taken to create and maintain these organizational designs. However, the final part of this section highlights LPL practices that have especially important effects on members' learning whether in districts, schools, networks, or teams.

District and School Designs Which Encourage Learning

Professional learning in whole districts and schools is enhanced when those structures combine features associated with both "enabling bureaucracies" and "learning organizations." The term "bureaucracy" is commonly associated with hierarchical structures, inflexible policies, and rigid procedures. A small but compelling body of evidence (e.g., Hoy & Sweetland, 2000; Mitchell et al, 2016) now suggests, however, that the formality, transparency, and predictability initially justifying the use of bureaucratic structures can be achieved in ways that enable rather than impede the learning and work of organizational members.

The standard rules, policies, and procedures of an enabling bureaucracy provide "flexible rules and regulations and an authority structure" (Mitchell, 2019, p. 625) that promotes learning and builds on the existing capacities of organizational members. More specifically, these rules and regulations that enable authentic communication between teachers and with administrators help rather than hinder the learning and work of teachers. Those rules also are guides to solutions rather than rigid procedures. In an enabling bureaucracy the school or district's administrators facilitate the mission of the school and enable teachers to enact what they learn about improving instruction.

While the quantity of literature about "learning organizations" far outweighs the literature about enabling bureaucracies, it is still surprisingly light on empirical evidence, especially evidence collected in school and district contexts. Nevertheless, results of this research stretch considerably beyond the structure, rules, and hierarchy identified in enabling bureaucracies. Results of three closely related studies summarized in Leithwood, Leonard, and Sharratt (1998), along with conclusions from Kool and Stoll's (2016) review, point to five sets of conditions within both districts and schools that foster much of their members' learning through organizational design— missions and visions, organizational cultures, participative structures, strategies for accomplishing key tasks, as well as polices and resources.

The missions and visions of districts include the learning of all students and are sources of learning for school staffs when they are well-understood, meaningful, and accessible. To foster learning in schools, district visions and missions must also engender a sense of commitment on the part of school staffs. District visions should serve as nonprescriptive clues about which initiatives, taken by schools, would be valued and supported by district personnel.

As in the case of district visions and missions, school visions and missions prompt learning when they are clear, accessible, and widely shared by staff. When these missions and visions are perceived as meaningful and when they are pervasive in conversations and decision-making throughout the school, they provide much of the motivation organizational members need to learn whatever it takes to progress toward their organizations' missions and visions (also see Sun & Leithwood, 2015).

"Collaborative and harmonious" capture much of what is important about both school and district cultures when they contribute to staff learning. Such learning is fostered in districts when there is a sense of community across the district. This sense of community is more likely when there is frequent interaction with other schools (for example, feeder schools), and when disagreements in the district are settled in ways that are perceived to be professional. District cultures also foster learning when the need for continuous change, innovation, and exploration is accepted, and when new initiatives are clearly built on previous work rather than being discontinuous with such work.

Norms of mutual support among teachers, respect for colleagues' ideas, and a willingness to take risks in attempting new practices are all aspects of school cultures that encourage teacher learning. Receiving honest, candid feedback from their colleagues is an important factor in the learning of many teachers. Teachers' commitments to their own learning can be reinforced by shared celebrations of successes by staff, along with a strong focus on the needs of all students. Collaborative and collegial school cultures promote informal sharing of ideas and materials among teachers, especially when continuous professional growth is a widely shared norm among staff (also see Louis and Lee, 2016).

Learning is encouraged by districts which provide ample opportunity for school-based staff to participate in shaping both district and school-level decisions (Leithwood, 2010). Participation in district decisions teaches those involved about the wider issues faced by the district and about those influences not readily evident in schools that are, nevertheless, germane to district decisions. Considerable delegation of decision-making to schools enhances opportunities for improving the collective problem-solving capacities of staff. Such decision-making also permits staff to create solutions which are sensitive to important aspects of the school's context.

School structures support professional learning when they allow for greater participation in school decision-making by teachers (e.g., Bektaş, Kılınç, Gümüş, 2022). These structures may include, for example, brief weekly planning meetings, frequent and often informal problem-solving sessions, regularly scheduled professional-development time in school, and common preparation periods for teachers who need to work together. When decisions are made by staff through consensus, something which seems more likely in smaller schools, more learning is likely to occur.

Districts encourage learning through the use of many different strategies for reaching out to schools as, for example, newsletters, workshops, informal lines of communication, and procedures for collecting and exchanging knowledge. Especially influential are strategies which have teaching as their explicit purpose such as workshops and mentoring programs. Strategies which buffer schools from excessive turbulence or from pressure from the community also contribute to teacher learning.

Clarifying short-term goals for improvement, and establishing personal, professional-growth goals are school strategies that assist teacher learning. This learning is extended when school goals and priorities are kept current through periodic review and revision and when there are well-designed processes for implementing specific program initiatives designed to accomplish such goals and priorities. Schools also foster the learning of their members when they limit themselves to a manageable number of priorities for action and when there is follow-through on plans for such action.

Districts encourage learning by providing social support (e.g., Pomaki et al, 2010) such as release time for teacher planning and professional development, especially when these resources can be used in flexible ways. Access to special expertise or "technical assistance" in the form of consultants and lead teachers, for example, also foster learning. Sufficient *resources* to support essential professional development in aid of their initiatives is a decided boost to teacher learning, as well as to teacher commitment and retention in schools; teacher colleagues are among the most valuable of those resources. Access to rich curriculum resources and to computer facilities encourages teachers' learning, as does access to technical assistance (consultants, etc.) when implementing new practices.

Network and Team Designs that Encourage Learning

Networks and teams are not identical structures. A network is a more-or-less formally interconnected group of persons with fluid, often voluntary membership and only a loosely defined lifespan. Peer principal leadership networks, often encouraged and supported by districts, exemplify the conception of networks top-of-mind in this chapter. These networks typically bring together school leaders for the purpose of finding solutions to problems more-or-less common across their schools. Principals included in two recent studies (e.g., Leithwood, 2018) ranked, among a dozen possible sources of their professional learning, participation in their peer leadership networks as second only to their own professional reading.

Teams, in contrast, are more formally interconnected groups of people with specified roles working toward a common goal in a single organizational entity. Senior district leadership teams composed of superintendents and other central office staff, as well as school leadership teams including principals, vice principals, and sometimes department heads, are examples of teams commonly found in educational environments. These district and school leadership teams are typically responsible for helping their organizations as a whole—or some significant component of their organization—achieve its vision and strategic goals. Whereas networks entail individual members learning together then acting apart, teams entail members both learning and acting together, often simultaneously, in order to accomplish common purposes.

This brief description of networks and teams mostly indicates how they are different. Furthermore, the lack of comparative research on networks and teams reinforces the impression that such differences are what matter most. But networks and teams have many things in common, especially with respect to design characteristics that promote the learning of their members: a relatively small number of people, individual members typically considered to have problem relevant expertise, interactions among members both expected and relatively frequent. Both networks and teams also have goals shared by members and almost always the expectation of action to solve a problem, preceded by significant learning about the nature of that problem and known solutions. Nonetheless, the next two sections summarize, separately, the design characteristics of networks and teams that foster learning based on the independent noncomparative evidence reported about these two structures.

Networks

As Liou and Daly (2020) argue, "leadership is ultimately defined and shaped by the social interactions leaders experience within their networks of contacts, making social influence key to their leading capacity" (p. 164). Evidence indicates that learning occurs in collegial networks when they have a sustained focus and clear expectations for improved outcomes such as student engagement and learning, in the case of school leadership networks. In networks such as these, the motivation of members to engage actively in their own learning is typically very high. Peer networks that significantly add to the learning of their members can vary in size and members may interact both in person and online, although Liou and Daly (2020) argue that greater importance should be awarded to in-person interaction. A well-functioning network builds on strong interpersonal relationships and contributes to the capacity of individual members by exposing them to the practices, dispositions, and ideas of others faced with similar tasks and responsibilities. This is the diffusion goal of networks, one that exploits the knowledge of some members by ensuring that such knowledge goes to scale through the learning of all or most members in the same network.

The chances of knowledge being widely diffused within a network depends, at least in part, on the perceived value of such knowledge to achieving goals members are pursuing within their own organizations, as well as the frequency and density of member interactions. These social processes also encourage network members to make explicit, for themselves and their colleagues, the large amounts of tacit knowledge (Polanyi, 1983) on which a large proportion of their expertise depends.

A network is also a structure which, under the right conditions, stimulates potentially rich interactions among members resulting in the learning of new and creative ideas or practices not initially part of the repertoire of any individual network member—the whole becomes more than the sum of its parts. This is the knowledge creation goal of networks. Knowledge creation is stimulated by a willingness on the part of participants to collaborate in the solving of some shared problem, as well as a willingness to genuinely listen to the ideas of one's network colleagues. Such listening entails a conscious change in mindset, from one that is primarily about assimilation of new ideas into one's existing understandings to one that is focused on the adaptation of one's existing understandings. Knowledge creation is also encouraged by the infusion of relevant ideas located in sources outside the network.

Teams

A number of individual, collective, and organizational factors help explain the learning that occurs in teams (e.g., Barnett & McCormick, 2012). Individual team members engage not just in systematic information processing, they actively process and integrate such information. These team members overtly reflect upon the teams's objectives, strategies, and processes and adapt them to current or anticipated circumstances. Individual members of teams that foster their learning are skilled communicators and problem-solvers, adept at conflict resolution and both willing and able to collaborate with other team members. Team members have considerable task-relevant knowledge, manage their own emotions and performance well. They set goals for their own contribution to the team's work, as well as help plan and coordinate team tasks.

Collectively, members of effective teams have shared mental models that enable them to form accurate understandings of team tasks and to coordinate and adapt their responses to the demands of those tasks and one another. The collective membership of effective teams resists disruptions and is attracted to and motivated to stay with the team. Internal team relationships are characterized by mutual trust, collaboration, reduced conflict, and increased commitment to the team and the organization.

Members of effective teams are collectively efficacious—confident about their capacities to learn whatever it takes to achieve the team's goals.

A handful of organizational conditions are also common to learning-rich teams. One set of such conditions, reflecting the "enabling bureaucracy" concept discussed earlier in the chapter, are team norms and procedures designed to assist and reward members to master their tasks and improve team functioning. The broader organization (and its managers) within which a team belongs is perceived by members as supportive of their work, placing a high value on learning and innovation. It also strongly encourages team members to invest effort in learning and implementing what is needed to achieve team goals.

Key Features of Leadership for Professional Learning (LPL)

Through Organizational Design

To this point in the chapter, LPL has been conceptualized as any set of actions a person or group takes to create and maintain organizational designs that contribute to members' learning. There is evidence to indicate, however, that at least nine sets of leadership practices make especially powerful contributions to members' learning whether in schools, districts, networks, or teams. While not all of these practices are self-evident in the organizational designs described above, they are part of one or more existing leadership models, in particular, transformational, functional, and servant leadership models.

The nine key LPL practices include the following:

1. *Clarifying goals and expectations.* Help organizational members develop a clear, agreed-on focus or goal for their learning and work, one that can be sustained over time along with explicit expectations for members' contributions (e.g., Lieberman and Grolnick, 1996).
2. *Distributing leadership based on expertise.* Encourage members to assume leadership roles when their expertise is aligned with their organizations' goals and strategic tasks (e.g., Mehra et al., 2006). Those to whom leadership is distributed should share their expertise in ways that promote the learning of colleagues.
3. *Monitoring progress.* Monitoring organizational progress allows leaders to feed back information to members so they can learn (assess and modify their activities) to better realize their collective purposes (e.g., Thiele et al., 2007).
4. *Supporting the basic functions of an organization.* Such support is likely to include locating resources needed for group tasks, encouraging stakeholder support, facilitating connections with sources of needed expertise, providing advice about a member's own organizational challenges, serving as a model of successful approaches to leadership and offering encouragement to organizational members (e.g., Rincon-Gallardo, 2020). Such "functional leadership" buffers network members from distractions to learning how to achieve the organization's collective purposes.

5. *Assisting in the development of productive interpersonal communication.* Interaction among organizational members is the foundation on which are built the social processes which spawn learning. Examples of how productive interpersonal communication among members might be refined include leaders modeling high-quality interpersonal relationships during interactions with organizational members and encouraging members to be aware of the quality of their own interpersonal skills. An important stimulus for learning in organizations is members genuinely listening to the ideas of their colleagues.
6. *Helping members access relevant ideas from outside their organization.* No matter the level of members' existing collective expertise, additional insights will almost always be available in relevant research found and shared with colleagues and by making connections with other people and organizations pursuing similar goals.
7. *Encouraging high levels of "task reflexivity."* High task reflexivity means that team members overtly reflect on their organization's objectives, strategies, and processes and adapt them to current or anticipated circumstances (e.g., Carter & West, 1998).
8. *Build one's own and one's organization's "positive psychological capital."* A growing body of evidence indicates that such capital includes both individual and collective forms of self-efficacy, hope, resilience, and optimism. Together, these dispositions promote problem-solving, persistence, and learning. Organizations whose members have such positive generalized beliefs about their capabilities and likely successes are more willing to learn, work hard, and persist in the face of challenge and adversity (Luthans, Luthans & Luthans, 2004).
9. *Be humble and encourage humility among organizational members.* A leader's humbleness serves to build an organizational climate of psychological safety and democracy which encourages the contribution of all members to their collective learning and goal achievement. Humility is also likely to help build trust among group members, a key condition for authentic communication. Humbleness on the part of leaders entails the following:

    (1) showing a willingness to evaluate oneself without positive or negative exaggeration;
    (2) showing appreciation for the unique strengths and contributions of others; and
    (3) showing openness to new ideas, feedback, and advice (Rego et al., 2017, p. 641).

Learning through Targeted Individual Intervention

As the previous section of the chapter explained, organizational designs can be significant sources of workplace learning. Both what is learned and how it is learned through even the most promising organizational designs, however, are typically difficult to predict and codify. This is because organizational members are steeped in their work, often in interaction with others, arriving at understandings that are often a composite of procedural know how, emotional responses and sensory impressions; those understandings are "multimodal," to use Billett and Choy's (2013) term.

Complex understandings such as these may be a product of self-regulated learning but often arise spontaneously and remain tacit (Polyani 1983). Learners often have little conscious control over such learning and may not consciously know what they know; this tacit knowledge is difficult to improve except over long periods of time during which learners may, for example, encounter some feedback that helps surface, assess, and possibly refine their knowledge. But feedback such as this is typically slow and its precision uncertain illustrating why spontaneous processes may vary considerably in their value to improve especially crucial educator capacities. Learning acquired through organizational design may also be difficult to transfer to other superficially different circumstances even though the underlying principles of what is learned may be quite relevant.

Limitations such as these on learning through organizational design make it a necessary but far from sufficient source for significant organizational advancement. Furthermore, surprisingly little attention by those focused on learning through organizational design is devoted to what is known about the cognitive processes involved in individual's learning even though organizational or collective learning depends fundamentally on the learning of many individuals.

Individual cognitive perspectives on learning, in contrast, aim to explain how knowledge stored in memory is adapted and extended in response to social experiences. These perspectives on learning identify processes associated with individual learners' acquisition of skills, knowledge, and dispositions; even when organizational designs do include provision for members' access to individual targeted learning, they rarely acknowledge differences in the social processes giving rise to these three sets of capacities. This section describes the cognitive processes underlying the acquisition of skills, knowledge, and dispositions and identifies leadership practices likely to nurture those processes.

Skill Learning

The foundation of a person's performance of a skill (e.g., execution of a leadership practice or an instructional strategy) is procedural knowledge. Such knowledge is stored in "procedural memory," one of two basic memory processes (Bransford, et al, 2004), as a list of things to do and a sequence about when to do them. By way of illustration, consider "Creating high performance expectations among staff," a skill commonly associated with successful leadership while high-performance expectations do not define the substance of organizational goals or directions, they signal the degree of effort expected to accomplish those goals, and the level of performance associated with the goals (e.g., achievement of the goals by all students not just some).

Now imagine a principal new to a school serving a high proportion of students from economically disadvantaged families struggling to make ends meet. After a few months in the school, the principal comes to appreciate that most staff members care a great deal about their students, spend considerable time offering students social support, and know the family circumstances of their student very well. Most staff members are also defensive about the relatively low academic achievement of these students but believe their paramount responsibility is for their students' social and emotional well-being. The principal believes, however, that the long-term well-being of these students is closely linked to their academic success and sets out to increase staff expectations for such achievement without diminishing the school's contribution to their students' well-being.

Among several of the elements of the skill included for this principal in "creating high performance expectations" are helping staff understand and eventually agree on the long-term value of their students' academic success, helping staff identify instructional strategies with the potential to improve their students' academic success, and providing constructive feedback to staff about how well those practices are being implemented. Each of these elements contains its own set of more specific skills and each can be enacted with more or less expertise.

Improving a novice learner's skill requires opportunities for the learner to acquire initial rudimentary understandings of the elements entailed in performing the skill, as well as the order of performance of those elements when order might be important (procedural knowledge). Learners then need opportunities to perform the skill, guided by those initial, rudimentary understandings of what is involved. Repeated cycles of feedback and performance gradually improve the learner's understanding of what is entailed in performing the skill and their performance until such understanding and performance approximates those who are at least competent at the skill.

Moving especially from competent to expert levels of skill depends on time spent in deliberate practice (Ericsson, 2006) focused on those aspects of a skill one is weakest at performing. Deliberate practice requires concentration and practice beyond the point of being able to concentrate does not do much to advance one's expertise. Furthermore, as expertise increases over time, there is a tendency for skills to become automated and consciously unavailable to the learner for further improvement. So, achieving high levels of expertise also depends on the motivation to continue achieving ever higher levels of expertise (Ryan & Deci, 2012) and the ability (or access to help) to retrieve and monitor one's performance.

High levels of expertise also depend on the learners' self-regulation of their own response to that performance that is, their ability to focus their thoughts, feelings, and actions on achieving their goals (Zimmerman, 2002), as well as on deep levels of domain-specific, propositional knowledge (Ericsson, 2006).

Based on the processes described above, those choosing to provide leadership to their colleagues for the acquisition of new skills should:

1. *Provide opportunities for learners to observe others* enacting the skill to be acquired in order to develop an initial understanding of what is involved in executing a skill.
2. *Make feedback available to learners* about the adequacy of her or his initial and subsequent performances of the skill.
3. *Ensure external encouragement and guidance* to persist through the repeated cycles of feedback and performance necessary to develop at least competent if not expert levels of skill performance.
4. *Model critical self-reflection* on one's own performance and demonstrate a commitment to continuous progress.

Learning Strategic Ideas, Concepts, and Theories

While procedural knowledge is the foundation of skill development, knowledge "about" something—facts, ideas, and concepts for example—depends on a type of knowledge often referred to as "propositional" or "declarative"; such knowledge is stored in "declarative memory," the second basic memory process (Bransford et al, 2004). Social construction theory aims to explain how propositional knowledge is developed. While rote learning will sometimes be sufficient to acquire new facts, acquiring more complex forms of new propositional knowledge (such as concepts) depends on learners making connections between what they already know and the new ideas or concepts to be learned. This process entails learners accommodating what they already know by adapting or adding to it in ways that make sense to them in the contexts in which they find themselves (Shunk, 2012). A personal level of understanding of new concepts or ideas is developed through such processes.

Piagetian notions about intellectual development (Kail & Bisanz, 1982) suggest that, in the face of potentially new ideas, the mind's default response is to attempt to assimilate or subsume them into one's existing understandings, avoiding the hard work of restructuring or significantly adding to one's existing understandings. The hard work of "accommodating" new knowledge is prompted by challenges to existing ways of understanding, clear definitions and explanations, as well as by experiences that distinguish new concepts and ideas from already understood concepts and ideas.

Consider, for example, the concept of equity conceived of as providing educational opportunities to students in proportion to their need. In practice, many teachers still believe that they are behaving equitably by trying to be "colour blind" or choosing to ignore significant differences among their students, treating them all the same. This understanding assumes the concept of "equitable" is the same as the concept of "equality," something close to "fairness" meaning that all students should be treated the same, independent of differences in need.

Four social processes that can be fostered by leaders are likely to help shift a teacher's understanding of equitable from providing all students with the same learning opportunities to providing students learning opportunities proportionate to need:

1. *Make connections between new concepts/ideas and existing understandings.* Most teachers are strongly committed to treating all students "fairly" and for some this means treating all students the same. One approach to helping these teachers develop a better concept of "equitable" is to build on their initial understanding and commitment to fairness. This might be done by providing evidence about the differences in students' starting points for learning. Such evidence nudges the "treat-everyone—the-same" views of fairness toward a more complex conception of fairness essentially by asking teachers if they really believe a race between two students is fair when one of them is given a 20-yard head start.
2. *Create experiences in which learners have their existing understandings challenged.* When some teachers have opportunities to better appreciate the challenging

family circumstances in which many of their struggling students live, they are much less likely to attribute their students' poor performance at school to lack of student effort and/or parental indifference (Leithwood & Patrician, 2015). With greater appreciation of the nature and extent of challenges faced by some of their students and families, these teachers often begin to provide learning conditions aimed at addressing the root causes of their students' struggles. Considerable evidence indicates that these conditions will sometimes include, for example, replacing punitive approaches to classroom discipline with alternatives such as "restorative justice" (Welsh & Little, 2018), increasing parents' expectations for their children's success at school and making use of cultural and linguistic differences among students as instructional assets.

3. *Provide examples and clear definitions.* School handbooks and parent newsletters explaining to parents, and indirectly to teachers, the school's commitment to treating students equitably is a potentially powerful way of influencing teachers' understandings of what the concept equitable means in their school.
4. *Make available and insist on learners having experiences that help distinguish new concepts and ideas from already understood concepts and ideas.* The concept of "equitable" can also be clarified for teachers by encouraging (insisting on) changes needed in some of their common instructional strategies if they are to be equitable. Student grouping practices is one such strategy. Since research on the effects of student grouping practices began some ten decades ago (Steenbergen-Hu. Makel & Olszewski-Kubilius, 2016), a large proportion of the teacher population has believed in the value of grouping all students within classes by ability levels, while almost all research results point to the value of mixed ability groups for struggling students, in particular. Kutnick et al. (2005) report evidence indicating that:

> students placed in lower-ability groups are likely to make less progress, become demotivated and develop anti school attitudes. These students are likely to experience poorer quality of teaching and a limited range of curricular opportunities, which may affect their later life chances.
>
> (p. 27)

When teachers begin to implement mixed ability groupings in their classes, with the support they need to do it well, they are likely to be pleasantly surprised with the success of their formerly struggling students. These experiences of success have the potential to disrupt teachers' understandings of the underlying causes of these students' struggles.

Learning Dispositions

While there are a great many human dispositions, our focus here is restricted, for illustrative purposes, to a selected set of socio-emotional dispositions that studies have demonstrated to enhance the quality of school leadership. These social emotional dispositions include perceiving and managing emotions, as well as acting in emotionally appropriate ways, largely reflecting the dimensions of emotional intelligence included in Mayer, Salovey & Caruso's (2004) influential framework. Social emotional dispositions such as these are strongly associated with school leaders' job satisfaction, improved management and coaching skills, teamwork and conflict management ability, along with positive attitudes toward work (e.g., Little, Gooty & Williams, 2016).

There is a broad consensus about the improvability of these social emotional dispositions (e.g., Schutte, Malouff &Thorsteinsson, 2013) through social processes aimed at increasing learners' sensitivity to their own and others' emotions. Leaders of professional learning can enhance their colleagues' social emotional dispositions by:

1. *Making available feedback for recognizing the emotions* of self and others from facial and voice cues, as well as awareness of one's own body states relating to emotions.
2. *Providing opportunities to practice and to receive feedback* for regulating one's own emotions, to differentiate between varying emotions and to improve knowledge about the causes and consequences of different emotions.
3. *Provide coaching about how to adjust the overt expression* of learners' own emotions so they are appropriate to the circumstances, and how to draw on positive moods to enhance creative thought.

Conclusion

Justifications for the most common conceptions of educational leadership ("instructional leadership," for example) depend on evidence demonstrating their effects on student learning. This chapter has assumed that significant contributions to both the amount and type of student learning depend crucially on the learning of educational professionals. It has argued that fostering such learning should be the central responsibility of those in both formal and informal leadership roles. Professional learning occurs in response to features of the organization in which educators work, as well as in response to something much closer to targeted tutoring and coaching. This is not an especially controversial argument. More controversial, however, is the extent to which many educational leaders have the capacities needed to enact a *Leadership for Professional Learning* role. "The devil is in the details" and this chapter has aimed to make explicit some of the most important of these details as sources of guidance for those who aspire to make significant contributions to the learning of their colleagues.

Note

1   Kools & Stoll (2016, p. 20).

References

Barnett, K., & McCormick, J. (2012). Leadership and team dynamics in senior executive leadership teams. *Educational Management Administration & Leadership, 40*(6), 653–71.

Bektaş, F., Kılınç, A. Ç., & Gümüş, S. (2022). The effects of distributed leadership on teacher professional learning: mediating roles of teacher trust in principal and teacher motivation. *Educational studies*, 48(5), 602–24.

Billett, S., & Choy, S. (2013). Learning through work: Emerging perspectives and new challenges. *Journal of Workplace Learning, 25*(4), 264–76.

Bransford, J. D., Brown, A. L., Cocking, R. R., Donovan, M. S., & Pellegrino, J. W. (2004). *How people learn.* National Academy Press.

Brown, J. S., Collins, A., & Duguid, P. (1989). Situated cognition and the culture of learning. *Educational Researcher, 18*(1), 32–42.

Carter, S. M., & West, M. A. (1998). Reflexivity, effectiveness, and mental health in BBC-TV production teams. *Small Group Research, 29*(5), 583–601.

Earl, L., Watson, N., Levin, B., Leithwood, K., & Fullan, M. (2003). *Watching and learning 3: Final report of the external evaluation of England's National Literacy and Numeracy Strategies.* Toronto, Ontario: OISE/UT, January.

Ericsson, A. (2006). The influence on expertise and deliberate practice on the development of superior expert performance. In Anders Ericsson, A. (Ed.), *Development of Professional Expertise: Toward measurement of expert performance and design of optimal learning environments* (pp. 637–706). Cambridge University Press.

Hoy, W., & Sweetland, S. R. (2000). School bureaucracies that work: Enabling, not coercive. *Journal School Leadership, 10*, 524–41.

Fenwick, T. (2013). Understanding transitions in professional practice and learning: Towards new questions for research. *Journal of Workplace Learning, 25*(6), 352–67.

Kail, R., & Bisanz, J. (1982). Information processing and cognitive development. *Advances in Child Development and Behavior, 17*, 45–81.

Kools, M., & Stoll, L. (2016). *What Makes a School a Learning Organisation?* OECD Education Working Papers, No. 137, OECD Publishing.

Kutnick, P., Sebba, J., Blatchford, P., Galton, M., & Thorp, J. (2005). *The effects of student grouping: Literature review.* Research Report 688, London, England.

Leithwood, K. (2010). Characteristics of school districts that are exceptionally effective in closing achievement gaps. *Leadership and Policy in Schools, 9*(3), 245–91.

Leithwood, K. (2018). Characteristics of effective leadership networks: A replication and extension. *School Leadership and Management, 39*(2), 145–17.

Leithwood, K., & Patrician, P. (2015). Changing the educational culture of the home to increase student success at school. *Societies, 5*(3), 664–85.

Leithwood, K., Leonard, L., & Sharratt, L. (1998). Conditions fostering organizational learning in schools. *Educational Administration Quarterly, 34*(2), 243–76.

Levitt, B., & March, J. G. (1988). Organizational learning. *Annual Review of Sociology, 14*(1), 319–338.

Lieberman, A., & Grolnick, M. (1996). Networks and reform in American education. *Teachers college record, 98*(1), 7–45.

Liou, Y.-H., & Daly, A. (2020). The networked leader: understanding peer influence in a system-wide leadership team. *School Leadership and Management, 40*(5), 2–3.

Little, L., Gooty, J., & Williams, M. (2016). The role of leader emotion management in leader—member exchange and follower outcomes. *The Leadership Quarterly, 27*(1), 85–97.

Louis, K., & Lee M. (2016). Teachers' capacity for organizational learning: The effects of school culture and context. *School Effectiveness and School Improvement, 27*(4), 534–56.

Luthans, F., Luthans, K., & Luthans, B. (2004). Positive psychological capital: Beyond human and social capital. *Business Horizons, 47*, 45–50.

Mehra, A., Smith, B. R., Dixon, A. L., & Robertson, B. (2006). Distributed leadership in teams: The network of leadership perceptions and team performance. *The Leadership Quarterly, 17*(3), 232–45.

Mayer, J. D., Salovey, P., & Caruso, D. R. (2004). Emotional intelligence: Theory, findings, and implications. *Psychological Inquiry, 15*(3), 197–215.

Mitchell, R. M. (2019). Enabling school structure & transformational school leadership: Promoting increased organizational citizenship and professional teacher behavior. *Leadership and Policy in Schools, 18*(4), 614–27.

Mitchell, R. M., Mendiola, B., Schumacker, R. E., & Lowery, X. M. (2016). Creating a school context of success: The role of enabling school structure and academic optimism. *Journal of Educational Administration, 54*(6), 626–46.

Murphy, P. K., & Knight, S. L. (2016). Exploring a century of advancements in the science of learning. *Review of Research in Education, 40*(1), 402–56.

Polanyi, M. (1983). *The tacit dimension*. Peter Smith.

Pomaki, G., DeLongis, A., Frey, D., Short, K., & Woehrle, T. (2010). When the going gets tough: Direct, buffering and indirect effects of social support on turnover intention. *Teaching and Teacher Education, 26*(6), 1340–6.

Rincon-Gallardo, S. (2020). Leading school networks to liberate learning: Three leadership roles. *School Leadership & Management, 40*(2–3), 146–62.

Rego, A., Owens, B., Leal, S., Melo, A. I., E Cunha, M. P., Gonçalves, L., & Ribeiro, P. (2017). How leader humility helps teams to be humbler, psychologically stronger, and more effective: A moderated mediation model. *The Leadership Quarterly, 28*(5), 639–58.

Rogoff, B., Callanan, M., Gutiérrez, K. D., & Erickson, F. (2016). The organization of informal learning. *Review of Research in Education, 40*(1), 356–401.

Ryan, R., & Deci, E. (2012). An overview of self-determination theory: An organismic dialectical perspective. In Deci, E. & Ryan, R. (Eds.), *Handbook of self-determination research* (pp. 3–33). University of Rochester Press.

Schunk, D. (2012). *Learning theories: An educational perspective* (6th ed.). Allyn & Bacon Publishers.

Schutte, N., Malouff, M., & Thorsteinsson, E. (2013). Increasing emotional intelligence through training. *The International Journal of Emotional Education, 5*(1), 56–72.

Steenbergen-Hu, S., Makel, M. C., & Olszewski-Kubilius, P. (2016). What one hundred years of research says about the effects of ability grouping and acceleration on K–12 students' academic achievement: Findings of two second-order meta-analyses. *Review of Educational Research, 86*(4), 849–99.

Stenmark, D. (2000). Leveraging tacit organizational knowledge. *Journal of Management Information Systems, 17*(3), 9–24.

Sun, J., & Leithwood, K. (2015). Direction-setting school leadership practices: A meta-analytic review of evidence about their influence. *School Effectiveness and School Improvement, 26*(4), 499–523.

Thiele, G., Devaux, A., & Velasco, C. (2007). Horizontal evaluation: Fostering knowledge sharing and program improvement within a network. *American Journal of Evaluation, 28*(4), 493–508.

Welsh, R. O., & Little, S. (2018). The school discipline dilemma: A comprehensive review of disparities and alternative approaches. *Review of Educational Research, 88*(5), 752–94.

Zimmerman, B. J. (2002). Becoming a self-regulated learner: An overview. *Theory into Practice, 41*(2), 64–70.

Part 2

Students, Leadership, and Networks

3

Leading toward Relational Inclusivity for Students Identified as Having Special Educational Needs and Disabilities

Christoforos Mamas and David Trautman

Developing a more inclusive educational system has been high on the agenda of most educational systems across the globe. Moving away from segregated special education provisions to more inclusive educational provisions for students with identified Special Educational Needs and Disabilities (SEND) has been a global trend since the 1990s. The Salamanca Statement and Framework for Action on Special Needs Education (UNESCO, 1994) reaffirmed the right to education of every individual and renewed the pledge made by the world community at the World Conference on Education for All (UNICEF, 1990) to ensure that right for all regardless of individual differences. One might argue that the 1994 Salamanca Statement gave birth to the idea and educational philosophy of inclusive education for all students, particularly those with disabilities.

Inclusive education was welcomed by educational stakeholders across the globe as a new philosophy of education that would create more equitable, socially just, and effective school systems for all children, especially those with SEND. However, it soon became apparent that grand declarations, without subsequent pedagogical, leadership, structural and cultural transformations, could hardly succeed. Despite the political and educational will for a more inclusive special education system, there have been numerous challenges in implementing meaningful and efficacious inclusive education for students with SEND. These challenges include schools' unpreparedness, lack of teacher training, societal barriers, such as negative attitudes toward diversity, and limited leadership action for inclusion, among others. In this chapter, we will be discussing one specific approach to fostering what we call "relational inclusivity": the use of a Social Network Analysis (SNA) Toolkit. In this chapter, we hope to equip school leaders with a concrete set of tools that enable them to drive a more inclusive school community. In fostering the development of relational leaders, we note that this does not include just those with formal influence and roles, but also influential individuals within the school community who occupy informal leadership positions, such as classroom teachers or counselors.

Our view reflected across the chapter is that enhancing relational inclusivity, equity, and social justice for all students—and particularly those with SEND—requires leadership which pays systematic attention to the relational aspects of schooling. This chapter is divided into three distinct sections intended to be used as a practical guide for exploring relational inclusivity. We begin by outlining a grounding framework, highlighting the foundations undergirding the notion of relational inclusivity as it pertains to equity. We then offer a step-by-step overview for implementation of the SNA Toolkit, a free, web-based platform that supports high-quality data collection to map out student peer social networks. We then integrate the relational inclusivity lens from the first section into an analysis of a sample data set to illustrate the avenues of exploration leaders can use to foster a healthier, happier, more inclusive school community.

Defining Relational Inclusivity

Despite the international momentum toward "inclusive education" or "inclusion" or "inclusivity," there is still much conceptual ambiguity in defining the term (Lindsay, 2003). In the context of this chapter, we use these terms interchangeably to refer to the various *models* of school organization that promote the involvement of SEND students in the general education environment. Despite the ambiguities, there are a few generally agreed upon tenets of these models. In contrast to the medical model of disability that views disability as an individual deficit, inclusive education stems from the social model of disability (Shakespeare, 2006). According to the latter, disability is defined as a social creation. That is, there is a limited set of biological human differences which are labeled as disability; it is not the differences themselves which cause someone to be disabled, but rather the social institutions around individuals which are unable to accommodate these differences. Therefore, in line with the social model of disability, Liasidou (2012) argues that "inclusive education refers to the restructuring of social and, by implication, educational settings in order to meet the needs of all learners irrespective of their diverse biographical, developmental and learning trajectories" (p. 5). Similarly, Florian (2008) defined inclusion in terms of a philosophy of education that promotes the education of all students in general education settings, and as a policy which is generally understood around the world as part of a human rights agenda that demands access to, and equity in, education (Florian et al., 2016).

One of the main justifications for including students with SEND in general education settings is for the opportunities to engage in social interactions with peers (Mamas et al., 2021). Among others, inclusive pedagogy aims to provide students with opportunities to experience meaningful social interactions and develop peer relationships (Freitag & Dunsmuir, 2015). Since the inception of the idea and educational philosophy of inclusion, it has been argued that the most significant indicator of the success of inclusion is the extent to which these students are accepted by their mainstream peers (Lewis, 2002). Unfortunately, as Connor and Berman (2019) argue, much of what is happening in educational practice in the name of inclusion has been a technical response to change rather than meaningful integration. They continue by concluding that "with the primary emphasis of programmatic management and formulas attached to funding, instead of being grounded in exponential possibilities of pedagogy, inclusive education ironically becomes understood in reductionist terms" (Connor & Berman, 2019, p. 923).

In this chapter, we argue for the concept of "relational inclusivity" as a fundamental ethical, moral, and pedagogical component to larger conceptualizations of inclusive education. By relational inclusivity, we mean the degree to which all students are connected into the social fabric of their educational environments. This rests on a fundamental belief that students' sense of belonging and community are integral to both their academic and civic success. We call it out as a separate term in order to emphasize that programmatic models of inclusion do not necessarily result in *actual* inclusion in all senses of the word. Instead, relational inclusivity needs to be actively monitored, developed, and maintained in order to ensure that students, and particularly those with SEND, are able to fully engage and actively participate in their educational contexts.

This is in close alignment with expectations for school leaders, if not in the concrete sense of accountability, then at the very least in espoused policy frameworks. In the California Professional Standards for Education Leaders (CPSEL), for example, leaders are expected to "facilitate safe, fair, and respectful environments that meet the intellectual, linguistic, cultural, social-emotional, and physical needs of each learner" (CTC, 2014, p. 7). This expectation is elaborated with several indicators, including creating a school climate of belonging, developing preventative plans, and monitoring diverse data sets for equity. The implications of this are clear: the environment we create in schools is not just to meet the academic needs of students; inclusive school communities also foster a sense of belonging and community for all students. It should be noted here that inclusion is not just about students with SEND, but about all students. Nevertheless, in the context of this chapter, we focus on students with SEND as a specific student group due to the long history of formal exclusion from and within school communities. We call on leaders to challenge this legacy by enhancing relational inclusivity for these students.

We argue that leaders who are truly committed to advancing transformative change in their school environments *must* attend to relational inclusivity as a way to combat long-standing inequities, particularly for students with SEND. The idea of relational leadership has been examined more in the prism of wider school reform and change (Daly, 2010; David, 2018; Moolenaar et al., 2010), however not specifically addressing the unique reform efforts within a special education context. Therefore, in this chapter, our aim is to provide a unique perspective on relational leadership in transforming special education toward more inclusive ends.

Schooling as Relational

The heavy emphasis in recent decades on the development of "twenty-first century learning," largely due to the changing demands of an increasingly connected global community, has resulted in a recasting of the various roles of schooling (Kereluik et al., 2013). Nevertheless, what has remained constant is the core role of educational spaces in developing students' knowledge, skills, and dispositions, which can be largely categorized into content knowledge, "meta knowledge" (defined largely around the Four

Cs: critical thinking, communication, collaboration, and creativity) and "humanistic knowledge" (for example, emotional intelligence and cultural competence) (Kereluik et al., 2013). In other words, schools are—and have been—spaces of learning beyond the development of academics for quite some time.

Like twenty-first century skills, social and emotional learning (SEL) has also grown in its prominence in educational discourse in the past quarter century, with clear implications for equity in schools (Jagers et al., 2019). In part, this is due to the recognition that academic learning is a social process which is fundamentally intertwined with students' social and emotional capabilities (Jones & Khan, 2017). Closely related to this is, of course, students' sense of belonging within their educational communities (Farrington, 2013; McMahon et al., 2008). Traditionally marginalized groups may be particularly subjected to both unconscious and explicit messages about the degree to which they belong in school (Ezikwelu, 2020; Walton & Cohen, 2007). SEND students, whose identities intersect with a variety of other forms of marginalization, are no exception. Importantly, student sense of belonging is not only impacted by teacher-student relationships, but peer relationships as well (Osterman, 2000).

Nevertheless, the measurement regimes for accountability in education have been largely focused on concrete academic progress through standardized testing (Lingard et al., 2013) and only proxy measures of the social dimension (often through suspension rate and absenteeism). Students' sense of belonging, their relationship to their educational communities, and overall social-emotional well-being are rarely, if ever, captured in this discourse, which tends to center explicitly on academic achievement or opportunity "gaps" between highly served social groups and students of color, students in poverty, and students with disabilities.

If we acknowledge the fundamental role of students' social capabilities in academic learning *and* the importance of the school in developing a democratic society (Jagers et al., 2019), then this calls for new ways of observing students' social environments in school. Fundamental to discussions of inclusion, therefore, needs to go beyond proxy measures of student learning and school climate. Instead, we need explicit and targeted ways to observe, measure, and reflect on the social environment of learning in schools. We believe that the SNA toolkit provides valuable insights to leaders looking to develop more systematic, iterative ways of understanding the relational dimension of school and that these insights are an important factor addressing educational inequities.

Students as Plural Actors

Further complicating the measurement paradigms in education is that the school is not a monolithic social space in which students engage. That is, individuals experience a plurality of experiences throughout the course of a day that result in a heterogeneous, or plurality, of ways that they show up in relational contexts (Lahire, 2011). In other words, in each of the different social contexts we navigate, we occupy different social positions (Lahire, 2011). Thus, as students navigate the course of their school day, they do not occupy a singular identity; what it means to be a student, a classmate, a group member, or the goalkeeper at recess can be radically different and sometimes even contradictory (Lahire, 2011). As such, when we seek to understand the student experience conceptualizing them solely as a student in the context of a classroom (or even more narrowly in terms of their academic performance), we lose an understanding of the student as a whole individual. Moreover, we lose the ability to think about the myriad ways students engage in social spaces with opportunities for both inclusion and exclusion.

The implications of this are that if we truly want to develop *inclusive* school communities, we have to see the student beyond their identified SEND and how they present themselves in the context of the classroom, group work, or academic assessment. How does the quiet child who accomplishes her work and gets along with others during collaborative class assignments experience the friendship sphere of the classroom? How does this translate to her social experience at recess? After school? While students may appear well-connected in certain contexts, they may not be so well-connected outside of these. To evaluate their relational connectedness, or inclusion, solely on the basis of how they perform in the classroom—assuming that teachers are even positioned to capture these observations given the multiplicity of their roles during instruction—ignores the fact that most of the student's social experience in school exists outside of directly observable social interactions.

Relational Inclusivity as Equity

In addition to the plurality of ways students show up in educational spaces, they also express a multitude of intersecting identities with larger social salience, such as race, class, gender, and disability status. We believe that layering these identities into analysis of relational inclusivity is imperative for equity-oriented leaders.

The implications for equity emerge, in part, when we start to uncover systematic patterns of inclusion and exclusion along an axis of identity within school communities. As noted above, this is typically seen through proxy measures such as suspension data and attendance data. And, when we look at data, we find that these proxy measures reveal a troubling story. More than 16 percent of the nearly 600,000 SEND students in California were chronically absent (missing 10 percent or more of the school year) in 2019 compared to 10.1 percent of the entire student population (CA School Dashboard, n.d., *a*). Moreover, 6.2 percent of SEND students were suspended at least once during that same school year compared to an overall rate of 3.4 percent (CA School Dashboard, n.d., *b*). While our focus is on students in special education in this chapter, it should be noted that there are several other student groups for whom schools are demonstrating concerning patterns, including African American students, homeless, and foster youth. Furthermore, what is not noted in the data cited above is the intersection of different identity labels, for example, suspension rates for African American students with disabilities, though research has shown disproportionate outcomes for youth who experience multiple forms of marginalization (Cruz et al., 2021).

To address these issues of equity, leaders need to take a more active approach by engaging critically in the ways that all their actions have implications for potential inclusion for some students and exclusion for others (Trautman et al., 2022). Ultimately, if school leaders want to create inclusive school communities—ones in which all students experience a sense of belonging, not only with the adults in the school, but other students—then they need to explicitly attend to the school as a complex social space. We also need concrete ways to assess and visualize this, not through reactive, post hoc data, but rather through consistent, systematic measurement combined with ongoing reflection. While social network data is not the only way to do this, we believe the SNA Toolkit is a promising tool for critical reflection among equity-oriented school leaders and educators.

This is for a few reasons. First, as we move toward *de jure* inclusion—models based on current policy frameworks—the question remains as to what forms of *de facto* exclusion remain in the classroom and school. To what extent are students with disabilities fully integrated into the academic and social fabric of the school? How are students socially impacted by different service delivery models? Second, we know that students with disabilities and students from other marginalized backgrounds are disproportionately represented in suspension and absenteeism data, which begs the question, to what extent is this driven by the social dynamics of school? Social network data can provide valuable insights as to students' sense of belonging and connectedness to their classroom communities, and school leaders can leverage this information to create more robust and holistic preventative plans that preempt these issues. Lastly, given our awareness of disability as a social construct (Smagorinsky et al., 2017), if we truly want to create a more just, loving, inclusive society, then we must support all children in recognizing the diverse abilities each individual brings to the table. Analyzing social network data allows us not only to consider the needs of students with disabilities and their inclusion, but also the students around them and their ability to engage constructively with difference. In this sense, inclusion is not solely in reference to students with disabilities, but the ways we prepare all students, across all lines of difference, to engage with one another.

Social Network Perspective

In this chapter, we approach leadership for relational inclusivity from a social network perspective. It is our belief that educational leadership should be intentional about cultivating and growing relationships among all members of a school community.

According to Kenis and Oerlemans (2007), a social network perspective focuses on the joint activities of, and continual exchanges between, participants in a social system or network. They argue that this perspective is characterized by an interest in the relationship patterns that connect the actors that make up a system's or a network's social structure. This book chapter considers that the social network perspective consists of the relationships among students and how these students are embedded within social networks of interconnected relationships that provide opportunities for or constraints in social interactions and other elements in their educational journeys. David (2018) notes that leadership is always relational, and relationships are the essence of leadership. David continues by arguing that relational leadership is not about describing another leadership style, but rather about a relational way of being that utilizes specific relational sensitivities. Thus, below we briefly describe three main assumptions that underpin a social network perspective and call specific attention to who they related to the context of a relational leader.

First, students/actors in a social network are interdependent rather than independent (Daly, 2012; Moolenaar et al., 2012; Wasserman & Faust, 1994). Thus, changes at the interpersonal level (e.g., friendship between two students) are expected to have an impact on the whole network level (e.g., the classroom level) and vice versa. From a relational leadership point of view, school leaders' role becomes pivotal in encouraging and generating whole school or classroom inclusive changes which can then have a positive impact on individual students, including students with SEND. Second, interpersonal relationships are seen as conduits for the flow or exchange of resources such as information, knowledge, materials, and others (Daly, 2012; Kilduff & Tsai, 2003; Moolenaar et al., 2012). Therefore, leaders should strive to create the conditions for students to grow and maintain such interpersonal relationships so that resources can flow through these relational ties. This can be particularly beneficial for students with SEND, as interpersonal relationships may reduce social isolation and exclusion that these students typically experience (Mamas et al., 2021). Third, the structure of a network has influence on the resources that flow to and from an actor (Borgatti & Foster, 2003; Daly, 2012). For example, being well connected to each other within a classroom or school (e.g., dense network) may have a positive impact on students' peer social acceptance, whereas a sparsely connected classroom or school network (e.g., students not well connected to each other) may be conducive toward marginalization and isolation, particularly for students with SEND. Therefore, it is imperative for relational leaders to be mindful of and be strategic about the structure of social networks within their schools.

We argue that in order to promote relational inclusion, school leaders should strive to create more socially responsive and networked school communities. It is our view that one way of achieving this is through the deployment of the SNA toolkit that we describe and discuss below.

Overview of the SNA Toolkit

The Social Network Analysis (SNA) Toolkit is an easy-to-use, free, web-based program which facilitates leaders' use of the social network perspective in advancing relational inclusivity. It was conceived, designed, and developed to enable educators conduct basic and descriptive SNA in order to understand the social dynamics within their settings. A noteworthy advantage is that it does not require any knowledge around social network methods; the necessary elements are built into the program. It is worth noting that there is a wide variety of SNA software, including UCINET, R, SIENA, Gephi, Pajek, and others. In our opinion, these software packages are not particularly educator-friendly and require some prerequisite SNA research knowledge. Mamas and Huang (2022) offer a close-up comparison between the SNA Toolkit and UCINET. The SNA Toolkit is currently hosted under the domain name Socionomy.net.

In the following subsections, we will guide the reader through some of the logistics and functions of the SNA Toolkit that can be particularly useful in launching a meaningful investigation into the degree of relational inclusivity in their school community. Any educator can use the Toolkit to take a snapshot of the social dynamics within their classroom at any given point in time. The SNA Toolkit can be used across the K-12 spectrum with the use of age-appropriate prompts when collecting relational data from students. School leaders or leadership teams can then examine that data closely and inform policy and instructional decisions at the school level.

Implementing the SNA Toolkit

At the school level, the school leader or leadership team can empower several educators to conduct such work in their classrooms so a "birds-eye view" of the whole school in terms of relationships may be obtained. In previous writings, we offered a more detailed overview of the Toolkit's functions (Mamas et al., 2019; Mamas & Huang, 2022). Here, we focus on presenting the basics of how the Toolkit may be used in general to transform special and inclusive education and, in doing so, enhance relational inclusion. Here are some suggestive steps to be followed by leaders and educators.

Step 1

First, the school leader or leadership team convenes educators to discuss vision for school improvement in relation to curating a more relationally responsive and caring school community. The SNA Toolkit is introduced during that initial meeting. The main functions of the Toolkit are explained to educators and they are invited to sign up. These main functions include collecting relational data (e.g., data on friendship ties, recess ties, or advice ties) as well as analyzing and interpreting the results from each classroom in a classroom-level and student-level report. The sign-up process is fairly straightforward. The school leader or someone appointed by them is responsible for signing up the whole school. Then, links are generated and sent to participating educators so they can register their classroom. Classroom registration on the Toolkit may be completed centrally at the school level. Even though registering a classroom on the Toolkit and adding the students for the first time is not very lengthy (about 15 minutes depending on classroom size), this is the lengthiest part of the whole process.

Step 2

After educators have signed up their classrooms, they will have access to the Toolkit's dashboard. On the dashboard, they can create as many classrooms as they want. As the Toolkit performs whole descriptive SNA, the networks examined should be bounded. This means that educators should populate each classroom with all the students rostered in the actual classroom environment (e.g., grade 4 homeroom). Classroom registration or creation involves setting the size of the classroom (e.g., twenty-five students), uploading students' names or unique identifiers and setting demographic information (e.g., gender, disability status, race/ethnicity, etc.). Educators have the option to manually add the names/identifiers and demographic information of their students or upload an Excel file. It is worth noting that the classroom has to be registered only once. After the classroom has been created, any number of relational surveys may be generated. Though the surveys are fully customizable, educators may opt to rely on pre-programmed, suggested questions. These survey questions include, for example: Who are your friends in the classroom? Who do you play with during recess? Who do you talk to if you are having a bad day at school? If your teacher is not available, who do you go to for advice on academic matters? Educators may also choose to add to the survey any age-appropriate relational questions they are interested in or remove questions they do not wish to use. The survey can be deployed as many times as educators see fit for longitudinal data collection.

Step 3

In order to disseminate the survey to their students, educators share a survey link with them, which is automatically generated by the Toolkit. Students then click on the link and respond to the survey. Upon completion and submission of the survey, the Toolkit generates the results for the classroom. The results include both a classroom report and an individualized report for each student. Educators have immediate access to those results and reports with a click of a button. The results include visual network maps (sociograms) for the classroom social networks based on each prompt/question in the survey. For example, the friendship question will yield the friendship network map for the classroom. Figure 3.1 shows one such network map.

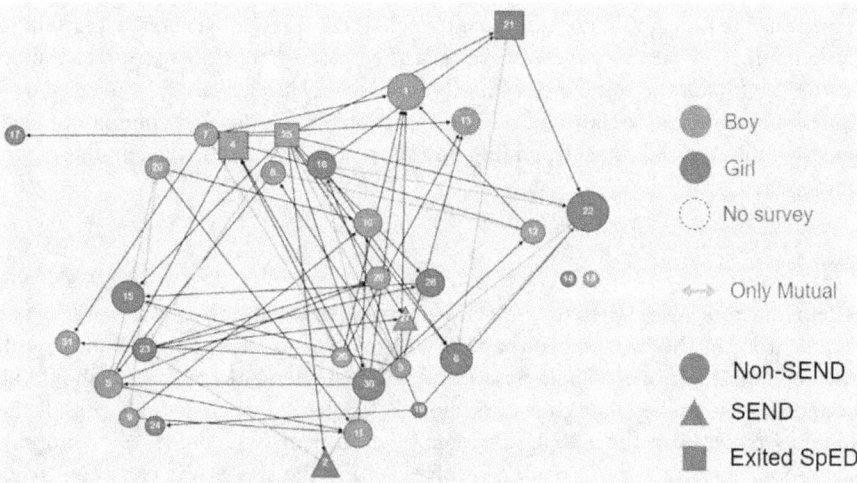

Figure 3.1 An example of a friendship network map.

Step 4

After the data have been collected and the reports produced, educators at the classroom level and the leadership team at the school level should make sense of it. Each question's network map can be customized to highlight information of interest to the school team, with options to change node size, color, and shape based on different measures and variables. In Figure 3.1, for example, each node (geometric shapes) represents a student in the classroom. The node size is based on the number of friendship nominations received from each student, or in-degree centrality (meaning that the more nominations received, the bigger the node size is). Alternatively, node size can be set to adjust according to other measures, such as out-degree centrality (number of nominations sent out by each student) or betweenness centrality, which represents the degree to which nodes stand between each other (depicting a student's role the flow of information from one part of the network to the other). In Figure 3.1, the different colors show the gender of students. These color schemes can also be adjusted for any other demographic variables in the dataset. In Figure 3.1, the triangular and square shapes represent students with SEND. In this case, triangular shapes show students with an IEP, whereas the square-shaped nodes show students who have exited their special education program. Of course, classroom educators can assign different attributes to node shapes. Arrows indicate the friendship nominations made by each student, with red double-edged arrows to show mutual friendship nominations. If any student does not complete the survey, their node is shown with a dotted outline.

In addition to examining the sociograms, educators should explore the descriptive SNA measures included in the classroom and student-level reports to help them make a better sense of their students' social dynamics. The classroom report includes the density for each classroom network. Network density shows the portion of the potential connections in a network that are actual connections, and it is represented by a percentage. For example, if the density within the friendship network of classroom is 23 percent, that means that out of a possible 100 connections, twenty-three exist. If all students were connected to each other with a friendship tie (a very unlikely scenario) the density would be 100 percent. A low network density may be a sign of a weakly connected classroom in which information, knowledge, and resources may be harder to flow. Having the ability to compare and contrast these measures across different time points can be particularly useful for educators to track the progress of their students in terms of social engagement and participation. Additionally, the average degree centrality for each of the networks is provided in the classroom report. In the case of the friendship network, the average degree centrality would show how many friendship nominations were received or sent out on average by each student. For example, if the average degree centrality were seven, this would mean that on average each student in that classroom received or sent out seven friendship nominations. Lastly, at the dyad level, reciprocity is also calculated which is a measure that shows how many of the ties in the network are reciprocated. A higher number of reciprocal ties may be a sign of a close-knit classroom community with higher relational inclusion.

Descriptive measures such as in-degree and out-degree centrality are also included in the student report. In-degree centrality shows the number of nominations received by each student. For example, in a friendship network, if the in-degree of student A is three, that means that three of their classmates identified them as their friend. This measure can show how sought-after a student is within each network in the classroom. On the flip side, out-degree centrality shows the outgoing nominations of a student. For example, if student A identifies eight students in the classroom as their friend, their out-degree would be eight. Comparing in-degree and out-degree centrality for student A, we may observe that student A has more outgoing friendship nominations (eight) than incoming (three), suggesting that this student may be overestimating the nature and depth of their classroom relationships. Additional measures are anticipated to be included in future iterations of both the Toolkit's classroom and student reports, which are revised as additional educator feedback is collected, new insights in research emerge, and as technology advances.

Relational Inclusivity and the Toolkit

In this section, we highlight a few noticings on Figure 3.1 to start illustrating some of the questions and ideas educators might want to consider when engaging with the data from a standpoint of relational inclusivity. The social network data in the map is a starting point for further investigation; analysis should prompt further questions. First, we look at students around the periphery. For example, you may notice three students (14, 18, and 19) with no in-degree nominations (as in, no one identified them as a friend). Of these, only one (19) identified other classmates as friends. Additionally, two other students (17, 24) have no outgoing nominations. Though none of these are students with SEND, educators might want to dig into the social dynamics for these students. Of note, four of these students identify as female. This might prompt educators to think specifically about the gendered dynamics of the classroom. Further, they may ask, what does their classroom engagement look like? What factors might be leading to their friendship isolation? Does this isolation extend into other networks in which they participate? Therefore, it is important to use the Toolkit to examine different networks that capture diverse domains of socioemotional and academic well-being of students. For example, friendship networks may be studied along with advice and trust networks.

A second noticing is that by and large, SEND students (2 and 27) appear to be relatively well-connected to other students, with Student 2 showing two reciprocal ties and 27 both giving and receiving friendship nominations. This might prompt educators to think about what aspects of the classroom community are contributing to this dynamic. Is it similar across classrooms in the school, or is this a unique case? Insight into the teaching and social practices facilitating this inclusion merits further investigation. On a similar note, we notice that students who have exited special education (4, 21, and 25) are similarly well-connected, with student 25 appearing to be a hub of social activity, particularly in relation to outgoing nominations. It is worth mentioning that the Toolkit should not be used exclusively to uncover what is "wrong" with relational inclusivity but rather to share what works well in specific classrooms.

Our intention here is not to provide a "cheat sheet" as to what leaders and educators should be noticing on the various network maps of their respective schools and classrooms. We rather see the Toolkit as a starting point for discussion on relational inclusivity, that is based on systematic data collection and evidence that can be made available quickly and at low cost. Therefore, we encourage educators and leaders to be creative and systematic with their noticings and design and implement subsequent pedagogical practices that will best serve the interests of their students, especially those who need the most support.

Implications for Leadership

In the above section, we highlighted some of the ways educators might engage the Toolkit to deepen their understanding of relational inclusivity and identify potential lines of inquiry. Building on this, here we outline some of the main reasons why using the SNA Toolkit may be catalytic toward achieving relational inclusivity. One main reason is that the Toolkit enables leaders to collect relational student data in a systematic manner. As we note above, the data in and of itself is meaningless; what is important from a leadership and instructional perspective is how we make sense of it and inform pedagogical decisions based on that data.

Inclusive education advocates argue that one of the main functions of inclusion is for students with SEND to benefit socially and emotionally by being active participants in the school community. However, overwhelming research evidence on the social participation (Koster et al., 2009) of these students has shown that in most cases students with SEND remain on the margins of their classrooms or school communities (Koster et al., 2010; Mamas et al., 2021). Therefore, it is imperative that social relationships and interactions can be captured and measured in a systematic and non-complicated manner. In Figure 3.1, we find that exclusion of students with SEND does *not* appear to be occurring socially in the context of friendship networks in the classroom. Leaders can work toward establishing a culture of inclusivity by using the Toolkit to get a "snapshot" of the social dynamics within their schools and, in doing so, identifying not just those students who may be at risk of exclusion and social isolation, but also "bright spots" where we see strong ties for traditionally marginalized students. As we note in the example, isolated students may be those with SEND but also other students too, including racially, ethnically, culturally, linguistically, and financially diverse students.

Another reason that is similar but particularly relevant to special education is to collect relational data as part of a student's Individual Education Plan (IEP) development and assessment. It is usually the case for students with IEPs/SEND to have goals related to social aspects of learning, such as developing friendships, participating in social activities, or minimizing loneliness and other. Educators are mandated to collect evidence to show how they are addressing such goals. One way of achieving this can be through the SNA Toolkit. These data can be then put together to monitor each student's progress on achieving their relational goals and minimizing their likelihood for social isolation.

A third reason is to examine the efficacy of school-wide policies or interventions aiming to enhance relational inclusivity and minimize social isolation not just for students with SEND, but for all students who have a higher risk of being marginalized. Having a readily available platform to collect relational data, such as the SNA Toolkit, affords the ability for immediate and continuous feedback on any school-wide intervention or policy aiming to enhance relational inclusivity and equity. Schools and classrooms can collect baseline data, implement their interventions, and engage in ongoing cycles of inquiry regarding observed changes. School leaders and educators are responsible for curating a dynamic, social learning process in more constructivist, student-centered learning environments. In doing so, we argue that there should be alignment of social intentionality with instructional programs. A curriculum that places emphasis on social and emotional aspects of learning is more likely to lead toward more inclusive and caring communities.

Conclusion

Educational leadership is admittedly vital in catalyzing wider educational reform and change (Daly, 2010; Datnow et al., 2002). The same can be assumed in reform and transformation of special education toward more inclusive ends. However, there is very little research addressing the role of relational leadership in transforming special education. Of particular concern for us is the manner in which inclusion is approached and addressed by school leaders. Part of this is confusion regarding the term. Norwich (2008) notes that inclusion has been conceptualized in varied ways and engendered multiple theoretical tensions and dilemmas. Liasidou (2012) describes inclusion as a semantic chameleon because it adopts a different color and meaning when used by different people, at different times, and in different places. In this chapter, we offer a definition of relational inclusivity both to provide clarity and to promote deeper thinking about the various facets of inclusive education.

As Rayner (2007) pointed out, managing inclusion should reflect an inclusive leadership characterized by an enduring concern for diversity, access, and achievement. We would add to Rayner's point by arguing that managing inclusion should also reflect an inclusive leadership style that is actively promoting positive and meaningful relationship building among students and school leaders are systematic about understanding and improving those relationships. Developing and promoting a relational school culture among students can be conducive toward reducing social isolation and marginalization for all students, particularly those with SEND and be a catalyst for increasing trust, respect, and mutual support among all students in the school. It can also be catalytic toward enhancing their academic success, as studies have shown a positive relationship between peer social networks and academic achievement of students (Cook & Kim, 2017; Ryabov, 2011).

A school leader who is committed toward creating more inclusive and socially responsive communities within their school can promote the use of the Toolkit among educators. It can also be beneficial to school leaders to keep monitoring school-wide initiatives that aim to create a more inclusive, socially responsive, and relational community. Creating the ideal school may be utopic, but this should not prevent leaders and educators alike from creating a better, safer, and more inclusive learning community. The Toolkit is not a panacea when it comes to relational inclusivity but can contribute toward meaningful inquiry in this direction. It is certainly rewarding to all involved in this important work when their students feel happier, more secure, more connected and have an enhanced sense of belonging and socioemotional well-being.

References

Borgatti, S. P., & Foster, P. C. (2003). The network paradigm in organizational research: A review and typology. *Journal of Management, 29*(6), 991–1013.

California Commission on Teacher Credentialing (CTC). (2014). *California Professional Standards for Education Leaders (CPSEL)*.

CA School Dashboard. (n.d., *a*). *State Summary, 2019: Academic Engagement*. Available at: https://www.caschooldashboard.org/reports/ca/2019/academic-engagement#chronic-absenteeism. Accessed: March 15, 2022.

CA School Dashboard. (n.d., *b*). *State Summary, 2019: Conditions and Climate*. Available at: https://www.caschooldashboard.org/reports/ca/2019/conditions-and-climate#suspension-rate. Accessed: March 15, 2022.

Connor, D. J., & Berman, D. (2019). (Be) Longing: A family's desire for authentic inclusion. *International Journal of Inclusive Education, 23*(9), 923–36.

Cook, N., & Kim, J. S. (2017). Peer influence on children's reading skills: A social network analysis of elementary school classrooms. *Journal of Educational Psychology, 109*(5), 727.

Cruz, R. A., Kulkarni, S. S., & Firestone, A. R. (2021). A QuantCrit analysis of context, discipline, special education, and disproportionality. *AERA Open*. Available at: https://doi.org/10.1177/23328584211041354

Daly, A. J. (2010). *Social network theory and educational change*. Harvard Education Press.

Daly, A. J. (2012). Data, dyads, and dynamics: Exploring data use and social networks in educational improvement. *Teachers College Record, 114*(11), 1–38.

Datnow, A., Hubbard, L., & Mehan, H. (2002). *Extending educational reform*. Taylor & Francis.

David, L. G. (2018). *Relational leadership in education: A phenomenon of inquiry and practice*. Routledge.

Ezikwelu, E. U. (2020). Institutional racism and campus racial climate: Struggles for sense of belonging and academic success among black students in the K-12 public schools. *Journal of Critical Thought and Praxis, 10*(1), 1–20.

Farrington, C. (2013). *Academic mindsets as a critical component of deeper learning*. William and Flora Hewlett Foundation. Available at: https://www.hewlett.org/wp-content/uploads/2016/08/Academic_Mindsets_as_a_Critical_Component_of_Deeper_Learning_CAMILLE_FARRINGTON_April_20_2013.pdf

Florian, L. (2008). Inclusion: Special or inclusive education: Future trends. *British Journal of Special Education, 35*(4), 202–8.

Florian, L., Black-Hawkins, K., & Rouse, M. (2016). *Achievement and inclusion in schools*. Routledge.

Freitag, S., & Dunsmuir, S. (2015). The inclusion of children with ASD: Using the theory of planned behaviour as a theoretical framework to explore peer attitudes. *International Journal of Disability, Development and Education, 62*(4), 405–21.

Jagers, R. J., Rivas-Drake, D., & Williams, B. (2019). Transformative social and emotional learning (SEL): Toward SEL in service of educational equity and excellence. *Educational Psychologist, 54*(3), 162–84.

Jones, S. M., & Kahn, J. (2017). *The evidence base for how we learn supporting students' social, emotional, and academic development*. National Commission on Social, Emotional, and Academic Development. The Aspen Institute.

Kenis, P. N., & Oerlemans, L. A. G. (2007). The social network perspective: Understanding the structure of cooperation. In *Oxford handbook of inter-organizational relationships* (pp. 289–312). Oxford University Press.

Kereluik, K., Mishra, P., Fahnoe, C., & Terry, L. (2013). What knowledge is of most worth: Teacher knowledge for 21st century learning. *Journal of Digital Learning in Teacher Education*, 29(4), 127–40.

Kilduff, M., & Tsai, W. (2003). *Social networks and organizations*. Sage Publications.

Koster, M., Timmerman, M. E., Nakken, H., Pijl, S. J., & van Houten, E. J. (2009). Evaluating social participation of pupils with special needs in regular primary schools: Examination of a teacher questionnaire. *European Journal of Psychological Assessment*, 25(4), 213–22.

Koster, M., Pijl, S. J., Nakken, H., & Van Houten, E. (2010). Social participation of students with special needs in regular primary education in the Netherlands. *International Journal of Disability, Development and Education*, 57(1), 59–75.

Lahire, B. (2011). *The plural actor*. D. Fernbach (Trans.). Polity. (Original work published 1998).

Lewis, A. (2002). *Children's understanding of disability*. Routledge.

Lindsay, G. (2003). Inclusive education: a critical perspective. *British Journal of Special Education*, 30(1), 3–12. DOI: 10.1111/1467-8527.00275

Liasidou, A. (2012). *Inclusive education, politics and policymaking*. Continuum.

Lingard, B., Martino, M., & Rezai-Rashti, G. (2013). Testing regimes, accountabilities and education policy: Commensurate global and national developments. *Journal of Education Policy*, 28(5), 539–56, DOI: 10.1080/02680939.2013.820042

Mamas, C., & Huang, H. (2022). Social network analysis software packages. In B. Frey (Ed.), *The SAGE encyclopedia of research design* (Vol. 1, pp. 1554–5). Sage Publications.

Mamas, C., Daly, A. J., Struyve, C., Kaimi, I., & Michail, G. (2019). Learning, friendship and social contexts: Introducing a social network analysis toolkit for socially responsive classrooms. *International Journal of Educational Management*, 33(6), 1255–70.

Mamas, C., Daly, A. J., Cohen, S. R., & Jones, G. (2021). Social participation of students with autism spectrum disorder in general education settings. *Learning, Culture and Social Interaction*, 28, 100467.

McMahon, S. D., Parnes, A. L., Keys, C. B., & Viola, J. J. (2008). School belonging among low-income urban youth with disabilities: Testing a theoretical model. *Psychology in the Schools*, 45(5), 387–401. DOI: 10.1002/pits.20304

Moolenaar, N. M., Daly, A. J., & Sleegers, P. J. (2010). Occupying the principal position: Examining relationships between transformational leadership, social network position, and schools' innovative climate. *Educational Administration Quarterly*, 46(5), 623–70.

Moolenaar, N. M., Sleegers, P. J., & Daly, A. J. (2012). Teaming up: Linking collaboration networks, collective efficacy, and student achievement. *Teaching and Teacher Education*, 28(2), 251–62.

Norwich, B. (2008). Dilemmas of difference, inclusion and disability: International perspectives on placement. *European Journal of Special Needs Education*, 23(4), 287–304.

Osterman, K. F. (2000). Students' need for belonging in the school community. *Review of Educational Research*, 70(3), 323–67. https://doi.org/10.3102/00346543070003323

Shakespeare, T. (2006). The social model of disability. *The Disability Studies Reader*, 2, 197–204.

Smagorinsky, P., Cole, M., & Willadino Braga, L. (2017). On the complementarity of cultural historical psychology and contemporary disability studies. In Esmonde, I., & Booker, A. N. (Eds.), *Power and privilege in the learning sciences: Critical and sociocultural theories of learning* (pp. 70–92). Routledge.

Trautman, D., Jones, M., Bagula, F., & Green, Z. (2022). Emancipatory leadership development in action: The RISE Urban Principal Pipeline. In Brown, K., Rodriguez, S., & Papa, R. (Eds.), *Recipes to Combat the "ISMS" Volume 2* (pp. 85–92). Lulu.

Rayner, S. (2007). *Managing special and inclusive education*. Sage.

Ryabov, I. (2011). Adolescent academic outcomes in school context: Network effects reexamined. *Journal of Adolescence, 34*(5), 915–27.

UNESCO (1994). *The salamanca statement and framework for action on special needs education*. UNESCO.

UNICEF (1990). *World conference on education for all: Meeting basic learning needs.* Jomtien, Thailand, March 5–9, 1990.

Walton, G. M., & Cohen, G. L. (2007). A question of belonging: Race, social fit, and achievement. *Journal of Personality and Social Psychology, 92*(1), 82–96. https://doi.org/10.1037/0022-3514.92.1.82

Wasserman, S., & Faust, K. (1994). *Social network analysis: Methods and applications*. Cambridge University Press.

The Impact of Support Networks on the Education and Development of Pre-Service Teachers

Chloe Eddy and Christopher Downey

Introduction

The Initial Teacher Education (ITE) phase in a teachers' career is one of the most critical; a year which Flores (2020, p. 1) describes as a "multi-dimensional process of teacher identity development which is influenced by personal, social and cognitive responses." Combined with the professional and academic requirements of pre-service teachers in England, graduate routes to ITE can be challenging. The road to qualified teacher status (QTS) is one that is defined by multiple transitions, multiple school placements, academic assignments and for most, the first time stepping in the classroom in a teaching capacity. When considering the impact of this on pre-service teachers, previous research has pointed to feelings of isolation, vulnerability, resentment, and burnout (Bloomfield, 2010; Smit *et al.*, 2021), while other studies point to the importance of impersonal trust and networks of support on positive outcomes of ITE (Liou *et al.*, 2017).

Despite these pressures, there is surprisingly little empirical research into the various support networks that enable pre-service teachers to progress and succeed. This is in spite of high levels of teacher attrition in the UK, with 22 percent of teachers leaving the profession within their first two years of teaching (Foster, 2019). Early career Secondary maths and science teachers, in particular, have above average attrition rates (Worth & De Lazzari, 2017). In light of this challenge, key stakeholders posit ITE as a strategic priority in improving the retention of early career teachers, such as initiatives outlined in the "Teacher Recruitment and Retention Strategy" (DfE, 2019). Part of this strategy focuses on developing early career teachers' resilience and self-efficacy by expanding their support networks, but it fails to recognize how support networks within ITE may also contribute to development.

Literature Review

As previously noted, the literature regarding the social networks of pre-service teachers is fairly modest. Therefore, when appropriate, reference has also been made to early career teachers. A social network perspective of ITE is introduced, as well as the concepts of self-efficacy and social capital theory. The links between support networks and the development of pre-service teachers are also considered.

A Social Network Perspective of Initial Teacher Education

The social side of pre-service education has been noted to be under-researched when compared to other areas of pre-service education, namely the focus of developing teaching competencies and pedagogical skills (Liou et al., 2017), and emotional intelligence (Trapp, 2010). Considering the construct of pre-service teachers' identities in their ITE year (which we know to be multifaceted and complex (Beijaard et al., 2004; Lutovac & Flores, 2021)) helps us to understand how complex the social landscape may be. In some ways the pre-service teacher views themselves as a student and a learner. Throughout the year they navigate the identity shift toward being a teacher, and a professional (Beltman et al., 2015). This can result in a complex set of relational networks that provide access to support through this transition in tapping into a range of sources of academic, professional, and emotional support.

The Networks of Pre-Service Teachers

Social network analysis (SNA) is an analytical and theoretical tool that enables the study of social structures within a population. Broadly speaking, network studies can be divided into "whole networks" which study the relationships within a specified population, or "egocentric" networks constructed around an individual (Wasserman & Faust, 1994). In the educational field, SNA became a significant method to explore the way teachers and schools interact with one other. Borgatti and Ofem (2010) point to two distinct reasons that SNA remains so integral to educational research. Firstly, SNA can be conducted at multiple levels of analysis; networks can be constructed around the individual, around teams, across organizations, and even across countries. Secondly, SNA allows for both quantitative and qualitative methods of data collection, "allowing for fuller descriptions of the social world that are both ethnographically grounded and quantitively rigorous," (Borgatti & Ofem, 2010, p. 18).

Borgatti and Ofem (2010) provide a typology of the types of SNA research, distinguishing between two broad domains. The first domain is the "theory of networks," in which research is interested in the antecedents of network variables, and network evolution. The second domain, "network theory," is more concerned with the consequences of the network on other variables. Both domains can be studied at three levels of analysis: the dyad level (between pairs of actors), the node level (around an individual), and finally at the group (whole network) level. At all levels, Wasserman and Faust (1994) point to the fact that the social network is a representation of the relational capital (represented by ties between nodes) among actors (individuals in the network). Thus, a key benefit of such an approach is that the researcher is able to identify the social and relational capital around the individual that is not possible through the use of statistics alone (Anscombe, 1973).

Much literature in the field of social network analysis, specifically related to the structure of networks, suggests that tightly knit networks with a higher density enable the efficient dissemination of information (Lin, 2001). Density in a network was defined by Boissevain (1974) as a measure of how many ties within a network exist compared to the potential number of ties that could exist. Therefore, a higher density within a network may suggest that information can flow across the network more efficiently (Inkpen & Tsang, 2005) because more actors are relationally tied to one another. Research on network density in teacher networks has broadly suggested this to be true. For example, professional collaboration has been argued to have positive effects on the educational outcomes of students (Tschannen-Moran & Barr, 2004). Daly et al.'s (2014a) study on teacher networks found that teachers' social capital had a direct influence on their students' performance, even when controlling for prior attainment and student demographics. Similarly, Berebitsky and Salloum (2017) also suggested in their longitudinal study of teacher networks in the US context that student performance improved as a result of collective efficacy through their network. Both Daly et al. (2014a) and Berebitsky and Salloum (2017) posit that the potential reason for this is that teacher performance improved as a result of collaboration through their network. This may be related to the flow of resources, advice, and expertise that is being shared rapidly amongst colleagues (Finnigan & Daly, 2012).

The Initial Teacher Education Context in the UK

The ITE landscape in England is one that has long been characterized by rapid and swift policy reform (La Velle *et al.*, 2020), and since the publication of an influential policy document "*The Importance of Teaching*" (DfE, 2010) ITE has been an area of intense scrutiny in England. ITE provision has become a key driver in raising pupil attainment and raising school standards (Barber & Mourshed, 2007). University Led (UL) routes to qualified teacher status (QTS) remained the most common route into teaching in England up until the government popularization of school direct (SD) routes (DfE, 2014), although salaried SD requires previous school-based work experience in order to qualify for the course. While some have described the shift toward school-led provision as fulfilling neoliberalist agendas within education (Furlong, 2013), others have pointed to the fact that both UL and SD routes into teaching can be very similar experiences, so the impact on program design and delivery is minimized (Brouwer *et al.*, 2020). However, the difference in the support networks of pre-service teachers following different routes into teaching is relatively under researched.

One feature common to both routes is the emphasis on practical, school-based experience. The current requirement of all ITE providers, whether UL or SD, is a minimum of 24 weeks practical experience in at least two schools (DfE, 2022). The ITE learning context, despite being 10–11 months, is full of major transitional periods for the pre-service teacher. This is not only the social shifts as they move from university to schools, but also the identity shift from student to teacher (Brown, 2006). Hence, when analyzing the ITE landscape with a network perspective, variety in the experience of pre-service teachers must be considered.

Theoretical Framework

Self-Efficacy and the Development of Pre-Service Teachers

Self-efficacy is a cognitive construct that is broadly understood to be the self-perceived belief in one's abilities to perform the cognitive and behavioral tasks that are required of them (Bandura, 1977). For teachers, studying self-efficacy has revealed that low self-efficacy is related to higher levels of classroom stress and low job satisfaction (Klassen & Chiu, 2010), as well as poorer student outcomes and teacher attrition (Huber et al., 2016). In many ways, teacher self-efficacy is well worthy of its own definition. Tschannen-Moran and Hoy (2001) defined teacher self-efficacy as the self-judgment of whether a teacher feels capable of bringing about desired outcomes for student learning and motivation, even in challenging contexts. Barni et al. (2019) expand upon this definition by including wider professional responsibilities and well-being in the school environment. In both instances, self-efficacy is a self-belief that can both grow and decline in relation to life experiences (Bandura, 1977), interactions with others (Liou & Daly, 2018), and experiences of success or failure (Skaalvik & Skaalvik, 2016). Therefore, one may posit that for teachers, self-efficacy cannot necessarily be considered to grow not just with time, but instead in relation to specific experiences and relationships.

This notion grows much more interesting when considering the perceived self-efficacy of pre-service teachers. For example, as Skaalvik and Skaalvik (2016) contend, self-efficacy may come as a result of mastery of experiences, which many pre-service teachers may not have had yet. This may explain the reason why feedback is so important to pre-service teachers (McCormack et al., 2006) as they aim to prescribe value to their teaching experiences. Like in service teachers, self-efficacy has also been related to the development of teaching competencies by Liou et al. (2017), and also to tie formation and the development of communication networks. Bjorklund et al. (2021) liken this to the importance of self-efficacy in trusting your peers and feeling like you belong in your network.

Network Theoretical Perspective of Social Capital in ITE

Social capital is defined by Woolcock (2001, p. 13) as "the norms and networks that enable people to act collectively," emphasizing the quality of the ties within a network as opposed to the quantity of ties. Coleman (1990) contends that social capital enables the flow and distribution of resources, and thus at the individual level, social capital is a valuable resource that enables people to achieve individual goals. What's more, Fukuyama (1995) posits social capital as a key driver of relational trust. The range of definitions alludes to the range of types of social capital that can be utilized by an individual, in the same way that individuals are part of a range of networks with differing functions (Little, 2010).

For teachers, social capital has been shown to be affected by the school leaders' attitudes toward teacher collaboration and collegiality, and the established ethos in the school (Penuel et al., 2009). Educational leaders therefore have a significant role to play in developing a supportive culture and modeling collaborative behaviors. In schools with high levels of social capital, information and resources are able to be shared more widely and more efficiently (Penuel et al., 2009) which in turn benefits student outcomes (Demir, 2021). Demir and Qureshi (2019) also report other benefits of social capital for teachers, namely continuous professional development, implementing school reform, and job retention and satisfaction.

For pre-service teachers, the role of social capital is more nuanced as the pre-service teacher is still navigating the dual identity of student and teacher in their ITE year. In terms of early career teachers, social capital may enhance the introduction and retention of people entering the profession (Demir, 2021), but less is known about the social capital of pre-service teachers (Brouwer et al., 2020). Mandzuk et al. (2005) studied the impact of a cohort model approach to ITE. For these pre-service teachers, the benefits of social capital were broadly similar to those of in-service teachers. Interestingly, the negative role of social capital was also explored. Some pre-service teachers struggled with the relationships within the university setting, citing issues of not feeling they fit in, or worrying if they seemed to be struggling more than their peers. Therefore, when studying pre-service teachers' development of social capital, these complexities should be carefully considered.

The Link between Support Networks and The Performance and Development of Pre-Service Teachers

While clear associations between teacher networks and professional development have been established in the literature, the evidence of this link in pre-service teachers is more sparse. More empirical studies engaging with the social networks of pre-service teachers are needed in order to begin making deliberate improvements to ITE programs (Civis et al., 2019). There is evidence to suggest that the relational capital of pre-service teachers can have an effect on their performance. In the US context, Liou et al. (2017) found that the social ties and peer trust amongst trainee teachers were positively associated with their teaching performance. What's more, several other studies have highlighted the significant role of social capital in developing innovative practices (Jensen, 2012), and speaking about classroom support (Steinbrecher & Hart, 2012). There is some counter evidence to suggest that the support networks of teachers have no significant impact on their perceived self-efficacy (Thomas et al., 2019).

In the context of early career teachers, networks in the very first few weeks of teaching were primarily focused on settling into the school, and then gradually developed into support networks that aided their professional development (Marz & Kelchtermans, 2020). While this study did not make associations between the networks of early career teachers and their teaching competence, it demonstrates how networks enabled them to feel they had developed as teachers. In a study of early career teachers in Wales, a lack of support networks was associated with early career teachers feeling unappreciated and resentful toward the older teachers in the school (McCormack & Thomas, 2003), as well as the fact designated mentors were themselves underprepared to support early career teachers' development.

Collectively, these studies outline the potential for stakeholders in ITE in not only facilitating the development of these networks, but utilizing them as a means to improve the performance outcomes of pre-service teachers. Attrition in the UK is high, and as previously mentioned, it has been established in the literature that the first two years of a teachers' career are critical in terms of attrition (Foster, 2019). Thus, research that aims to directly capture the consequences of the social networks of pre-service teachers is integral to the education sector. In light of this identified gap in the literature, this study will address the following research questions.

Research Questions

1. To what extent is the growth in observation scores and perceived self-efficacy predicted by characteristics of the pre-service teacher's social support network?
2. To what extent is the growth in observation scores and perceived self-efficacy predicted by the pre-service teacher's views on social networks and support?

Methodology

The following chapter presents the methodological aspects of the study. It begins by introducing the research design of the study. The participants are described, as well as all variables and measures utilized in the data analysis. Finally, the analytic approach toward the development of a latent growth curve model is described, including how the null (or unconditional) models were built.

Research Design

The study utilized a longitudinal survey design, with data being collected at four strategically timed data collection points in order to reflect some of the key transitional periods that pre-service teachers experience during the ITE program. Full network data were collected in order to create egocentric networks of each pre-service teacher. Internal network data involved participants selecting from a class roster those peers to whom they had reached out for support in the previous month. External network data collection provided participants the opportunity to share their wider support network, for example mentors, colleagues, family members, and friends external to their course peer group. Demographic data on age and sex were collected, as well as whether participants were enrolled as maths or science subject specialists, and whether they were pursuing the School Direct (SD) course or University Led (UL) course. Other contextual data collected related to the pre-service teachers' views on support, networks, and trust. Data were collected via an online questionnaire that took approximately 20 minutes to complete.

Applying Borgatti and Ofem's (2010) typology of network research, this study falls within the "type 4: individual social capital" domain, in which the consequences of occupying a certain space within a network is examined at the individual (node) level. As the research hypotheses of this study are concerned the exploration of the dependent variables related to the pre-service teachers' individual level attributes, the decision to utilize a data set with an egocentric network design (as opposed to whole networks) was therefore appropriate. What's more, as a key assumption within structural equation modeling is independent of cases in order to avoid predictable biases (Kaplan, 2000) egocentric data were more appropriate than the whole network data. This is because the network data collected were around the individual's own network, and focused on support-seeking behaviors as opposed to **who** was providing support. This is in line with other social network studies imploring a SEM approach, for example Liu et al. (2018, p. 715) who state "specifically, the edges in a social network are conditionally independent given levels of covariates and latent personality traits."

Sampling and Participants

The sample was collected through a convenience sampling procedure, a form of non-probability sampling. Participants were invited to partake in the study if they were enrolled on a selected maths and science secondary ITE program in England. While non-probability sampling comes with certain inferential limitations, the nature of this SNA study deems the use of probability sampling inappropriate. The sampling of a specifically chosen class reflects a true social landscape, and external validity can be justified on the basis that this sample may be applicable to other similar samples, that is other cohorts of science and maths secondary PGCE students.

Participants were informed about the purpose of their participation and invited to provide consent at all four data collection points. This resulted in a sample of n = 74 participants, with a mixture of maths and science students, and SD and UL students. Attrition from the study was relatively low, but in some circumstances reflected withdrawal from the course (n = 11) as well as non-response meaning that missing data could not be considered to be based on random events or actions. The response rate at data collection 1 was 98.64 percent, at data collection 2 was 82.43 percent, at data collection 3 was 82.43 percent, and at data collection 4 was 81.08 percent. Serva et al. (2011) state that a major advantage of LGM, in comparison to other longitudinal methods of data analysis (like Repeated Measures ANOVA), is that LGM can still run despite missingness in the data. However, Serva et al. (2011) also acknowledge that too much missing data can affect the validity of the results. As such, it is recommended that for at least the repeated measures dependent variable, participants should have at least 2 time points in order to be able to calculate a slope. Eight participants only had one observation score/self-efficacy score, and thus were removed from the LGM analysis. This resulted in a final sample of n = 66.

Due to the nature of the different ITE routes, the SD trainee teachers spent much more of their time in school placements, and had fewer training days within the university. Table 4.1 presents some of the patterns in demographic distribution of the participants.

Table 4.1 A crosstabulation of the sample of pre-service teachers showing demographic characteristics of the participants

		Programme		Total
		UL	SD	
Subject	Maths	24	7	31
	Science	26	9	35
Age	20–24	34	2	36
	25–29	13	4	17
	30–34	1	4	5
	35–39	0	3	3
	40–44	2	2	4
	45–49	0	1	1
Sex	Male	24	8	32
	Female	26	8	34

Note. n = 66.

Dependent Variables

Teachers' Observation Scores

A key dependent variable consists of mean lesson observation scores assigned to the pre-service teachers at four key moments throughout their ITE program. The scores ranged from 0 to 8, with a score of 4 and above generally considered to be a "pass" on the course supporting a recommendation for Qualified Teacher Status. The observation scores were judged by mentors in the placement school, with these values reflecting the average observation score assigned to each pre-service teacher over the previous few months of the placement. To reflect the four data collection points throughout the course, this study referred to these measures as **OBS1-OBS4**. The use of teachers' observation scores may seem controversial (see, for example, issues of validity and observation bias; Fauth *et al.*, 2020; and ethical issues; NASUWT: the teachers' union, 2022). There are significant justifications for this choice that must be borne in mind. The observation scores (at each time point) are an average over multiple lesson observations, and are not single snapshots of teacher performance. Secondly, these measures are being observed longitudinally, so this study is more interested in the growth of scores rather than the specific values.

Perceived Self-Efficacy

A measure of self-efficacy was collected at all four data collection points in the study. Three scales (instructional strategies = three items, student motivation = four items, and classroom management, five items) were used, the mean of each scale creating a metric for perceived self-efficacy (**Development 1–Development 4**). The scale, initially developed by Tschannen-Moran and Hoy (2001) is well cited and robust (Nie et al., 2012) and has previously been used when studying pre-service teachers (Pfitzner-Eden, 2014). It also has a high internal consistency ($\alpha = 0.96$) (Bokhove & Downey, 2018).

Independent Variables

Demographic Variables

Demographic variables were collected. They included Biological sex (0 = Male, 1 = female), Subject (0 = Maths, 1 = Science), Age (five-year ordinal categories from 20 to 59) and Programme type (0 = University Led, 1 = School Direct).

Network Variables

Data on the egocentric networks of pre-service teachers were captured at each of the four data collection points. Participants were asked via a questionnaire to indicate to whom they had reached out for support in the past month. Coromina and Coenders (2005) indicate that online questionnaire data collection for egocentric network data is suitable in terms of its reliability and validity.

Internal ties described the number of actors within the class the participant had approached for support. Similarly, external ties described the number of actors external to the class whom the participant had turned to for support. The sum of these two values provided each pre-service teacher with an out-degree value at each time point, which measured the total support-seeking behavior of the individual, measured by the total number of actors in their network. The first of these measures was used in this study when exploring the total support seeking behavior (TotalOut1). Finally, Krackhardt and Stern's (1988) External-Internal (E-I) Index was calculated:

$$EI\ Index = \frac{E-I}{E+I}$$

The resulting value ranges from −1 to +1, with values closer to −1 indicating homophily in the network (more ties are within the group) and values closer to +1 indicating heterophily in the network (more ties are external to the group). A value of 0, therefore, would indicate an equal number of ties are external and internal. E-I indexes were calculated, again, at each of the four time points, but the initial measurement is used in this study (E-I1). The justification for this choice was the focus on growth—the intercept plays a key part in the growth model and provides a foundation for growth. This is also why the first measurement was used in further psychometric variables. Ultimately, the insufficient sample size of the study meant it was unable to support modeling the network change as a time varying construct, but this would be an interesting avenue for future studies to explore.

Psychometric Variables

A peer trust scale contained six items relating to the participants' attitudes toward trust, scored on a Likert-type response scale (1= very strongly disagree, 9 = very strongly agree). The scale was adapted by Bokhove and Downey (2018) from previous work by Daly and Chrispeels (2008) and Hoy and Tschannen-Moran (2003). This measure was taken three times across the year. The decision was made to use the first measure of trust in the ITE year, as it served as a baseline value (trust1). While this study could not calculate the Cronbach's Alpha, Bokhove and Downey (2018) reported that the internal consistency of the scale was high across all waves ($\alpha = 0.95$).

Views on support were captured at three data collection points throughout the year through a scale consisting of thirteen items, the first of which resulted in a value for views on support (support1). The Likert-type scale (1=strongly disagree, 6= strongly agree) sought views and attitudes toward support, for example, if they view support seeking as negative or positive. Bokhove and Downey (2018) found the internal consistency of the scale to be relatively low ($\alpha = 0.61$) but Nunallay and Bernstein (1994) suggest this is still an acceptable value.

Views on network intentionality were collected via a scale consisting of twenty-two items at three points throughout the study, with the first data collection providing a measure of network intentionality (network1). The purpose of the scale was to attempt to quantify how intentional, or pro-active, participants were in regard to developing their network. Again, each item utilized a Likert response scale (1= strongly disagree, 5= strongly agree), and internal consistency of the scale was reported to be high ($\alpha = 0.81$).

Data Analysis

Graphs, crosstabulations, and descriptive statistics were generated via SPSS version 26 (IBM, 2019). SPSS AMOS version 28 (Arbuckle, 2014) was used to build the latent growth curve models in order to assess the growth trajectory of teaching observation scores and self-efficacy across time, in relation to the other independent variables. The dataset was transformed from long format into wide format to enable it to be used successfully in AMOS.

Establishing the Null (Unconditional) Models

As suggested by Chan and Schmitt (2000) and Serva et al. (2011) an unconditional "null" model was built that had the best fit to the focal variables. For the current study, this was the dependent variables of pre-service teachers' observation scores and perceived self-efficacy scores, each measured at four time points. We followed the guidance of Chan and Schmitt (2000) by building multiple initial models to provide us with the foundation to analyze the effects of various factors on that growth over time. These consisted of a no-growth model (intercept only); a free-from growth model, and a growth linear model.

Line graphs demonstrating the mean trajectory of observation and perceived self-efficacy (Figure 4.1a and Figure 4.1b, respectively) were constructed. This enabled visual examination of the growth curves. As seen in Figure 4.1, the observation scores over time suggest possible quadratic growth over time. Therefore, an additional quadratic model was constructed and tested for fit.

As suggested by Hooper *et al.* (2008), a range of fit indices were reported in order to assess the best fit of the models to the data. A significant issue with this study is the relatively modest sample size, and thus fit indices were selected on the basis that they were least sensitive to sample size. An exception to this is the chi-Square statistic, which should be reported at all times (Hooper *et al.*, 2008) with a nonsignificant value of chi-

a. Mean trajectory of observation scores over time

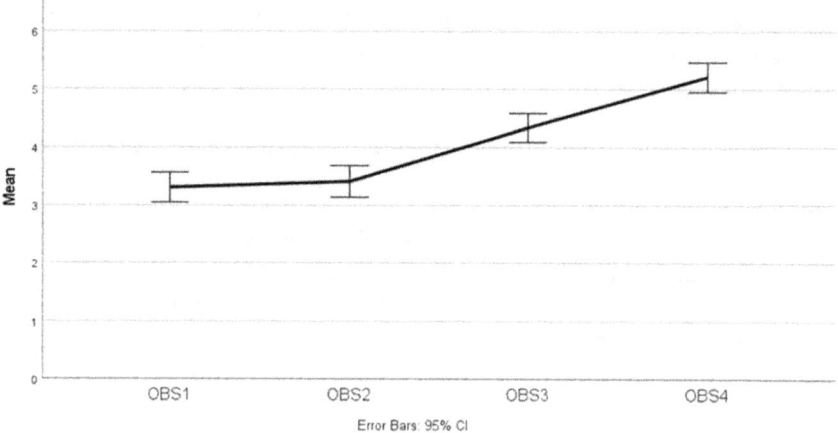

b. Mean trajectory of perceived self-efficacy over time

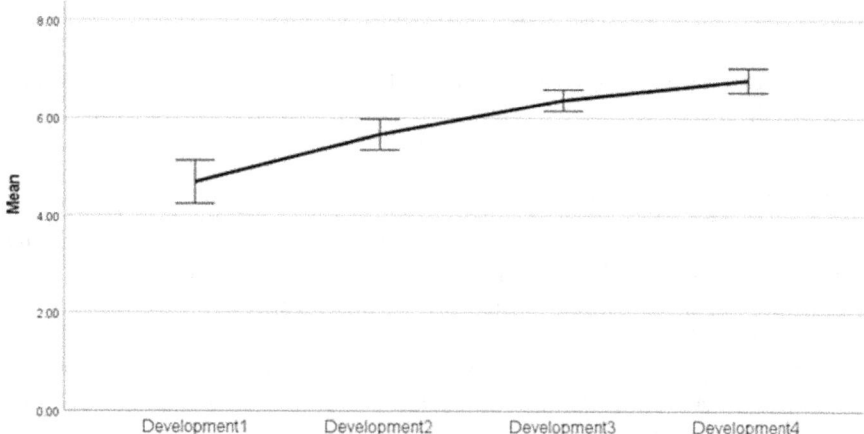

Figure 4.1 Simple mean line graph demonstrating the mean trajectory over time.

square indicative of good model fit (Elizar & Mochamad, 2017). The comparative fit index (CFI) was selected as it was argued to be least sensitive to sample size (Fan *et al.*, 1999) with values exceeding 0.93 indicating good fit (Byrne, 1998). While the normed fit index (NFI) can underestimate the fit of models with a small sample (Ullman, 2007) it was selected as it is good for assessing fit as covariates are added (Hammervold & Olsson, 2012). A value exceeding 0.90 suggests good fit (Schumacker & Lomax, 2004). The Tucker-Lewis index (TLI) was selected as it is relatively independent of sample size (Marsh *et al.*, 2004). A value of 0.90 and over is considered acceptable fit (Hu & Bentler, 1999). The root-mean-square error of approximation (RMSEA) was also argued to be least susceptible to small samples (Fan *et al.*, 1999) with values smaller than 0.05 indicating a close fit (Browne & Cudeck, 1993), and 0.05–0.08 indicating an acceptable fit (Fabrigar *et al.*, 1999).

Table 4.2 presents the fit indices for each of the unconditional models. The free-form model was considered to have good fit to the data for growth models of both lesson observation scores and perceived self-efficacy.

Table 4.2 Model fit indices for null LGM for observation scores and development scores (perceived self-efficacy) over time

	No-growth Model	Free-form Model	Linear Model	Quadratic Model
Observation scores				
Chi-Square	289.377	11.924	75.222	4.265
Degrees of freedom	11	6	8	3
p-value	$p < .001$	0.064	$p < .001$	0.234
RMSEA	0.589	0.116	0.341	0.076
CFI	0.000	0.971	0.664	0.994
NFI	−0.368	0.944	0.642	0.980
TLI	−0.256	0.951	0.580	0.979
Development scores				
Chi-Square	190.402	11.318	31.169	13.71
Degrees of freedom	11	6	8	5
p-value	$p < .001$	0.079	$p < .001$	0.018
RMSEA	0.473	0.11	0.199	0.154
CFI	0.000	0.931	0.693	0.884
NFI	−1.231	0.907	0.635	0.839
TLI	−1.164	0.882	0.616	0.769

Results and Discussion

This section presents the results of the latent growth curve analyses and answers the established research questions.

Establishing the Basic Growth Model

Establishing a well-fitting latent growth curve model helps us establish the trajectory of development in the capability of the pre-service teachers. It also provides the analytical foundation that allows us to address our research questions. A dual-domain growth curve model was constructed to consider the effects of factors on both dependent variables. RQs 1 and 2 are concerned with the characteristics of the networks of pre-service teachers, and their views about networking with others, and how these factors relate to the initial levels and growth in lesson observation scores and perceived self-efficacy. Demographic variables of age, sex, program of study (UL or SD), and subject specialism (mathematics or science) were added to the model to explore their predictive value. Variables were added one at a time to model 1 (see Figure 4.2).

Covariances were added between disturbance terms to indicate the variance between slope and intercepts, as in model 1. These indicate that the growth in pre-

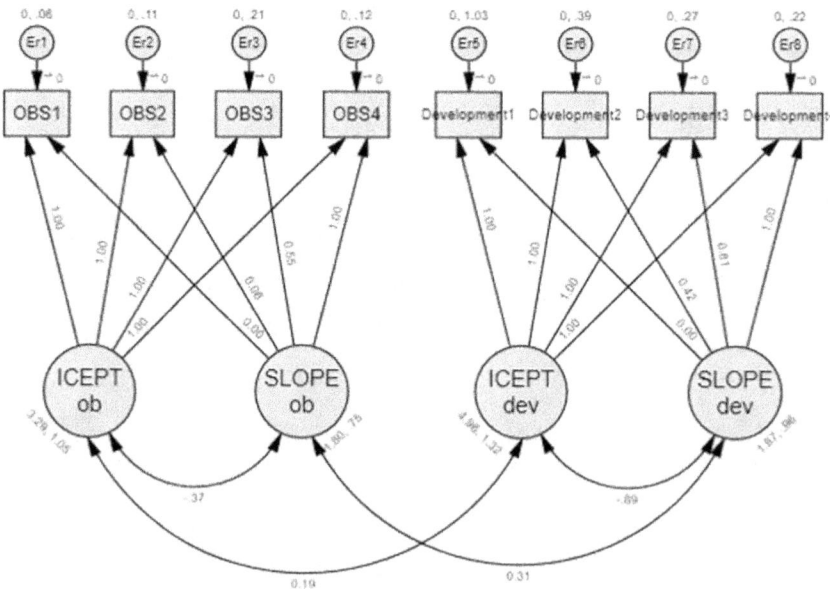

Figure 4.2 Latent growth curve model of observation scores (Ob) and perceived self-efficacy (dev) with standardized coefficients (model 1).

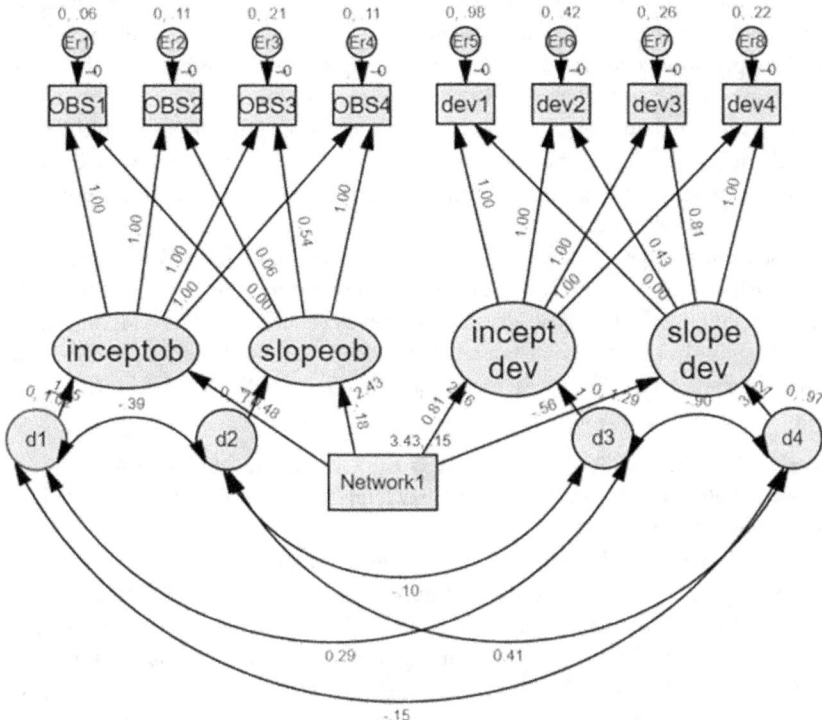

Figure 4.3 Latent growth curve model of observation scores (Ob) and perceived self-efficacy (Dev) with network intentionality at time 1 as a predictor, and showing standardized coefficients.

service teachers' observation scores and self-efficacy appeared to be moderately correlated. This finding is consistent with previous research on self-efficacy (Bandura, 1977), as it adds confirmation to the notion that teacher self-efficacy and actual performance on a task are two different concepts (Tschannen-Moran & Hoy, 2001).

Figure 4.3 shows an example of the model with a predictor variable added. The results of the analysis are presented in Table 4.3, reporting the regression weights between the predictive variables and the slope and intercept factors for both observation scores and self-efficacy. Chi-square remained nonsignificant in the model (X^2 = 15.432, p = 0.751), and the rest of the fit indices were suggestive of good model fit (CFI = 0.972, NFI = 0.953, TLI = 0.95, RMSEA = 0.032). The values of the slope means suggest that observation scores and perceived self-efficacy both demonstrate significant patterns of growth across the duration of the program of study.

Demographic Predictors

Demographic variables were added to the model, to assess if they were predictive of initial levels of self-efficacy and observation scores, and the growth of self-efficacy and observation scores (Table 4.3). The *subject* specialism of the pre-service teachers (mathematics or science) was not a significant predictor in the model, nor was the *age* of the pre-service teachers. By contrast, biological sex was predictive of the initial observation scores with female pre-service teachers attaining higher observation scores on average than their male peers. The nature of the *programme* of study, namely whether the pre-service teachers were part of School Direct (SD) course or a University Led (UL) course, was a significant predictor, both of initial observation scores and of initial perceived self-efficacy.

These results suggest that students enrolled on the School Direct course had higher initial levels of both self-efficacy and observation scores but this did not appear to lead to more rapid growth of their observed or perceived capabilities as developing teachers. We suggest this initial difference is a result of previous school-based experience that all student teachers on the SD courses are required to have (DfE, 2014). This finding also supports the conclusions drawn from Bokhove and Downey (2018).

Research Question 1: To What Extent Is the Growth in Observation Scores and Perceived Self-Efficacy Predicted by Characteristics of the Pre-Service Teacher's Social Support Network?

Adjusting for the balance of different types of supporters in the networks of the pre-service teachers was achieved by adding the *E-I index* of network homophily as a predictor. The overall model was still deemed to have good fit to the data (Table 4.3). This measure of the balance of different types of supporter in the network was not a significant predictor of observation scores nor of perceived self-efficacy. By contrast the total initial outdegree score was found to be a significant predictor of the growth of self-efficacy scores over time. The addition of this factor to the model also maintained good fit to the data (Table 4.3)

These results suggest that those pre-service teachers with a greater tendency to reach out to others at the start of the course were also more likely to experience growth in their self-efficacy scores, with a greater sense of capability in developing instructional strategies and both motivating and managing students in the classroom. What seems less important is the balance of different actors to whom the pre-service teachers are reaching out in their networks. Whether they are reaching out to peers on the course, or to those beyond the course such as mentors, family, or friends, the important thing may simply be a disposition to seek support from others.

One possible suggestion for this finding from a social capital perspective may be that a high volume of initial support seeking behavior may allow for pre-service teachers to have wider access to resources and support (Penuel *et al.*, 2009) which has been noted to have a positive impact on continuous professional development (Demir, 2019). This finding should be interpreted with caution, as this study was unable to provide evidence of the quality of support ties. For example, having a very large number of ties does not necessarily mean you have access to an equal number of quality ties (Mandzuk *et al.*, 2005). Future studies should therefore aim to assess the perceived usefulness of such relational capital before this finding can be confirmed.

Table 4.3 Predictive variables and their respective fit indices and regression weights to the slopes and intercepts of observation scores and self-efficacy

Predictor	Model Fit			Intercept OB			Slope OB			Intercept DEV			Slope DEV		
	X^2	CFI	RMSEA	b	β	R^2	b	β	R^2	b	β	R^2	b	β	R^2
Age	20.69	0.96	0.09	0.129	0.195	0.038	0.113	0.196	0.038	0.207	0.274	0.075	-0.102	-0.159	0.025
Sex	21.42	0.96	0.09	.643**	.313**	0.098	-0.131	-0.074	0.006	-0.014	-0.006	0	0.498	0.245	0.06
Programme	24.53	0.95	0.1	.533**	.238**	0.057	0.066	0.034	0.001	1.181***	.452***	0.204	-0.7	-0.317	0.1
Subject	20.39	0.96	0.09	-0.034	-0.016	0	-0.161	-0.091	0.008	-0.532	-0.225	0.051	0.193	0.096	0.009
E-I index	18.69	0.97	0.08	0.351	0.162	0.026	0.199	0.106	0.011	0.451	0.18	0.033	-0.244	-0.115	0.013
Total Out	24.82	0.94	0.06	-0.022	-0.189	0.036	0.023	0.23	0.053	-0.037	-0.268	0.072	.048**	.389**	0.152
Trust	15.75	0.97	0.07	0.033	0.052	0.003	-0.095	-0.173	0.03	.242**	.333**	0.111	-.206*	-.337*	0.113
Support	28.62	0.93	0.12	0.14	0.076	0.006	0.297	0.187	0.035	.937**	.451**	0.204	-0.416	-0.244	0.059
Network	22.7	0.95	0.09	0.479	0.182	0.047	-0.181	-0.08	0.072	0.811	0.268	0.006	-0.564	-0.218	0.033

Note. X^2 was non significant in all models, with 22 degrees of freedom.
*** p <.001, ** p <.01, *p <.05.

Research Question 2: To What Extent Is the Growth in Observation Scores and Perceived Self-Efficacy Predicted by the Pre-Service Teacher's Views on Social Networks and Support?

The addition of the *network* intentionality score of pre-service teachers was neither predictive of growth in their observation scores nor of growth in perceived self-efficacy over time (Table 4.3).

Adding pre-service teachers' initial views on peer *trust* did not significantly affect the overall good fit of the model and resulted in significant predictive power for of both higher levels of perceived self-efficacy and increased growth in self-efficacy. Having positive views about reaching out for *support* at the start of the course was also predictive of higher initial perceived self-efficacy but not of growth in self-efficacy across the course. This last outcome is somewhat more tentative since there was a drop in the ability of the model to fit the data, based on one of the measures assessing overall model fit (RMSEA).

These results would suggest that high levels of peer trust and positive initial views on the benefits of seeking support at the start of the course are both linked with a heightened initial sense of capability among pre-service teachers' in the areas of instructional practice, student motivation, and classroom management. High initial levels of initial peer trust may also be linked to more rapid growth of their perceived capability across the duration of the course. We suggest that student teachers entering ITE programs with positive views on the benefits of reaching out to others for support also hold high views about their own beliefs, linked to the concept of collective self-efficacy that has been observed amongst teachers (Skaalivik & Skaalvik, 2016).

Conclusions

Limitations

The participant group for this study was relatively small, reflecting only a single cohort in a single higher education institution. While the nature of social network analysis often leads to whole cohort selection, as opposed to probability sampling, the transferability of these findings should not be overstated. As such, this study would benefit from replication to strengthen the validity of these findings, especially in larger cohorts in a variety of contexts. A larger sample size would also enable more complex latent growth curve models to be constructed. For example, this study was limited to adding one predictor variable to the model at a time. A larger sample would have allowed each predictor to be added cumulatively. Likewise, only the initial levels of predictor variables could be modeled. A larger participant group would allow changes in these predictors to also be modeled over the duration of the course as time varying constructs, and thus would allow for more nuanced analysis.

This study was also limited in the sense that it only had access to the longitudinal, egocentric data around individuals while they were pre-service. An interesting line of enquiry for future research may consider whether the additional transition to early career teacher has an impact on social networks and outcomes. As noted in this study, the ITE year is characterized by multiple transitions, whereas the early-career phase is likely to be a more stable experience. Therefore, research that follows pre-services teachers into their early careers is much needed and may shed additional light on the significance of social networks on the ongoing development of professional capabilities.

Implications

We believe this study makes a valuable contribution to the small but growing body of literature on the social networks of pre-service teachers. A key and significant finding suggests that actively reaching out to others at the start of the pre-service year and having positive views toward seeking support are both linked to the growth of perceived self-efficacy over time. Self-efficacy is linked to a broad number of positive outcomes and was shown in this study to be linked to growth in lesson observation scores across the pre-service year. Those in key leadership roles informing the design and implementation of ITE curricula may wish to incorporate an explicit focus on network building and developing confidence and trust to seek support from others, especially as part of the introductory period to pre-service program of study. This may include providing strategies for effectively growing and utilizing a network of supporters.

The growth in self-efficacy of pre-service teachers would also be beneficial in terms of public policy. As previously mentioned, the attrition of teachers is at an all-time high, with the first two years of teaching being particularly critical in retaining teachers. As self-efficacy has previously been linked with teacher retention, initiatives that aim to develop the relational networks of pre-service teachers may be one way of keeping talented teachers in the profession.

The aim of the current study was to examine the predictive potential of pre-service teachers' social networks and views on networks on their perceived self-efficacy and observation scores across an ITE year. Latent growth curve modeling revealed some key and significant findings, mainly regarding levels of self-efficacy. Network variables were found to be nonsignificant in relation to the baseline levels and growth of observation scores, leading to the conclusion that there are other variables that better predict observation scores. The field of social network analysis of pre-service teachers would benefit from further study to replicate these findings on a much larger scale.

References

Anscombe, F. J. (1973). Graphs in statistical analysis. *The American Statistician, 27*(1), 17–21. https://doi.org/10.2307/2682899

Arbuckle, J. L. (2014). Amos (Version 23.0) [Computer Program]. IBM SPSS.

Bandura, A. (1977). Self-efficacy theory: Toward a unifying theory of behavioural change. *Psychological Review, 84*(2), 191–215. https://doi.org/10.1037/0033-295X.84.2.191

Barber, M., & Mourshed, M. (2007). *How the World's Best-Performing School Systems Come Out on Top*. Available at: https://tinyurl.com/697e5rta

Barni, D., Francesca, D., & Paula, B. (2019). Teachers' self-efficacy: The role of personal values and motivations for teaching. *Frontiers in Psychology, 10*. https://doi.org/10.3389/fpsyg.2019.01645

Beijaard, D., Meijer, P. C., & Verloop, N. (2004). Reconsidering research on teachers' professional identity. *Teaching and Teacher Education, 20*(2), 107–28. https://doi.org/10.1016/j.tate.2003.07.001

Beltman, S., Glass, C., Dinham, J., Chalk, B., & Nguyen, B. (2015). Drawing identity: Beginning pre-service teachers' professional identities. *Issues in Educational Research, 25*(3), 225–45. https://doi.org/10.3316/informit.535515724376399

Berebitsky, D., & Salloum, S. (2017). The relationship between collective efficacy and teachers' social networks in urban middle schools. *AERA Open, 3*(4), 1–11. https://doi.org/10.1177/2332858417743927

Bjorklund, P., Warstadt, M., & Daly, A. (2021). Finding satisfaction in belonging: Preservice teacher subjective well-being and its relationship to belonging, trust, and self-efficacy. *Frontiers in Education, 6*. https://doi.org/10.3389/feduc.2021.639435

Boissevain, J. (1974). Towards a sociology of social anthropology. *Theory and Society, 1*, 211–30.

Bokhove, C., & Downey, C. (2018). Mapping changes in support: A longitudinal analysis of networks of pre-service mathematics and science teachers. *Oxford Review of Education, 44*(3), 383–402. https://doi.org/10.1080/03054985.2017.1400427

Borgatti, S., & Ofem, B. (2010). Social network theory and analysis. In Daly, A. (Ed.), *Social Network Theory and Educational Change* (pp. 17–30). Harvard Educational Press.

Bloomfield, D. (2010). Emotions and "getting by": A pre-service teacher navigating professional experience. *Asia-Pacific Journal of Teacher Education, 38*(3), 221–34. https://doi.org/10.1080/1359866X.2010.494005

Brouwer, J., Downey, C., & Bokhove, C. (2020). The development of communication networks of pre-service teachers on a school-led and university-led programme of initial teacher education in England. *International Journal of Educational Research, 100*(2020), 1–13. https://doi.org/10.1016/j.ijer.2020.101542

Brown, T. (2006). Negotiating psychological disturbance in pre-service teacher education. *Teaching and Teacher Education, 22*(6), 675–89. https://doi.org/10.1016/j.tate.2006.03.006

Browne, M. W., & Cudeck, R. (1993). Alternative ways of assessing model fit. In Bollen, K. A. & Long, J. S. (Eds.), *Testing structural equation models* (pp. 136–62). Sage Publications.

Byrne, B. M. (1998). *Structural equation modeling with LISREL, PRELIS and SIMPLIS: Basic concepts, applications and programming*. Lawrence Erlbaum Associates.

Chan, D., & Schmitt, N. (2000). Inter-individual differences in intra-individual changes in proactivity during organizational entry: A latent growth modeling approach to understanding newcomer adaptation. *Journal of Applied Psychology, 85*(2), 190–210. https://doi.org/10.1037/0021-9010.85.2.190

Civis, M., Diaz-Gibson, J., Lopez, S., & Moolenaar, N. (2019). Collaborative and innovative climates in pre-service teacher programs: The role of social capital. *International Journal of Educational Research, 98*, 224–36. https://doi.org/10.1016/j.ijer.2019.08.019

Coleman, J. S. (1990). Commentary: Social institutions and social theory. *American Sociological Review, 55*(3), 333–9. https://doi.org/10.2307/2095759

Coromina, L., & Coenders, G. (2005). Reliability and validity of egocentered network data collected via web: A meta-analysis of multilevel, multitrait, multimethod studies. *Social Networks, 28*(3), 209–31. https://doi.org/10.1016/j.socnet.2005.07.006

Daly, A. J., & Chrispeels, J. (2008). A question of trust: Predictive conditions for adaptive and technical leadership in educational contexts. *Leadership and Policy in Schools*, 7(1), 30–63. https://doi.org/10.1080/15700760701655508

Daly, A. J., Der-Martirosian, C., Moolenaar, N., & Liou, Y.-H. (2014a). Accessing capital resources: Investigating the effects of teacher human and social capital on student achievement. *Teachers College Record*, 116(7), 1–42.

Demir, E. K. (2021). The role of social capital for teacher professional learning and student achievement: A systematic literature review. *Educational Research Review*, 33(2021), 1–33. https://doi.org/10.1016/j.edurev.2021.100391

Demir, E. K., & Qureshi, A. (2019). Pakistani science teachers' experiences of professional development: A phenomenological case study. *Journal of Science Teacher Education*, 30(8), 838–55. https://doi.org/10.1080/1046560X.2019.1607707

Department for Education, Teacher Recruitment and Retention Strategy, 2019. Available at: https://assets.publishing.service.gov.uk/government/uploads/system/uploads/attachment_data/file/786856/DFE_Teacher_Retention_Strategy_Report.pdf. Accessed: March 19, 2022.

Department for Education, The Importance of Teaching, 2010. Available at: https://assets.publishing.service.gov.uk/government/uploads/system/uploads/attachment_data/file/175429/CM-7980.pdf. Accessed: March 14, 2022.

DfE (2014). *Initial teacher training performance profiles: 2013 to 2014 academic year*. Department for Education.

Elizar, S., & Mochamad, A. W. (2017). Model of construction waste management using AMOS-SEM for Indonesian infrastructure projects. *MATEC Web of Conferences*, 138(05005), 1–8. https://doi.org/10.1051/matecconf/201713805005

Fabrigar, L. R., Wegener, D. T., MacCallum, R. C., & Strahan, E. J. (1999). Evaluating the use of exploratory factor analysis in psychological research. *Psychological methods*, 4(3), 272. https://doi.org/10.1037/1082-989X.4.3.272

Fan, X., Thompson, B., & Wang, L. (1999). Effects of sample size, estimation methods, and model specification on structural equation modeling fit indexes. *Structural Equation Modeling*, 6(1), 56–83. https://doi.org/10.1080/10705519909540119

Fauth, B., Wagner, W., Bertram, C., Göllner, R., Roloff, J., Lüdtke, O., Polikoff, M. S., Klusmann, U., & Trautwein, U. (2020). Don't blame the teacher? The need to account for classroom characteristics in evaluations of teaching quality. *Journal of Educational Psychology*, 112(6), 1284–302. https://doi.org/10.1037/edu0000416

Finnigan, K. S., & Daly, A. J. (2012). Mind the gap: Organizational learning and improvement in an underperforming urban system. *American Journal of Education*, 119(1), 41–71. https://doi.org/10.1086/667700

Flores, M. A. (2020). Feeling like a student but thinking like a teacher: A study of the development of professional identity in initial teacher education. *Journal of Education for Teaching*, 46(2), 145–58. https://doi.org/10.1080/02607476.2020.1724659

Foster, D. (2019). *Teacher recruitment and retention in England* (House of Commons No. 7222). London: House of Commons.

Fukuyama, F. (1995). *Trust: The social virtues and the creation of prosperity*. The Free Press.

Furlong, J. (2013, January). Globalisation, neoliberalism, and the reform of teacher education in England. *The Educational Forum*, 77(1), 28–50, DOI: 10.1080/00131725.2013.739017

Hammervold, R., & Olsson, U. H. (2012). Testing structural equation models: The impact of error variances in the data generating process. *Quality and Quantity*, 46(5), 1547–70. https://doi.org/10.1007/s11135-011-9466-5

Hooper, D., Coughlan, J., & Mullen, M. (2008). Structural equation modelling: Guidelines for determining model fit. *Electronic Journal of Business Research Methods, 6*(1), 53–60. https://doi.org/10.21427/D7CF7R

Hoy, W. K., & Tschannen-Moran, M. (2003). The conceptualization and measurement of faculty trust in schools: The omnibus T-Scale. In Hoy, W. K., & Miskel, C. G. (Eds.), *Studies in leading and organizing schools* (pp. 181–208). Information Age Publishing.

Hu, L. T., & Bentler, P. M. (1999). Cut off criteria for fit indexes in covariance structure analysis: Conventional criteria versus new alternatives. *Structural Equation Modeling, 6*(1), 1–55. https://doi.org/10.1080/10705519909540118

Huber, M., Fruth, J., Avila-John, A., & Lopez-Ramirez, E. (2016). Teacher self-efficacy and student outcomes: A transactional approach to prevention. *Journal of Education and Human Development, 5*(1), 46–54. https://doi.org/10.15640/jehd.v5n1a5

Inkpen, A. C., & Tsang, E. W. K. (2005). Social capital, networks, and knowledge transfer. *Academy of Management Review, 30*(1), 146–65.

Jensen, A. (2012). Digital culture, and the viewing/participating pre-service teacher: (Re)envisioning theatre teacher training for a social media culture. *Research in Drama Education, 17*(4), 553–68.

Kaplan, D. (2000). *Structural equation modelling: Foundations and extensions.* Sage Publications.

Klassen, R., & Chiu, M. M. (2010). Effects on teachers' self-efficacy and job satisfaction: Teacher gender, years of experience, and job stress. *Journal of Educational Psychology, 102*(3), 741–56. https://doi.org/10.1037/a0019237d

Krackhardt, D., & Stern, R. (1988). Informal networks and organizational crises: An experimental simulation. *Social Psychology Quarterly, 51*(2), 123–40. https://doi.org/10.2307/2786835

La Velle, L., Newman, S., Montgomery, C., & Hyatt, D. (2020). Initial teacher education in England and the Covid-19 pandemic: Challenges and opportunities. *Journal of Education for Teaching, 46*(4), 596–608. https://doi.org/10.1080/02607476.2020.1803051

Lin, N. (2001). *Social capital: A theory of social structure and action.* Cambridge University Press.

Liou, Y. H., & Daly, A. J. (2018). Evolving relationships of pre-service teachers In Yoon, S. A., & Baker-Doyle, K. J. (Eds.), *Networked by design: Interventions for teachers to develop social capital* (pp. 85–110). Routledge.

Liou, Y. H., Daly, A. J., Canrinus, E. T., Forbes, C. A., Moolenaar, N. M., Cornelissen, F., Van Lare, M., & Hsiao, J. (2017). Mapping the social side of pre-service teachers: Connecting closeness, trust, and efficacy with performance. *Teachers and Teaching, 23*(6), 635–57. https://doi.org/10.1080/13540602.2016.1218329

Little, J. W. (2010). Foreword. In Daly, A. J. (Ed.), *Social network theory and educational change* (pp. xi–xiv). Harvard Education Press.

Liu, H., Hoon Jin, I., & Zhang, Z. (2018). Structural equation modeling of social networks: Specification, estimation, and application. *Multivariate Behavioral Research, 53*(5), 714–30. https://doi.org/10.1080/00273171.2018.1479629

Lutovac, S., & Flores, M. A. (2021). Those who fail should not be teachers': Pre-service teachers' understandings of failure and teacher identity development. *Journal of Education for Teaching, 47*(3), 379–94. https://doi.org/10.1080/02607476.2021.1891833

Mandzuk, D., Hasinoff, S., & Seifert, K. (2005). Inside a student cohort: Teacher education from a social capital perspective. *Canadian Journal of Education, 28*(1), 168–84. https://doi.org/10.2307/1602159

Marsh, H. W., Hau, K. T., & Wen, Z. (2004). In search of golden rules: Comment on hypothesis-testing approaches to setting cut off values for fit indexes and dangers in overgeneralizing Hu and Bentler's findings. *Structural Equation Modeling, 11*(3), 320–41. https://doi.org/10.1207/s15328007sem1103_2

Marz, V., & Kelchtermans, G. (2020). The networking teacher in action: A qualitative analysis of early career teachers' induction process. *Teacher and Teacher Education, 87*(4). https://doi.org/10.1016/j.tate.2019.102933

McCormack, A., & Thomas, K. (2003). Is survival enough? Induction experiences of beginning teachers within a New South Wales context. *Asia-Pacific Journal of Teacher Education, 31*(2), 125–38. https://doi.org/10.1080/13598660301610

McCormack, A., Gore, J., & Thomas, K. (2006). Early career teacher professional learning. *Asia Pacific Journal of Teacher Education, 34*(1), 95–113. https://doi.org/10.1080/13598660500480282

NASUWT: The Teachers' Union. (2022). *Grading of Lesson Observations*. Available at: https://www.nasuwt.org.uk/advice/performance-management/lesson-observation.html. Accessed: March 17, 2022.

Nie, Y., Lau, S., & Liau, A. (2012). The teacher efficacy scale: A reliability and validity study. *The Asia-Pacific Education Researcher, 21*(2), 414–21. https://doi.org/10497/14287

Penuel, W., Fishman, B., Gallagher, L., Korbak, C., & Lopez-Prado, B. (2009). Is alignment enough? Investigating the effects of state policies and professional development on science curriculum implementation. *Science Education Policy, 93*(4), 656–77. https://doi.org/10.1002/sce.20321

Pfitzner-Eden, F., Thiel, F., & Horsley, J. (2014). An adapted measure of teacher self-efficacy for pre-service teachers: Exploring its validity across 2 countries. *Zeitschrift fur Padagogische Psychologie, 28*(3), 83–92. https://doi.org/10.1024/1010-0652/a000125

Serva, M. A., Kher, H., & Laurenceau, J. (2011). Using latent growth modeling to understand longitudinal effects in MIS theory: A primer. *Communications of the Association for Information Systems, 28*(14), 213–32. https://doi.org/10.17705/1CAIS.02814

Schumacker, R. E., & Lomax, R. G. (2004). *A beginner's guide to structural equation modeling* (2nd ed.). Lawrence Erlbaum Associates Publishers.

Skaalvik, E. M., & Skaalvik, S. (2016). Teacher stress and teacher self-efficacy as predictors of engagement, emotional exhaustion, and motivation to leave the teaching profession. *Creative Education, 7*, 1785–99. https://doi.org/10.4236/ce.2016.713182

Smit, R., Robin, N., & Rietz, F. (2021). Emotional experiences of secondary pre-service teachers conducting practical work in a science lab course: Individual differences and prediction of teacher efficacy. *Disciplinary and Interdisciplinary Science Education Research, 3*(5), 1–17. https://doi.org/10.1186/s43031-021-00034-x

Steinbrecher, T., & Hart, J. (2012). Examining teachers' personal and professional use of Facebook: Recommendations for teacher education programming. *Journal of Technology and Teacher Education, 20*(1), 71–88.

Thomas, L., Tuytens, M., Devos, G., Kelchtermans, G., & Vanderlinde, R. (2019). Beginning teachers' professional support: A mixed methods social network study. *Teaching and Teacher Education, 83*, 134–47. https://doi.org/10.1016/j.tate.2019.04.008

Trapp, C. S. (2010). *The association among emotional intelligence, resilience, and academic performance of preservice teachers*. University of Phoenix.

Tschannen-Moran, M., & Barr, M. (2004). Fostering student learning: The relationship of collective teacher efficacy and student achievement. *Leadership and Policy in Schools*, *3*(3), 189–209. https://doi.org/10.1080/15700760490503706

Tschannen-Moran, M., & Hoy, A. W. (2001). Teacher efficacy: Capturing an elusive construct. *Teaching and Teacher Education*, *17*(7), 783–805. https://doi.org/10.1016/S0742-051X(01)00036-1

Ullman, J. B. (2007). Structural equation modelling. In Tabachnick, B. G., & Fidell, L. S. (Eds.), *Using multivariate statistics* (pp. 676–768). Pearson Education.

Wasserman, S., & Faust, K. (1994). *Social network analysis: Methods and applications*. Cambridge University Press.

Woolcock, M. (2001). The place of social capital in understanding social and economic outcomes. *Canadian Journal of Policy Research*, *2*(1), 11–17. https://doi.org/10.1.1.463.2107

Worth, J., & De Lazzari, G. (2017). *Teacher retention and turnover research. Research update 1: Teacher retention by subject*. NFER.

5

Strong Ties and Social Boundaries: Social Networks and Program Influence on Pre-Service Teachers' Social Justice Teacher Identities

Peter Bjorklund Jr.

Teachers' practice and pedagogy are inextricably linked to teacher identity, which influences most aspects of teachers' work, from lesson planning to relationships with students (Beauchamp & Thomas, 2009; Danielewicz, 2001). Hamachek (1999) contended that being aware of who one is as a teacher and how one is perceived by others is a critical step in becoming a good teacher. Moreover, he asserted, *"[c]onsciously, we teach what we know; unconsciously, we teach who we are"* (italics in original, p. 209). For pre-service teachers (PSTs) and new teachers, having an awareness and intentionality about developing a teacher identity provides a strong foundation on which to build pedagogy, agency, resilience, and practice (e.g., Beauchamp & Thomas, 2009; Beijaard et al., 2004). Thus, one of the core functions of teacher education programs (TEPs) is to shape pre-service teachers' (PSTs') teacher identities (Danielewicz, 2001; Farnsworth, 2010).

At the same time, one of the main goals of TEPs in democratic societies is to work toward social justice and train teachers who can disrupt systemic inequities (Zeichner, 2006). Recently there has been increased overlap between the social justice teacher education literature and the teacher identity literature (Boylan & Woolsey, 2015). The resulting scholarship underscores that all PSTs and teachers have a relationship with social justice and that social justice beliefs are deeply intertwined with teacher identity (Boylan & Woolsey, 2015). Moreover, social justice teacher identities, like any identity, are influenced through social interaction (Boylan & Woolsey, 2015). As such, the purpose of this chapter is to examine how PSTs' interactions with their peers and with their TEP influence their social justice teacher identities.[1]

The term *social justice* is widely used in TEPs and in teacher education research (Chubbuck & Zembylas, 2016; Enterline et al., 2008). Zeichner (2006) contended that it is difficult to find a TEP in the United States that does not claim to prepare teachers to work toward social justice in their classrooms. Teaching for social justice is rooted in an understanding that systemic oppression and wide disparities exist in "educational opportunities, resources, achievement, [and] in positive outcomes between minority and/or low-income students and their White middle-class counterparts" (Cochran-Smith et al., 2009a, p. 350). This stance is often paired with the idea that teachers are both educators and advocates committed to reducing these disparities and disrupting systems that perpetuate inequity (Cochran-Smith, 2010; Cochran-Smith et al., 2009b). Teaching for social justice is ultimately grounded in the idea that the main goal of teaching is "enhancing students' learning and life chances by challenging inequities in school and society" (Cochran-Smith et al., 2009a, p. 350).

PSTs' social justice teacher identity is integral not only to how they learn and teach but also to how they will ultimately shape their classrooms to address systemic oppression (Chubbock & Zembylas, 2016; Farnsworth, 2010). Moreover, PSTs' histories and views on social justice influence their experiences as teachers and their identity development (Boylan & Woolsey, 2015; Olsen, 2008; 2011). Teacher identity formation—like all identity formation—is a dynamic and inherently social process that is constantly being negotiated (Beauchamp & Thomas, 2009; Burke & Stets, 1999, 2009). Identities are generally developed and legitimated through interactions with others in various social contexts (Burke & Stets, 2009; McCall & Simmons, 1978). Despite this, few studies have examined the role that interactions with peers and professors play in social justice teacher identity development (e.g., Boylan & Woolsey, 2015). This mixed-methods chapter adds to the literature by exploring how PSTs' relationships with their peers and their program are related to their social justice teacher identities. I used social network analysis, classroom observations, and interviews in a connected mixed-methods approach (Creswell & Plano Clark, 2011) to answer the following research questions:

> RQ1: Is there a relationship between PSTs' close relationships with diverse peers and a social justice teacher identity?
> RQ2: Is there a relationship between PSTs' value consonance with their TEP and a social justice teacher identity?
> RQ3: How does interaction with the TEP and peers shape PSTs' social justice teacher identity?

Below I explore the literature regarding teacher education for social justice, social justice teacher identity, and theory of social networks. I then describe my qualitative and quantitative methods and the findings. I conclude with implications for PSTs, TEPs, and further research.

Literature Review

Social Justice in Teacher Education

Despite (or because of) its ubiquity in TEPs and teacher education research, social justice is both ambiguous and undertheorized (Cochran-Smith, 2010; Cochran-Smith et al., 2009b; Enterline et al., 2008). Although critiques of social justice teacher education argue that it is focused on attitudes and beliefs and not on content (Cochran-Smith et al., 2009b), it is fundamentally intended to "enhance students' learning and their life chances by challenging the inequities of school and society" (Enterline et al., 2008, p. 270). Improving social justice is arguably one of the fundamental goals of teacher education in democratic societies (Zeichner, 2006).

Social justice teacher education is meant to give PSTs the tools they need to teach for social justice in K–12 settings (Cochran-Smith et al., 2009a), including to the ability to disrupt inequities and to think about and interpret their work through a social justice lens (Cochran-Smith et al., 2009b). It "also involves how teachers pose questions, make decisions, and form relationships with students and how they work with colleagues, families, communities, and social groups" (Cochran-Smith et al., 2009a, p. 350). One through line in the literature on social justice teacher education is the idea of a distributive justice and the need to recognize and respect marginalized social groups (Boylan & Woolsey, 2015; Cochran-Smith, 2010; Enterline et al., 2008).

Social Justice Teacher Identity

Using an Identity Theory lens (Burke & Stets, 2009), I define social justice teacher identity as the meaning PSTs give to their role as teachers in relation to social justice beliefs and principles (Boylan & Woolsey, 2015; Burke & Stets, 2009). As mentioned above, social justice teacher identity (as with all identities) is negotiated through social interaction (Boylan & Woolsey, 2015; Burke & Stets, 2009). Identities generally have socially constructed meanings that dictate behavior within that identity (Stryker, 1980). That said, identity and these behaviors are not fully determined by these socially constructed meanings—individuals continually negotiate these meanings via interaction with others in social contexts (Burke & Stets, 2009; Stryker, 1980). For example, people seek to validate or verify their identities through interaction with others and these interactions can strengthen, alter, or change those identities (Burke & Stets, 1999, 2009). In short, meanings attached to an identity—like social justice identity—are shaped through interactions with others in specific social contexts (Burke & Stets, 2009; McCall & Simmons, 1978).

PSTs' social justice identity is integral to shaping how they learn and how they understand themselves and the work of teaching (Farnsworth, 2010). Importantly, identity is not only about who someone is and what they do; it is also about who someone is *not* and what they will *not* do (Benson, 2003). This is an important distinction for social justice identity, as it implies that the meaning teachers ascribe to teaching for social justice can predict what they will or will not do for their students. For example, if teachers refuse to see differences between groups of students, they are essentially erasing their students' identities and maintaining the status quo, which benefits dominant social groups (Boylen & Wollsey, 2015). Moreover, teachers who do not value social justice may be resistant to learning practices and methods associated with it or they will not be inclined to have necessary but difficult conversations about race and inequity (Daniel, 2009).

Teachers' and PSTs' actions, experiences, and pedagogy are filtered through their beliefs and their social justice identities (Enterline et al., 2008). Their social justice teacher identities are shaped by interactions with peers and by their programs (Olsen, 2011). This chapter explores the social side of social justice teacher identity development by examining the role of interactions with peers and the TEP in its development. Social network theory, which I discuss next, provides further context for the research.

Social Network Theory

Social network theory "provides a formal and conceptual way to think about the social world" (Wasserman & Faust, 1994, p. 11). The study of social networks is grounded in the notion that relationships among interacting units are related to the actions of individuals (Borgatti et al., 2018). Since identity formation is inherently social, it makes sense to use social networks as an avenue to learn more about how social interactions are related to PSTs' identity formation.

Social networks consist of *actors* (people, organizations, companies, etc.)—also called *nodes*—who are connected by relationships or *ties* to one another. A tie between two actors can denote a variety of relationships: kinship, work colleague, collaborator, or, in the case of this study, close friends. Additionally, ties can be considered weak or strong based on the type of tie, the content of the tie, or the frequency of the interaction embodied in the tie (Marsden & Campbell, 1984, 2012). Social network structures and ties within those networks can influence actors' ideas, attitudes, and actions (Centola, 2018; Granovetter, 1973). Both tie strength and network composition have been shown to influence identity, beliefs, and actions.

Tie strength can have an effect on the importance of relationships and how much influence they have on actors' beliefs and actions (Centola, 2018; Coburn, 2012). Friendship ties are often considered strong ties, and friends can have an outsized influence on the beliefs, attitudes, and actions of actors (Carter et al., 2019; Davies et al., 2011; Pettigrew & Tropp, 2006). Friendship interactions can have a strong influence on attitudes and beliefs because they are characterized by shared goals, cooperation, and multiple equal-status interactions that take place over long periods of time (Pettigrew & Tropp, 2006). McAdam and Paulsen (1993) note, "[t]he fact that we are embedded in many relationships means that any major decision we are contemplating will likely be mediated by a significant subset of those relationships" (p. 646). I argue that this notion applies to decisions about how to teach and PSTs social justice identity development as well. I incorporate strong ties into my analysis by using a multiplex network (discussed more below).

Scholars have found a relationship between the composition of an actor's network and a variety of outcomes (e.g., Carter et al., 2019; Leahy & Chopik, 2020; Levitan & Visser, 2009). Having a diverse network composition (i.e., having friends outside of one's ethno-racial group) is related to increased positive feelings about diversity and outgroups (Bahns et al., 2015; Davies et al., 2011; Pettigrew & Tropp, 2006). A recent study of the ethno-racial composition of college students' networks found that a network with a higher percentage of friends who identify as underrepresented minorities was related to increased feelings of perceived injustice and involvement in collective action (Carter et al., 2019). The authors state, "diverse friendship networks are a foundational component of students' attitudes, and the diversity of these networks shapes the way that they perceive, and how they engage with the world around them" (Carter et al., 2019, p. 57). In this study, I will expand on this literature by exploring the relationship between network composition and social justice teacher identity.

Methods and Data

Data for this chapter were collected from PSTs enrolled in a master's of education credentialing program at a large public university in the southwestern United States. The program had an explicit social justice bent, with a commitment to equity and partnerships with low-income schools. The program placed all participants in schools with underserved populations for their student-teaching placements. The program worked in a cohort model, with the same students grouped together for several classes during a semester or quarter and over the course of the school year.

I used a concurrent mixed-methods design to collect data (Creswell & Plano Clark, 2011). Specifically, I administered surveys to two cohorts of PSTs in the final month of their program. The findings in this chapter draw from three interviews with each participant: the first in October/November 2018, the second in January/February 2019, and the third in May/June 2019. To analyze my data, I used a connected mixed-methods approach—quantitative data from the survey informed part of the qualitative data analysis (Creswell & Plano Clark, 2011).

Quantitative Data

Survey Sample

As mentioned above, I surveyed the students in two cohorts—one multiple-subject cohort ($n=38$) and one single-subject cohort ($n=25$)—in a graduate-level TEP in May 2019. Multiple-subject teachers teach primary grades (i.e., Kindergarten through sixth grade), while single-subject teachers typically teach middle and high school and focus on a single subject (e.g., science, math, or history). The survey measured two networks with the following prompts:

- **Close relationship network prompt:** *Of the cohort members, with whom do you have a close relationship? By "close," we mean a person whom you trust with personal information and/or spend time with in informal settings.*
- **Advice network prompt:** *Please select the frequency of interaction with members of the cohort from whom you seek advice regarding the improvement of your teaching practice.*

The close relationship network was a binary network where participants either selected a cohort mate as a close relationship (1) or did not select them (0). In the advice network, I asked about the frequency with which they sought advice from other members of their cohort. Their options for frequency of interaction were *once a quarter* (1), *monthly* (2), *weekly or almost weekly* (3), or *daily or almost daily* (4). For the analysis described in this chapter, the advice network was dichotomized to reflect a strong-tie network. As such, a tie existed when an individual sought advice weekly/almost weekly or daily/almost daily.

I then combined the two networks into a multiplex network, which represents the overlap of two or more relationships (Scott, 2013; Verbrugge, 1979). *Multiplex ties* are considered strong and enduring, as they represent relationships with multiple facets and multiple dimensions (Granovetter, 1973; Scott, 2013). In the current study, for a tie to exist in the multiplex network, it had to exist in both the close relationship network *and* the strong-tie advice network. Multiplex ties expand the ways and dimensions through which people know and interact with each other and represent stronger relationships between people (Small, 2017). Strong ties are indicative of closer relationships, and education research has found that stronger ties tend to be a greater source of influence than weaker ties on practices, beliefs, and uptake and implementation of new practices (Coburn et al., 2012; Frank et al., 2004).

Table 5.1 Sample demographics

	Mean	**SD**	**Min.**	**Max.**
Demographics				
Female	.89	-	0.0	1.0
Multiple-subject cohort	.60	-	0.0	1.0
Ethno-racial identity				
White	.44			
Latina/o	.18			
Asian	.24			
Black	.02			
More than one group identity	.13			
Undergraduate GPA	3.41	.29	2.88	4.00
Independent Variables				
Value Fit	7.15	1.52	2.33	9.00
EI Index by Ethno-Racial Identity (x10)	.98	6.41	−10.00	10.00
Dependent Variable				
Teaching for Social Justice Beliefs	7.74	1.16	3.50	9.00

Note. Values for ethno-racial identity do not add to 100 percent due to rounding.

To improve validity of my networks, each participant was given a roster of their cohort to refer to as they named peers from whom they sought advice (Scott, 2013). Further, I piloted the survey in the spring of the prior academic year with a separate cohort of PSTs and conducted follow-up cognitive interviews with three pilot study participants. In the interviews, participants were asked to put the network prompts in their own words and explain some of their choices. This allowed me to test whether they understood the questions as intended (Fowler, 2014).

Of the PSTs surveyed I obtained a 100 percent response rate, and my overall sample for the survey was 63 PSTs (see Table 5.1). Sixty percent of the sample were in the multiple-subject cohort, and 89 percent of the sample identified as female. PSTs who identified as White made up 44 percent of the total sample; PSTs who identified as Asian were 24 percent of the sample, and Latinas/os represented 18 percent of the sample; those who identified with more than one ethno-racial group comprised 13 percent of the sample; and PSTs who identified as Black made up 2 percent. Participants' average undergraduate GPA was 3.41, with a minimum of 2.88 and a maximum of 4.00. All PSTs in the sample had been in a school placement and were either student-teaching or interning when they took the survey. Interns were single-subject candidates who were the teacher of record for one class without being fully credentialed.

Survey Variables

Dependent Variable: LTSJ-B Scale. To measure social justice teacher identity, I used the Learning to Teach for Social Justice-Beliefs (LTSJ-B) scale (Enterline et al., 2008). This scale was specifically designed to measure PSTs' beliefs about teaching for social justice (Enterline et al., 2008). Participants were asked to indicate the extent to which they believed twelve items like, "*Good teaching incorporates diverse cultures and experiences into classroom lessons.*" Items were measured on a scale ranging from 1 (*strongly disagree*) to 9 (*strongly agree*), high score on this scale indicates a stronger sense that teaching for social justice is core to the individual's mission as a teacher ($\alpha=.88$). It is worth noting that the LTSJ-B is a proxy for social justice teacher identity. Using an Identity Theory lens, I defined social justice teacher identity as the meaning PSTs give to their role as teachers in relation to social justice beliefs and principles. I argue that this scale offers evidence of participants' social justice beliefs and principals, which inform the meaning that they ascribe to their role as teachers thus it is a good proxy—albeit imperfect—measure of social justice teacher identity.

Independent Variable: Value Consonance. To explore the relationship between the program and PSTs' social justice identities, I used a value consonance scale (Skaalvik & Skaalvik, 2011). This three-item scale measured how much participants believed their views and beliefs about teaching and education were consonant with the TEP, for example "*I feel like this program shares my views of what constitutes good teaching.*" The scale ranged from 1 (*strongly disagree*) to 9 (*strongly agree*), with a higher score indicating a stronger sense of value consonance ($\alpha=.86$).

Independent Variable: Ethno-Racial EI Index. Finally, to measure the relationship between social peers in participants' social networks and social justice teacher identity,

I used an ethno-racial external-internal (EI) index (Borgatti et al., 2018). As discussed above, ethno-racially diverse friendships can increase awareness of social justice issues and foster positive feelings about people in outgroups (Carter et al., 2019; Davies et al., 2011). As such I explored ethno-racial network composition in my multiplex network. To measure network composition, I found the EI index using UCINET (Borgatti et al., 2002) for each participant based on their self-identified ethno-racial group.

An EI index is a measure of the proportion of people in an actor's ego network who are from the same group (internal) or a different group (external). The EI index ranges from—1.0 to 1.0, where a score of—1.0 indicates complete homogeneity in network ties (i.e., all the people in the actor's ego network identify with the same ethno-racial group as the participant) and a score of 1.0 indicates complete heterogeneity in network ties (i.e., all of the people in the actor's ego network identify with a different ethno-racial group than the actor). In short, a score that is closer to—1.0 indicates more relationships with peers with the same ethno-racial identity and a score that is closer to 1.0 indicates more relationships with peers with a different ethno-racial identity. I multiplied the EI index by 10 to make it easier to interpret in my regression.

Survey Data Analysis

To analyze the quantitative data, I conducted a hierarchical ordinary least squares (OLS) multiple regression (Petrocelli, 2003). A hierarchical OLS regression involves including several predictor variables into a regression in a sequential manner to explore the importance of each set of predictors. The change in the amount of variance explained by a model (ΔR^2) and change in the F-statistic (ΔF) between sets of predictors measures the predictive power of the model.

I entered variables in two steps. In Step 1, I included control variables: gender identity, undergraduate GPA, ethno-racial identity, and cohort. All of these variables have been found to have an association with how people experience their TEP and how they understand their teacher identities (e.g., Brown, 2014; Bullough & Knowles, 1990; Olsen, 2008). In Step 2, I entered my variables of interest—value fit and ethno-racial EI index—into the model, not only to explore the individual relationship these variables have with social justice teacher identity but also to see how they changed the R^2 as a pair.

Qualitative Data

Sampling and Data Collection

After the initial survey in the fall of 2018, I selected sixteen PSTs to interview over the course of the year based on social network position as measured by an initial survey given in Fall 2018 (Daly, 2010; Liou & Bjorklund, 2023). More specifically, I selected interviewees who were central actors and peripheral actors (as measured by indegree and outdegree) as well as participants who fell between the central actors and peripheral actors in the close relationship and advice networks. This selection process was part of a longitudinal project on teacher identity development. I chose to select interviewees based on network position so that I could use the interviews to get a better understanding about how, if at all, network position was related to teacher identity development. Table 5.2 lists the sixteen participants as well as their cohort and ethno-racial identification.

I conducted three semi-structured interviews (Merriam & Tisdell, 2016) with the sixteen participants three times over the academic year—in October/November 2018, in January/February 2019, and in May 2019. Each interview was transcribed verbatim. I also attended one 3-hour class every week for the entire year for each cohort (two classes per week) to conduct observations and write fieldnotes (Emerson et al., 2011). This amounted to forty-five three-hour observations across the two cohorts over the academic year. During the observations, I focused particular attention on the sixteen selected participants and their social interactions with their peers. I typed fieldnotes as soon as possible after the end of each observed class (Emerson et al., 2011). The observations gave me a better sense of the social dynamics within each cohort, helped me to triangulate my qualitative findings (Merriam & Tisdell, 2016), and helped me make sense of the social networks.

Table 5.2 Interview participants

Name (Grade or Subject)	Cohort	Self-Identified Ethno-Racial Group
Joelle (Kindergarten)	Multiple-Subject	White
Anna (1st Grade)	Multiple-Subject	Mexican
Cate (3rd Grade)	Multiple-Subject	Middle Eastern
Tina (3rd Grade)	Multiple-Subject	White
Janice (4th/5th Grade Split)	Multiple-Subject	Chinese-American
Leila (Kindergarten)	Multiple-Subject	Mexican
Tara (Kindergarten)	Multiple-Subject	Mexican
Karen (6th Grade)	Multiple-Subject	Black
Marta (World Languages)	Single-Subject	Mexican
Jaime (ELA)	Single-Subject	Mexican
Logan (World Languages)	Single-Subject	Black and Chinese
Sofia (ELA)	Single-Subject	Mexican
James (Math)	Single-Subject	Mexican and White
Diana (Science)	Single-Subject	White
Julia (Science)	Single-Subject	Mexican
Kaleb (ELA)	Single-Subject	White

Note. All names are pseudonyms. ELA = English language arts.

To validate analysis of participants via their interviews, I conducted a participant check after the completion of their program (Merriam & Tisdell, 2016). Based on prior interviews and interactions with the participants, I created short narratives (memos) that described them as teachers and described their feelings about teaching for social justice. I read each participant their memo and gave them a copy to review. The participants all agreed that my analysis captured their understandings of themselves as teachers.

Interview Coding and Analysis

All qualitative data were uploaded into NVIVO software for coding, and then I used a two-cycle coding process (Miles et al., 2014; Saldaña, 2016). Guided by the quantitative results in the first coding cycle, I read the interviews from each participant and coded any passages related to issues of teaching for social justice (Cochran-Smith, 2010; Cochran-Smith et al., 2009a)—for example, discussions about race, equity, structural inequality, teaching students from minoritized backgrounds, and so on. I also coded any passages that were related to their interactions with peers and the TEP and to how their peers and the program shaped their teacher identities.

After one round of coding, I ran queries in NVIVO to extract coded excerpts. I then reviewed the data to find overarching patterns and create a smaller number of codes that captured these broader patterns and themes (Miles et al., 2014). In the second cycle of coding, I took a deductive approach to search for emerging themes (Miles et al., 2014; Saldaña, 2016). The following themes emerged:

- **Close relationship influences on social justice teacher identity:** These codes were expressions of the ways that peers who were considered friends influenced the social justice teacher identities of participants.
- **Boundary making:** These codes included instances where participants drew clear boundaries between themselves and their peers in their program.
- **Program influence:** These codes were expressions of participants' feelings about how the program impacted their social justice teacher identities.

The goal of gathering these qualitative data was to get a better explanation for the quantitative results and a deeper understanding of how PSTs' networks and the TEP impacted social justice teacher identity for the sixteen participants.

Findings

Quantitative Results

As noted above, I ran a hierarchical OLS (Petrocelli, 2003); Table 5.3 shows the results. In Step 1, I included demographic variables described above which accounted for over one quarter of the variance in the outcome variable ($R^2=.26$, $F=2.89$, $p<.05$). In Step 2,

Table 5.3 Hierarchical OLS regression on teaching for social justice beliefs

	Teaching for Social Justice Beliefs	Standardized Coefficients of Significant Variables
Step 1		
Control Variables		
R^2	.26	
F	2.89*	
Step 2		
Value Consonance	.17*	.31
	(.07)	
EI Index by Ethno-Racial Identity (x10)	.06***	.47
	(.02)	
ΔR^2	.19	
ΔF	5.54***	
Intercept	3.20*	
R^2	.45	

Note. Control variables include gender identity, undergraduate GPA, ethno-racial identity, and cohort. Standard errors are in parentheses.
*p <.05. **p <.01. ***p <.001.

I added the variables of interest, which increased the explanatory power of the model by 19 percent (ΔR^2=.19, ΔF=5.54, $p<.001$). Value consonance was significant and positively related to social justice beliefs (b=.17 p<.05), as was the EI index (b=.06, $p<.001$). Here, a one-unit increase in the EI index (x10) was related to a .062 increase in social justice beliefs. In other words, participants with a higher number of strong ties with people outside of their ethno-racial group reported a stronger social justice identity, controlling for demographics. The standardized coefficients show that the EI index (β=.47, $p<.001$) had a stronger relationship with social justice beliefs than value consonance (β=.31, $p<.05$). These findings indicate that a one-standard-deviation increase in the EI index was associated with almost a one-half-standard-deviation increase in social justice beliefs. The final model accounted for almost half of the variance in the outcome variable (R^2=.45). Next, drawing from the interview data, I explore the mechanisms that are potentially driving these results.

Qualitative Results

Close Peers Shape Social Justice Identities

The quantitative results described above indicate that a participant's social justice beliefs were positively related to the proportion of people in their network who identified with different ethno-racial groups than their own. The results potentially support the notion that PSTs' social justice identity is influenced through social practice and interaction with others (Boylan & Woolsey, 2015), as having more friendships in the cohort with people outside of the participant's ethno-racial identity was related to stronger social justice identity.

Interviews and observations showed that participants often had relationships with diverse peers, and these relationships were integral to their social justice teacher identities. The evidence suggests that many close relationships in the program formed because of similar social justice identities (Vaisey & Lizardo, 2010). Participants in the current study felt like their close peers helped them to shape or solidify the social justice identities that they entered the program with but did not change them drastically (Olsen, 2011).

Cate, for example, was a PST in the multiple-subject cohort who identified as Middle Eastern. She had an EI index of 10, indicating that all of her close friends identified with a different ethno-racial group than hers. She came into the program with very strong views about the work of teaching. She developed close friendships with three women, two of whom identified as Latina and one of whom identified as White; she felt like her friends' experiences strengthened her social justice teacher identity. She explained how they shaped her understanding of herself as a teacher:

> Marisol and Tara, they're both ... English is their second language, like me. And I think we share in this idea of drawing from a student's funds of knowledge. You give value to someone's culture, you give value to their past, their language, their heritage. ... Me and Marisol actually [did] our first project in this program ... on funds of knowledge. ... And we grew closer because of that. My relationships with them have strengthened my resolve to value the strengths and diversity that my students bring to the classroom.

Cate's experiences before the program strongly influenced her social justice teacher identity and she was able to find close friends in Marisol and Tara, whom she felt shared similar backgrounds and social justice identities. Cate was able to learn and grow with her friends as they strengthened and broadened the beliefs she came to the program with. Other research has shown that PSTs' histories of diversity and social justice prior to entering the TEP tend to have a strong influence on their social justice identities (Olsen, 2011).

Studying social justice topics drew Cate closer to her peers and strengthened her resolve in valuing her students. She believed that being a teacher meant celebrating the cultural assets and funds of knowledge that her students brought to the classroom. Utilizing students' funds of knowledge in the classroom is a valuable tool in teaching for social justice, as it challenges the ideas of what knowledge counts as valid in the classroom (Moll et al., 1992). Cate's views on teaching for social justice issues were part of what drew her to become friends with Marisol and Tara (Vaisey & Lizardo, 2010). At the same time, it seems that being in a network with like-minded people strengthened her beliefs and social justice teacher identity (Levitan & Visser, 2009). Engaging in relationships with her friends in the cohort helped Cate bolster her social justice identity and gave her a space where that identity could be nurtured and strengthened.

In contrast, Janice had an EI index of −10, indicating that her network consisted of peers who identified with the same ethno-racial group that she did. She was a candidate in the multiple-subject cohort and identified as Chinese American. Janice said she would often talk about privileging care and love toward her students in her teaching as a way to address the issues she saw in her community. She credited her close friends in the program with helping her to shape and solidify her pedagogy of care:

> I think in general we still believe pretty similar ideas, about caring for our students and everything, but ... our dialogue about it really helps solidify my beliefs. I mean, I think that teaching is ... caring for our students ... But also, to see it as a way that we can also express our love for them ... even though they might not have a lot of support from their families and things like that.

Cochran-Smith (2010) averred that a common theme at the heart of teaching for justice is care and love for students. That said, caring teachers can maintain the status quo by conflating care with expecting less from students of color and not setting high standards for them (Nieto, 2008). Janice's conversations with her close friends in the cohort solidified her beliefs about care and making sure her students knew they were loved. But she seemed to view her students through a deficit lens: she indicated that she thought they may not have love and support from their families so it was incumbent upon her to give it to them.

Janice's current students were mostly Black or Latina/o; this view that their families did not love and support them is part and parcel of deficit views of minoritized families that are rampant in schools (Cochran-Smith, 2010; Valencia, 2010). While Janice's close peers were able to solidify her notion of caring as social justice identity, they may also have reinforced her deficit frames. Carter et al. (2019) found that more diverse networks increased college students' sense of injustice and propensity toward collective action. Conversely, they also found that less diverse networks decreased actors' sense of injustice and propensity toward collective action. Janice's close friends were people with similar backgrounds and ethno-racial identities. As such, the lack of close relationships with others outside of her own experiences may have limited her ability to move past a deficit mindset of her students.

These results support the quantitative findings related to the EI index. The two participants above represent the two extremes of the EI index, but the relationships between their peers and their social justice identities were similar to the participants in the middle of the EI index spectrum as well. Across all interviews, close peers shaped participants' social justice identities. Many participants came to the TEP with social justice identities based on past experiences, and the relationships they had with their peers did not seem to play a radical role in changing them—rather, their peers helped to hone and solidify those beliefs (Levitan & Visser, 2009; Olsen, 2011). Complex ideas about teaching and learning are facilitated through strong relationships (Coburn et al., 2012). As such, it is clear that the close relationships in the cohort had a meaningful, but not necessarily transformational impact on participants' social justice identities. Interestingly, peers from the cohort who were outside of their friend group also helped shape participants' social justice identities in meaningful ways—through the creation of boundaries.

Setting Boundaries to Define Social Justice Identities

An interesting finding from the interview data was that connections in participants' social networks were important to identity formation, but similarly important was who was *not* in their social networks. As participants formed strong bonds with their friend groups, they also created symbolic social boundaries (Binder & Abel, 2019; Carter, 2006; Lamont & Molnár, 2002) between themselves and others via their social justice identities. In most social activities, individuals create social boundaries or distinctions to identify themselves as a group apart from others (Binder & Abel, 2019; Carter, 2006; Lamont & Molnár, 2002). As noted earlier, identities and understanding of self are grounded in who we are and what we will do, but also in who we are *not* and what we will *not* do (Benson, 2003). Put succinctly, "I am what I can and will do, but also ... what I cannot do and will resist doing" (Benson, 2003, p. 64).

In both cohorts, participants tended to form boundaries by describing peers they thought were not meeting the ideal of social justice set by the program. Kara was the only Black woman in the multiple-subject cohort. She had a group of friends with whom she interacted, but she said she did not feel like they had an influence on her as a teacher. It seemed like the people she was not friends with had a stronger influence on her social justice identity. Describing some of her peers outside of her friend group, Kara said:

> … Half of them [have] White savior complex, even if they don't realize. … Just like … "Oh my god, I'm going to go in and save all of these kids, and be the best teacher ever." There's nothing wrong with wanting to be the best teacher, but it's different when you want to be the best teacher because you actually want to teach the kids, and when you think you're saving them from life.

Kara set boundaries around her group, herself, and others in the program by saying that they had White savior complexes. Ziechner (2018) noted that TEPs and their training programs often maintain a discourse of "'Helperism,' the emphasis to save students from their broken communities rather than recognizing and building on the strengths and funds of knowledge that exist in these communities" (p. 270). Kara acknowledged what she saw as "helperism" in her peers and set her social justice identity in contrast to them.

Sofia was a single-subject English Language Arts (ELA) teacher who identified as Mexican. After college she found work as a long-term substitute which she said shaped her teacher identity. She felt like there was a group of peers in her cohort who were unnecessarily punitive toward their students and did not value the same types of lessons about equity and inclusion. She set clear boundaries around her social justice teacher identity and how it contrasted with some of her peers. She began by saying how her peers would talk about their students in a demeaning way:

> Like, they're just like, "This essay's trash." I wouldn't tell my students that. ... Yeah. Or like, "Referral. You get a referral. You get a referral." I don't do that ... Now that I've been taking all these classes ... I gained all this knowledge. With them, the way, you know, when they share their stories, it's like, that's what I used to do when I had no knowledge of how to interact with students. ... We have been taught to kind of talk to [students] and see what's going on. Like, it's not their fault. Something's going on.

When I asked Sofia whether she thought these individuals were rejecting what they were being taught in the TEP, she responded, "Oh, yeah. Totally 'cause their comments are like, 'Oh, this is so stupid. This is a waste of time.' They'll be grading or they'll be lesson planning while we're supposed to be doing something else."

Sofia set boundaries between herself and her peers who she felt like were not living up to the ideals of the program. Moreover, she felt like her peers were teaching in a way that was antithetical to what they had learned in the program. Minoritized students, most frequently Black students, are disproportionally disciplined and excluded from classroom instruction (e.g., Gregory et al., 2010; Kennedy-Lewis & Murphy, 2016). Sofia learned that talking to students and seeing why they might be misbehaving—instead of acting punitively—was a more equitable approach. Communication between students and teachers, like Sofia advocated for, could potentially lead to increased trust and better communication between minoritized students and their teachers (Gregory & Weinstein, 2008). Sofia saw her peers as disinterested in an equitable approach to teaching—she saw them as the type of teacher she did not want to be, and drew her social justice identity in contrast to them.

Strong Program Influence on Social Justice Identity, but Race is Missing

The final question guiding this chapter examined how the program influenced the social justice identity of the participants. The quantitative findings showed a positive relationship between value consonance and social justice beliefs. In other words, the more the participants felt that their values were aligned with the program, the stronger their feelings about teaching for social justice. The qualitative findings support these findings and show that the social justice stance of the program had an impact on the social justice identities of the PSTs in the program. All participants, to varying degrees, indicated that the program had an influence on their social justice identities. For instance, when asked how much the program influenced her ability to address issues of equity in the classroom, Julia, a single-subject science teacher who identified as Mexican said:

A huge degree. I feel like I've learned so much about having culturally responsive pedagogies through the program and really getting to know my kids and what they need specifically … it has been so eye-opening, and it has really challenged what I believe and really made me look at my own bias … and really putting that at the forefront of my teaching. Every day I always look back and think, "What could I have done different?"

Julia felt like the program had given her valuable insights about teaching that shaped her social justice identity. In this excerpt, she noted how the program forced her to challenge herself and her biases. In fact, fundamental to teaching for social justice is challenging beliefs and stereotypes and examining how they maintain the status quo (Cochran-Smith, 2010; Cochran-Smith et al., 2009a). Moreover, a significant part of teaching for social justice is constantly reflecting on oneself and on one's pedagogy in an effort to make it more equitable (Athanases & Oliveira, 2008). To Julia, working toward more socially just practice was at the heart of what it means to be a teacher. It seems that Julia felt the program had instilled a social justice identity that was weaved into her work in the classroom.

Jaime was a PST in the single-subject cohort who identified as Mexican. During our interviews, he was teaching middle school ELA. When I asked him asked how the program had influenced his understanding of himself as a teacher he said:

The program, I think it shaped me … being equitable, making sure that diversity is visible in the curriculum. And, for example, I think the program has shaped me into being somebody that is actively changing and challenging the canon of literature that is taught in the classroom. … For example, I was talking to another English teacher … about starting the Greek [mythology] unit. And I told him, "You know what? I'm also going to allow them to learn myths about their own cultures because it's a diverse classroom. … For example, I'm going to teach them myths from Cambodia and Laos, etc." It's more so because I look at my classroom and I don't see White kids, period. There's just no White kids in my classroom.

Jaime was openly challenging the Western Canon taught in schools by bringing stories and myths that are relevant to his students, which scholars have noted as integral to teaching for social justice (Cochran-Smith, 2010; Cochran-Smith et al., 2009a). He felt like the program helped him to be more aware of his students' backgrounds and to introduce a culturally relevant pedagogy (Ladson-Billings, 1995) that drew upon the knowledge that his students brought from their homes and histories (Moll et al., 1992). Other participants in the study also believed the program had shaped their ideas about teaching for social justice and making their classrooms more equitable. These results support the quantitative findings, as participants who felt like their beliefs aligned with the program felt like they were learning from the program and felt a stronger social justice identity relative to peers who potentially felt lower levels of value consonance with the program.

It is worth noting, however, that participants felt like the program prepared them to be more equity minded, but almost none of them felt like the program prepared them to address issues of race in the classroom. Many TEPs have only a token class about race and racism (Chapman, 2011); few incorporate it throughout the program. In her interview at the end of the year, Janice seemed to point to this happening in this TEP as well. She saidWhen I think about race, it's more of our class with Sandra, where I think she was the main person really pushing for that and having that conversation. I'm not so sure whether they really talk about it in other parts of the program. I feel like they just really gave us that one class to think about it.

Janice's sentiment seemed to mirror the literature regarding discussions of race in TEPs: They are limited to a single class and do not go very deep into the topic (Young, 2016). Kara had a sharper critique of the programs lack of attention to race in the program:

First of all, they don't really talk about race in the classroom that much. I haven't noticed it. They don't bring it up … They talk about socioeconomic [status], … and autism, and ADHD, and deaf, and blind, but they don't really talk about race at all … They don't even teach about it. They just assume equity is making sure that your instruction is different for all kids …

Kara felt like the program equated equity and race, and that it gave scant explicit attention to issues of race and equity in the classroom. She noted that they are not the same and that she was upset by the lack of attention to it; she did not feel like the program was giving her the tools to talk about, think about, or adequately address race.

Whiteness is pervasive in TEPs (Brown, 2014; Sleeter, 2001). One way Whiteness seemed to manifest itself in this particular program was the lack of explicit attention to issues of race throughout coursework and the dedication of just part of one course to it (Chapman, 2011). Other issues of equity were discussed, but many participants stated that race was talked about infrequently, if at all, in the program (Young, 2016). The lack of explicit discussion of race by the TEP was a form of colorblindness in that it conflated equity with fairness for all and did not explicitly address issues of racism.

Discussion and Conclusion

In this mixed-methods study, I explored the roles of peer interaction and a TEP in shaping PSTs' social justice teacher identities. Quantitative results indicated that the ethno-racial network composition was related to social justice teacher identity. This supports prior research that showed that having more diverse close friendships is related to more positive views on diversity and awareness of social injustice (Bahns et al., 2015; Carter et al., 2019). The qualitative findings also support the quantitative findings as friend groups often enhanced or shaped social justice beliefs that PSTs brought with them to the TEP (Olsen, 2011; Vaisey & Lizardo, 2010). Moreover, they show that peers outside PSTs' friend groups influenced their social justice identities, as they drew social boundaries between themselves and those peers who they felt were anathema to their social justice teacher identities.

The quantitative results further showed that value consonance—the belief that one's values aligned with the program—was positively related to PSTs' social justice identities and beliefs. The qualitative data supported this finding and showed that participants' social justice identities were strongly shaped by what they had learned in their TEP. The qualitative findings in fact expanded on the quantitative findings by showing that the program had little influence on PSTs' views specifically about race, racism, and racial justice. Potential implications for TEPs are explored below.

Ideas of social justice and diversity are ubiquitous in TEPs (Cochran-Smith, 2010; Cochran-Smith et al., 2009b; Zeichner, 2006, 2018). Despite a large number of critics (Cochran-Smith et al., 2009b), social justice teacher education, if done well, can serve as a bedrock for equitable teaching practices that expand educational opportunities and fight systemic barriers (Cochran-Smith, 2010). Additionally, the benefits and pitfalls of diversity in TEPs have received the attention of numerous scholars in the past fifteen years (e.g., Ball & Tyson, 2011; Brown, 2014; Chapman, 2011; Sleeter & Milner, 2011). Overall, scholarship indicates that the benefits of diversity in TEPs are manifold and increasing the racial and ethnic diversity of the teacher workforce should be central to a teacher education system that wants to put well-prepared teachers in all schools for all students (Ball & Tyson, 2011). PSTs from minoritized backgrounds not only benefit the students they will ultimately teach but also their peers, as they bring cultural experiences and knowledge to TEPs that helps teachers become more effective (Sleeter & Milner, 2011).

While there is a wealth of literature exploring the benefits of more diverse TEPs broadly, little research has more pointedly investigated the role of diverse friendships in TEPs. This chapter adds to the literature by beginning to explore the connections between diverse friendships and a social justice teacher identity. Close friendships can play a meaningful role in shaping PSTs' social justice identity and attitudes about teaching, as these types of relationships require a level of trust and interaction over time. As such, TEPs may want to pay attention to the friendships being formed in their programs and the social networks in which these relationships are embedded. This knowledge may give them a better understanding of their PSTs networks, the diversity of those networks, and how those networks interact with PSTs' social justice identities.

For participants in this study, peer relationships and the TEP played an outsized role in shaping social justice identities—all of the participants were impacted by their interactions with peers and what they learned in the program. That said, they also felt their program was lacking robust discussion of race. It would be impossible to expect TEPs to completely prepare PSTs to address issues of race, but they must give PSTs a framework or tools to better address racism in the classroom (Cochran-Smith, 2010). For example, Richard Milner (2007) offered a framework for reflecting on race in educational research that could be applied to teachers and classroom settings. TEPs may want to consider the types of tools or frameworks that they are giving their PSTs to address issues of racial inequity in the classroom.

Lastly, Centola (2020) notes that "social relations do not appear out of nowhere. Rather they emerge from social contexts that we inhabit ... this means that for people to form ties, there must be a social setting where they can meet one another." (p. 121). For TEPs this means that they may want to explore the social contexts that they create for PSTs to interact and form trusting ties. What opportunities are they giving their PSTs to meet and form ties? What social contexts are they opening up so that PSTs can exchange ideas and facilitate strong relationships? TEPs cannot make PSTs be friends with each other, but they can create social contexts that allow for friendships to form and strategically shape social networks to benefit their PSTs and help shape their social justice identities (Centola, 2018).

Overall, the results presented in this chapter support the idea that PSTs' social justice identities are influenced through social interaction (Boylan & Woolsey, 2015). Future work should continue to explore the social side of social justice identity. TEPs should consider examining their PSTs' social networks and the contexts that are created to foster them. Whether PSTs or teachers are aware of it or not, they all have a relationship to social justice, and it manifests in their social justice identity and how they teach their students (Boylan & Woolsey, 2015).

Note

1   Throughout the chapter, the terms *social justice identity* and *social justice teacher identity* are used interchangeably.

References

Athanases, S. Z., & De Oliveira, L. C. (2008). Advocacy for equity in classrooms and beyond: New teachers' challenges and responses. *Teachers College Record, 110*(1), 64–104.

Ball, A. F., & Tyson, C. A. (2011). *Studying diversity in teacher education*. Rowman & Littlefield Publishers, Inc.

Beauchamp, C., & Thomas, L. (2009). Understanding teacher identity: An overview of issues in the literature and implications for teacher education. *Cambridge Journal of Education, 39*, 175–89.

Beijaard, D., Meijer, P. C., & Verloop N. (2004). Reconsidering teachers' professional identity. *Training and Teacher Education, 20*, 107–28.

Benson, C. (2003). The unthinkable boundaries of self: The role of negative emotional boundaries in the formation, maintenance and transformation of identities. In R. Harré & F. Moghaddam (Eds.), *The self and others: Positioning individuals and groups in personal, political, and cultural contexts* (pp. 61–84). Westport, Connecticut, London: Praeger.

Binder, A. J., & Abel, A. R. (2019). Symbolically maintained inequality: How Harvard and Stanford students construct boundaries among elite universities. *Sociology of Education, 92*(1), 41–58.

Bahns, A. J., Springer, L. S., & The, C. (2015). Fostering diverse friendships: The role of beliefs about the value of diversity. *Group Processes & Intergroup Relations, 18*(4), 475–88.

Borgatti, S. P., Everett, M. G., & Freeman, L. C. (2002). *Ucinet 6 for Windows: Software for social network analysis [Computer software]*. Harvard, MA: Analytic Technologies.

Borgatti, S. P., Everett, M. G., & Johnson, J. C. (2018). *Analyzing social networks*. Washington, DC: Sage Publications.

Boylan, M., & Woolsey, I. (2015). Teacher education for social justice: Mapping identity spaces. *Teaching and Teacher Education, 46*, 62–71.

Brown, K. D. (2014). Teaching in color: A critical race theory in education analysis of the literature on preservice teachers of color and teacher education in the U.S. *Race Ethnicity and Education, 17*, 326–45.

Bullough, R. V., Jr., & Knowles, J. G. (1990). Becoming a teacher: Struggles of a second-career beginning teacher. *International Journal of Qualitative Studies in Education, 3*, 101–12.

Burke, P. J., & Stets, J. E. (1999). Trust and commitment through self-verification. *Social Psychology Quarterly, 62*, 347–66.

Burke, P. J., & Stets, J. E. (2009). *Identity theory*. Oxford, UK: Oxford University Press.

Carter, E. R., Brady, S. T., Murdock-Perriera, L. A., Gilbertson, M. K., Ablorh, T., & Murphy, M. C. (2019). The racial composition of students' friendship networks predicts perceptions of injustice and involvement in collective action. *Journal of Theoretical Social Psychology, 3*(1), 49–61.

Carter, P. L. (2006). Straddling boundaries: Identity, culture, and school. *Sociology of Education, 79*(4), 304–28.

Centola, D. (2018). *How behavior spreads: The science of complex contagions*. Princeton University Press.

Chapman, T. K. (2011). A critical race theory analysis of past and present institutional processes and policies in teacher education. In Ball, A. F. & Tyson, C. A. (Eds.), *Studying diversity in teacher education* (pp. 237–56). Rowman & Littlefield Publishers, Inc.

Chubbuck, S. M., & Zembylas, M. (2016). Social justice and teacher education: Context, theory, and practice. In Loughran, J. & Hamilton, M. L. (Eds.), *International handbook of teacher education* (pp. 463–501). Springer.

Coburn, C. E., Russell, J. L., Kaufman, J. H., & Stein, M. K. (2012). Supporting sustainability: Teachers' advice networks and ambitious instructional reform. *American Journal of Education, 119*(1), 137–82.

Cochran-Smith, M. (2010). Toward a theory of teacher education for social justice. In Hargreaves, A., Lieberman, A., Fullan, M., & Hopkins, D. (Eds.), *Second international handbook of educational change* (pp. 445–68). Springer.

Cochran-Smith, M., Barnatt, J., Lahann, R., Shakman, K., & Terrell, D. (2009b). Teacher education for social justice: Critiquing the critiques. In Ayers, W., Quinn, T. & Stovall, D. (Eds.), *The handbook of social justice in education* (pp. 625–39). Routledge.

Cochran-Smith, M., Shakman, K., Jong, C., Terrell, D. G., Barnatt, J., & McQuillan, P. (2009a). Good and just teaching: The case for social justice in teacher education. *American Journal of Education, 115*(3), 347–77.

Creswell, J. W., & Plano Clark, V. L. (2011). *Designing and conducting mixed methods research* (2nd ed.). Sage Publications.

Daly, A. J. (2010). *Social network theory and educational change*. Cambridge, MA: Harvard Education Press.

Daniel, B. J. (2009). Conversations on race in teacher education cohorts. *Teaching Education, 20*(2), 175–88.

Danielewicz, J. (2001). *Teaching selves: Identity, pedagogy, and teacher education*. Albany, NY: State University of New York Press.

Davies, K., Tropp, L. R., Aron, A., Pettigrew, T. F., & Wright, S. C. (2011). Cross-group friendships and intergroup attitudes: A meta-analytic review. *Personality and Social Psychology Review, 15*(4), 332–51.

Emerson, E. M., Fretz, R. I., & Shaw, L. L. (2011). *Writing ethnographic fieldnotes* (2nd ed.). Chicago, IL: University of Chicago Press.

Enterline, S., Cochran-Smith, M., Ludlow, L. H., & Mitescu, E. (2008). Learning to teach for social justice: Measuring change in the beliefs of teacher candidates. *The New Educator, 4*(4), 267–90.

Farnsworth, V. (2010). Conceptualizing identity, learning and social justice in community-based learning. *Teaching and Teacher Education, 26*(7), 1481–9.

Fowler, F. J., Jr. (2014). *Survey research methods* (5th ed.). Sage Publications.

Frank, K. A., Zhao, Y., & Borman, K. (2004). Social capital and the diffusion of innovations within organizations: The case of computer technology in schools. *Sociology of Education, 77*(2), 148–71.

Granovetter, M. S. (1973). The strength of weak ties. *American Journal of Sociology, 78*, 1360–80.

Gregory, A., & Weinstein, R. S. (2008). The discipline gap and African Americans: Defiance or cooperation in the high school classroom. *Journal of School Psychology, 46*(4), 455–75.

Gregory, A., Skiba, R. J., & Noguera, P. A. (2010). The achievement gap and the discipline gap: Two sides of the same coin? *Educational Researcher, 39*(1), 59–68.

Hamachek, D. (1999). Effective teachers: What they do, how they do it, and the importance of self-knowledge. In Lipka, R. P. & Brinthaupt, T. M. (Eds.), *The role of self in teacher development* (pp. 77–95). Albany: State University of New York Press.

Kennedy-Lewis, B. L., & Murphy, A. S. (2016). Listening to "frequent flyers": What persistently disciplined students have to say about being labeled as "bad." *Teachers College Record, 118*(1), 1–40.

Ladson-Billings, G. (1995). But that's just good teaching! The case for culturally relevant pedagogy. *Theory into Practice, 34*(3), 159–65.

Lamont, M., & Molnár, V. (2002). The study of boundaries in the social sciences. *Annual Review of Sociology, 28*(1), 167–95.

Leahy, K. E., & Chopik, W. J. (2020). The effect of social network size and composition on the link between discrimination and health among sexual minorities. *Journal of Aging and Health, 32*(9), 1214–21.

Levitan, L. C., & Visser, P. S. (2009). Social network composition and attitude strength: Exploring the dynamics within newly formed social networks. *Journal of Experimental Social Psychology, 45*(5), 1057–67.

Liou, Y.-H. & Bjorklund, P., Jr. (2023). Understanding the shaping of school teacher networks amidst reform: Collaborative structure, network intentionality, closeness, and school climates. Manuscript under review.

Marsden, P. V., & Campbell, K. E. (1984). Measuring tie strength. *Social Forces, 63*, 482–501.

Marsden, P. V., & Campbell, K. E. (2012). Reflections on conceptualizing and measuring tie strength. *Social Forces, 91*(1), 17–23.

McAdam, D., & Paulsen, R. (1993). Specifying the relationship between social ties and activism. *American Journal of Sociology, 99*(3), 640–67.

McCall, G. J., & Simmons, J. L. (1978). *Identities and interactions: An examination of human association in everyday life*. Free Press.

Merriam, S. B., & Tisdell, E. J. (2016). *Qualitative research: A guide to design and implementation* (4th ed.). Jossey-Bass.

Miles, M. B., Huberman, M. A., & Saldaña, J. (2014). *Qualitative data analysis: A methods sourcebook* (3rd ed.). Thousand Oaks, CA: Sage Publications.

Milner IV, H. R. (2007). Race, culture, and researcher positionality: Working through dangers seen, unseen, and unforeseen. *Educational Researcher, 36*(7), 388–400.

Moll, L. C., Amanti, C., Neff, D., & Gonzalez, N. (1992). Funds of knowledge for teaching: Using a qualitative approach to connect homes and classrooms. *Theory into Practice, 31*(2), 132–41.

Nieto, S. (2008). Nice is not enough: Defining caring for students of color. In Pollock, M. (Ed.), *Everyday anti-racism: Getting real about race in school* (pp. 28–31). The New Press.

Olsen, B. (2008). How reasons for entry into the profession illuminate teacher identity development. *Teacher Education Quarterly, 35*(3), 23–40.

Olsen, B. (2011). "I am large, I contain multitudes": Teacher identity as a useful frame for research, practice, and diversity in teacher education. In Ball, A. F. & Tyson, C. A. (Eds.), *Studying diversity in teacher education* (pp. 357–274). Rowman & Littlefield Publishers, Inc.

Petrocelli, J. V. (2003). Hierarchical multiple regression in counseling research: Common problems and possible remedies. *Measurement and Evaluation in Counseling and Development, 36*(1), 9–22.

Pettigrew, T. F., & Tropp, L. R. (2006). A meta-analytic test of intergroup contact theory. *Journal of Personality and Social Psychology, 90*(5), 751.

Saldaña, J. (2016). *The coding manual for qualitative reserachers* (3rd ed.). Sage Publications.

Scott, J. (2013). *Social network analysis* (2nd ed.). Sage Publications.

Skaalvik, E. M., & Skaalvik, S. (2011). Teacher job satisfaction and motivation to leave the teaching profession: Relations with school context, feeling of belonging, and emotional exhaustion. *Teaching and Teacher Education, 27*(6), 1029–38.

Sleeter, C. E. (2001). Preparing teachers for culturally diverse schools: Research and the overwhelming presence of whiteness. *Journal of teacher education, 52*(2), 94–106.

Sleeter, C. E., & Milner, H. R. (2011). Researching successful efforts in teacher education to diversify teachers. In Ball, A. F. & Tyson, C. A. (Eds.), *Studying diversity in teacher education* (pp. 81–104). Rowman & Littlefield Publishers, Inc.

Small, M. L. (2017). *Someone to talk to*. Oxford University Press.

Stryker, S. (1980). *Symbolic interactionism: A social structural version*. Caldwell, NJ: Blackburn.

Vaisey, S., & Lizardo, O. (2010). Can cultural worldviews influence network composition? *Social Forces, 88*(4), 1595–618.

Valencia, R. R. (2010). *Dismantling contemporary deficit thinking: Educational thought and practice*. Routledge.

Verbrugge, L. M. (1979). Multiplexity in adult friendships. *Social Forces, 57*(4), 1286–309.

Wasserman, S., & Faust, K. (1994). *Social network analysis: Methods and applications*. Cambridge University Press.

Young, K. S. (2016). How student teachers (don't) talk about race: An intersectional analysis. *Race Ethnicity and Education, 19*(1), 67–95.

Zeichner, K. M. (2006). Reflections of a university-based teacher educator on the future of college-and university-based teacher education. *Journal of Teacher Education, 57*(3), 326–40.

Zeichner, K. M. (2018). *The struggle for the soul of teacher education*. Routledge.

Part 3

School-Wide Networks

6

Teachers' Interactions about Multilingual Learner Instruction: Considerations for Elementary School Leaders in the United States

Megan Hopkins, Lisa Matsukata, and Tracy M. Sweet

Since the 1990s, changing labor markets and economic conditions in the United States have meant that more immigrant families are settling outside of traditional receiving destinations (e.g., California, Florida, New York). It is now common for US schools in small Midwestern towns and large Southeastern cities (often termed the "New Latino Diaspora") to serve large and/or growing numbers of immigrant students, many of whom are identified as English learners (ELs; Hamann et al., 2015). ELs, who we refer to as multilingual learners (MLs) to foreground their linguistic giftedness, are defined in US federal education policy as students whose "proficiency in speaking, reading, writing, or understanding the English language may be sufficient to deny the individual the ability to successfully achieve in classrooms where the language of instruction is English" (20 U.S. Code § 7801).

Though often treated as a monolithic group, MLs speak over 400 languages and dialects, are US- and foreign-born, and come from a wide range of socioeconomic and racial/ethnic backgrounds (National Academies of Sciences, Engineering, & Medicine [NASEM], 2017). These trends indicate that schools across the country are becoming more linguistically, culturally, ethnically, and racially diverse, especially in locales where such diversity has not been the norm. Yet the majority of teachers in US schools do not feel adequately prepared to teach MLs (NASEM, 2017), nor do they receive the professional learning (PL) needed to feel capable of supporting MLs' linguistic and academic development (Santibañez & Gándara, 2018). Although some locally based efforts provide teachers with PL opportunities focused on ML instruction (see Brooks & Adams, 2015; Hansen-Thomas et al., 2014; Kim et al., 2018; Penner-Williams et al., 2017; Teemant et al., 2016), the reach of these opportunities is often limited to small groups of teachers working in a handful of schools. Most teachers, then, are likely learning how to teach MLs on the job, in their interactions with colleagues.

It is thus important for school leaders to understand whether and how teachers have on-the-job opportunities to learn about ML instruction. Such understandings are foundational for organizational change efforts that promote ML-focused teacher learning and capacity development. To inform these efforts, we use social network analysis to explore the factors shaping teachers' interactions related to ML instruction. We focused our inquiry on elementary (i.e., kindergarten through sixth grade) schools, as these schools tend to serve the largest proportions of ML students in the United States (National Center for Education Statistics, 2021). The eight schools in our study are located in two midsized suburban districts, one in the Northeastern United States and one in the Midwestern United States. While both districts were experiencing new and rapid ML population growth, MLs represented a full 25–30 percent of students in the Northeastern schools, but just 5–10 percent of students in the Midwestern schools.

Compared to schools serving large ML populations (i.e., high-density ML schools), low-density ML schools face heightened challenges with respect to obtaining sufficient resources for ML programs and services and accessing PL support for teachers (Coady, 2020). We thus consider the following questions:

(1) What factors predicted ML-related instructional interactions among teachers?; and
(2) How did these factors differ between low- and high-density ML schools?

Below, we describe the social network theory guiding our research and compare and contrast findings across districts and schools. We conclude by discussing our findings specifically in relation to their implications for school leaders.

Social Network Theory and Teacher Interactions

Social networks are important for supporting the development of social capital, or the knowledge and resources that become available through social relationships (Lin, 2001). For teachers, the networks they engage in with colleagues have the potential to foster the exchange of advice and information, which can facilitate their professional learning and growth (Coburn, 2001; Frank et al., 2011; Spillane et al., 2012). These on-the-job learning opportunities have been shown to be important for shaping teachers' instructional practices and beliefs in subjects like mathematics and reading (see, for example, Hopkins, et al., 2013; Parise & Spillane, 2010; Penuel et al., 2013; Shirrell et al., 2019). However, few studies have examined teachers' advice and information networks related specially to ML instruction (see Hopkins et al., 2019, for an exception). Further, whereas much prior research explores the effects of teachers' instructional networks on classroom practice or student achievement (e.g., Leana & Pil, 2006; Penuel et al., 2013; Shirrell et al., 2019), fewer studies explore the factors predicting the presence of these network ties (Spillane et al., 2012). The extant literature indicates that these factors reside at both the individual and organizational levels, which we describe below.

Individual Factors Shaping Network Ties

Research in education and beyond draws on homophily theory to explain the individual factors shaping the development of social network ties. The familiar phrase "birds of a feather flock together" captures the theory's basic idea, which suggests that individuals tend to interact with others who are from similar backgrounds in terms of race, ethnicity, gender, and education (McPherson et al., 2001; Monge & Contractor, 2003). One study examining teachers' network formation across thirty schools in a midsized US district showed that teachers from the same racial or ethnic backgrounds, as well as those who shared the same gender identity, were significantly more likely to seek each other out for instructional advice and information (Spillane et al., 2012). Based on these findings, we hypothesized that teachers who reported the same race, ethnicity, and/or gender would be more likely to have ML-related instructional ties.

Spillane and colleagues (2012) also examined whether and how teachers' prior professional experiences predicted teachers' tie formation. Specifically, they asked teachers to report their years of teaching experience and the number of PL hours they participated in over the last year. With respect to teaching experience, teachers with more years of experience were less likely to seek out instructional advice or information than teachers with fewer years of experience. In terms of PL hours, teachers tended to seek out others for advice or information who had participated in more PL hours than they had. Overall, these findings suggest that instructional advice and information tended to flow from more to less experienced and knowledgeable teachers. We thus hypothesized that teachers with fewer years of experience and who had participated in fewer PL hours would be more likely to seek out ML-related instructional advice. In the next section, we discuss factors beyond the individual level that shape teachers' interactions.

Organizational Factors Shaping Network Ties

Beyond the individual level, teachers are situated within organizations whose structures can either enable or constrain their interactions. Schools are organized in particular ways to facilitate the coordination of teaching and learning, and these structures shape whether and how teachers have opportunities to collaborate. For instance, teachers tend to interact more frequently with colleagues who are assigned teach in the same grade or department (Hopkins et al., 2015; Spillane et al., 2012, 2015), given that they teach similar material or might be required to meet to coordinate instruction (Bidwell & Yasumoto, 1999; Daly et al., 2010; Spillane et al., 2016). We thus hypothesized that teachers who taught the same grade would be more likely to exchange ML-related instructional advice and information.

Formal positions are another aspect of the organizational structure that shapes teachers' networks. In studies examining teachers' advice and information ties related to reading and math instruction, teachers who held formal leadership positions as instructional coaches, department chairs, or mentor teachers were more likely to be sought out for advice or information than teachers without such designations (Hopkins et al., 2013; Spillane et al., 2012, 2015). Related to ML instruction, the extant literature suggests that teachers whose roles focus on supporting MLs' language development (e.g., English-as-a-second-language (ESL) specialists) are important sources of advice or information for their colleagues (Hopkins et al., 2019). Based on these findings, we hypothesized that ESL teachers would be more likely to be sought out for ML-related instructional advice than other teachers.

Beyond formal structures, aspects of the school culture can shape whether and how teacher interact about instructional matters. For example, teachers are more likely to ask each other questions, admit they do not have an answer, openly discuss problems, seek help, and learn from mistakes in schools characterized by high levels of trust (Leana & Pil, 2017; Lee et al., 2011; Liou & Daly, 2014). In schools experiencing demographic change, trust may be particularly important for shaping teachers' ML-related ties, as teachers may not feel confident in their abilities to work with MLs and need to trust their colleagues in order to feel comfortable seeking ML-related advice. We thus hypothesized that teachers who reported higher levels of trust would be more likely to seek out ML-related instructional advice.

As another organizational factor, we considered the demographics of the student population (Datnow et al., 2002), specifically the size of the ML population. As alluded to above, the proportion of MLs at a school has been found to influence the provision of resources, personnel, and professional learning, such that schools serving low-density ML populations often struggle to offer support to ML students and teachers (Hopkins et al., 2022; Weddle et al., 2021). We thus assumed that teachers in low-density ML schools may have more limited opportunities to learn about MLs from their colleagues than teachers in high-density schools.

Methodological Approach

Our inquiry is situated across two research projects examining elementary teachers' instructional advice and information networks. In both projects, we collected surveys and interviews and utilized a sequential explanatory mixed methods approach in which interview data helped to elucidate findings from our survey analysis. Although each district had between 10 and 12 elementary schools, our analysis focused on the four schools in each district serving MLs. In the Midwestern district, MLs were bussed to these four schools to centralize support; in the Northeastern district, residential segregation meant that only four schools served MLs. Below, we describe these contexts in more detail and outline our data collection and analysis processes.

District Contexts

In our low-density ML context in the Midwest, the district served a predominantly White population (80 percent) alongside growing numbers of Latino students (10 percent), as well as small populations of Black (5 percent) and Asian (3 percent) students, many of whom were recent immigrants or refugees from Sudan, Somalia,

Table 6.1 Demographics of schools in the study sample

School	Size	% EL	Students % White	% Latinx	% Black	% Economically Disadvantaged	Teachers Gen. Ed.	ESL
Midwest								
Bryant	400	5	77	10	9	30	30	1
Torres	500	4	70	15	10	35	30	2
Ashton	450	9	70	20	4	35	30	1
Loma	420	12	65	20	12	45	30	2
Northeast								
Riley	440	25	10	80	4	75	20	1
Kent	750	30	15	80	3	70	30	2
Mann	450	25	10	85	2	80	30	2
Edgemont	850	25	15	80	3	75	40	4

Note. Numbers are rounded to preserve confidentiality.

Vietnam, and Nepal. About 5 percent of students in the district were identified as English learners, representing a twofold increase from ten years prior. Across the four schools included in our study, MLs represented between 5 and 12 percent of students (see Table 1).

In contrast, the higher-density Northeast district served a larger, and still growing, population of Latinx students (40 percent), many of whom were first- or second-generation immigrants from the Dominican Republic. Compared to the Midwest, the Northeastern district served a smaller White population (6 percent), and about 10 percent of students in the Northeast district were formally identified as English learners. As can be seen in Table 1, the Northeastern schools in our study served about twice as many MLs and Latino students than the district as a whole.

Though situated in two distinct contexts, all eight schools relied on pull-out English language development (ELD) instruction to meet MLs' linguistic needs, which was organized by ESL teachers. Within this approach, ESL teachers often separated MLs from their grade-level classroom for a portion of the school day to teach ELD in small groups.

Teacher Surveys

Data Collection

Teachers in all eight schools completed a staff survey via Qualtrics in either spring 2016 or 2017 that gathered information about their instructional networks, perceptions of school culture, professional experiences, and demographics. Our analysis drew from survey data collected from 121 teachers in four Midwestern schools, with school response rates ranging from 83 to 94 percent. Similarly, 119 teachers completed the survey in the Northeast district, with response rates ranging from 72 to 89 percent across schools.

Social network items asked teachers to indicate from whom they sought advice or information related to curriculum, teaching, and/or student learning during the last school year. Respondents were then prompted to indicate the topic around which they sought advice or information, including content area (e.g., reading or math) and student population (e.g., MLs). In the Midwest district, teachers listed up to twelve individuals from whom they sought advice or information. Teachers in the Northeast district, in contrast, selected individuals from a school roster. Although only four respondents in the Northeast selected more than twelve people, this difference in data collection likely limits our findings in unmeasurable ways.

Additional survey items sought to measure aspects of school culture, including teacher trust. Other items asked respondents about their involvement in ML-related PL, years of teaching experience, assigned grade level(s), and whether or not they were an ESL teacher. The survey also included demographic questions (e.g., race/ethnicity, gender). Survey data were downloaded, cleaned, and imported into R for analysis.

Data Analysis

We built a series of hierarchical latent space models (HLSMs; Sweet et al., 2013) to compare the factors predicting teachers' ML-related ties across schools. HLSMs accommodate covariate effects, which allowed us to model the eight school networks concurrently. The HLSM assumes that networks are independent of one another and treats them as isolated. Another assumption of the HLSM is that each individual has a position in a latent or unobserved social space; thus, it models the probability of observing a tie between two actors in a network as a function of covariates and the distance between latent space positions. After controlling for covariates, individuals whose positions are close together are more likely to have a tie than individuals whose positions are far apart.

Our dependent variable in each HLSM was the presence of an ML-related instructional tie between two teachers. For every pair of teachers i and j, if i turned to j for advice, the $i{\to}j$ relationship was assigned a value of 1. If i did not turn to j for advice, the relationship was assigned a value of 0. We included both individual- and dyadic-level measures as independent variables, as described below.

Individual-Level Measures. Based on our review of prior literature (see above), we included professional learning, years of experience, ESL teacher, and teacher trust in our models at the individual level.

Professional Learning. The survey asked respondents to report the number of PL hours they participated in during the last year pertaining to ML instruction and/or adapting instruction to MLs' language proficiency levels. Responses included the following: (0) None; (1) Less than 4 hours; (2) 4–8 hours; (3) 9–16 hours (1–2 days); (4) 17–32 hours (3–4 days); (5) 33 hours or more (5+ days). For each response level, we used the median number of hours in the range, except for the last level, where we used 40 hours.

Years of Experience. We included teachers' responses to the question, "How many years have you worked as a teacher at this school?" as a continuous variable ranging from 1 to 30.

ESL Teacher. In the Midwest district, we used rosters to identify ESL teachers; in the Northeast district, the survey included an item explicitly asking if respondents were ESL teachers. This variable was dichotomous with a value of 1 if respondents were ESL teachers and 0 otherwise.

Teacher Trust. The survey asked respondents to indicate their agreement with five statements used and validated by the Consortium on Chicago School Research (2003) pertaining to their level of trust in teachers at their school. Statements included, "It's okay in this school to discuss feelings, worries, and frustrations with other teachers," and "Teachers respect other teachers who take the lead in school improvement efforts." Respondents indicated their agreement on a 1-5 Likert scale from strongly disagree to strongly agree. Aligned with prior studies, these items demonstrated internal consistency (Midwest α=0.91; Northeast α=0.94).

Dyadic-Level Measures. We included two dyadic-level measures: same grade and difference in PL. We did not include same race/ethnicity or same gender, given that a multilevel regression analysis revealed little variation on these variables in either district (i.e., most if not all teachers in both districts identified as white women).

Same Grade. The questionnaire asked teachers to indicate the grade level(s) they taught. We used that information to create a same-grade variable that had a value of 1 if two teachers taught the same grade and 0 if they did not.

Difference in PL. This dyadic indicator uses the PL item described above and includes a value of the difference between two teachers on their reported ML-related PL hours.

Network Modeling. In our models, Y_{ij} is the value of a tie from teacher i to teacher j, so that $Y_{ijk} = 1$ indicates that i receives advice or information from teacher j in school k. Otherwise, $Y_{ijk} = 0$. The HLSM is given as:

$$\log \frac{P(Y_{ijk}=1)}{1-P(Y_{ijk}=1)} = \beta_0 + \beta_1 X_{1ijk} + \ldots + \beta_8 X_{8ijk} - \left| Z_i - Z_j \right|,$$

where Y_{ijk} represents an EL-related instructional tie, X_{ijk} is a set of individual- or dyadic-level covariates, and Z_i and Z_j are the latent space positions for individuals i and j, respectively. We separated covariates for advice seekers and providers, and built both fixed effects and random effects models, the latter of which allowed covariate effects to vary by school. Given that there was substantial variation across schools on key variables, we present results from the random effects models below.

Teacher Interviews

Data Collection

We examined HLSM results to select two schools in each district to conduct follow-up interviews. Given that the effects of teacher trust and ESL teacher varied across schools, we were interested in understanding the factors shaping these effects, and whether and how they varied between low- and high-density ML contexts. As such, we selected the schools where ESL teachers were significant providers and seekers of ML-related advice and information and/or where teacher trust was a significant factor shaping teachers' networks.

At the end of the survey, teachers were asked if they would be willing to participate in a follow-up interview. Based on those who responded affirmatively, we identified participants in the four selected schools to ensure the inclusion of teachers who had opportunities to exchange ML-related advice and those who did not, as well as teachers who represented different grade levels. We also invited all ESL teachers to participate in an interview. Overall, we conducted thirteen interviews at Torres and Ashton Elementary in the Midwestern district (eleven grade-level teachers, two ESL teachers) and five interviews at Riley and Edgemont Elementary in the Northeastern district (two ESL teachers, three grade-level teachers). The difference in number was related to the fact that the Midwestern interviews were conducted in person, while the Northeastern interviews were conducted via Zoom. These differences in format and number are limitations to generalizability; nonetheless, they helped to contextualize findings and inform future research.

Interview protocols were developed to understand the factors shaping teachers' opportunities to learn about MLs, through both formal PL and in interaction with colleagues. Interviewees were first asked to describe what they knew about MLs in their school and how the ML population had changed over time. Then, questions focused on ML instructional programs, including how they were structured and staffed. Next, participants responded to questions about PL opportunities related to ML instruction offered by their school, district, or otherwise. Then, the interviewer presented a series of prompts regarding how teachers learned about ML instruction on the job, including whether and how they collaborated with others around ML instruction. Interviews lasted between 30 minutes and one hour and were transcribed verbatim, with transcripts uploaded to Dedoose for analysis.

Data Analysis

Interview analysis was conducted iteratively as we built the HLSMs, as we were interested in understanding any differences in HLSM results between schools. As such, we coded transcripts for descriptions of teachers' formal PL opportunities as well as their on-the-job learning opportunities, the latter of which included collaborations and interactions with colleagues about ML instruction. Within these coded excerpts, we looked for descriptions of the factors shaping these interactions. We were particularly interested in examining how formal roles (i.e., ESL teacher) and school culture (i.e., teacher trust) shaped teachers' ML instructional ties. We drafted memos around key themes for each school, then compared and contrasted themes across schools and districts. In our comparisons, we paid particular attention to how these factors varied between the low-density and high-density ML schools.

Teachers' Interactions about Multilingual Learner Instruction

We begin by presenting results for the individual and organizational factors included in the random effects HLSMs. As noted above, our model selection process revealed little to no variation in the gender and race/ethnicity variables in both districts; thus, we did not include these variables in our final models. Further, the PL variable was highly correlated with the ESL teacher variable, meaning that ESL teachers tended to be one of the only staff members to have participated in ML-related PL at their schools. As such, the models we report include only the ESL teacher variable. Below, we report parameter estimates across schools for the effects of 1) being an ESL teacher and 2) teacher trust on seeking and providing advice, given that these factors were the only two that varied across schools. To elucidate our findings, we present network diagrams and draw on interview themes to contextualize similarities and differences.

For both years of experience and grade level, HLSM findings were consistent across schools and aligned with prior research on teachers' instructional networks. We thus do not delve into them deeply except to say that, overall, we observed a negative effect of years of experience on seeking ML-related instructional advice, meaning that teachers who had been working in their schools longer were less likely to seek ML-related instructional advice or information. Additionally, teaching the same grade significantly predicted the presence of an ML-related instructional tie between teachers in all eight schools.

The Effects of Being an ESL Teacher

We observed a small to moderate effect of being an ESL teacher on seeking ML-related instructional advice or information (see Table 2). In the Northeastern district, ESL teachers in all four schools were significantly more likely than grade-level teachers to seek out ML-related instructional advice (i.e., the 95 percent confidence interval does not include zero). This was only true at Ashton Elementary in the Midwestern district, as there was no effect of being an ESL teacher on ML-related advice seeking in the other three schools. These trends are evident in Figure 6.1, where the ESL teacher (indicated as a blue node) at Ashton district had three outgoing ties, and ESL teachers in all four schools in the Northeast district had several more outgoing ties, suggesting that ESL teachers in the four high-density ML schools tended to have higher out-degree centrality than ESL teachers in low-density MLs schools.

Table 6.2 Hierarchical latent space models with regression coefficient estimates and intervals, showing results for the ESL teacher variable only

	Seeker ESL Teacher		Provider ESL Teacher	
School	Posterior Mean	95% Credible Interval	Posterior Mean	95% Credible Interval
Midwest				
Bryant	−0.17	[−2.24, 1.75]	3.52	[1.82, 5.42]*
Torres	0.80	[−1.39, 3.08]	1.43	[−0.80, 3.63]
Ashton	2.55	[0.68, 4.58]*	2.71	[0.91, 4.55]*
Loma	0.39	[−1.58, 2.27]	3.12	[1.55, 4.89]*
Northeast				
Riley	3.84	[2.22, 5.50]*	1.85	[0.30, 3.45]*
Kent	1.52	[−0.02, 3.00]**	3.78	[2.31, 5.26]*
Mann	2.43	[1.06, 4.03]*	0.23	[−1.27, 1.86]
Edgemont	1.65	[0.63, 2.63]*	2.41	[1.39, 3.48]*

Note. *Strong evidence that the covariate is predictive of ML-related advice or information seeking. **Weak evidence that the covariate is predictive of ML-related advice or information seeking.

Our interview analysis suggests that these trends may be related to differences in how ESL teachers organized ELD supports. One of the two ESL teachers at Ashton described her approach to ELD as "parallel teaching," which meant that she sometimes taught alongside a grade-level teacher: "We teach in parallel, where there's two lessons going on where it's like, 'You do this lesson, I'll do this lesson with the ELs and other students who need help,' and then it's whole group." This approach to ELD necessitated that the ESL teacher seek out grade-level teachers for advice and information to plan ahead of time. In contrast, the ESL teacher at Thorn took a more passive approach to working with grade-level teachers, so as "not to add another thing to their plates." She described waiting for teachers to come to her to ask for ML-related advice or information, rather than going to them: "If a teacher wants me to come in and teach some vocabulary lessons or something like that I might do that throughout the year."

In the Northeast, ESL teachers only offered pull-out ELD instruction to MLs at the most beginning ELP levels. Otherwise, they worked with grade-level teachers to ensure that MLs received in-class support; this approach required frequent communication. The ESL teacher at Riley noted that she sought out grade-level teachers during their "morning planning periods," because "they might have had the same experience [with a student] and know how to handle something I'm asking about." ESL teachers at Riley and Edgemont were also responsible for keeping track of all MLs' linguistic and academic progress; thus, they regularly had to seek out grade-level teachers for information. As an Edgemont teacher noted, "They [ESL teachers] have systems to track students' progress all the way from the time they enter the district until they leave the district. They are very extensive in making sure that these students are becoming proficient."

Compared with advice seeking, results for ML-related instructional advice or information providing were more similar across districts, where being an ESL teacher had a significant effect in three of four schools in each district. This finding indicates that, in general, ESL teachers tended to be sought out for ML-related advice or information more than grade-level teachers. We can observe this trend in Figure 6.1, where ESL teachers tend to have many incoming ties, suggesting that they had high in-degree centrality in their schools' ML-related instructional networks. An exception to this trend can be observed in Torres in the Midwest, where ESL teachers were isolated from their colleagues and neither incoming nor outgoing ML-related ties. We offer a potential explanation for this anomaly below.

Aligned with the HLSM results, our interview data revealed that ESL teachers were viewed as important sources of ML-related advice and information. An Edgemont teacher described frequent interactions with one of her school's ESL teachers:

> I meet with her daily. Daily! She comes to pick up the kids [MLs] in the classroom, and then it's this one needs this, this one ... it's a regular ongoing communication. It has to be because our school is mostly English learners.

Because she served so many MLs, this teacher felt a need to seek out the ESL teacher frequently to support her instruction. A teacher at Riley indicated that, although the district served a large ML population, little, if any, relevant ML-related PL opportunities had been provided: "One thing I wish that we had is more professional development for teachers. The ones we have now are kind of useless. We need something more that relates to EL learners." Because grade-level teachers had few PL opportunities, they likely needed to seek out on-the-job learning opportunities from someone they viewed as an expert in ML instruction: the ESL teacher.

Teachers viewed ESL teachers as experts not only because they held ESL-specific positions, but also because they occasionally gave presentations on ML instruction during staff meetings, shared materials during grade-level meetings, or sent ML strategies to teachers via email. These learning opportunities were described by teachers at Riley and Edgemont in the Northeast district, as well as at Ashton in the Midwest district. In contrast, the ESL teacher at Torres was relatively new to the school and still getting to know her colleagues: "I've kind of gradually been getting to know the teachers and how they teach and what they want." Given that the Torres ESL teacher did not openly share her expertise, her colleagues may not have viewed her as someone they could or should seek out for ML-related advice. Additionally, given the low density of MLs at Torres (i.e., MLs represented 4 percent of students), teachers may not yet have felt a need to seek out ML-related instructional advice like teachers at higher-density schools (e.g., Riley and Edgemont).

Effects of Teacher Trust

Turning to teacher trust, our HLSM results indicated no effect of trust on ML-related advice and information providing at any of the eight schools (i.e., the 95 percent confidence interval includes zero). However, there was substantial variation in the effect of teacher trust on ML-related advice and information seeking. Whereas trust was not a significant predictor of ML-related advice seeking in five schools, there was a negative effect of trust on seeking ML-related advice or information in two schools in the Northeast (Riley and Edgemont), and a positive effect of trust on seeking ML-related advice or information in one school in the Midwest (Torres; see Table 3).

This negative effect indicates that teachers at Riley and Edgemont who reported lower levels of trust in their colleagues were more likely to seek out ML-related advice or information (see Table 2). Our interview findings suggest that, although teachers at these two Northeastern schools may not have felt a strong sense of trust in their colleagues, they turned to them for ML-related advice or information out of necessity, given the high number of MLs in their classrooms. A teacher at Riley indicated that some teachers were not open to the changing population: "It's definitely made things challenging. We've had to change the way that we teach. A lot of people in general have to change their thought process. Some teachers haven't been very welcoming of the change." Given differences in their reception of MLs, teacher trust may have been strained. Nonetheless, this teacher noted that, "It's such a common thing to have more Spanish speaking students than English speaking students in our classes," making it necessary for all teachers to seek out advice and information related to teaching MLs.

In contrast, the positive effect of teacher trust at Torres in the Midwestern district indicates that teachers who reported higher levels of trust were more likely to seek

Table 6.3 Hierarchical latent space models with regression coefficient estimates and intervals, showing results for the teacher trust variable only

School	Seeker Teacher Trust		Provider Teacher Trust	
	Posterior Mean	95% Credible Interval	Posterior Mean	95% Credible Interval
Midwest				
Bryant	−0.07	[−1.40, 1.28]	0.02	[−1.38, 1.34]
Torres	1.66	[0.22, 3.18]*	0.08	[−1.31, 1.49]
Ashton	−0.60	[−2.24, 1.02]	0.46	[−1.15, 2.20]
Loma	−0.40	[−1.65, 0.85]	−0.24	[−1.52, 0.96]
Northeast				
Riley	−2.91	[−4.47, −1.46]*	0.88	[−0.52, 2.38]
Kent	−0.64	[−1.49, 0.18]	−0.27	[−1.07, 0.55]
Mann	0.17	[−0.33, 0.65]	−0.13	[−0.58, 0.34]
Edgemont	−0.84	[−1.63, −0.07]*	0.45	[−0.33, 1.25]

Note. *Strong evidence that the covariate is predictive of EL-related advice or information seeking.

ML-related advice or information. As described above, Torres was also the only school where there was no effect of being an ESL teacher on advice seeking and providing (see Table 1), and where ESL teachers were isolated in the school's ML-related advice or information network (see Figure 6.1). Thus, it may be that, because ESL teachers did not interact with grade-level teachers about ML instruction, grade-level teachers sought out colleagues who they trusted for ML-related advice. Our interview data from Torres suggest that trusting relationships were present in grade-level teams, with one teacher describing her team's interactions related to MLs:

> When we plan together, we just make sure we're all on the same page and that we're all aware of what's coming up. We have to try to be on top of things and organized so things are ready to go to provide those kids with what they need.

While some teachers at Torres sought out grade-level colleagues, others stated that they were the only teacher serving MLs at their grade level, given the small ML population at the school. As such, they might seek out a colleague teaching MLs at another grade level, but who they knew well: "I would just go to Susan [for advice] who's now in fifth grade but used to work with me in second." This quote suggests that teachers trusted others with whom they had prior experience collaborating, and this trust informed their ML-related advice seeking behaviors.

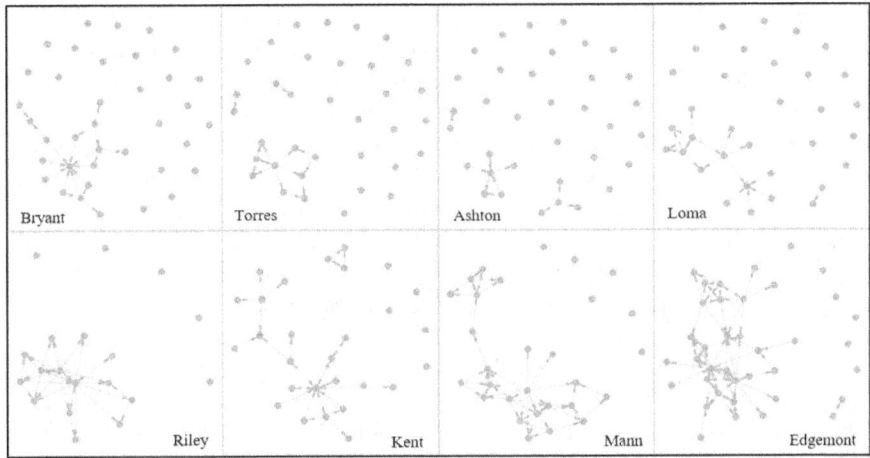

Figure 6.1 Multilingual learner instructional advice or information networks, by school.

Note. ESL teachers are indicated by blue nodes.

Discussion

In this chapter, we sought to identify the factors that predict elementary teachers' ML-related instructional advice seeking and providing ties in two US school districts. Both districts were undergoing demographic change, yet schools in the Midwestern district served low-density ML populations, and schools in the Northeastern district served higher-density ML populations. We examined how various individual- and organizational-level factors shaped teachers' social networks related to ML instruction in four schools in each district, as we theorized that these networks provided teachers with on-the-job learning opportunities. Such on-the-job learning opportunities are especially important for teachers of MLs, as many feel unprepared to support MLs' linguistic and academic development (NASEM, 2017), yet they tend to have few ML-related PL opportunities (Santibañez & Gándara, 2018). Our findings revealed two important factors shaping teachers' opportunities to learn about MLs on the job: having an ESL teacher at the school and teacher trust.

ESL Teachers as Leaders of Professional Learning

Overall, our findings suggest that ESL teachers served as informal leaders who facilitated teachers' on-the-job learning about ML instruction. First, our social network analysis showed that being an ESL teacher was a significant predictor of ML-related advice and information providing in three of four schools in each district. Regardless of ML density, ESL teachers appeared to be important sources of ML-related advice or information. This finding aligns with prior research examining the effect of formal leadership positions (e.g., instructional coach) on advice and information providing related to language arts and mathematics instruction (Hopkins et al., 2015; Spillane et al., 2012; Spillane et al., 2015). At the schools in our study, ESL teachers were positioned as informal ML leaders and instructional experts, as they were given time at staff meetings to share strategies, and often attended grade-level meetings or sent ML-related information to teachers via email. Grade-level teachers described interacting frequently with ESL teachers, in part because they were provided few formal PL opportunities related to ML instruction. In schools where being an ESL teacher did not predict ML-related advice providing (e.g., Torres), interview data indicated that the ESL teacher took a more passive role in supporting ML-related interactions.

Second, our analysis showed that being an ESL teacher significantly predicted ML-related advice and information seeking. This finding contrasts with prior research, which finds no significant effect of formal position on advice seeking (Spillane et al., 2012; Spillane et al., 2015). Being an ESL teacher was a significant predictor of ML-related advice seeking in all four schools in the Northeast district, but in only one Midwestern school. This difference between districts indicates that ESL teachers in the Midwest may have been more isolated compared to ESL teachers in the Northeast, which we also observed in network diagrams (see Figure 6.1). Thus, ESL teachers in low-density schools may have had fewer opportunities to interact with grade-level teachers, and our interview data suggest that this may have been related to the ESL teacher's approach to organizing ELD instruction. Whereas ESL teachers at Ashton, Riley, and Edgemont described working alongside grade-level teachers to co-plan, co-teach, or share student progress, the ESL teacher at Torres Elementary described waiting for grade-level teachers to reach out to her for assistance. Further, given the low density of MLs in the Midwest schools, grade-level teachers may have been less motivated to seek out ML-related instructional advice and information.

Teacher Trust in the Context of Multilingual Learner Density

With respect to teacher trust, prior literature suggests that higher levels of trust can facilitate work-related interactions among teachers (Moolenaar et al., 2014; Van Maele et al., 2015); however, our findings revealed conflicting results. Specifically, we observed a positive seeker effect of teacher trust in one school in the Midwestern district, yet a negative seeker effect of trust in two schools in the Northeastern district. Interviews indicated that these negative effects may have been related to ML density, where teachers in schools with larger ML populations (e.g., Riley and Edgemont where MLs were 25 percent of students) may have felt a sense of urgency to seek out ML-related advice or information, even if they did not feel a sense of trust in colleagues. Some teachers even described hostility toward the growing ML population, which could engender limited trust among teachers; yet, they noted that instructional improvement was needed. Thus, it could be that teachers at Riley and Edgemont were more motivated to improve their instruction of MLs than teachers at the other two Northeastern schools, where trust had no effect on advice seeking.

In contrast with these two high-density schools, we observed a positive effect of teacher trust on ML-related advice and information seeking at Torres in the Midwestern district, where MLs represented just 4 percent of students. Absent an ESL teacher who sought opportunities to engage with grade-level teachers at Torres, it appears that teachers relied on colleagues who they trusted for ML-related advice. Given the small size of the ML population in the Midwest, only a handful of teachers at Torres may have had MLs in their classrooms. This small group of teachers may have been more selective with their ML-related instructional interactions, choosing colleagues with whom they had prior experience and had thus developed a certain level of trust.

Implications

Our findings have several implications for school leaders who seek to support teachers' on-the-job opportunities to learn about ML instruction. First, given that our findings suggest that ESL teachers were important leaders in ML-related instructional networks, school leaders can consider how ESL teachers' work with grade-level teachers is structured, and whether ESL teachers receive appropriate preparation to fulfill these leadership roles. In many cases, ESL teachers are assumed to have lower status than grade-level teachers (e.g., Arkoudis, 2006; McClure & Cahnmann-Taylor, 2010), and are not treated as instructional leaders even though they may act like one (Hopkins et al., 2019). Given their important roles in providing ML-related instructional advice and information, however, it may be important for school leaders to reconsider and redefine the ESL teachers' role in both high- and low-density ML contexts. For instance, providing structured time for ESL and grade-level teachers to collaborate may be one way to support the development of ML-related social capital within schools. Additionally, elevating the status of the ESL teacher could be facilitated by offering ESL workshops that grade-level teachers are required to attend, with opportunities for follow-up discussions and ongoing engagement.

Second, school leaders can consider how teacher trust may shape teachers' ML-related instructional networks. In higher-density schools experiencing rapid demographic change, teachers may seek out others for ML-related advice out of necessity even if they do not feel a sense of trust. To facilitate more trusting interactions, leaders can consider explicitly addressing teachers' concerns about the new student population and directly attending to negative biases and assumptions. ESL teachers can aid in this work, collaborating with other school leaders to facilitate formal PL opportunities. Similarly, in lower density schools, leaders can consider how to bring the ESL teacher into a more central position among the trusting relations that already exist. Overall, ensuring that teachers have opportunities to develop trust may be useful in further fostering the exchange of ML-related advice and information in schools. Given the exploratory nature of our findings, additional research examining how teacher trust intersects with ESL teacher leadership across high- and low-density ML schools is needed, particularly as leaders in districts and schools across the United States engage in efforts to promote ML-related learning opportunities among their teaching staff.

Finally, although the nature of our sample did not allow us to examine the relevance of homophily theory in shaping teachers' ML-related instructional ties, it is important for leaders to consider how similarities and/or differences in teachers' race, ethnicity, gender identity, and linguistic background may influence the development of teacher trust and thus who interacts with whom in a school community (Bristol & Sherrill, 2019). Although more research is needed to examine whether and how these demographic factors shape teachers' ML-related networks, teachers from linguistically diverse backgrounds may bring expertise that would benefit their colleagues (Hopkins, 2013), and leaders can consider how to elevate these linguistic and experiential assets within and between districts and schools.

References

Arkoudis, S. (2006). Negotiating the rough ground between ESL and mainstream teachers. *International Journal of Bilingual Education and Bilingualism*, 9, 415–33.

Bidwell, C. E., & Yasumoto, J. Y. (1999). The collegial focus: Teaching fields, collegial relationships, and instructional practice in American high schools. *Sociology of Education*, 72(4), 234.

Bristol, T. J., & Shirrell, M. (2019). Who is here to help me? The work-related social networks of staff of color in two mid-sized districts. *American Educational Research Journal*, 56(3), 868–98.

Brooks, K., & Adams, S. R. (2015). Developing agency for advocacy: Collaborative inquiry-focused school-change projects as transformative learning for practicing teachers. *The New Educator*, 11(4), 292–308.

Coady, M. (2020). Rural English learner education: A review of research and call for a national agenda. *Educational Researcher*, 49(7), 524–32.

Coburn, C. E. (2001). Collective sensemaking about reading: How teachers mediate reading policy in their professional communities. *Educational Evaluation and Policy Analysis*, 23(2), 145–70.

Consortium on Chicago School Research. (2003). *Key Measures of School Development*. Retrieved from: https://consortium.uchicago.edu/web_reports/keymeasures_alpha_version/keymeasures.html#professionalcapacity.

Daly, A. J., Moolenaar, N. M., Bolivar, M., & Burke, P. (2010). Relationships in reform: The role of teachers' social networks. *Journal of Educational Administration*, 48, 359–91.

Datnow, A., Mehan, H., & Hubbard, L. (2002). *Extending educational reform from one school to many*. Routledge.

Frank, K. A., Zhao, Y., Penuel, W. R., Ellefson, N., & Porter, S. (2011). Focus, fiddle, and friends: Experiences that transform knowledge for the implementation of innovations. *Sociology of Education*, 84(2), 137–56.

Hamann, E., Wortham, S., & Murillo, E. G. (Eds.). (2015). *Revisiting education in the new Latino diaspora*. Ablex Publishing.

Hansen-Thomas, H., Dunlap, K., Casey, P. J., & Starrett, T. (2014). Teacher development: De facto teacher leaders for English language learners. *International Journal of Learning, Teaching and Educational Research*, 5(1), 35–47.

Hopkins, M., Lowenhaupt, R., & Sweet, T. M. (2015). Organizing English learner instruction in new immigrant destinations: District infrastructure and subject-specific school practice. *American Educational Research Journal*, 52(3), 408–39.

Hopkins, M., Gluckman, M., & Vahdani, T. (2019). Emergent change: A network analysis of elementary teachers' learning about English learner instruction. *American Educational Research Journal, 56*(6), 2295–332.

Hopkins, M., Spillane, J. P., Jakopovic, P., & Heaton, R. M. (2013). Infrastructure redesign and instructional reform in mathematics: Formal structure and teacher leadership. *Elementary School Journal, 114*(2), 200–24.

Hopkins, M., Weddle, H., Lavadenz, M., Vahdani, T., & Murillo, M. (2022). Examining the English learner policy ecology: How educators navigated the provision of designated English language development (ELD) support at the secondary level. *Peabody Journal of Education, 97*(1), 47–61.

Kim, S., Song, K., & Coppersmith, S. (2018). Creating an interactive virtual community of linguistically and culturally responsive content teacher-learners to serve English learners. *Contemporary Issues in Technology and Teacher Education, 18*(2), 442–66.

Leana, C. R., & Pil, F. K. (2006). Social capital and organizational performance: Evidence from urban public schools. *Organization Science, 17*(3), 353–66.

Leana, C. R., & Pil, F. K. (2017). Social capital: An untapped resource for educational improvement. In Quintero, E. (Eds.), *Teaching in Context: The Social Side of Education Reform*. Harvard Education Press.

Lee, J. C., Zhang, Z., & Yin, H. (2011). A multilevel analysis of the impact of a professional learning community, faculty trust in colleagues and collective efficacy on teacher commitment to students. *Teaching and Teacher Education, 27*(5), 820–30.

Lin, N. (2001). *Social capital: A theory of social structure and action*. Cambridge University Press.

Liou, Y., & Daly, A. J. (2014). Closer to learning: Social networks, trust, and professional communities. *Journal of School Leadership, 24*(4), 753–95.

McClure, G., & Cahnmann-Taylor, M. (2010). Pushing back against push-in: ESOL teacher resistance and the complexities of coteaching. *TESOL Journal, 1*, 101–29.

McPherson, M., Smith-Lovin, L., & Cook, J. M. (2001). Birds of a feather: Homophily in social networks. *Annual Review of Sociology, 27*(1), 415–44.

Monge, P. R., & Contractor, N. S. (2003). *Theories of communication networks*. Oxford University Press.

Moolenaar, N. M., Karsten, S., Sleegers, P., & Daly, A. J. (2014). Linking social networks and trust at multiple levels: Examining Dutch elementary schools. In Van Maele D., Forsyth, P. & Van Houtte, M. (Eds.), *Trust and School Life* (pp. 207–28). Springer.

National Academies of Science, Engineering, and Medicine. (2017). *Promoting the educational success of children and youth learning English: Promising futures*. Washington, DC: The National Academies Press.

National Center for Education Statistics. (2021). *English Language Learners in Public Schools*. Retrieved from: https://nces.ed.gov/programs/coe/indicator/cgf.

Parise, L. M., & Spillane, J. P. (2010). Teacher learning and instructional change: How formal and on-the-job learning opportunities predict change in elementary school teachers' practice. *Elementary School Journal, 110*(3), 323–46.

Penner-Williams, J., Díaz, E. I., & Gonzales Worthen, D. (2017). PLCs: Key PD component in learning transfer for teachers of English learners. *Teaching and Teacher Education, 65*, 215–29.

Penuel, W. R., Frank, K. A., Sun, M., Kim, C. M., & Singleton, C. A. (2013). The organization as a filter of institutional diffusion. *Teachers College Record, 115*(1), 1–33.

Santibañez, L., & Gándara, P. (2018). *Teachers of English Language Learners in Secondary Schools: Gaps in Preparation and Support*. The Civil Rights Project/Proyecto Derechos Civiles at UCLA.

Shirrell, M., Hopkins, M., & Spillane, J. P. (2019). Educational infrastructure, professional learning, and changes in teachers' instructional practices and beliefs. *Professional Development in Education*, 45(4), 599–613.

Spillane, J. P., Kim, C. M., & Frank, K. A. (2012). Instructional advice and information seeking behavior in elementary schools: Exploring tie formation as a building block in social capital development. *American Educational Research Journal*, 49(6), 1112–45.

Spillane, J. P., Hopkins, M., & Sweet, T. (2015). Intra- and inter-school interactions about instruction: Exploring the conditions for social capital development. *American Journal of Education*, 122(1), 71–110.

Spillane, J. P., Shirrell, M., & Hopkins, M. (2016). Designing and deploying a professional learning community (PLC) organizational routine: Bureaucratic and collegial arrangements in tandem. *Les Dossiers des Sciences de l'Éducation*, 35, 97–122.

Sweet, T. M., Thomas, A. C., & Junker, B. W. (2013). Hierarchical network models for education research: Hierarchical latent space models. *Journal of Educational and Behavioral Statistics*, 38, 295–318.

Teemant, A., Hausman, C. S., & Kigamwa, J. C. (2016). The effects of higher order thinking on student achievement and English proficiency. *INTESOL Journal*, 13(1), 1–22.

Van Maele, D., Moolenaar, N. M., & Daly, A. J. (2015). All for one and one for all: A social network perspective on the effects of social influence on teacher trust. In DiPaola, M. & Hoy, W. K. (Eds.), *Leadership and School Quality* (pp. 171–96). Information Age Publishing.

Weddle, H., Yoshisato, M., & Hopkins, M. (2021). Professional learning for secondary teachers of English learners in an urban school district: Examining systems of support. *Journal of Professional Capital & Community*. https://doi.org/10.1108/JPCC-11-2020-0084.

Teacher Collaboration in Times of Change—Enhancing Existing Research in Norway through A Social Network Analysis Perspective

Esther T. Canrinus and Jo Inge Johansen Frøytlog

Introduction

While teacher collaboration has been a focal point in Norwegian schools for decades (Carlsten et al., 2021), a recently implemented curriculum, also known as LK20, has set in motion conditions for teacher collaboration and knowledge sharing. The main aim of this chapter is to outline some analytical possibilities that follow from a social network analysis (SNA) perspective on teacher collaboration and knowledge sharing in teams in this specific context. Norwegian secondary schools commonly feature teacher teams as a collaborative configuration (e.g., Liebech-Lien, 2021) that is critical for fostering a professional learning community (Stoll et al., 2006).

In the following section, we describe relevant policy documents as a first step to clarify the wider political context in which Norwegian teachers operate. Our focus is on the political ambitions and expectations related to collaboration and knowledge-sharing practices for quality education. Second, we zoom in on the collaborative configuration of the team and present Norwegian research on teacher collaboration and knowledge sharing in schools. Throughout this chapter, we highlight collaborating teachers in secondary education. Research has suggested that secondary school teachers engage in less formal collaboration than their counterparts in primary schools in Norway (Dahl, 2016; Munthe, 2003). However, teachers teaching in secondary schools also tend to report a strong experience of being part of a supportive and collaborative culture (Carlsten et al., 2020). Together, these findings suggest that important collaborative efforts may be expressed informally and may be worth investigating further. We will argue that an SNA perspective can complement existing research and methodologies and enrich our understanding of the relationship between informal and formal collaborative processes in teams of collaborating teachers.

Norway's Perspective on Teacher Collaboration

Political ambitions to strengthen schools as learning organizations, with teacher collaboration being a core component, are by no means new in the Norwegian context. Almost twenty years ago, the White Paper Culture for learning (*Kultur for læring*; Kunnskapsdepartementet, 2004) identified a need to strengthen learning cultures in Norwegian schools. This ambition was further themed and specified with the subsequent introduction of a national curriculum reform in 2006 and in a series of policy documents since then (e.g., Meld. St. 18 (2014–2015)). The White Paper Motivation—Mastering—Possibilities (*Motivasjon—Mestring—Muligheter*), for example, aimed to increase students' motivation and sense of mastery and underlined the importance of strong professional communities of teachers in attaining this aim (Kunnskapsdepartementet, 2011). Based on this policy, teachers' professional development was moved into school and put forward as a collective process. The White Paper Desire to learn—Early intervention and quality in school (*Lærelyst—tidlig innsats og kvalitet I skolen*; Kunnskapsdepartementet, 2016a) offered justification for strengthening schools as learning organizations by problematizing quality differences between classes, schools, and school districts. This latter report also highlighted that the most important component in efforts to enhance schools as learning organizations is the teacher. The report further stated that schools offer better conditions as sites for working to systematically develop the quality of education through teacher collaboration and participation in knowledge-sharing practices about teaching.

Since 2020, a new national curriculum has been gradually implemented. The Norwegian Directorate for Education and Training involved teachers, educational researchers, and other stakeholders in the development of this curriculum, aiming to make both the developmental and implementation process more "bottom-up" (Utdanningsdirektoratet, 2021). The implementation of the new curriculum established conditions for teacher collaboration and knowledge sharing in Norwegian schools in several ways. First, the new curriculum was the result of increased recognition that desired changes in schools and classrooms must be anchored in existing practices locally, as argued in the White Paper Subjects—specialization—understanding—A renewal of the curriculum (*Fag—Fordypning —Forståelse. En fornyelse av Kunnskapsløftet*; Kunnskapsdepartementet, 2016b). Such local practices are complex conglomerates of informal and formal elements that connect wider sociocultural contexts to specific ways of "getting things done" in the classroom. The new curriculum stresses that collaboration is perceived as relevant not only inside schools, but also within the wider context in which the school is located. Second, the overarching part of the new curriculum, which establishes the values and principles of activities in schools, explicitly states that "teachers who jointly reflect on and assess the planning and implementation of teaching develop a richer understanding of good pedagogical practice" (translated by the author, Kunnskapsdepartementet, 2017). Thus, teacher collaboration and knowledge sharing about teaching to enhance the quality of education are expected to characterize teachers' professional practice in schools. Third, the new curriculum broadly highlights concepts such as deep learning and competencies across subjects, challenging educators to teach in ways that strengthen connections and coherence in students' learning experiences across subjects. Strengthening coherence implies creating a shared vision through dialogue (Canrinus, Klette, & Hammerness, 2019; Hammerness, 2006), in this case implying collaboration and connections between teachers across subjects.

Based on the policy documents addressed here, we conclude that the importance of teacher collaboration for teaching and school development is emphasized in Norway. Such collaboration has been further actualized with the recent implementation of a new curriculum.

How Are School Teams Generally Organized?

The formal structure in Norway makes the school principal responsible for the implementation of new policies, curricula, and focus areas established by policy. Additionally, the principal is responsible for how teachers spend their time in school. Besides teaching, teachers' time is divided between "common time," often focused on areas of development and new policies, and time with their team, which often entails practical aspects of teachers' work (Kvam, 2021). Internationally, Norway has the highest proportion of teachers indicating they collaborate with their colleagues to ensure fair and relevant student assessment (Carlsten et al., 2020). This finding was unsurprising, as Norwegian educational policy has been particularly focused on this topic for the past decade (Kunnskapsdepartementet, 2011). As such, this is a clear example of how principals have chosen to highlight this focus area in their choice of topic during "common time."

Results from the 2018 Teaching and Learning International Survey (TALIS) study among lower secondary school teachers showed that nearly all Nordic countries scored high when it came to the participation of teachers in team meetings (Carlsten et al., 2020). In lower secondary education, principals may organize teachers into interdisciplinary teams responsible for one student group throughout years 8–10 or into grade-level teams responsible for one specific grade level (Liebech-Lien, 2021). However, TALIS 208 results indicated that providing feedback based on observations of each other's teaching is nearly nonexistent in these countries (Carlsten et al., 2020). The TALIS 2018 results further showed that collaboration was primarily related to practical and coordinating activities for Norwegian teachers in lower secondary education. Again, collaboration directly linked to the teaching context was reported less frequently (Carlsten et al., 2020). Yet, teachers also collaborate, seek help from colleagues, and discuss their work on their own initiative and during informal interactions (Hermansen, 2016; Kvam, 2021).

Schools differ in how they organize their "common time" and team time. Nevertheless, the collaboration is mostly formally organized, controlled, and directed by the principal. The overarching idea that collaboration is important is clearly present in the principals' choices regarding how to organize teachers and creating time for formal collaboration. Less is known about informal collaboration between teachers and between teachers and their principal.

Norwegian Studies on Teacher Collaboration

Internationally, research has clearly shown that collaborative and supportive activities contribute to teachers' teaching practices (e.g., Levine & Marcus, 2010; Liou et al., 2017; López Solé et al., 2018) and their self-efficacy (e.g., Çoban et al., 2020; Liou et al., 2017). Norwegian studies have shown similar results. In this section, we present research on teacher collaboration and knowledge sharing, which can happen both within and outside of teacher teams. Hatlevik and Hatlevik (2018) concluded that collegial collaboration among teachers has a positive association with the use of information communication technology (ICT) in their teaching practice. They also found a positive association between collegial collaboration and teachers' self-efficacy in ICT use for instructional purposes. Caspersen and Raaen (2014) focused on newly beginning teachers and compared their findings with results from more experienced teachers. Their findings suggest that the influence of support from colleagues and superiors on teachers' self-efficacy becomes stronger over time. In a different study with different outcome measures, Ertesvåg and Roland (2015) showed that schools in which teachers reported weaker collaborative activity had higher levels of reported bullying among students. Teachers in schools with higher levels of collaborative activity also reported higher levels of authority in their classes, which was a buffer for bullying (Ertesvåg & Roland, 2015).

Furthermore, teacher collaboration and teacher social capital are important parts of and contribute to teachers' professional development (Demir, 2021; Liou & Canrinus, 2020; Shea et al., 2018; Vangrieken et al., 2017). The positive influence of collaboration on teachers' professional development observed in international studies was also observed in a large-scale longitudinal study in Norway by Ertesvåg in 2014. This study compared schools that implemented one of two interventions aimed at strengthening teachers' classroom management and reducing and preventing problem behavior. Both interventions included collaborative activity, yet the schools where teachers reported high levels of collaborative activity during the intervention improved more than schools with lower levels of reported collaborative activity (Ertesvåg, 2014). In a smaller study investigating the difference between two schools in an assessment for learning project, Hermansen (2016) stressed the importance of the schools' organizational routines and "recourses" for the development of collective practice. In one school, the teachers participating in the assessment for learning project were positioned more as knowledge brokers for individual teachers, whereas the participating teachers in the other school had made the project a collective endeavor. Hermansen (2016) does not portray one type of routine as preferred over the other yet presents a clear discussion of the consequences of the contrasting approaches to knowledge work. A more recent study also underlined the importance of school culture for the sharing of knowledge within schools. In their study, Morud and Rokkones (2020) observed differences between the interviewed groups of teachers who were enrolled in one of three professional development courses. Schools differed in their routines for sharing and collaboration at the school leadership level, as well as at the level of colleagues. The studies by Hermansen (2016) and Morud and Rokkones (2020) both underlined the importance of support from the school leader for collaborative processes and knowledge sharing. This finding is not surprising. As mentioned in Part 3 of this chapter, school leaders are responsible for guiding how teachers spend their time and which topics or developments they pursue.

The teachers in the study by Morud and Rokkones (2020) felt that their newly gained knowledge and experience from their professional development were not put to use in their school. As other international studies have indicated (e.g., Borko et al., 2010; Sleegers et al., 2005), sending one or some teachers to a professional development program does not lead to structural change within a school or to the professional development of the school as a whole. Again, the new curriculum implemented in Norway also stresses the importance of teachers' active participation in their professional learning communities for the continued development of schools (Kunnskapsdepartementet, 2017). This approach aligns with earlier policy in which the Norwegian government moved teacher professional development in lower secondary schools mainly into schools. This shift resulted in strengthened collaboration and school development (Lødding et al., 2018). Moreover, comparative research has shown that, compared to other countries, Norway has the highest proportion of teachers participating in professional development together with colleagues (Carlsten et al., 2020).

Although Norway may stand out internationally in this regard, recent research from Chile and Portugal has suggested that teachers' own perceptions of the value of collaboration are more influential than differences between countries or schools for collaboration factors (e.g., affinity with colleagues or a stimulating school culture) and experiences (Ávalos-Bevan & Flores, 2021). Regarding Norwegian teachers' perceptions of collaboration and knowledge sharing, research conducted in the south of Norway reported that vocational education teachers' beliefs about collaboration and sharing knowledge with their colleagues were important for these teachers' intention to participate in professional development (Canrinus, Dalehefte, & Myhre, 2019). Kvam (2021) conducted an interview study on teachers' perceptions of knowledge development among teachers and found that teachers view conversations with colleagues as helpful for knowledge development. However, the teachers mentioned conditions which needed to be in place for such conversations to be effective. The interviewed teachers stated that they need to feel ownership of the collaboration and should be able to discuss challenges that are authentic to their teaching (Kvam, 2021). Therefore, Kvam (2021) stressed that support structures should be put into place to ensure that these knowledge processes among teachers will not stand alone but will remain a collective process. As such, the principal will play an important role in leading such processes.

As mentioned at the beginning of this chapter, the extent of collaboration between teachers typically differs depending on the level of education in which the teachers teach, with more collaboration in primary education (Dahl, 2016; Munthe, 2003). Studies in Norway (in line with international studies; see Demir, 2021, for a review) have demonstrated that differences in perceptions likewise exist between beginning and experienced teachers in secondary education (e.g., Caspersen & Raaen, 2014; Ertesvåg, 2014). Beginning and experienced teachers differ in how they perceive the level of support received from colleagues or superiors and in the extent to which they collaborate. In a study on teaching learners with reading difficulties, Grimsæth and Holgersen (2015) reported that novice teachers in particular are in need of support and collaboration to learn about teaching practices helpful for learners with reading difficulties. Based on survey data, Caspersen and Raaen (2014) found that novice and experienced teachers perceived similar levels of collegial support, but novice teachers perceived that they received somewhat less professional support from their superiors compared to experienced teachers. Yet, based on interviews and observations from the same study, Caspersen and Raaen (2014) revealed a discrepancy between what was actually offered to beginning teachers and what these teachers perceived as being offered. These findings show that understanding team collaboration requires taking into account the school level and the teachers' level of experience. Moreover, interview data might not be sufficient to understand how teachers, teams, and school leaders collaborate.

Most Norwegian studies examining teachers have used a qualitative approach. Hermansen and colleagues (2018), in their review study of research on teachers' roles, concluded that nearly 75 percent of the 163 included studies were qualitative studies. Most often, these studies used semi-structured interviews as the method of data collection (Hermansen et al., 2018). However, these methods are not necessarily well suited for including a relational perspective. Results based on such methods often provide a summary of teachers' perspectives of teacher collaboration. To understand how the new curriculum, which has a strong focus on collaboration, is implemented in schools, a different way of investigating teachers, principals, and collaboration is needed in Norway.

Teacher Collaboration in Times of Change: A SNA Perspective to Enhance Existing Research in Norway

Collaboration and the sharing of knowledge are at the heart of professionalism, and many have argued that professionalism is therefore fundamentally relational (e.g., Frelin, 2013; Styhre, 2016). Additionally, the implementation of new reforms, such as the new curriculum in Norwegian schools, is a collaborative and interactive process between and among teachers and educational leaders (Moolenaar & Daly, 2012). When teachers work as professionals in teams during new curriculum implementation, this relational epistemology directs attention to the social terrain of the team—that is, how the participating teachers become socially constituted through the activity.

In the research plan to evaluate the implementation process of the new curriculum in Norway, one of the aims is to bring forward how school leaders and teachers use the new curriculum (Karseth, 2019). The methods proposed in this evaluation include observations during "common time," team time, and leadership time, combined with individual interviews with school leaders, principals, and teachers (Karseth, 2019). The ambitious nature of this project does justice to the fact that multiple actors are involved in the implementation process. Nevertheless, we believe that the project plan describes methods that could be successfully complemented with a SNA perspective to systematically map the interrelatedness of actors across contexts. Such interrelatedness concerns the balance between formal and informal knowledge distribution, as well as the balance between various forms of support and autonomous learning *within* formal networks of connected teachers and school leaders. Whereas the formalized contexts are clearly at the forefront of the mentioned plan to evaluate the implementation process of the new curriculum in Norway, we also know that learning processes take place outside such contexts (see Hermansen, 2016; Kvam, 2021). Although research has shown that mandatory participation in networks can help teachers appreciate the benefits of such networks (van Amersfoort et al., 2019), the content addressed in formal situations might not be the content the teachers need collegial support with, and this support might be sought outside formalized contexts. It remains unclear to what extent the formal and the informal overlap and influence each other in Norwegian schools. Moreover, the analytic focus on interrelatedness that we propose is particularly relevant to understanding the continuity of the reform after the initial implementation (e.g., Coburn et al., 2012; Datnow, 2012).

Little is known about the interconnectedness of Norwegian teachers from an SNA perspective or about the more informal processes in which the teachers engage. These informal connections are important, as they influence who can access new "recourses" at which time and in what way (Hermansen, 2016; Li, 2007). In Norway, formal collaboration between teachers is mainly managed by the school principal or team heads, formally giving the school principal and team heads a central position. We saw this position of the school principal reflected in the answers given in a pilot study we recently conducted at a school southeastern Norway. Most of our thirty-nine participating teachers mentioned their school principal as an important person in their formal work with implementing the new curriculum, suggesting that the principal had a high degree and closeness centrality. Yet, finding a balance between support from formal leadership and self-organized teams is key to networked learning (Pettersson & Olofsson, 2019). We know little about the balance between the supporting structures offered by formal leadership and teachers' autonomous learning and development in Norwegian schools. Questions arise about what balance is most beneficial for specific outcomes, such as the implementation of a new curriculum. Are the formalized settings also the places where teachers obtain the information they need? With whom do teachers collaborate, in what way, and why do they choose those collaborative partners? What does the connection between the formal and informal collaboration processes look like? What do these structures, their similarities, and their differences imply for the implementation of new policies? These are all examples of relevant research questions that a SNA approach could shed light on in the Norwegian context and thus complement other methods.

A mixed methods approach to obtaining network data would be valuable to find answers to these questions. For example, combining observational data with self-report data on who teachers actually collaborate with formally and who they turn to for advice will shed light on the level of overlap that may exist between the formal and informal networks, both as observed and as self-reported. A sociocentric approach as a starting point may then lead to an egocentric approach to zoom in on key actors in both the formal and the informal advice network. An advice network related to the implementation and use of the new curriculum, in addition to a collaboration network, would provide information on the level of embeddedness of the new curriculum in the schools. Density, centrality, and brokerage measures would be relevant to include, as well as a focus on, the directionality of the relationships (in- and outdegree; cf. Sinnema et al., 2021). To evaluate the implementation of the new reform, studies should consider the interconnectedness and the formal and informal position of teachers within the whole school, as well as within their team.

As seen in Hermansen's (2016) study, the way knowledge is distributed in a school can vary considerably from school to school. The school principal has an important position and role in structuring how knowledge is gained, maintained, and distributed in schools in Norway. Previous studies have investigated principals' positions in their networks of other principals (e.g., Daly et al., 2014; Rehm et al., 2021). We propose investigating their position and participation in schools and school teams to understand how reforms are implemented and continued in Norwegian schools. This approach will furthermore reveal the extent to which teacher teams operate autonomously and how teachers' level of autonomy relates to outcome measures, such as reform implementation. Previous research has shown that autonomy is a key factor in motivational processes (Ryan & Deci, 2017); in turn, motivational processes are influential for action taking related to implementation of reforms (Liou et al., 2019). Furthermore, an approach investigating principals' positions will provide information on the extent to which leadership is distributed in Norwegian schools and the extent to which this is related to various outcome measures. In addition, survey data on the social network could be combined with interview data on the working climate, for example, to provide information on the extent to which the social structure contributes to the implementation process of reforms above and beyond the working climate. Again, combining ego-centric approaches (e.g., focusing on the principal) and sociocentric approaches (e.g., focusing on specific school teams including the principal) would be valuable. Examining the level of reciprocity would, in this case, provide information on how and to what extent autonomous teams collaborate with other teams on the reform and in what way the school principal is included in this process.

As mentioned, the aim of the Norwegian Directorate for Education and Training was to ensure a bottom-up process of the development and implementation of the new curriculum (Utdanningsdirektoratet, 2021). The new curriculum also stresses the importance of collaboration between teachers. To determine whether the goal of the directorate is achieved and whether the new curriculum has led to further collaboration between teachers, the interconnectedness of teachers and the influence of their school principal should be studied. Moreover, the methodology in such a study should be able to illuminate the interrelatedness and interconnectedness of the various actors in relation to each other. We believe that taking an SNA perspective would be a highly suitable approach in this case. Such an approach will offer school leaders and teachers information on where to strengthen their linkages to facilitate the flow of their social capital related to the new curriculum. Furthermore, it will offer policymakers insight into whether they achieved their goal of making the implementation process a bottom-up process. Lastly, it will offer policymakers information on the extent to which the new curriculum has truly been set in motion as an integral part of schools.

In conclusion, we would like to underscore that studying the relationships and networks of teachers is important not only for implementing new policy or curricula, but also for understanding the conditions for collaboration between teachers and for their professional learning (Levine & Marcus, 2010). Who do teachers turn to for help? Are teams really collaborating, or are there specific people who ensure that changes are implemented? Can teachers be a leading team in times of change? To find answers to these questions, researchers in Norway should focus on the interaction between teachers, as Kvam also called for in 2018. Similarly, Jensen and colleagues (2022) stressed the importance of shifting the focus from teachers as individuals to the collective community. Internationally, research on teachers' social capital has been booming, and we expect this trend to influence Norwegian education and policy as well. Taking a SNA perspective and mapping the interconnectedness of teachers when studying policy implementation, collaboration, and knowledge processes within teacher teams will contribute to understanding how teachers are a key part of a leading team in times of change.

References

Ávalos-Bevan, B., & Flores, M. A. (2021). School-based teacher collaboration in Chile and Portugal. *Compare: A Journal of Comparative and International Education*, Advance online publication. https://doi.org/10.1080/03057925.2020.1854085.

Borko, H., Jacobs, J., & Koellner, K. (2010). Contemporary approaches to teacher professional development. In Peterson, P. L., Baker, E., & McGaw, B. (Eds.), *Third international encyclopedia of education* (pp. 548–56). Oxford: Elsevier.

Canrinus, E. T., Dalehefte, I. M., & Myhre, S. (2019). VET teachers' beliefs on collaboration, identity, and status and their relationship with professional development. *Pedagogische Studiën*, 96(6), 463–80.

Canrinus, E. T., Klette, K., & Hammerness, K. (2019). Diversity in coherence: Strengths and opportunities of three programs. *Journal of Teacher Education*, 70(3), 192–205.

Carlsten, T. C., Throndsen, I., & Björnsson, J. K. (2020). *TALIS 2018—Flere hovedfunn fra ungdomstrinnet* [TALIS 2018—More main findings from lower secondary education]. University of Oslo. Retrieved from https://hdl.handle.net/11250/2726536.

Carlsten, T. C., Throndsen, I., & Björnsson, J. K. (2021). Profesjonelle fellesskap på ungdomstrinnet som del av skolens utvikling [Professional communities in lower secondary education as part of school development]. In Björnsson, J. K. (Ed.), *Hva kan vi lære av TALIS 2018? Gode relasjoner som grunnlag for læring* [What can we learn from TALIS 2018? Good relations as a base for learning] (pp. 87–106). Cappelen Damm Akademisk.

Caspersen, J., & Raaen, F. D. (2014). Novice teachers and how they cope. *Teachers and Teaching*, 20(2), 189–211.

Çoban, Ö., Özdemir, N., & Bellibaş, M. Ş. (2020). Trust in principals, leaders' focus on instruction, teacher collaboration, and teacher self-efficacy: Testing a multilevel mediation model. *Educational Management Administration & Leadership*. Advance online publication. https://doi.org/10.1177/1741143220968170.

Coburn, C. E., Russell, J. L., Kaufman, J. H., & Stein, M. K. (2012). Supporting sustainability: Teachers' advice networks and ambitious instructional reform. *American Journal of Education, 119*(1), 137–82.

Dahl, T. (2016). *Norske lærere og skoleledere i TALIS-undersøkelsene. En re-analyse av TALIS-dataene*. [Norwegian teachers and head teachers in the TALIS surveys. A reanalysis of the TALIS data]. Oslo and Akershus University College of Applied Sciences.

Datnow, A. (2012). Teacher agency in educational reform: Lessons from social networks research. *American Journal of Education, 119*(1), 193–201.

Daly, A., Liou, YH., & Moolenaar, N. (2014). The principal connection: Trust and innovative climate in a network of reform. In Van Maele, D., Forsyth, P. & Van Houtte, M. (Eds.). *Trust and school life* (pp. 285 311). Dordrecht: Springer. https://doi.org/10.1007/978-94-017-8014-8_13.

Demir, E. K. (2021). The role of social capital for teacher professional learning and student achievement: A systematic literature review. *Educational Research Review, 33*, 100391.

Ertesvåg, S. K. (2014). Teachers' collaborative activity in school-wide interventions. *Social Psychology of Education, 17*(4), 565–88.

Ertesvåg, S. K., & Roland, E. (2015). Professional cultures and rates of bullying. *School Effectiveness and School Improvement, 26*(2), 195–214.

Frelin, A. (2013). *Exploring relational professionalism in schools*. Sense Publishers.

Grimsæth, G., & Holgersen, H. (2015). Nyutdannede allmennlærere og deres opplevelse av faglig kompetanse i leseopplæring generelt og av elever med lesevansker spesielt [Newly qualified general teachers and their experience of professional competence in reading instruction in general and of students with reading difficulties in particular]. *Acta Didactica Norge, 9*(1), 14–17.

Hammerness, K. (2006). From coherence in theory to coherence in practice. *Teachers College Record, 108*(7), 1241–65.

Hatlevik, I. K., & Hatlevik, O. E. (2018). Examining the relationship between teachers' ICT self-efficacy for educational purposes, collegial collaboration, lack of facilitation and the use of ICT in teaching practice. *Frontiers in Psychology, 9*, 935. https://doi.org/10.3389/fpsyg.2018.00935.

Hermansen, H. (2016). Teachers' knowledge work in collective practice development: Approaches to introducing assessment for learning at the school level. *Scandinavian Journal of Educational Research, 60*(6), 679–93.

Hermansen, H., Lorentzen, M., Mausethagen, S., & Zlatanovic, T. (2018). Hva kjennetegner forskning på lærerrollen under Kunnskapsløftet? En forskningskartlegging av studier av norske lærere, lærerstudenter og lærerutdannere [What characterizes research on the teacher's role during the new curriculum?]. *Acta Didactica Norge, 12*(1), 1–36. https://doi.org/10.5617/adno.4351.

Jensen, K. I., Bærøe Nerland, M., & Tronsmo, E. (2022). Changing cultural conditions for knowledge sharing in the teaching profession: A theoretical reinterpretation of findings across three research projects. *Professions and Professionalism, 11*(3). https://doi.org/10.7577/pp.4267.

Karseth, B. (2019). *Prosjektbeskrivelse. Evaluering av fagfornyelsen: Intensjoner, prosesser og praksiser* [Project description. Evaluation of the new curriculum: Intentions, processes, and practice]. University of Oslo.

Kunnskapsdepartementet. (2004). *Kultur for læring* [Culture for learning]. Ministry of Education and Research. https://www.regjeringen.no/no/dokumenter/stmeld-nr-030-2003-2004-/id404433/?ch=1.

Kunnskapsdepartementet. (2011). *Motivasjon—Mestring—Muligheter. Ungdomstrinnet (Meld. St. 22 (2010–2011))* [Motivation—mastering—possibilities. Lower secondary education]. Ministry of Education and Research. https://www.regjeringen.no/no/dokumenter/meld-st-22-2010-2011/id641251/.

Kunnskapsdepartementet. (2016a). *Lærelyst—tidlig innsats og kvalitet i skolen (Meld. St. 21 (2016–2017))* [Desire to learn—Early intervention and quality in school]. Ministry of Education and Research. https://www.regjeringen.no/no/dokumenter/meld.-st.-21-20162017/id2544344/.

Kunnskapsdepartementet. (2016b). *Fag—Fordypning—Forståelse—En fornyelse av Kunnskapsløftet (Meld. St. 28 (2015–2016))* [Subjects—specialization—understanding—A renewal of the curriculum]. Ministry of Education and Research. https://www.regjeringen.no/no/dokumenter/meld.-st.-28-20152016/id2483955/.

Kunnskapsdepartementet. (2017). *Overordnet del—verdier og prinsipper for grunnopplæringen.* [Core curriculum—values and principles for primary and secondary education]. Ministry of Education and Research. https://www.regjeringen.no/no/dokumenter/verdier-og-prinsipper-for-grunnopplaringen/id2570003/.

Kvam, E. K. (2018). Untapped learning potential? A study of teachers' conversations with colleagues in primary schools in Norway. *Cambridge Journal of Education, 48*(6), 697–714.

Kvam, E. K. (2021). Knowledge development in the teaching profession: An interview study of collective knowledge processes in primary schools in Norway. *Professional Development in Education.* Advance online publication. https://doi.org/10.1080/19415257.2021.1876146.

Levine, T. H., & Marcus, A. S. (2010). How the structure and focus of teachers' collaborative activities facilitate and constrain teacher learning. *Teaching and Teacher Education, 26*(3), 389–98.

Li, P. P. (2007). Social tie, social capital, and social behavior: Toward an integrative model of informal exchange. *Asia Pacific Journal of Management, 24*(2), 227–46.

Liebech-Lien, B. (2021). Teacher teams–A support or a barrier to practicing cooperative learning? *Teaching and Teacher Education, 106,* 103453.

Liou, Y.-H., & Canrinus, E. T. (2020). A capital framework for professional learning and practice. *International Journal of Educational Research, 100,* 101527. https://doi.org/10.1016/j.ijer.2019.101527.

Liou, Y. H., Daly, A. J., Canrinus, E. T., Forbes, C. A., Moolenaar, N. M., Cornelissen, F., Van Lare, M., & Hsiao, J. (2017). Mapping the social side of pre-service teachers: Connecting closeness, trust, and efficacy with performance. *Teachers and Teaching, 23*(6), 635–57.

Liou, Y. H., Canrinus, E. T., & Daly, A. J. (2019). Activating the implementers: The role of organizational expectations, teacher beliefs, and motivation in bringing about reform. *Teaching and Teacher Education, 79,* 60–72.

López Solé, S., Civís Zaragoza, M., & Díazgibson, J. (2018). Improving interaction in teacher training programmes: The rise of the social dimension in pre-service teacher education. *Teachers and Teaching, 24*(6), 644–58.

Lødding, B., Gjerustad, C., Rønsen, E., Bubikova-Moan, J., Jarness, V., & Røsdal, T. (2018). *Sluttrapport fra evalueringen av virkemidlene i satsingen ungdomstrinn i utvikling* [Final report of the evaluation of the instruments in the investment in the development of lower secondary education]. NIFU.

Meld. St. 18 (2014–15). *Konsentrasjon for kvalitet. Strukturreform i universitets- og høgskolesektoren* [Concentration for quality. Structural reform in the university and college sector]. Kunnskapsdepartementet.

Moolenaar, N. M., & Daly, A. J. (2012). Social networks in education: Exploring the social side of the reform equation. *American Journal of Education, 119*(1), 1–6.

Morud, E. B., & Rokkones, K. L. (2020). Deling av kunnskap og kompetanse er ingen selvfølge for deltakere i Yrkesfaglærerløftet [Sharing knowledge and competence is not a matter of course for participants in the Vocational Teacher Strategy]. *Skandinavisk Tidsskrift for Yrker og Profesjoner i Utvikling, 5*(1), 129–44.

Munthe, E. (2003). Teachers' workplace and professional certainty. *Teaching and Teacher Education, 19*, 801–13.

Pettersson, F., & Olofsson, A. D. (2019). Learning to teach in a remote school context: Exploring the organisation of teachers' professional development of digital competence through networked learning. In Littlejohn, A., Jaldemark, J., Vrieling-Teunter, E., & Nijland, F. (Eds.), *Networked professional learning*. (pp. 167–85). Cham: Springer.

Rehm, M., Daly, A., Bjorklund, P., Liou, Y. H., & Del fresno, M. (2021). The social continuum of educational leadership: Exploring the offline and online social networks of elementary principals. *The Elementary School Journal, 122*(1), 112–35.

Ryan, R. M., & Deci, E. L. (2017). *Self-determination theory: Basic psychological needs in motivation, development, and wellness.* Guilford Publications.

Shea, L. M., Sandholtz, J. H., & Shanahan, T. B. (2018). We are all talking: A whole-school approach to professional development for teachers of English learners. *Professional Development in Education, 44*(2), 190–208.

Sinnema, C., Liou, Y. H., Daly, A., Cann, R., & Rodway, J. (2021). When seekers reap rewards and providers pay a price: The role of relationships and discussion in improving practice in a community of learning. *Teaching and Teacher Education, 107*, 103474.

Sleegers, P., Bolhuis, S., & Geijsel, F. (2005). School improvement within a knowledge economy: Fostering professional learning from a multidimensional perspective. In Bascia, N., Cumming, A., Datnow, A., Leithwood, K., & Livingstone, D. (Eds.), *International handbook of educational policy* (pp. 527–43). Springer.

Stoll, L., Bolam, R., McMahon, A., Wallace, M., & Thomas, S. (2006). Professional learning communities. A review of the literature. *Journal of Educational Change, 7*(4), 221–58.

Styhre, A. (2016). *Knowledge sharing in professions: Roles and identity in expert communities.* Routledge.

Utdanningsdirektoratet. (2021). *Slik ble læreplanene utviklet* [How the curriculum was developed]. https://www.udir.no/laring-og-trivsel/lareplanverket/fagfornyelsen/slik-ble-lareplanene-utviklet/.

van Amersfoort, D., Korenhof, M., Nijland, F., De laat, M., & Vermeulen, M. (2019). Value creation in teacher learning networks. In Littlejohn, A., Jaldemark, J., Vrieling-Teunter, E., & Nijland, F. (Eds.), *Networked professional learning* (pp. 187–205). Cham: Springer.

Vangrieken, K., Meredith, C., Packer, T., & Kyndt, E. (2017). Teacher communities as a context for professional development: A systematic review. *Teaching and Teacher Education, 61*, 47–59.

8

Structures That Support Leader Development and School Improvement: Insights from Mixed Method Research

Darren Bryant and Allen Walker

Introduction

This chapter examines how principals design and enact educational infrastructure that enhances middle leadership capacity. Middle leaders (MLs) typically include teachers with formal leadership responsibilities on the school's organizational hierarchy or specialists, such as special needs or technology coordinators, who provide advice to senior leaders (SLs) and support teachers and students (Bryant, 2019; DeNobile, 2019). MLs are typically appointed because of their experience as teachers and specialized expertise rather than leadership training or skill. However, they need situated support to develop their leadership skillsets, because leading differs from teaching (Irvine & Brundrett, 2017). Accordingly, we examine how changes in school-based educational infrastructure that senior leadership teams design can build MLs' capacities as leaders. Cohen and colleagues (2018) define educational infrastructure as "the coordinated roles, structures, and resources that school systems design and use to support and coordinate instruction, maintain instructional quality, and enable instructional improvement" (p. 205). Through qualitative and social network analyses (SNA), we suggest how a principal-led design of school-based educational infrastructure influences interactions among leaders and teachers that enhance middle leadership development. This approach adopts the perspective that leadership occurs through social interactions among leaders and followers (Kwok et al., 2018).

Drawing on the concept of educational infrastructure, we consider how school-based designs influence the professional learning of MLs. This chapter differs from much current research on educational infrastructure that focuses on teachers' professional learning and infrastructure designed by school systems rather than school leaders (Shirrell et al., 2019). It builds on our prior identification of three such models (Bryant & Walker, 2022) that principals intentionally crafted to support MLs' development.

To provide a context for the study, we first highlight the principalship's importance to professional learning generally and then to middle leadership specifically. We then review recent literature on the potential of school-based educational infrastructure to drive capacity building. We further interrogate the model by applying SNA to illuminate the nature of interactions among leaders and teachers. This serves to assess the model's potential to shape interactions, triangulate the qualitative data, and suggest possibilities for enhancing the model's design. We conclude the chapter by discussing the implications of this study for research and practice.

Literature Review

In this section, we present prior research and theoretical perspectives that inform our study and explain educational infrastructure's potential to shape professional interactions that support MLs' capacity development.

Professional Learning

Developing professionals in schools involves building individual and collective capacity (Day et al., 2011). To accomplish this, leaders provide support for individual needs and construct situated opportunities for professional learning through formal and informal mechanisms outside or within the school. Formal professional learning includes out-of-school activities such as participation in seminars, conferences, and postgraduate study. On-the-job learning occurs through situated interactions within schools through intentional designs or unplanned professional engagements. The former comprises planned activities such as lesson observations, giving and receiving feedback, or action research (Thurlings et al., 2015). School cultures with strong learning orientations stimulate informal professional learning opportunities through spontaneous discussion, peer-to-peer consultation, or other collaborative activities. Hence, professional capacity development is linked with vision-setting activities that lead to improved schools.

Middle Leadership

Increasingly, research in educational leadership points to the pivotal role that MLs play in schools. Effective MLs work closely with principals, other leaders, teachers, teaching teams, and other stakeholders to meet mission-critical goals. Hence, MLs play a crucial role in the school improvement process and in building teacher capacity (Bryant, 2019; DeNobile, 2019).

The above suggests important implications for MLs. Firstly, that principal leadership is often distributed to MLs. To support this distribution, senior leaders (SLs, i.e., principals and vice-principals) and more experienced or specialized MLs share responsibility for developing teachers and less experienced MLs (Bryant, 2019; Bryant et al., 2020). Secondly, MLs need leadership skillsets that differ from teaching expertise

(Irvine & Brundrett, 2017). This means principals' responsibilities for developing people must encapsulate all formal leaders, including those in the middle (Bryant & Walker, 2022).

Professional Learning and Educational Infrastructure

Effective professional learning in schools is not left to chance. Instead, leaders align resources and shape cultures (Walker, 2012). Work by Spillane and colleagues (see below) point to the potential of educational infrastructure to enhance professional learning. Infrastructure can include roles, for example, senior, middle, and teacher leaders, routines such as team meetings or instructional rounds, and tools inclusive of guidelines, curriculum, protocols, and procedures (Spillane & Coldren, 2011). An intentionally designed educational infrastructure can shape professional interactions and leadership practices among teachers and leaders and develop individual and collective capacities (Spillane et al., 2018).

Building Middle Leadership Capacity

Given MLs' role in school improvement, their leadership development is crucial. Typically, MLs' capacity develops through formal and on-the-job avenues. The former includes externally planned professional development. The efficacy of such learning depends on its application to real-world practices. On-the-job professional learning occurs through situated professional practices such as participation in learning communities. Although principals play a crucial part in establishing leader development strategies, their direct engagement with MLs may be limited to coaching, mentoring, and job shadowing (Lipscombe et al., 2023), or through providing opportunities to lead and reflect (Irvine & Brundrett, 2017). Even though MLs prefer on-the-job professional development, the availability of time and resources hinders such practices, often resulting in *ad hoc* support from principals (Gurr, 2019). MLs, therefore, tend to manage their own development (Lillejord & Børte, 2019).

Educational Infrastructure for Building Middle Leadership Capacity

Organizational approaches to developing MLs include shaping supportive cultures, structures, and policies that are actualized through (re-)designing or (re-)aligning school-based educational infrastructure (Spillane & Coldren, 2011). For instance, Shirrell et al., (2019) found that exposure to colleagues' reform-oriented practices changed teachers' practices. This resulted when educational infrastructure, such as instructional coaches, focused on instructional interactions.

Bryant et al., (2020) examined the role of MLs in developing teachers' instructional capacity. They found that school-based educational infrastructure supported MLs in maintaining teachers' focus on student learning. MLs actively defined, redefined, and co-constructed responsibilities. They employed curricular standards, protocols, and routines to create opportunities that encouraged feedback and reflection. Such infrastructure prioritized the "central idea and how to excel at it" (p. 6). Further, the intentional designs around MLs' role definitions, peer interactions, and team membership compositions reflected purposeful targets, such as curriculum articulation. Using social network analysis (SNA), Bryant et al., (2020) compared the advice-seeking pattern between MLs and teachers across two academic years. This yielded insights into how interactions develop with new roles, team compositions, purposes, and routines. Gradually, informal social interactions, like spontaneous conversations, reflected less dependency on SLs and structured routines. Notably, program coordinators (PCs) became the focal point of capacity-building advice-seeking by lower-tier MLs, such as subject leaders, who closely supported teachers' instructional capacity. PCs emerged as pivotal to building the capacity of subject and year-level leaders. The study, therefore, demonstrated the potential of infrastructure to support MLs' work in building others' capacity by influencing interaction processes.

Given the importance of school-based infrastructure to *in-situ* development, we (Bryant & Walker, 2022) used qualitative data to cross-examine how principals designed infrastructure to facilitate interactions that build leadership capacities. We categorized the emerging infrastructure designs into multiple models. These models were explicitly associated with the schools' mission and agendas, which required site-based professional capacity development and embedded a range of supports to facilitate MLs' development and that of teachers. The models differed across schools regarding their formality, routines, and tools, such as linkages to performance appraisal, school initiatives, and resource deployment.

Together, the above demonstrates the potential influence of educational infrastructure on social interactions among staff that build instructional and leadership capacity. Our research shows the decisive role of MLs in developing professional capacity and how school-based educational infrastructure supports and enhances leadership development. This chapter examines school-based educational infrastructure using qualitative interviews and social network data to analyze one school-based model—the cascade model (Bryant & Walker, 2022).

Research Design

Site Selection

The study employed a nonrandom purposeful sampling strategy focused on ML development (Patton, 2002). The selected school was a K-12 international school located in Tokyo. International schools have considerable autonomy over staffing, curriculum, assessment, and organizational structure. The school offered three International Baccalaureate (IB) programs, the Primary Years, Middle Years, and Diploma Programs. We selected the school because (a) SLs were actively engaged in designing educational infrastructure to address instructional improvement and professional development,

(b) MLs were a vital part of this infrastructure, and (c) IB authorization supported such engagement given IB's external mandates around professional learning and curriculum leadership roles. Although this school type differs from public schools in Japan, our research in Hong Kong suggests that the findings would be relevant to other IB schools or to semi-autonomous schools such as academies and charter schools (Bryant & Walker, 2022).

Mixed Methods

We employed a parallel mixed methods research design that utilizes SNA to interrogate qualitative findings (Yousefi Nooraie et al., 2020). Qualitative and social network data collection occurred concurrently with analyses conducted separately and then compared. This was further interrogated by the second round of analysis, which resulted in the model presented below. SNA provides perspectives that further illuminate the qualitative findings of how capacity-building responsibilities and interactions are distributed (Daly, 2010). Reciprocally, the qualitative analysis provides explication that SNA may lack (Yousefi Nooraie et al., 2020). In this way, mixed methods produce a fuller image of phenomena, that is, educational infrastructure, rather than "mutual confirmation or validation" (Gorard & Taylor, 2004, p. 45). We adopt the perspective that when dealing with small samples or poor response rates, qualitative data can help make sense of social networks (Williams & Shepherd, 2017).

Qualitative Data and Analysis

The qualitative data for Japan School (N=21) is derived from semi-structured interviews with (a) all SLs (n=3), that is, the Head of School (responsible for the K-12 school operations), the primary principal (K–Grade 5) and secondary principal (Grade 6–Grade12); (b) all IB PCs (n=3) who are responsible for the Primary, Middle Years, and Diploma Programs; (c) all subject leaders, which the school termed subject area coordinators (SACs, n=7) and; (d) a small number of teachers (n=5). All participated in 45-minute individual semi-structured interviews conducted in English. Table 1 exemplifies the nature of the interview questions and collected data.

We analyzed the data by applying codes derived from the theoretical perspectives framed in the literature review. These included the following: MLs' role definition, leadership practices, organizational structures, tools, and routines that supported MLs' development and work. We specifically related leadership roles and practices to the tools and routines by plotting the relevant codes on schema, similar to sociograms. This process led to the development of auditable figures that formed the basis of the cascade model.

The Social Network Data and Analysis

We employed SNA to examine the interrelationships depicted in the qualitative model, inclusive of formal and informal interactions (Lima, 2010; Moolenaar, 2012).

Table 8.1 Sample interview questions by topic

Topics	Sample interview questions for SLs and MLs
Roles and structures	How is leadership structured to address the school mission or other core purpose?
Leadership practices	Do MLs collaborate or co-lead with other leaders? What supports this?
Tools and Routines	How do you use tools such as common planners, templates, protocols, or frameworks to achieve goals?
Supportive and inhibiting conditions	What is done in this school to support MLs development? How does this help you in your work?

Participants nominated up to three advisors from the school staff list in response to prompts on (a) teaching and learning and (b) school capacity building (See Box 1). The limit of three nominees compelled participants to identify significant advisors whom they most frequently approached for advice (Lima, 2010).

Thirty participants from a staff of sixty-four completed the survey—a response rate of about 47 percent. This is problematic for the accuracy of SNA due to the loss of possible ties (Robins et al., 2004). Only one SL (n=1, 33 percent of N) and two PCs (n=2, 67 percent of N) participated in the SNA survey. However, arguably SNA alone, even with a reasonable response rate, is insufficient to describe how interactions are shaped (Yousefi Nooraie et al., 2020). SNA paired with qualitative data can help researchers make sense of social structures from varied perspectives (Edwards, 2010). Hence, the quantitative data explain and illuminate the qualitative findings (Guetterman et al., 2015). We trialed this approach in a previous study, which also suffered a poor response rate. Still, participants agreed that our interpretations successfully captured and described their interactions and leadership structure (Bryant et al., 2020).

Again, this study investigates how leaders enacted their leadership to create professional learning opportunities *in-situ* within the designed structure. The qualitative data describes the dimensions (the "What") and the context (the "How" and "Why") of the leadership structures and enactment. The SNA reveals the pattern (the "How") and the depth (the "How much") of the interactions.

We combined the mixed methods findings into one table, paring the qualitative and qualitative findings according to the relationship between groups. Table 1 indicates sets of relationships among leaders and teachers, the leadership practices associated with teaching and learning, and capacity building. It aligns the respective leadership practices to SNA, represented as the number of ties and percentage of reported ties (ignoring the ties' direction) connecting various leadership levels and teachers across the school. "Ties" refer to the relationship between two people (Prell, 2012). Each tie connects a respondent to an advisor nominated in the questionnaire (see Box 1). Figure 8.2 represents such relationships with arrows from respondents to nominated advisors. We interpret these ties as interaction, communication, and coordination

> **Box 1**
>
> *Advice-Seeking Questionnaire*
>
> Part A
> **Who do you frequently seek advice from for matters related to Teaching and Learning?**
> Examples include
>
> - Improving your practices related to instruction or assessment.
> - Developing curriculum.
> - Implementing new methods of teaching and learning.
> - Implementing new technologies.
> - Learning new strategies to support students with Special Needs.
> - Analyzing data related to student learning.
>
> [List of names with check boxes]
>
> Part B
> **Who do you frequently seek advice from for matters related to School Capacity Building?**
> Examples include
>
> - Understanding school policies and strategic aims.
> - Developing your own or others' professional knowledge and skills.
> - Seeking support through activities such as mentoring or coaching.
> - Understanding or supporting school-wide initiatives.
> - Collaborating with parent groups.
> - Developing strategies for school improvement.
>
> [List of names with check boxes]

between members of a relatively small sample (Clifton & Webster, 2017). Ties with arrows in both directions (i.e., participants seeking advice from one another) are counted as two ties, implying stronger professional interaction. We indicate the number of ties for different sets of relationships under the "Ties" column in Table 2. We derived ten relationship combinations from the leader and teacher roles. The "SNA" column adjacent to the "Ties" column represents the ties linking identified relationships as a percentage of all nominated ties. Table 2 is best read in conjunction with the cascade model (Figure 8.1). This provides a better sense of how two methods (qualitative study as the spine and quantitative analysis as the ribs) create the skeleton of the proposed leadership structure.

Table 8.2 Leadership practices and distribution of interactions among leaders and teachers

Group	Relationship	Leadership enactment (Teaching and Learning related)	Ties	SNA	Leadership Enactment (Capacity building related)	Ties	SNA
1	Among Senior Leaders (Head of School, Principals)	• Co-design goals • Co-design strategies toward goals • Set structural measures to evaluate performance	2	2.27%	• Develop structure to recognize performance and explore professional growth • Create opportunities for interactions and enhance situ-PD exposures	2	2.41%
2	Senior Leaders and Program Coordinators	• Co-interpret and enforce IB policies • Distribute leadership to oversee programs and curriculum • Co-supervise teachers' performance	4	4.55%	• Co-design strategic plan for school capacity building • Mentoring and coaching • Review support process for teachers	4	4.82%
3	Senior Leaders and Subject Area Coordinators	• Delegate/distribute leadership to oversee subject areas • Co-supervise teachers' performance	2	2.27%	• Mentoring and coaching • Facilitate support process for teachers	6	7.23%
4	Senior Leaders and Teachers	• Communicate expectations • Formal observation and assessment • Demonstrate pedagogical practices	14	15.91%	• Review appraisal for professional growth • Informal advice seeking • Workshop • Structure hiring and promotion system to illuminate career path and select suitable leaders	25	30.12%
5	Among Program Coordinators	• Align curriculum across year programs • Review IB inspections for curriculum development	0	0.00%	• Co-design teachers' capacity building strategies • Review IB inspections for capacity building • Involve collaboration with parents	0	0.00%

#	Group	Activities	Count	%	Activities	Count	%
6	Program Coordinators and Subject Area Coordinators	• Analysis data for curriculum enhancement • Action research • Co-construct instructional goals with SACs • Share pedagogical strategies • Coordinating SACs work; • Facilitating horizontal curriculum alignment	8	9.09%	• Mentoring and coaching leadership skills • Enhance communication and coordinating between SACs and teachers • Developing and implementing workshops	9	10.84%
7	Program Coordinators and Teachers	• Feedback on teachers' classroom observations • Conferences to review and develop instruction • Promote strategies for teaching • Align collaboration across year levels	20	22.73%	• Setup mentoring program for new teachers • Schedule and develop professional learning session • Individual mentoring and coaching	16	19.28%
8	Among Subject Area Coordinators	• Comment on teachers' performance at class • Share practical pedagogical practices • Coordinate for horizontal curriculum alignment	2	2.27%		0	0.00%
9	Subject Area Coordinators and Teachers	• Coordinate between Senior Leaders and teachers • Coordinate among subject teachers • Standardize assessment practices • Daily support and advice to achieve goals	19	21.59%	• Mentoring and coaching • Reviewing student learning data and advise teachers • Coordinating between SLs and teachers	10	12.05%
10	Among Teachers	• Horizontal alignment • Cross-school facilitation	17	19.32%	Peer observation	11	13.25%
	Total		88			83	

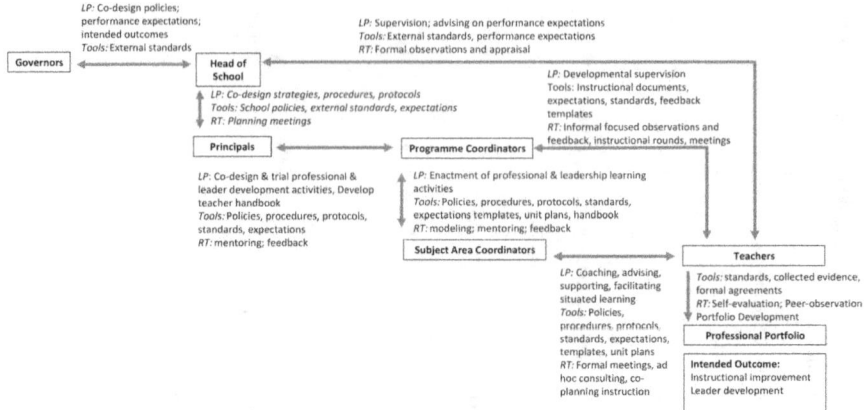

Figure 8.1 Cascade design of educational infrastructure (adapted from Bryant & Walker, 2022).

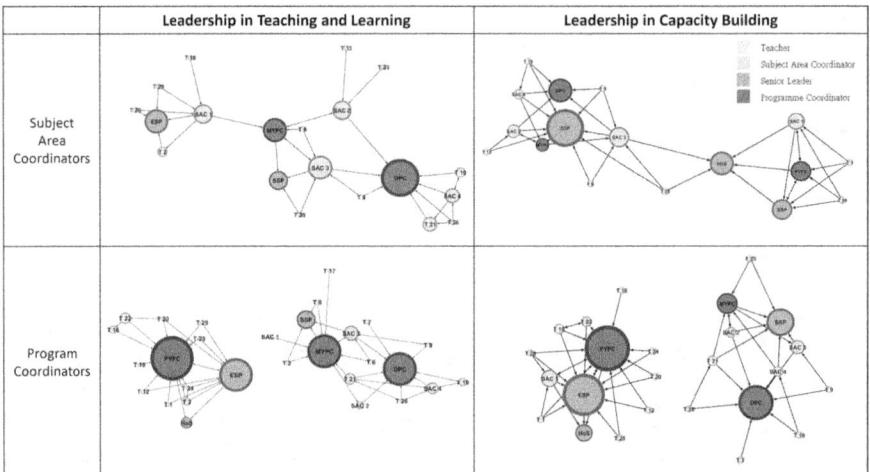

Figure 8.2 Middle leaders advise networks for teaching and learning and capacity building.

Findings

In this section, we present the Cascade model to explain how it was derived from data. We first explain the model holistically and then explore the network relationships and the core infrastructure that supports it.

The Cascade Model: Connecting Roles, Routines, Tools, and Practices

We adopted the term "cascade" to imply an interconnected but tiered approach to structuring professional learning. While reflecting organizational hierarchy, it demonstrates unique relational ties between roles at different levels. Each tie reflects defined purposes and leadership practices supported by specific tools and routines. Responsibilities for capacity building connect through intentionally designed interactions among various combinations of SLs, MLs, and teachers. In other words, in addition to role definition, the SLs who designed the model aimed to account for the types of interactions that would best support situated capacity development. The model, therefore, is holistic in that it accounts for potential interactions among all staff. Additionally, it accounts for leadership practices and capacity development necessary to build teachers' instructional capacity and support a portfolio-based performance appraisal system. Figure 8.1 illustrates the cascade design and the roles (formal positions), leadership practices (LP), tools, and routines (RT) that make the interactions work.

Below we elaborate on the design with reference to qualitative data and the SNA that illuminates interactions among SLs, MLs, and teachers.

To further investigate the interrelationships of various leaders, we created a series of network maps. Each network map shows advisory ties related to specific leadership roles and to teachers. Given that the focus of this study is on Middle Leadership, we include in Figure 8.2 network maps for two sets of MLs. The top row shows SACs' network as givers and receivers of advice for teaching and learning and capacity building, respectively. The second row does so for PCs.

Next, we discuss the findings with reference to the qualitative and social network data summarized in the figures and tables.

The Head of School and School Governors

Figure 8.1 depicts the interactions and infrastructure that support the cascade model. Initially, the Head of School and school governors set the intended outcome for the model in which instructional improvement was linked to six professional standards to be assessed through portfolio assessment and observations.

> Our board decides what success is ... If I don't have policies, job descriptions, and support measures in place to define our expectations and what success means, then I'm not setting [teachers] up for success ...
>
> (Head of School)

The Head of School and governors established policies related to formal job descriptions, linking incentives with job performance. They put expectations for summative appraisal into place, that is, using a portfolio to evidence meeting the six instructional standards.

> One of the first things that we did was to bring in a comprehensive appraisal system, and the reason wasn't to give critical feedback so much [as] to recognize staff and, of course, to support them in their professional growth.
>
> (Head of School)

The Head of School clarified that the model was framed around the formative potential of appraisal to support professional growth. As we explicate the model, we see how this growth entails both instructional and leadership capacity. The latter was an essential part of the process of building instructional capacity. As we discuss below, roles, routines, tools, and leadership practices (labeled in Figure 8.1) work collectively and are holistically enacted.

Senior Leaders and Program Coordinators

To meet the formative purposes of performance appraisal, the Head and Principals defined support strategies and procedures to support implementation, including updating the teacher handbook, detailing expectations around instructional planning and assessment, and delineating MLs' roles. By using performance appraisal as an anchor for instructional and leader development, the SLs were responsible for formal teacher evaluation, freeing PCs and SACs to provide sustained and collegial formative support to teachers. The qualitative data suggested two ways in which SLs and MLs collaborated to provide support for teachers:

> Sometimes the middle leaders will talk with me first ... [They] can follow up without a teacher feeling it's the SAC who makes the final evaluation.
>
> (Secondary School Principal)

Principals would work with PCs and sometimes SACs around teacher appraisal. The principal, responsible for formal appraisal, would discuss teacher progress with MLs. However, MLs formed a buffer between the principal and teachers so that direct feedback and support could be addressed as a formative process and not be conflated with summative performance appraisal. This also frees MLs from "difficult decisions" regarding contractual matters or unmet performance expectations.

In a second area of leadership, principals worked with PCs to develop capacity directly. As the PCs were highly experienced teachers in IB programs, ongoing discussion addressed how PCs could build the capacity of subject heads to work effectively with teachers:

> [I used a] workshop-style so that the coordinator was able to give the SACs some tools to work with the subject teachers on how you would review a unit plan, how you would decide on whether [an] assessment [strategy] was meaningful ...
>
> (Secondary School Principal)

The secondary school principal explained that in the first year of implementing the instructional improvement strategy, he took the initiative to develop "a year's agenda with 4 or 5 focuses ..." around curriculum coordination. He then worked with PCs to build their capacity allowing them subsequently to develop similar skills in SACs. In the following year, the PCs identified foci for SACs' development. As the secondary school principal explained: "I'm increasingly trying to delegate a bit more curriculum leadership to the coordinators." This enabled him to focus on "initiatives or goals." In other words, the design deliberately accounted for the purposeful engagement of leaders at different levels in the organization to build others' capacity in a devolving flow.

Mentoring PCs in their roles formed a clear priority for the secondary school principal. PCs also reported an important role in co-interpreting with principals the performance standards and appraisal system. For instance, the primary year's PC used a constitutional metaphor to explain his function:

[Regarding] school policies and strategic aims ... [The Elementary School Principal] and I side-by-side interpret those laws all the time—like [how] the United States Congress, the judges interpret the laws and decide how they're going to be written and whether they need to be tweaked or not; I'm doing that all the time.

(Primary PC)

Thus, in both elementary and secondary sections, the close collaboration among the respective principals and PCs in interpreting and enacting school policies and goals was evident as they worked together to co-construct routines for SACs' development.

The SNA also shed some light on their collaborative work in developing SAC's capacity. The number of ties between the SLs and PCs in leading teaching and learning (4 ties 4.55 percent) and capacity building (4 ties 4.82 percent) is relatively low. The SLs and PCs only account for 9 percent of the respondents (N=64), and the response rate of SLs is poor (33 percent). However, the number of ties between the SLs and PCs remain stable across the two domains, indicating substantial interactions. Combining the SNA with the interview data, which reported the intensive interaction between the school principals and PCs, strengthens our perspective that their collaboration was close, sustainable, and inclusive despite absent SNA data.

The SNA, however, indicates different patterns of interaction among principals, PCs and SACs. In the capacity development domain, SLs collectively held more prominent roles, as measured by SACs' advice-seeking (6 ties, representing 7.23 percent of reported advice-seeking), as compared to teaching and learning (2 ties at 2.27 percent). In contrast, PC roles in both domains were relatively consistent in the measure of ties and proportion of advice-seeking (approximately 9 percent to 10 percent). The SNA data, while modest, corroborates the qualitative data, which suggests, a devolving distribution of curriculum and instructional leadership responsibility to PCs. In other words, the increasing pattern of proportional advice-seeking moving from SLs to PCs reinforces the cascade concept: that those leaders in closer proximity to the daily work of SACs are more engaged in advice-seeking for teaching and learning. However, the PC networks presented in Figure 8.2 indicate a bifurcation of elementary and secondary schools with no ties connecting the two. Indeed, interview data revealed that PCs and SACs in the elementary and secondary sections had limited interaction.

The first set of relationships in the cascade model reveals a few insights:

1. It illustrates the potential SLs see for PCs to build SACs' capacity. This capacity-building is co-constructed as illustrated by the planned leadership and instruction activities and the advice patterns shared among SLs, PCs, and SACs.
2. It shows a distinct role for SLs as mentors and coaches of PCs, and the latter for SACs. At the same time, as reinforced by social network data, SLs retain a developmental role in building SACs' capacity and are particularly consulted for this purpose.
3. It illustrates that SLs and PCs work to co-construct roles, routines, and tools and identify specific leadership practices to develop SACs. Still, these fall within the overall parameters set by school governors and SLs.

Program Coordinators and Subject Area Coordinators

Our analysis of the qualitative data suggests close interaction among the two tiers of MLs, that is, PCs and SACs, as they work to develop teachers' capacity. The MYP coordinator related that he worked directly with SACs in workshops on understanding how assessment works in the MYP. The workshop routine echoes the strategy conducted by the principals with PCs. PCs and SACs also worked together to use IB assessment guidelines to support teacher reflection on assessment practices. Monthly meetings provided a routine to identify and develop strategies, such as workshops, to improve instruction. This enabled SACs to implement instructional skill development strategies with subject area staff.

PCs and SACs worked together to initiate curriculum development plans for teachers. However, the process also allowed for two directions of interaction, as related by a SAC:

> This year we [the subject team] have developed two new plans. One person generally has the driving idea and then the other person joins in and helps direct it. [...] We'll fill in a planner and bring it to the PCs and principal, and then we together will discuss it in the meeting. If the central idea is a bit weak, and we'll tighten a few bits of the language up. Maybe we'll change one of the concepts if we discuss it and if we come up with a thought from a different angle that we've not thought of before.
>
> (Mathematics Subject Area Coordinator)

This approach allowed SACs to work with PCs and the secondary school principal to formalize an instructional planning approach originating from the instructional team, involving PCs and SLs in aligning planning with the school's overall strategic direction.

In addition to instruction and curriculum planning, the PCs designed a program for SACs on running department meetings. They identified priority areas based on accreditation exercises and aligned them with strategies to develop instructional capacity. Topics included pedagogical approaches and lesson planning. PCs and SACs provided feedback to colleagues through walkthroughs. They also targeted managerial development strategies. SACs presented "how they organize their department" (DP PC) and the structures instituted to provide feedback to colleagues. This routine allowed SACs to share effective practices with peers and obtain feedback from PCs. For example, one SAC used electronic notepads to provide feedback on planning documents, which everyone could then access and "stay up-to-date."

Despite the PCs workshop approach to developing SACs, an interesting finding around advice-seeking practices was the lack of nomination by SACs of other SACs for both teaching and learning and capacity building. The first row of Figure 8.2 illustrates how SACs give and receive advice from more senior leaders and teachers but not each other. This is illustrated in the SAC network (Figure 8.1), which depicts proximity to PCs, SLs, and teachers but not to each other. This may reflect the research design whereby participants identified their top three advisors. If allowed to nominate an unlimited number of advisors, the results may have shown SACs advising each other. Nonetheless, the forced prioritization reveals the influence of the model design around capacity development as flowing from SLs to more junior leaders rather than prioritizing peer-to-peer development. This design takes advantage of departmental/subject organizational structures. Similarly, the focus for improvement, that is, on learning and assessment rather than on the horizontal curriculum articulation, may lend itself to subject-specific disciplinary practices.

Program Coordinators and Teachers

As indicated above, various leaders interact collaboratively or individually with teachers and teaching teams. The MYP coordinator related that much work entailed helping teachers to understand criterion-referenced assessment practices and "dealing with teachers in individual departments to sort through that and ultimately being comfortable" with the required skillset. Similarly, the PYP coordinator explained that his job focused on improving instruction and assessment; this entailed, "teaching teachers how to implement the curriculum." The DP coordinator also outlined his role in providing focused feedback to teachers on curriculum and assessment implementation. An example of this included a subject teacher inviting the DP coordinator to observe him introducing an instructional strategy to students for the first time. The DP coordinator observed only the agreed part of the lesson, electronically recorded his feedback, and immediately sent it to the teacher. The feedback provided a basis for a post-lesson discussion about the effectiveness of the lesson and how it might be improved.

Our social network analyses reflected the PCs' direct engagement with individual teachers around teaching and learning. Predominantly, teachers viewed PCs as influential advisors in this domain (20 ties at 22.73 percent of advice-giving across the model). However, they were also perceived as necessary for capacity building, although with fewer ties (n=16) and a smaller proportion of advising (19.28 percent) in this domain.

Subject Area Coordinators and Teachers

Similarly, SACs discussed how they supported teacher development: "My job is to listen to teachers and support their new ideas ... [and] filter down new initiatives." One SAC explained that this involved managerial processes such as "keeping track of documents and making sure that things get done" and a leadership orientation around maintaining "the overarching vision and sense of community." Another related that his role entailed:

> ... supporting individual subject teachers in their teaching ... I go and observe math teacher's lessons and if I see something that they could improve, or if they have anything that they want to improve, then I would sit with them and go through some of the ways that they could improve.

Teachers reiterated this role for SACs:

> [My SAC] also helps me with things, like inquiry-based teaching, that I may not know or lack experience in ... So, I ask him for feedback on how you use provocations or how to set up the lines of inquiry.

The SACs exercised responsibilities as communication brokers between teachers, SLs, and curriculum administrators. Their leadership directly supported improved teaching and learning within the scope of the school's vision. This involved developing plans at the team level and working with more senior leaders to enhance and ensure their fit with the schools' direction. Like PCs, SACs were consulted primarily around support for teaching and learning (n=19 ties at 21.59 percent of overall advising) with more limited advising for capacity building (n=10 ties at 12.05 percent of advice-giving across the network). Such a difference reflects constraints of significant curriculum responsibilities but relatively limited release time of only one class per year.

Senior Leaders and Teachers

Finally, teachers sought advice from SLs. This reflects the intentional design of the model where principals conduct performance appraisals leading to contract renewal decisions, inclusive of evaluating portfolios and formal observations. This differed from PCs and SACs who contributed to appraisal indirectly through the formative processes described above.

SLs' engagement with teachers is reflected in the SNA. The proportion of advice-seeking for capacity building (n=25 ties at 30.12 percent of advising) is more significant than the proportion in teaching and learning (n=14 ties at 15.91 percent). This finding suggests that although the model distributes responsibilities across the two domains, teachers perceive the SLs as the main influencers of capacity building, or at least of how teachers' capacities are evaluated. The notable interaction findings between SLs and teachers further strengthen our observation that the SLs played a key role in building teachers' capacities within the cascade model.

The Holistic Model

As articulated previously, the cascade model was designed to improve instruction and build capacity that focused on a discrete set of performance indicators and to build the middle leadership skills necessary to foster such improvement. The qualitative data suggest distinct layers of leadership activity with specific roles and interactions that draw on designed tools and routines. To a large extent, the model was designed *pre-hoc*, with deliberate purposes, roles, tools, and routines formulated at an early stage. The qualitative evidence suggests that the model supported both purposes. However, the SNA lends three further insights not fully captured by the qualitative analysis.

First, as leadership roles move closer (cascading downwards) to proximity with teachers, the emphasis on advice-seeking (as indicated by the number of ties and their overall proportions) shifts from capacity building to teaching and learning orientations. SLs' interactions with both SACs and teachers are more strongly skewed toward capacity building, whereas advising ties for PCs and SACs is predominantly oriented to teaching and learning. Interestingly, the PCs, who fall between SLs and SACs, engage with SACs around the two domains with almost equal emphasis but with teachers more so on teaching and learning. This may mean that teachers have more significant concerns with teaching and learning and that their interactions with PCs center mainly on this domain. This may also reflect their preference to receive capacity-building advice from SLs.

Second, although the proportional distribution of advice-seeking across the two domains varies with the leadership level, it becomes clear that all leaders are engaged in both domains and that teachers view all leaders as potential sources of advice in both domains. However, they clearly distinguish among leaders based on the nature of advising, even within the different domains. This suggests that the cascade model represents a model of leadership distribution rather than a mere transmission of modeled practices down the hierarchy. Furthermore, advising around capacity development tends to target those with performance appraisal roles, but advice-seeking around learning and teaching is more broadly distributed. The role design of the different leadership positions likely influences teachers' advice-seeking decisions. Third, largely absent from the model were horizontal patterns of advice-seeking across subjects and among PCs. While this may reflect the limitations of the research design (with only three nominees as advisors permitted), it may also reflect the priorities of developing skill sets around instruction that may largely be subject-based in nature.

Discussion and Conclusion

To date, the corpus of research on middle leadership development focuses on practices such as mentoring, coaching, job-shadowing, and the opportunity to lead. These require intensive and sustained support from SLs (Irvine & Brundrett, 2017; Lipscombe et al., 2020; Thurlings et al., 2015) which often limits broad-based on-the-job leader development (Gurr, 2019). More recently, research illustrates the potential of educational infrastructure to support teachers' job-embedded professional learning (Shirrell et al., 2019; Lillejord & Børte, 2019) but has not articulated how these translate into holistic school-based designs (see Bryant & Walker, 2022). In our study, the Cascade model enacted formal policies and procedures, utilized layers of leadership and team roles, and articulated supportive routines and tools to create an intentional structure. Importantly, the design was linked to specific school agendas, with SLs playing the key roles of designing the models' parameters, sustaining its enactment, and building layered connections.

The SLs were intentional about educational infrastructure designs that were linked to context and key school goals. This places teacher and leader development as core, connected facets of organizational redesign (Day et al., 2011) rather than as peripheral or *ad hoc* activities (Gurr, 2019; Lipscombe et al., 2023). The cascade model involved formal role redesigns, connections to the performance appraisal framework, the development of overarching policies, and routines to intentionally influence professional interactions. Accordingly, SLs invested energy in designing, connecting, and energizing the models rather than providing support for all MLs individually. While the model served to explicitly develop leadership capacity with responsibilities for professional learning increasingly being devolved to different MLs, our SNA analysis showed a direct and crucial set of interactions among principals and teachers as essential to providing clarity around meeting capacity-building targets. We infer that while such designs may indeed lift some direct development activities and interactions from SLs (as observed by the secondary school principal), their involvement in both formal (appraisal, career-pathways) and informal advising remains essential.

Supporting Middle Leader Capacity

The Cascade model provided highly structured support for middle leadership development and teachers' professional learning. The model offers a potential leadership pipeline whereby MLs at different tiers and some teacher leaders have opportunity to lead with close support from experienced leaders. This was partially facilitated by utilizing the formative facets of performance appraisal (connecting MLs to teachers) while separating it from summative evaluation (connecting SLs to teachers). Our SNA findings corroborate this analysis by demonstrating shifts in advising ties; ML-teacher ties were more strongly represented in improving teaching and learning, with SL-teacher ties skewed toward capacity building. This indicates that teachers distinguish among middle and senior leadership roles. Further, the distinct leadership practices enacted by different tiers of MLs with teachers show how deliberate designs can position MLs as key builders of instructional and leadership capacity. The MLs work in partnership with SLs rather than just conduits of information (Bennett et al., 2007).

Layered Infrastructure

While the design opened opportunities to lead, it also incorporated specific activities, such as coaching, modeling, and guided reflection. Although noted in the literature (Irvine & Brundrett, 2017; Lipscombe et al., 2023), such leadership activities tend not to fall within intentional, holistic models that articulate educational infrastructure in layers of practice and interrelationships driven by school priorities. The cascade model reinforces the potential of embedded capacity building and affirms that educational infrastructure supports *in-situ* learning and successful reform (Bryant et al., 2020; Shirrell et al., 2019; Spillane et al., 2018). It supports research findings that effective leaders focus on constructing conditions and educational infrastructure that builds capacity (Parise and Spillane, 2010) while showing how MLs share influence and responsibility for this. Thus, an investment in designs that maximize professional interactions evidently pays off in terms of building capacity across the school.

Whilst the SNA, albeit partially representative, suggests that such designs focus interactions among teachers and layers of leaders, this model showed limited interdisciplinary engagement. This was true among PCs and SACs. The strong vertical interactions, as opposed to horizontal, may reflect the uniqueness of a design that emphasizes capacity development and the developmental stage of the school, which had only recently identified instructional capacity development as a core need. However, our other research indicates that subtle changes to educational infrastructures, such as ML's role definition, and team membership, purposes, and routines, can shift interactions from disciplinary to cross-curricular orientations (Bryant et al., 2020). Other infrastructure models may be better positioned to facilitate such an aim (Bryant & Walker, 2022).

Potential of Mixed Methods for Understanding Principal-Led Structures

This study utilized interview data to model the design and flow of educational infrastructure for instructional and capacity building. Concurrently conducted SNA further interrogated the interrelationships of participants represented in the model. As such, this study makes several contributions. First, research that couples qualitative interview and SN analyses is rare in the literature, as is analyzing in-service learning through social network data (Van Waes et al., 2016). This study contributes to that nascent corpus. Second, the study further illustrates the potential of one method addressing the others' limitations. For instance, whereas qualitative data permit explication of the nature of interactions among participants in defined roles, the SNA indicates the relative density of interactions among different tiers of leaders and teachers in the model. At times this yielded surprising results, which suggested a second look at the qualitative data, such as the scarcity of horizontal ties among MLs. Reciprocally, the depth of the qualitative data may compensate for the low SNA response rates by detailing the nature of measured interactions. The deliberate intention of the secondary school principal to model practices to PCs who in turn modeled them to SACs is a case in point. This helps to explain the model's strong vertical orientation toward capacity building. Third, the research points to the potential of deliberate *pre-hoc* designs that take a holistic vantage toward linking educational infrastructure to capacity development. While the qualitative data construct the model, the SNA provides insight into the relative density of interactions provided for different tiers. Finally, as evidenced by the SNA, principals and heads of schools who intentionally construct such designs and play active, ongoing roles in their enactment positively influence interaction levels and ML development. This finding supports the notion that effective distributed leadership requires strong principal leadership.

Acknowledgments

We thank Mr. Wong Yiu Lun for his support as Senior Research Assistant. We acknowledge funding support from IB Research.

References

Bennett, N., Woods, P., Wise, C., & Newton, W. (2007). Understandings of middle leadership in secondary schools: A review of empirical research. *School Leadership & Management*, 27(5), 453–70.

Bryant, D. A. (2019). Conditions that support middle leaders' work in organizational and system leadership: Hong Kong case studies. *School Leadership & Management*, 39(5), 415–33.

Bryant, D. A., & Walker, A. (2021). School designs that enhance leadership capacity. *Australian Educational Leader*, 43(2), 24–8.

Bryant, D. A., & Walker, A. (2022). Principal-designed structures that enhance middle leaders' professional learning. *Educational Management Administration & Leadership*, 1–20. https://doi.org/10.1177%2F17411432221084154.

Bryant, D. A., Wong, Y. L., & Adames, A. (2020). How middle leaders support in-service teachers' on-site professional learning. *International Journal of Educational Research*, 100(1), 101530.

Clifton, A., & Webster, G. D. (2017). An introduction to social network analysis for personality and social psychologists. *Social Psychological and Personality Science*, 8(4), 442–53.

Cohen, D. K., Spillane, J. P., & Peurach, D. J. (2018). The dilemmas of educational reform. *Educational Researcher*, 47(3), 204–12.

Daly, A. J. (2010). Mapping the terrain: Social network theory and educational change. In Daly, A. J. (Eds.), *Social network theory and educational change* (pp. 1–16). Cambridge, MA: Harvard Education Press.

Day, C., Sammons, P., Leithwood, K., Hopkins, D., Gu, Q., Brown, E., & Ahtaridou, E. (2011). *Successful school leadership: Linking with learning and achievement*. Berkshire, England: Open University Press.

DeNobile, J. (2019). The roles of middle leaders in schools: Developing a conceptual framework for research. *Leading and Managing*, 25, 1–14.

Edwards, G. (2010). *Mixed Methods Approaches to Social Networks Analysis (Rev. Pap. NCRM/015)*. Southampton, England: ESRC National Centre for Research Methods. https://eprints.ncrm.ac.uk/id/eprint/842

Gorard, S., & Taylor, C. (2004). *Combining methods in educational and social research*. Maidenhead: Open University Press.

Guetterman, T. C., Fetters, M. D., & Creswell, J. W. (2015). Integrating quantitative and qualitative results in health science mixed methods research through joint displays. *Annals of Family Medicine*, *13*(6), 554–61.

Gurr, D. (2019). School middle leaders in Australia, Chile and Singapore. *School Leadership and Management*, *39*, 278–96.

Irvine, P. A., & Brundrett, M. (2017). Negotiating the next step: The part that experience plays with middle leaders' development as they move into their new role. *Educational Management Administration & Leadership*, *47*, 74–90.

Kwok, N., Hanig, S., Brown, D. J., & Shen, W. (2018). How leader role identity influences the process of leader emergence: A social network analysis. *The Leadership Quarterly*, *29*(6), 648–62.

Leithwood, K., Harris, A., & Hopkins, D. (2020). Seven strong claims about successful school leadership revisited. *School Leadership & Management*, *40*(1), 5–22.

Lillejord, S., & Børte, K. (2019). Middle leaders and the teaching profession: Building intelligent accountability from within. *Journal of Educational Change*, *21*, 83–107.

Lima, J. Á. (2010). Studies of networks in education: Methods for collecting and managing high-quality data. In Daly, A. J. (Eds.), *Social network theory and educational change* (pp. 243–58). Cambridge, Mass: Harvard Education Press.

Lipscombe, K., Tindall-Ford, S., & Grootenboer, P. (2020). Middle leading and influence in two Australian schools. *Educational Management Administration & Leadership*, *48*(6), 1063–79.

Lipscombe, K., Tindall-Ford, S., & Lamanna, J. (2023). School middle leadership: A systematic review. *Educational Management Administration & Leadership*, *51*(2), 270–88.

Moolenaar, N. (2012). A social network perspective on teacher collaboration in schools: Theory, methodology, and applications. *American Journal of Education*, *119*(1), 7–39.

Parise, L. M., & Spillane, J. P. (2010). Teacher learning and instructional change: How formal and on-the-job learning opportunities predict change in elementary school teachers' practice. *The Elementary School Journal*, *110*, 323–46.

Patton, M. Q. (2002). *Qualitative research & evaluation methods*. Thousand Oaks, CA: Sage Publications, Inc.

Prell, C. (2012). *Social network analysis: History, theory & methodology*. London: Sage Publications.

Robins, G., Pattison, P., & Woolcock, J. (2004). Missing data in networks: Exponential random graph (p*) models for networks with non-respondents. *Social Networks*, *26*(3), 257–83.

Shirrell, M., Hopkins, M., & Spillane, J. P. (2019). Educational infrastructure, professional learning, and changes in teachers' instructional practices and beliefs. *Professional Development in Education*, *45*, 599–613.

Spillane, J. P., & Coldren, A. (2011). *Diagnosis and design for school improvement: Using a distributed perspective to lead and manage change*. New York: Teachers College Press.

Spillane, J. P., Hopkins, M., & Sweet, T. M. (2018). School district educational infrastructure and change at scale: Teacher peer interactions and their beliefs about mathematics instruction. *American Educational Research Journal*, *55*(3), 532–71.

Thurlings, M., Evers, A. T., & Vermeulen, M. (2015). Toward a model of explaining teachers' innovative behavior: A literature review. *Review of Educational Research*, *85*(3), 430–71.

Van Waes, S., Moolenaar, N. M., Daly, A. J., Heldens, H. H. P. F., Donche, V., Van Petegem, P., & Van den bossche, P. (2016). The networked instructor: The quality of networks in different stages of professional development. *Teaching and Teacher Education, 59,* 295–308.

Walker, A. (2012). Leaders seeking resonance: Managing the connectors that bind schools. *International Journal of Leadership in Education, 15*(2), 237–53, DOI: 10.1080/13603124.2011.626079

Williams, T. A., & Shepherd, D. A. (2017). Mixed method social network analysis: Combining inductive concept development, content analysis, and secondary data for quantitative analysis. *Organizational Research Methods, 20*(2), 268–98. https://doi.org/10.1177/1094428115610807.

Yousefi Nooraie, R., Sale, J. E. M., Marin, A., & Ross, L. E. (2020). Social network analysis: An example of fusion between quantitative and qualitative methods. *Journal of Mixed Methods Research, 14*(1), 110–24.

Part 4

System-Wide Leadership Networks

Competition to Cross-School Collaboration: A Social Network Perspective of Local System Leadership in England

Sotiria Kanavidou and Christopher Downey

Introduction

Recent policies and research literature have acknowledged the influential role of Professional Learning Networks as an enriched collaborative learning environment that has the potential to enhance capacity-building between schools and thereby the quality of education (DfE, 2010; Hubers & Poortman, 2018). There is a growing recognition that networking and collaboration in PLNs can support educators to exchange innovative ideas and resources with external partners (e.g., other schools) in order to enhance teaching practice and students' learning (Chapman, 2016; Hargreaves, 2018). Collaboration among school leaders in a PLN has been found to influence different aspects of professional practice, such as the analysis and use of students' data in informing improvement initiatives (Schildkamp et al., 2018; Van Gasse et al., 2017). Engaging in collaboration beyond school boundaries can generate a sense of collective commitment in improving not merely the individual school's capabilities but the professional development opportunities of school staff across the PLN (Brown et al., 2020; Ehren & Godfrey, 2017; Varga-Atkins et al., 2010).

The empirical research surrounding the functioning of PLNs is relatively sparse. It requires the use of methodologies that can capture how resources are mobilized across boundaries in the system through a network of interpersonal relations (e.g., Azorin et al., 2020; Brown & Flood, 2019). The use of network analysis techniques and associated metrics may facilitate the focus on the role played by relational networks. To respond to this paucity of research, Sinnema et al. (2020) utilized Social Network Analysis (SNA) to examine how collaboration networks among school leaders can provide them with access to professional expertise. Their findings revealed that SNA constitutes an innovative analytical approach to map the structural features that may facilitate or impede the flow of resources (e.g., know-how, innovative practices) across a PLN, revealing the relational processes that promote or hinder educational improvement. However, we have a more limited understanding of the way social ties (relations) develop between school leaders across multiple areas of practice, as well as the factors that may affect school leaders' actions in initiating these collaborative ties. In a changing educational community of multiple relations, it seems a reasonable assumption to expect tie creation based on formal and informal (e.g., friendship) aspects, as well as relational (e.g., competition), cognitive (e.g., self-efficacy), and personal (e.g., work-experience) characteristics (Daly, 2010). In this line, recent studies suggest that sustainable inter-school partnerships require the contribution of multiple actors in the collaborative improvement effort, although, prior studies have merely concentrated on the professional networks of head teachers (Coldron et al., 2014) or teachers (Moolenaar et al., 2014). A limited number of studies examined the role of school leaders across different leadership levels (e.g., middle leaders) in brokering professional development opportunities across PLNs (Finnigan et al., 2021; Hadfield, 2007).

We examine the social networks of one PLN, a formal network of five schools in the South of England that already work in close partnership with one another. Specifically, we pay attention to interactions across the PLN that involve collaboration on a) teaching and learning and b) analysis of students' data and c) designing/refining professional development activities for staff. We also collect friendship networks in order to better adjust for trust between leaders in our analysis of these professional networks (Downey, 2018; Liou et al., 2017). To conceptualize the research, the study draws upon social capital and social network theory, given the intention to further understand the structural and attitudinal mechanisms that may account for features in the network of relations that spans across the schools in the PLN.

The purpose of the study is to examine the structural characteristics of school leaders' collaboration networks across a PLN in England. In addition, the study aims to examine whether the presence of professional ties between school leaders is related to competition, self-efficacy, work experience, and friendship.

The research questions of the study are as follows:

RQ1. Within the context of the PLN, what are the structural properties of school leaders' collaborative networks in the areas of learning and teaching, use of data and professional development?

RQ2. In networks related to learning and teaching, use of data and professional development, to what extent is the presence of collaborative ties between school leaders associated with competition, self-efficacy, work experience and friendship?

The review of the literature will first provide a brief overview of the study's theoretical background, the dimensions of inter-school collaboration and the role of competition, self-efficacy, work experience, and friendship in the formation of social networks. We follow with a discussion of the methodology and findings to answer the study's research questions.

Literature Review

School Leaders Networking and Collaboration within a PLN

Research on school-to-school collaboration and the development of shared practice among school leaders in a PLN increasingly focuses on social interactions as a means for leveraging reform (Brown, 2020; Liou & Daly, 2020). PLNs are considered to be dynamic social contexts where school practitioners can access, make use of, or mobilize resources (e.g., materials, innovative strategies) that emerge from social relations in order to generate improvement (Armstrong et al., 2021; Hargreaves, 2018; Rincón-Gallardo & Fullan, 2016). Thus, the professional learning of school leaders in a PLN cannot be examined as an individualized process, but rather as an interpersonal practice that emerges from a web of social interactions (Brown & Poortman, 2018).

Both social capital theory and social network theory are increasingly used as theoretical underpinnings to explain the processes and structures that support professional learning in a PLN (e.g., Chapman et al., 2016; Liou & Daly, 2014). Lin (2001) defines social capital as "the resources embedded in social relations and social structure which can be mobilized when an actor wishes to increase the likelihood of success in purposive action" (p. 24). Adapting Lin's definition in the present context, school leaders interact and exchange knowledge and information through collaborative networks that potentially generate attitudinal and behavioral change (Daly, 2010). These channels can be created through formal (collaboration) or informal (e.g., friendship) connections (Carolan, 2013). Prior studies confirmed that social capital can enhance leadership capacity (Spillane & Kim, 2012), teaching quality (Daly & Stoll, 2018), and organizational innovativeness (Diaz-Gibson et al., 2014) in PLNs.

Social network theory emphasizes the importance of these patterns of social relations (network structure) in leveraging social capital across the PLN (Burt, 1992). Network theorists and research scholars advocated that this pattern of collaborative relationships and the exchange (or not) of resources can influence the behaviors and beliefs of entities (e.g., individuals, groups) (e.g., Coleman, 1990; Daly et al., 2015). In fact, Daly (2010) recommended a distinction between endogenous and exogenous mechanisms that may affect tie creation. Endogenous mechanisms aim to explain the development of ties based on structural effects of the network (e.g., reciprocity). Exogenous mechanisms explain external factors that may affect the tie formation, such as personal characteristics and other network effects (e.g., friendship). We are interested to examine this interaction between endogenous (outdegree; tie development) and exogenous mechanisms that may affect networking and collaboration.

Forms of Collaboration within PLN

The emergence of the school networking movement provided an increasing number of evidence of how collaboration across schools can promote the effectiveness of schooling and subsequently student capabilities (Greany, 2015; Hopkins, 2016; Leithwood & Azah, 2016). School leaders' collaboration with other colleagues across a PLN provides them the opportunity to access resources (e.g., knowledge, materials) that other individuals and groups maintain, promoting collaborative inquiry and teaching quality (Daly & Stoll, 2018).

Collaboration among school leaders in a PLN can develop to take different forms. For instance, Daly et al., (2010) focused on educators' professional networks in learning and teaching. The authors concluded that high-density networks enhanced educators' sense of groupness and organizational innovativeness and subsequently their participation in the decision-making. In one more case, Varga-Atkins et al. (2010) utilized a large-scale survey and semi-structured interviews with different stakeholders across a PLN to capture the potential of networked collaboration in improving the professional practice of educators. Their participants reported that they benefited from innovative professional development opportunities and the culture of collective professional learning across the partnership. In his think pieces, Hargreaves (2010, 2011, 2012) underscored the importance of joined professional practice among network members in securing the sustainability of the PLN. In addition, Sinnema et al. (2020) focused on the use of data networks across a PLN in New Zealand. In line with Daly's argument, their findings supported that the structure of social interactions between and among school practitioners may place some individuals in a prominent place in accessing resources and improving their professional practice. Thus, the success with which innovative professional practice and expertise are shared and utilized in a PLN relies on system leaders that share insights about their practices across school boundaries and help each other make sense of the innovative practice (Hopkins, 2016). While, in terms of informal relations, friendship networks can be a useful aid of personal support and interpersonal trust, thereby a facilitator for the exchange of innovative ideas between educational actors (Steglich et al., 2010). Different measures of the characteristics of social networks may provide insights into how collaboration can accomplish those functions (Borgatti et al., 2018).

Competition, Self-Efficacy, and Work-Experience

National and international policies and programs tend to encourage competition and inter-school collaboration in order to increase schools' innovativeness and performance (Milward & Provan, 2006; Pino-Yancovic et al., 2019; Sandals & Bryant, 2014). The English educational system constitutes the precursor of collaborative improvement efforts since the government initiated numerous programs (e.g., The Extended Schools, 2006) and structures (e.g., federations) to "secure 'buy-in' from parents, teachers and other stakeholders since these are essential for legitimacy" within the marketized educational context (Greany, 2018, p. 66). The publication of the 2010 White Paper and the Blueprint for a Self-Improving School (Cruddas, 2015; DfE, 2010) crystalized internally driven reform, combining autonomy with accountability. Armstrong and Ainscow (2018) and Muijs and Rumyantseva (2014) aimed to articulate how educational institutions can help one another to improve their capabilities and capitalize on the benefits of clusters of schools within an educational context that promotes competition. The authors emphasized the need for expertise exchange as the driving force that motivates school leaders to engage in collective decision-making. By contrast, in network terms, Burt (2002) explained that competition between different/

disconnected groups tends to limit the development of ties and hinders the groups' access to external expertise. Therefore, the dynamics of competition could affect collaborative activity in the current context.

In line with the above characteristics, self-efficacy (sense of efficacy) has been studied excessively in educational settings as a factor that affects teachers' collaboration and interdependency in social relationships (Kurz & Knight, 2004; Moolenaar et al., 2011). A limited number of studies have introduced the notion of self-efficacy in the field of educational leadership, examining leader efficacy in school organizational settings and how leaders' attitudes concerning their own ability to learn and lead are associated with successful reform efforts (Daly et al., 2015; Leithwood & Jantzi, 2008). Liou and Daly's (2020) social network findings revealed that school leaders who reported higher levels of self-efficacy actively engaged in policy implementation and reform efforts, compared to their less efficacious colleagues.

In addition, prior studies found that demographic characteristics such as work experience affect professional relationships. Utilizing network data and tools, Daly and colleagues (Daly et al., 2014; Daly et al., 2015) found that school leaders' work experience increased their confidence in "sending" professional ties. Moolenaar et al., (2014) explained that educators that work for many years in education may have acquired advanced knowledge which in turn affects their tendency in developing collaborative ties with colleagues.

The study aims to understand the connection between the presence of collaborative ties and these characteristics.

Methodology

Research Design and Setting

A case study design incorporating network data generated using questionnaires was adopted to capture the professional network interactions of a PLN: the Lakeside PLN. Case study designs allow the investigation of real-life situations, including group behaviors, beliefs, and interactions (Yin, 2017) such as those taking place in a PLN context. The current case study focused on five schools that comprise a formal PLN in the South of England. The Lakeside educates approximately 4000 students.

The member schools represent both primary, secondary, six form, and special education sectors suggesting a diversity of contexts and patterns of interactions in the present PLN. In fact, from 2017, when the Lakeside was funded, till today Ofsted[1] inspection reports reflected improved outcomes, across areas such as student progress and quality of teaching. Lakeside has also developed a diagnostic hub to better manage data of the organization, including data of pupils in need, their well-being, attainment, and behavior, in order to increase the quality of the provision that can be provided. Meanwhile, school leaders across the Lakeside design innovative professional development activities to increase the effectiveness of schooling. Finally, the Lakeside presents an innovative model of system leadership as some senior and middle school leaders are appointed to work across the partnership, rather than in a single school, promoting shared vision and practice. As such, this PLN serves as an exceptional case to understand network dynamics.

Participants

Due to the study's interest in school leaders' social roles across different leadership positions in developing social ties and mobilizing social capital within this PLN, the study includes all the certified staff members that hold a formal leadership position. Prior studies suggest that network census provides a more valid understanding of network dynamics (such as levels of connectivity), reducing potential bias because of misleading network boundary specifications (Kossinets, 2006; Žnidaršič, et al., 2018). All 153 middle, senior, and executive level leaders across the five schools were invited to participate. The response rate was 76 percent. Accumulative evidence suggests that a 75 percent response rate or greater can increase the researchers' confidence regarding the reliable interpretation of network interactions (e.g., Borgatti et al., 2018; Daly & Liou, 2020).

Based on the participants' main role in the network, the sample comprised of Members of the Executive (N=11), Secondary Senior Leadership Team (SLT) (N=21), Primary SLT (N=3), Middle Leaders (N=62), Support Staff (N=16), Special Provision SLT (N=4). The majority of the participants were females (64 percent), and forty-two of them were males. When the data collection started, participants have been working in their current position of responsibility for an average 4.17 years (SD 4.14), in the current school for 9.66 years (SD 9.43), and as educators for 14.61 years (SD 8.67).

Procedure

The data of the study were collected during May 2021. An online cross-sectional network survey was administrated via emails to identify the different social and professional relationships developed by school leaders within this larger cross-school network. The study's design was reviewed and approved by the University's Research Committee. The participants were informed about the study's purposes, process, and ethical concerns and they were asked to provide their informed consent at the beginning of the survey. The duration of the survey was 30 minutes.

Data Collection and Analysis

For the network data, the school leaders of the study were asked to assess the frequency of interactions from a list of their colleagues with whom they collaborate around a) teaching and learning, b) use of data, c) designing/refining professional development activities for teachers, on a 4-point Likert type scale from 1 (a few times per year) to 4 (daily). These questions had a common stem "During the last six months with whom did you collaborate." To define the network questions and secure the validity of the results we drew evidence from empirical studies concerning inter-school collaboration and collaborative improvement efforts (Armstrong & Ainscow, 2018; Greany, 2018) and social network studies (Daly & Finnigan, 2010; Rodway et al., 2021; Sinnema et al., 2020). The network questions were piloted with three school leaders that work in similar contexts to enhance the likelihood of collecting reliable data.

The bounded/saturated strategy of name presentation (a fixed choice name generating roster), as opposed to free choice, was chosen in order to reduce memory bias and subsequently increase the validity of the results (Scott, 2012). For the data analysis, we selected interactions that occur more often (i.e., monthly to daily). For the friendship networks, school leaders were asked which of their colleagues they considered to be a personal friend. A set of demographic characteristics were examined. The networks were scored on a dichotomous scale (1 = presence of a tie, 0 = absence of a tie).

Self-efficacy (sixteen items, α = 0.92) was assessed utilizing a modified version of the Leadership Efficacy Scale initially designed by Tschannen-Moran and Gareis (2004) and validated by Daly et al., (2015) that examines the perceptions of efficacy for instructional improvement. The efficacy scale comprised of sixteen items with a common stem, "In your current role as a leader, to what extent can you ... generate enthusiasm for a shared vision?" Responses for each item were based on a 9-point Likert scale (1= Not at all to 9 = A great deal).

Competition (thirteen items, α = 0.97) was examined using a scale that was developed based on previous studies (Helmreich et al., 1978; Wang, Wang & Liu et al., 2018) and adapted in the current context. Examples of the items are "I enjoy working in situations involving competition with others" and "It is important for me to perform better than others on a task." Participants responded to each item on a 6-point Likert scale (1 = "strongly disagree" to 6= strongly agree).

In the present context, the psychometric properties of the competition scale were accessed using principal component analysis (PCA) and the Oblimin with Kaiser Normalization method. The component analysis yielded a single-factor solution which explained 72.5 percent of the common variance. The "Competition" factor included the thirteen items, yielding loadings from 0.90 to 0.76 and the internal reliability of Cronbach α was 0.97. Appendix 9.A presents the factor loadings of the competition scale.

The NetDraw software (Borgatti, 2002) was used to visualize the networks in the form of network graphs. The UCINET 6.0 software package (Borgatti et al., 2002) was used to calculate a series of metrics at a whole network (PLN level) and group level. The whole-network level analysis included density (assesses the number of existing ties compared to the possible maximum number of ties across the bounded context), reciprocity (assesses the number of mutual ties), fragmentation (assesses the network disconnectedness), and centralization measures to understand the overall connectivity of the PLN. To examine the diversity of leaders' networks, the External and Internal (E-I) index was calculated at a group level. This measure assesses whether school leaders interact with actors in their school/group (internal tie-I) or other schools or/and groups (External tie-E). Krackhardt and Stem (1998) explained that the E-I index receives values between +1 (indicates only external ties, heterogeneity) and −1 (indicates only internal ties, homophily).

Additionally, a multiple regression[2] was employed to answer the second research question. Considering the study's focus on factors that affect tie presence among school leaders, the actor outdegree was used as the dependent variable which refers to school leaders' activity in developing ("sending") professional ties. However, the independent variables were as follows: (a) the sum of participants' responses about competition and self-efficacy, (b) the dyadic interactions about friendship, and (c) school leaders' work experience in education. Due to the fact that school leaders are nested within the same school or group and PLN, the assumption regarding the independence of observations is violated. To address this issue, the study utilizes quadratic assignment procedures that use permutation tests to control the context's interdependence (Krackhardt, 1988). In addition, the collinearity of the three network relations was assessed, using the Quadratic Assignment Procedure (QAP). The correlations among the network structures were weak to medium, yielding values from .28 to .52. This finding suggests that the learning and teaching, use of data, and professional development relations represent different concepts and therefore we can proceed with the analysis.

Findings

RQ1: Within the Context of the PLN, What Are the Structural Properties of School Leaders' Collaborative Networks in The Areas of Learning and Teaching, Use of Data and Professional Development?

The study focused on learning and teaching, use of data, and professional development collaborative relations. Table 9.1 presents cohesion measures for the present case. The learning and teaching professional network indicated the highest density, which shows that 5 percent of the maximum possible collaborative ties have been developed among school leaders. The density scores of the networks regarding the use of data and professional development were lower, yielding values of 2.7 percent and 1.6 percent, respectively, indicating that professional activity across these areas of practice is relatively sparse compared to prior studies concerning inter-school collaboration (Rodway et al., 2021; Sinnema et al., 2020). Centrality scores suggest that the knowledge and resource exchange through collaborative ties around learning and teaching (0.660) depends on a limited number of school leaders who seem to act as "source of knowledge," in comparison with the use of data and professional development, where the "know how" is almost equally distributed among the school leaders.

As Table 9.1 shows, the degree of fragmentation varied across the three networks. Based on fragmentation scores, these three network structures seem to have disconnected parts, considering that 46–74 percent of school leaders work in isolation which in turn can hinder the successful implementation of educational reforms. In terms of the network's reciprocity, the learning and teaching network indicated the lowest reciprocity (0.13), a score that revealed that one out of every ten ties in the learning and teaching network was mutual. The reciprocity scores of the use of data and professional development were higher, suggesting that two out of ten ties were mutual. Despite the variations and differences among the three relations, the findings highlight the need for coordinated efforts to support school leaders to diagnose the potentials of their networks and build collaborative patterns that allow the leverage of social capital across the PLN.

Table 9.1 Cohesion measures for the professional learning network

	Learning and Teaching	Use of Data	Professional Development
Number of ties	1170	628	378
Centralization	0.657	0.177	0.133
Network Density	0.050	0.027	0.016
Reciprocity	0.134	0.261	0.228
Fragmentation	0.462	0.576	0.741

Figure 9.1 presents network visualizations for these three professional relations. The visualizations show that Executive (circles) and Senior leaders (square) have an active role in initiating ties and bridging otherwise disconnected parts of the PLN (boxes; middle leaders).

Due to the increased recognition of the potential of inter-school collaboration, and the transition from within-school networking (i.e., collaborating with colleagues that work in the same school, Internal) to inter-school partnerships (i.e., collaborating with colleagues that work in another school, External) an External-Internal (E-I) index was calculated for each of the schools/sites in the PLN (see Table 9.2). The positive values of the E-I revealed that collaboration among schools/sites in the PLN is largely heterogeneous. More specifically, the learning and teaching network presents a disposition toward external ties (E-I= 0.167, p.=.000). In addition, the use of data and professional development networks exhibited positive values (E-I= 0.133 and 0.101, p.=.000, respectively), indicating a tenable level of boundary spanning across schools/sites. Considering that the E-I scores are affected by network size (i.e., number of leaders in the group), the more secure comparison between sub-groups is the comparison between groups having the same size. For instance, intra-group collaboration in Secondary School A may allow resource exchange between sixty-five school leaders. However, the two primary schools might have fewer opportunities to access internal knowledge, developing as a result, external connections to increase their capacity (n=6 and 5). Therefore, the re-scaled E-I was used.

Table 9.2 presents the E-I scores based on participants' site in the PLN.

Considering the increasing interest of research and practice in understanding school leaders' social role across different leadership positions in brokering social capital within the PLN, we calculated the E-I index for each of the roles across the leadership teams. Table 9.3 shows that the learning and teaching network (E-I= 360, p. 000) is highly heterogeneous and less homogenous compared to the networks regarding the use of data (E-I= 273, p. 000) and professional development (E-I= 232, p. 000). Senior leaders seem to have a strong tendency in developing external ties. Middle leaders have indicated a combination of internal and external ties, yielding values close to 0. Considering the two tables, as well as the figures above, it can be

Competition to Cross-School Collaboration

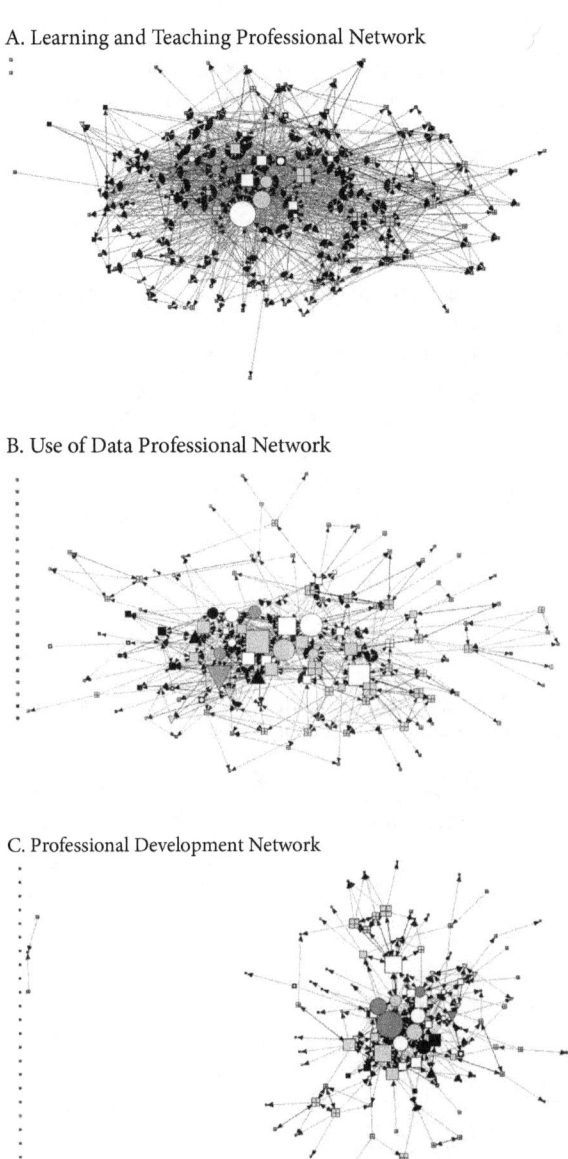

Figure 9.1 Network visualizations for three professional relations.

Note. The size of the nodes indicates outdegree centrality; the greater number of sending/outgoing ties, the greater the node size. The shape of the nodes illustrates school leaders' role in the partnership; circle: Members of the Executive, square: Secondary SLT, Up Triangle: Primary SLT, circle in a box: Special/Alternative Provision SLT, Box: Middle Leaders, Down Triangle: Central Services Officers. The colour of the nodes indicates the main school/site that the participants belong; Light grey: Secondary School, Black: Primary school; White: Cross-Network Leaders, Dark Grey: Central Officers and Central Services. The colour of ties indicates reciprocal (thick black) or non-reciprocal (thin grey) interactions.

argued that senior leaders that work across the Lakeside (e.g., orange circle) seem to have a prominent role in connecting parts of the organization by "sending" professional ties. Similarly, support staff that work for the organization rather than the school seem to have a strong tendency toward external ties. Overall, school leaders across different schools/sites and roles develop intra-school collaboration relationships that enable bonding of social capital, as well as inter-school interactions that facilitate access to innovative ideas and form an innovative model of system leadership.

RQ2: To What Extent Does Collaboration about Learning and Teaching, Use of Data Professional Development between School Leaders Relate to Years of Work Experience, Friendship, Self-Efficacy, and Competition?

The second research question of the study was to examine the degree to which school leaders' outdegree was associated with competition, self-efficacy, work experience, and friendship. Out-degree represents school leaders' actions in "sending" collaborative ties, which can be considered the basis of strategic synergies and collective improvement. The findings (see Table 9.4) revealed that competition was significantly and positively associated with school leaders' outdegree across the three areas of practice, explaining 10–13 percent of the variance. This finding suggests that school leaders who perceive their working environment to be competitive are

Table 9.2 E-I index for the learning and teaching, professional development and use of data professional networks based on the participants' school/site

	Learning and Teaching	Use of Data	Professional Development
Secondary School A (n=65)	−0.185	−0.204	−0.288
Secondary School B (n=36)	0.004	−0.030	−0.061
Primary School A (n=5)	0.360	0.586	0.289
Primary School B (n=6)	0.319	0.304	0.179
Cross-Network Leaders (n=22)	0.472	0.400	0.169
Executive Officers (n=3)	0.925	0.862	0.826
Central Services (n=16)	0.708	1.000	0.368
Alternative Provision Unit (n=6)	0.390	0.048	0.077
Network Overall (n=117)	0.167	0.133	0.101

Table 9.3 E-I index for the learning and teaching, professional development and use of data professional networks based on the participants' role

	Learning and Teaching	Use of Data	Professional Development
Members of the Exec (n=11)	0.612	0.550	0.314
Secondary SLT (n=21)	0.375	0.196	0.145
Primary SLT (n=3)	0.871	0.900	0.800
Special Provision SLT (n=4)	0.605	0.419	0.444
Middle Leaders (n=62)	0.075	0.066	0.029
Support Staff (n=16)	0.681	1.000	0.913
Network Overall	0.361	0.273	0.232

more likely to develop collaborative ties with colleagues. In practice, this finding reflects that collaboration and competition co-exist in English school leaders' interactions. In this line, self-efficacy was significantly and positively associated with school leaders' activity in developing collaborative ties with colleagues. School leaders who reported higher self-efficacy tended to develop a greater number of outgoing ties.

Similarly, the study revealed that school leaders who were working in education for more years tended to develop more outgoing ties. In practice, school leaders that work for several years in education may have acquired the knowledge and practices to successfully construct outgoing ties, in order to leverage reform. While, friendship was a significant and positive predictor of school leaders' outdegree regarding the use of data and professional development, highlighting the influence of informal relations in collaborative activity. However, friendship was negatively and significantly associated with the development of outgoing ties around learning and teaching. In this respect, friendship can be perceived as an indicator of personal support or interpersonal trust.

Discussion

From Competition to Inter-School Collaboration

The study's findings revealed that competition positively affected the actors' activity in developing collaborative ties with colleagues. Prior studies discussed that

Table 9.4 Regression analysis

Variables	Learning and Teaching		Use of Data		Professional Development	
	Unstandardized Coefficients	Standardized Coefficients	Unstandardized Coefficients	Standardized Coefficients	Unstandardized Coefficients	Standardized Coefficients
Intercept	0.222***	–	0.2621***	–	0.168***	–
Competition	0.038***	0.293	0.032***	0.260	0.027***	0.206
Self-efficacy	0.017***	0.209	0.022***	0.233	0.023***	0.271
Work-Experience	0.000***	0.062	0.004**	0.066	0.000***	0.039
Friendship	−0.018***	−0.077	0.057***	0.059	0.023***	0.065
R2	0.175***		0.190***		0.170***	

Note. **$p<0.01$; ***$p<0.001$.

competition constitutes an internal component of the educational practice in English schools, influencing the interactions between schools (Armstrong and Ainscow, 2018; Hopkins, 2016). Muijs and Rumyantseva (2014) explained that the inter-school relations in England seem to combine cooperation and competition, the so-called co-opetition. Hargreaves (2012) noted that competition could enhance school leaders' intention to access innovative ideas and resources in order to increase their capabilities in the education market. Researching these dynamics, Coldron et al., (2014) found that head teachers leading "outstanding" schools impeded to lead the network feeling that their schools were more competitive in the education market. This finding reveals the complexity of inter-school relations and mobilized social capital as well as the need for additional in-depth qualitative data. An increased understanding of these aspects can support school practitioners and policymakers to design activities and programs to invite the educational community in schools and distribute responsibilities, increasing network capabilities and preventing this hierarchical categorization.

Based on the network visualizations, it can be argued that a major component of middle leaders is connected to the networks with a limited number of ties which in turn limits their access to social capital (e.g., innovative ideas). In fact, these ties are directed from senior leaders to their colleagues that work in middle leadership roles. Considering the relatively hierarchical pattern of collaboration and the limited reciprocity in these interactions, it could be assumed that a part of these ties may represent information exchange or monitoring in increasing the teaching quality, the professional development outcomes, and the overall accountability of the Lakeside rather than collaboration. Although the prominent role of senior leaders and the centralized governance is in line with the existing research literature (Ehren & Godfrey, 2017; Greany, 2018), successful collaborative outcomes assume the mutual contribution from both sides (Hargreaves, 2018). Milward and Provan (2006, p. 22) commented that this form of governance "can create a complex governing administration, with increased costs and decreased transparency" where decision-making is mainly concentrated on performance and accountability. Findings from the research can be a useful aid for school leaders to acquire a deeper understanding of the resources available to them and their schools and initiate efforts to distribute responsibilities and support peripheral educators.

Collaborative Patterns and Cross-School Leadership

The density scores revealed that school leaders' professional networks are sparse in comparison to recent empirical studies regarding intra- and inter-group collaboration (e.g., Downey, 2018; Rodway et al., 2021). This finding is consistent with prior studies, such as the ones by Sinnema et al., (2020) and Finnigan et al., (2021) who found that cross-school collaborative networks tend to be sparse which often result in fragmented and highly centralized patterns of collaborative activity. One potential explanation of this finding may be related to the different interpretations and meanings that school leaders can attach to these collaborative relationships. Although we included an explanation for each network question (e.g., examples of student data include internal and external assessment data, attendance, and behavior data), the design or refinement of professional development activities within a PLN, for instance, can include different responsibilities for senior leaders compared to middle leaders. At the same time, Muijs (2015) explained that high density is not always an indicator of sustainable collaborative activity, because high density prevents actors from searching for innovative resources from external collaborators, such as the wider community.

In addition, the high scores of E-I index indicate that inter-school collaboration networks in the present PLN are heterogeneous. Almost all the school sites of the PLN are mobilizing, at least to some extent, social capital across the traditional school boundaries in improving learning and teaching, use of data, and professional development. Drawing evidence from international settings, this finding is inconsistent with Sinnema et al.'s (2020) study who found that collaboration and advice-seeking in a PLN in New Zealand are mainly based on intra-school relations. The present context can provide insights regarding an innovative approach to leadership, considering that school leaders who occupy executive positions and have the formal hierarchy have been assigned to work beyond school boundaries. Cross-Network leaders seem to have a prominent role in shaping the network structure. Much of the existing knowledge on inter-school collaboration draws evidence from formal leaders' reports (Daly et al., 2015). This study can contribute to the existing knowledge by including middle leaders. Findings from the study could be used to expand concepts related to system leadership and may assist governors and school leaders to make more well-informed and well-theorized decisions in organizing professional development opportunities for educators.

Self-Efficacy and Demographic Characteristics

The study found that self-efficacy was positively linked to school leaders' tendency in sending professional ties. In line with the study's findings, previous studies found that self-efficacy is positively associated with increased teaching quality and leadership capacity (Daly & Moolenaar, 2011). At the same time, friendship was positively associated with school leaders' activity in developing synergies about the use of data and professional development. Recent studies suggest that friendship can be perceived as a proxy of trust that seems to initiate voluntary and rewarding interactions (Block, 2015; Daly et al., 2015; Downey, 2018). However, friendship was negatively associated with the presence of ties around learning and teaching. Combining this finding with the discussion above, a potential interpretation could be that the more a school leader trusts a collaborator the less likely they are to monitor their teaching practice. Finally, in line with the study, Moolenaar et al., (2014) and Daly et al., (2015) found that demographic characteristics such as work experience affect professional relationships. To the best of our knowledge, this study is the only one that attempts to capture inter-school collaborative structures at a system level and examines factors that may hinder or facilitate the sustainability of inter-school arrangements. The research will allow a better understanding of how relational, cognitive characteristics, as well as socio-demographic characteristics contribute to variations in the quality of school leaders' professional networks. This information has important implications for the implementation of prevention and intervention programs that attempt to promote collaboration across school arrangements.

Innovative Analytical Approaches

Although several studies have focused on the potential of inter-school collaboration (Azorin, 2020; Brown & Flood, 2019; Chapman et al., 2016), these studies might not use "methods, metrics, and tools grounded in research that can support the measurement of progress and insights for improvement" (Sinnema et al., 2020, p. 13). This study applied network theory and tools to capture how school leaders' collaborative relationships can enhance the flow of social capital and therefore educational improvement. Current English government policies could utilize such evidence to motivate school practitioners to actively engage with research in understanding the potential of their network through the use of research evidence and SNA.

Limitations and Future Research

The present study contributes to the existing knowledge by providing insights into the social structures of a local school partnership in England. However, numerous limitations need to be considered during the interpretation of the research findings revealed. Due to the fact that this design focused on a single case, the generalization of the findings needs to be treated with caution. This PLN was carefully selected based on multiple criteria highlighted in the literature, which suggests that researchers, policymakers, and practitioners could use the findings to inform improvement efforts. This quantitative study draws evidence from well-theorized (e.g., Daly, 2010; Lin, 2010) and empirically justified (Brown et al., 2020) tools and metrics. However, qualitative studies can provide deeper insights into the perspectives of stakeholders in different positions and schools. In addition, existing research in the field suggests that the examination of multiple relations, such as communication and advice-seeking, can provide insights into diverse patterns of collaborative activity. (Liou & Daly, 2018). The cross-sectional orientation of the design allowed the mapping of collaborative structures; however, future studies need to adopt longitudinal designs, aiming to unravel the collaborative dynamics of PLNs. Considering the research findings, school practitioners need to use these network findings to design context-specific improvement efforts.

Appendix

Appendix 9.A Factor loading of the competition scale

Survey Items (a=97)	Factor Loadings
Much of what I have learned about being a good educator came from watching and talking with my peers	0.906
A student's success in the school is a reflection of my own efforts	0.891
It is important for me to perform better than others on a task	0.889
Everybody is concerned with us finishing well in the school performance tables	0.882
I try harder when I am in competition with other people	0.875
I enjoy working in situations involving competition with others	0.874
Everybody is concerned with achieving higher performance than other comparable schools	0.873
In general, generating competition among staff in schools is an effective way to boost performance	0.855
I feel that winning is important in and outside of work	0.848
The amount of recognition you get in this school depends on how your students' performance in tests compares to other schools' students	0.817
The use of student data is an appropriate way to determine staff pay	0.812
My co-workers frequently compare their results with mine	0.776
My Head teacher frequently compares my results with those of other educators	0.754

Notes

1 Office for Standards in Education (Ofsted) is responsible for the inspection of state schools in the UK, evaluating a wide range of areas, such as leadership and teaching quality.
2 The choice of the variables for the regression analysis was based on the literature and is in line with the study's focus on the factors that affect the presence of inter-school synergies. In addition, different models were performed (e.g., focusing on indegree) and the present models were considered to offer the more meaningful results.

References

Armstrong, P. W., & Ainscow, M. (2018). School-to-school support within a competitive education system: views from the inside. *School Effectiveness and School Improvement*, 29(4), 614–33. https://doi.org/10.1080/09243453.2018.1499534

Armstrong, P. W., Brown, C., & Chapman, C. J. (2021). School-to-school collaboration in England: A configurative review of the empirical evidence. *Review of Education*, 9(1), 319–51. https://doi.org/10.1002/rev3.3248

Azorín, C. (2020). Leading networks. *School Leadership & Management*, 40(2–3), 105–10.

Azorín, C., Harris, A., & Jones, M. (2020). Taking a distributed perspective on leading professional learning networks. *School Leadership & Management*, 40(2–3), 111–27. https://doi.org/10.1080/13632434.2019.1647418

Block, P. (2015). Reciprocity, transitivity, and the mysterious three-cycle. *Social Networks*, 40, 163–73. https://doi.org/10.1016/j.socnet.2014.10.005

Borgatti, S. P. (2002). *NetDraw: Graph visualization software*. Harvard: Analytic Technologies.

Borgatti, S. P., Everett, M. G., & Freeman, L. C. (2002). *UCINET 6 for Windows: Software for social network analysis*. Harvard: Analytic Technologies.

Borgatti, S. P., Everett, M. G., & Johnson, J. C. (2018). *Analyzing social networks*. London: Sage Publications.

Brown, C. (2020). *The networked school leader: how to improve teaching and student outcomes using learning networks*. Bingley: Emerald Group Publishing.

Brown, C., & Flood, J. (2019). *Formalise, Prioritise and Mobilise: How school leaders secure the benefits of professional learning networks*. Bingley: Emerald Group Publishing.

Brown, C., & Poortman, C. L. (Eds.). (2018). *Networks for learning: Effective collaboration for teacher, school and system improvement*. New York: Routledge.

Brown, C., Flood, J., Armstrong, P., MacGregor, S., & Chinas, C. (2020). Is distributed leadership an effective approach for mobilising professional capital across professional learning networks? Exploring a case from England. *Journal of Professional Capital and Community*, 6(1), 64–78. https://doi.org/10.1108/JPCC-02-2020-0010

Burt, R. (1992). *Structural holes: The social structure of competition*. Cambridge: Harvard University Press.

Burt, R. S. (2002). The social capital of structural holes. In Guillen, M. F., Collins, R., England, P. & Meyer, M. (Eds.), *The new economic sociology: Developments in an emerging field* (pp. 148–89). New York: Russell Sage Foundation.

Carolan, B. V. (2013). *Social network analysis and education: Theory, methods & applications*. Washington: Sage Publications.

Chapman, C. (2016). Networking for educational equity: rethinking improvement within, between and beyond schools. In Harris, A. & Jones, M. (Eds.), *Leading Futures: Global Perspectives on Educational Leadership*. London: Sage Publications.

Chapman, C., Chestnutt, H., Friel, N., Hall, S., & Lowden, K. (2016). Professional capital and collaborative inquiry networks for educational equity and improvement?. *Journal of Professional Capital and Community*, 1(3), 178–97. 10.1108/JPCC-03-2016-0007

Coldron, J. M., Crawford, M., Jones, S., & Simkins, T. (2014). The restructuring of schooling in England: The responses of well-positioned headteachers'. *Educational Management Administration and Leadership*, 42(3), 387–403. https://doi.org/10.1177/1741143214521592

Coleman, J. S. (1990). *Foundations of social theory*. Cambridge, MA: Belknap Press.

Cruddas, L. (2015). *Leading the way: Blueprint for a self-improving system*. Association of School and College Leaders (ASCL).

Daly, A. J. (2010). *Social Network Theory and Educational Change*. Cambridge, MA: Harvard University Press.

Daly, A. J., & Finnigan, K. S. (2010). A bridge between worlds: Understanding network structure to understand change strategy. *Journal of Educational Change*, 11, 111–38.

Daly, A. J., & Stoll, L. (2018). Looking back and moving forward: where to next for networks of learning? In *Networks for learning* (205–14). Routledge.

Daly, A. J., Moolenaar, N. M., Bolivar, J. M., & Burke, P. (2010). Relationships in reform: The role of teachers' social networks. *Journal of educational administration*, 48(3), 359–91. 10.1108/09578231011041062

Daly, A. J., Moolenaar, N. M., Der-Martirosian, C., & Liou, Y. H. (2014). Accessing capital resources: Investigating the effects of teacher human and social capital on student achievement. *Teachers College Record*, 116(7), 1–42.

Daly, A. J., Moolenaar, N. M., Liou, Y. H., Tuytens, M., & Del Fresno, M. (2015). Why so difficult? Exploring negative relationships between educational leaders: The role of trust, climate, and efficacy. *American Journal of Education*, 122(1), 1–38. https://doi.org/10.1086/683288

Department for Education (2010). *The importance of teaching. Cm 7980*. London: Department of Education. https://assets.publishing.service.gov.uk/government/uploads/system/uploads/attachment_data/file/175429/CM-7980.pdf

Díaz-Gibson, J., Zaragoza, M., & Guàrdia-Olmos, J. (2014). Strengthening education through collaborative networks: Leading the cultural change. *School Leadership & Management*, 34(2), 179–200. https://doi.org/10.1080/13632434.2013.856296

Downey, C. (2018). Utilising social network analysis to identify the estructural features of teachers' knowledge and resource-sharing networks within schools. *Profesorado. Revista de Currículum y Formación de Profesorado*, 22(2), 133–59. http://hdl.handle.net/10481/53095

Ehren, M. C. M. & Godfrey, D. (2017). External accountability of collaborative arrangements: A case study of a multi academy trust in England. *Educational Assessment, Evaluation and Accountability*, 29(4), 339–62.

Finnigan, K. S., Daly, A. J., Caduff, A., & Leal, C. C. (2021). Broken Bridges: The Role of Brokers in Connecting Educational Leaders Around Research Evidence. In *Networks, Knowledge Brokers, and the Public Policymaking Process* (pp. 129–53). Cham: Palgrave Macmillan.

Greany, T. (2015). More fragmented, and yet more networked: Analysing the responses of two local authorities in England to the coalition's self-improving school-led system' reforms. *London Review of Education*, 13(2), 125–43.

Greany, T. (2018). Innovation is possible, it's just not easy: Improvement, innovation and legitimacy in England's autonomous and accountable school system. *Educational Management Administration & Leadership, 46*(1), 65–85. https://doi.org/10.1177/1741143216659297

Hadfield, M. (2007). Co-leaders and middle leaders: The dynamic between leaders and followers in networks of schools. *School Leadership and Management, 27*(3), 259–83. https://doi.org/10.1080/13632430701379552

Hargreaves, D. (2010). *Creating a self-improving school system.* National Council.

Hargreaves, D. (2011). *Leading a self-improving school system.* National Council.

Hargreaves, D. (2012). *End game: A self-improving school system.* National Council.

Hargreaves, A. (2018). "Foreword." In Brown, C., & Poortman, C. L. (Eds.), *Networks for learning, effective collaboration for teacher school and system improvement* (pp. xxi–xxii). Abingdon: Routledge.

Helmreich, R. L., Beane, W., Lucker, G. W., & Spence, J. T. (1978). Achievement motivation and scientific attainment. *Personality and Social Psychology Bulletin, 4*(2), 222–6. https://doi.org/10.1177/014616727800400209

Hopkins, D. (2016). Building capacity for school improvement in multi-academy trusts—from the inside out. *SSAT Journal, 7*, 19–29.

Hubers, M. D., & Poortman, C. L. (2018). Establishing sustainable school improvement through professional learning networks. In *Networks for learning* (194–204). Routledge.

Kossinets, G. (2006). Effects of missing data in social networks. *Social Networks, 28*, 247–68. https://doi.org/10.1016/j.socnet.2005.07.002

Krackhardt, D. (1988). Predicting with networks: Nonparametric multiple regression analysis of dyadic data. *Social Networks, 10*(4), 359–81.

Krackhardt, D., & Stern, R. N. (1988). Informal networks and organizational crises: An experimental simulation. *Social psychology quarterly*, 123–40. https://doi.org/10.2307/2786835

Kurz, T. B., & Knight, S. L. (2004). An exploration of the relationship among teacher efficacy, collective teacher efficacy, and goal consensus. *Learning Environments Research, 7*(2), 111–28. https://doi.org/10.1023/B:LERI.0000037198.37750.0e

Leithwood, K., & Azah, V. N. (2016). Characteristics of effective leadership networks. *Journal of Educational Administration.* 54(4), 409–33 https://doi.org/10.1080/13632434.2018.1470503

Leithwood, K., & Jantzi, D. (2008). Linking leadership to student learning: The contributions of leader efficacy. *Educational Administration Quarterly, 44*(4), 496–528. https://doi.org/10.1177/0013161X08321501

Lin, N. (2001). *Social capital: A theory of social structure and action.* Cambridge University Press.

Liou, Y. H., & Daly, A. J. (2014). Closer to learning: Social networks, trust, and professional communities. *Journal of School Leadership, 24*(4), 753–95.

Liou, Y.-H., & Daly, A. J. (2018). Broken bridges: A social network perspective on urban high school leadership. *Journal of Educational Administration, 56*(5), 562–84. https://doi.org/10.1108/JEA-01-2018-0010

Liou, Y.-H., & Daly, A. J. (2020). Investigating leader self-efficacy through policy engagement and social network position. *Educational Policy, 34*(3), 411–48.

Liou, Y. H., & Daly, A. J. (2020). The networked leader: Understanding peer influence in a system wide leadership team. *School Leadership & Management, 40*(2–3), 163–82. https://doi.org/10.1080/13632434.2019.1686611

Liou, Y. H., Daly, A. J., Canrinus, E. T., Forbes, C. A., Moolenaar, N. M., Cornelissen, F., … & Hsiao, J. (2017). Mapping the social side of pre-service teachers: Connecting closeness, trust, and efficacy with performance. *Teachers and Teaching, 23*(6), 635–57.

Milward, H. B., & Provan, K. G. (2006). *A manager's guide to choosing and using collaborative networks (Vol. 8)*. Washington, DC: IBM Center for the Business of Government.

Moolenaar, N., Daly, A., & Sleegers, P. (2011). Ties with potential: Social network structure and innovative climate in Dutch schools. *Teachers College Record, 113*(9), 1983–2017. https://doi.org/10.1177/016146811111300906

Moolenaar, N. M., Daly, A. J., Cornelissen, F., Liou, Y. H., Caillier, S., Riordan, R., & Cohen, N. A. (2014). Linked to innovation: Shaping an innovative climate through network intentionality and educators' social network position. *Journal of Educational Change, 15*(2), 99–123.

Muijs, D. (2015). Improving schools through collaboration: A mixed methods study of school-to-school partnerships in the primary sector. *Oxford Review of Education, 41*(5), 563–86. https://doi.org/10.1080/03054985.2015.1047824

Muijs, D., & Rumyantseva, N. (2014). Coopetition in education: Collaborating in a competitive environment. *Journal of Educational Change, 15*(1), 1–18.

Pino-Yancovic, M., Parrao, C. G., Ahumada, L., & Gonzalez, A. (2019). Promoting collaboration in a competitive context: School improvement networks in Chile. *Journal of Educational Administration, 58*(2), 208–26.

Rincón-Gallardo, S., & Fullan, M. (2016). Essential features of effective networks in education. *Journal of Professional Capital and Community. 1*(1), 5–2.

Rodway, J., MacGregor, S., Daly, A., Liou, Y. H., Yonezawa, S., & Pollock, M. (2021). A network case of knowledge brokering. *Journal of Professional Capital and Community, 6*(2), 148–63. 10.1108/JPCC-11-2020-0089

Sandals, L., & Bryant, B. (2014). *The evolving education system in England: A "temperature check"*. London: Department for Education.

Schildkamp, K., Nehez, J., & Blossing, U. (2018). From data to learning: A data team professional learning network. In *Networks for learning* (pp. 75–91). Routledge.

Scott, J. (2012). *What is social network analysis?*. Bloomsbury Academic.

Sinnema, C., Daly, A. J., Liou, Y. H., & Rodway, J. (2020). Exploring the communities of learning policy in New Zealand using social network analysis: A case study of leadership, expertise, and networks. *International Journal of Educational Research, 99*, 1–16. https://doi.org/10.1016/j.ijer.2019.10.002

Spillane, J. P., & Kim, C. M. (2012). An exploratory analysis of formal school leaders' positioning in instructional advice and information networks in elementary schools. *American Journal of Education, 119*(1), 73–102. https://doi.org/10.1086/667755

Steglich, C., Snijders, T. A., & Pearson, M. (2010). Dynamic networks and behavior: Separating selection from influence. *Sociological Methodology, 40*(1), 329–93. https://doi.org/10.1111/j.1467-9531.2010.01225.x

Tschannen-Moran, M., & Gareis, C. R. (2004). Principals' sense of efficacy. *Journal of Educational Administration, 42*(5), 573–85.

Van Gasse, R., Vanlommel, K., Vanhoof, J., & Van Petegem, P. (2017). Individual, co-operative and collaborative data use: A conceptual and empirical exploration. *British Educational Research Journal, 43*(3), 608–26. https://doi.org/10.1002/berj.3277

Varga-Atkins, T., O'Brien, M., Burton, D., Campbell, A., & Qualter, A. (2010). The importance of interplay between school-based and networked professional development: School professionals' experiences of inter-school collaborations in learning networks. *Journal of Educational Change, 11*(3), 241–72.

Wang, H., Wang, L., & Liu, C. (2018). Employee competitive attitude and competitive behavior promote job-crafting and performance: A two-component dynamic model. *Frontiers in Psychology, 9*, 22–3. https://doi.org/10.3389/fpsyg.2018.02223

Yin, R. K. (2017). *Case study research and applications: Design and methods*. Sage publications.

Žnidaršič, A., Ferligoj, A., & Doreian, P. (2018). Stability of centrality measures in valued networks regarding different actor non-response treatments and macro-network structures. *Network Science, 6*(1), 1–33. https://doi.org/10.1017/nws.2017.29

10

In Pursuit of Community of Learning: Investigating a Cross-School Leadership Team

Joelle Rodway, Rachel Cann, and Claire Sinnema

When educators collaborate to improve teaching and learning, it often leads to improvements in student, school, and system performance (ERO, 2016; Hargreaves & O'Connor, 2018). In New Zealand, this potential for collaboration to improve outcomes for students is at the heart of the Communities of Learning-Kāhui Ako policy. The policy outlines how groups of schools—Communities of Learning (CoLs)—should work together to address a common goal focused on improving student outcomes, specifically leveraging both within school and across school collaboration in order to achieve the desired outcome(s). In this chapter, we examine the collaboration patterns in one such CoL to explore how this policy is enacted in practice.

For decades, research has shown that collaboration among colleagues increases teacher learning (Datnow & Park, 2018; Goddard et al., 2007; Rosenholtz, 1989) and improves teacher practice and outcomes for students (Stoll & Louis, 2007). Collaboration occurs through social interactions, either within schools or across a number of schools. Social network analysis (SNA) is a method that has been used to examine the interactions between educators in schools and has demonstrated their impact on innovation (Liou & Daly, 2018), curriculum and policy implementation (Coburn & Russell, 2008; Hopkins et al., 2017), and student achievement (Daly et al., 2014). This has led to interest from education systems around the world in promoting the use of collaborative networks that promote teacher learning in order to raise student achievement.

Multi-school networks are increasingly common internationally, for example Multi-Academy Trusts (MATs) in England, Boards of Multiple Schools (BMSs) in the Netherlands, Charter Management Organisations (CMOs) in the USA, and Communities of Learning-Kāhui Ako in New Zealand (Greany, 2021; Greany & Kamp, 2022; Wylie, 2016). We focus on the Communities of Learning-Kāhui Ako (CoL) policy in New Zealand. The policy aims to create system-wide change through purposeful collaboration that grows the capabilities of CoL members (Wylie, 2016). The Ministry of Education outlines best practices for collaboration: CoL members understand and agree about the purpose of working together; they work toward common goals using a process that values everyone's input whilst also questioning and analyzing information; and relationships that are based on trust, respect, and support, so that all members of the CoL have a sense of belonging and there are opportunities to share leadership (Ministry of Education, 2015).

The CoL policy is supported by several other policies that foreground the importance of relationships and collaboration. The standards for the teaching profession emphasize the importance of collaborative relationships (Education Council, 2017) and school leaders are expected to "establish, cultivate and sustain positive relationships with others, within collaborative and relational teams and networks" in order to successfully lead change (Education Council, 2018, p. 19). Indeed, schools are evaluated by the quality of the relationships they foster and their collaborative practices focused on improving teaching and learning (ERO, 2016).

The size of CoLs varies from four to over twenty schools. Each CoL identifies "achievement challenges" focused on measurable student outcomes, and uses collaboration as a vehicle to improve teaching practice that should, in turn, improve outcomes for students (Wylie, 2016). Within each CoL there are three main leadership roles: the overall CoL leadership role held by a CoL principal (CP), an across school lead role (ASL), and a within-school lead role (WSL) (Ministry of Education, 2016a). Each role is focused on building collaboration within the CoL. The CoL principal provides "leadership in building productive collaboration within Communities of Learning" (Ministry of Education, 2016a, p. 7). People in both the ASL and WSL roles are expected to work directly with each other and teachers from other schools to support CoL achievement objectives through the use of effective inquiry approaches (Ministry of Education, 2016a). However, the description of the ASL and WSL roles in regard to best practice have a different focus with ASLs focused on "promoting best teaching practice across a Community of Learning" (Ministry of Education, 2016a, p. 9) whilst the WSLs focus on "promoting best teaching practice within a school" (Ministry of Education, 2016a, p. 11).

At the end of 2014, the first eleven CoLs had been approved (Wylie, 2016), and by the beginning of 2021 there were 220 CoLs comprising 74 percent of the schools in New Zealand (Ministry of Education, 2021). We focus on one such CoL, the Pohutukawa CoL (a pseudonym), that was three years into its journey of establishing its across school network. The Pohutukawa CoL was chosen as it was established during the early stages of the CoL policy, and was therefore among the CoLs that have had the greatest amount of time to establish collaboration. By examining the interactions between educators in the Pohutukawa CoL, we explore what New Zealand's policy of across school collaboration looks like in practice. Through the application of social network theory and analysis, this chapter will answer these research questions:

- To what extent is collaboration *within* and *across* schools in the Pohutukawa CoL evident?
- To what extent are members of the CoL leadership team collaborating with each other?
- To what extent are members of the CoL leadership team central in the collaboration network as a whole?

Literature Review

Social network theory provides a framework for us to explore the implementation of the *Communities of Learning-Kāhui Ako* policy. The importance of relationships, a key idea woven throughout many of New Zealand's educational policies, is also a central idea in social network theory. Social network theory describes how relational patterns between people enable and/or constrain the flow of resources (Cross & Parker, 2004; Wasserman & Faust, 1994). The resources embedded in these relational ties are known as social capital, and can be leveraged in order to create human capital in terms of the knowledge, skills, and capabilities that people possess (Coleman, 1988).

By applying concepts from social network theory, we identify the patterns of collaboration that constitute an informal network, which is important as the social network structure in schools often deviates from the formal leadership structure (Moolenaar, 2012). For example, across a sample of thirty elementary schools on average only 49 percent of formal leaders were key advice givers in the network (Spillane, Healy & Kim, 2010).

The most common approach to analyzing social networks in educational settings is the bounded-saturated approach, in which all members of a defined group (e.g., a school) are surveyed to capture each individual's relationships with other people in the network (Borgatti et al., 2018; Hanneman & Riddle, 2005; Moolenaar, 2012). When coupled with high response rates, this approach helps to build a full and rich picture of the interactions between all people in the network (Hanneman & Riddle, 2005; Scott, 2000). Networks can be focused on different types of interactions such as advice seeking, friendship, or lesson planning (Moolenaar, 2012). Measures of the network as a whole can be useful in evaluating the effectiveness of the network and so are well suited to understand policies that have networks, relationships, and collaboration at their heart. For example, the frequency of interactions within a network gives an idea of the total amount of network activity, which in this case is important as "effective collaboration is characterised by dense, frequent sharing of knowledge among participants" (ERO, 2016, p. 15). In addition to measures that characterize activity across the whole network, individual measures focusing on the number of ties possessed by an individual (or ego) can be used to capture an individual's position in a social network and the contribution they make to it (Borgatti et al., 2018). The frequency of individual participation has been linked to desirable outcomes for that individual, such as the number of advice seeking ties and improvements in teacher learning and practice (Sinnema et al., 2021).

To further explore the role of particular individuals, we can also examine their "ego network" (or personal network), which shows the ties between one individual (called "ego") and any people to whom they are connected (called "alters"). In this case, the ego network is extracted from the data for the whole network for the CoL as shown in Figure 10.1. The advantage of extracting the ego network from the whole network data is that it includes accurate information on the alter's attributes; it highlights connections between alters; and, it shows ego's incoming ties from their alters (Perry et al., 2018).

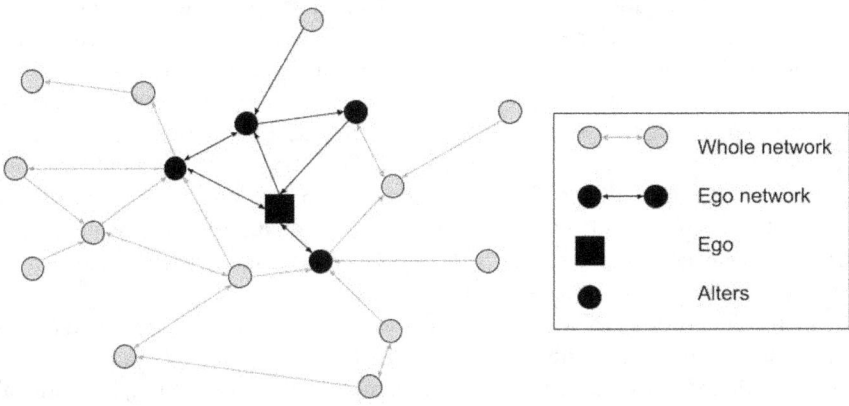

Figure 10.1 Example of extracting an ego network from a larger network.

By examining the ego networks of the CoL leaders, we can understand the role they play in the larger network and obtain more information than is provided by simply considering the number of ties they have. For example, in the ego networks we can see if ties are between people in different schools, and if ties are unidirectional or reciprocated.

In the context of the *Communities of Learning-Kāhui Ako* policy, we would expect to see those with formal leadership roles playing key roles in the collaboration network. In particular:

- The CP and ASL should have many across school ties as they lead collaboration and promote best teaching practice across the COL;
- The WSLs should have many within school ties as they promote best teaching practice within their school;
- The CP, ASL, and WSLs should have ties with each other as they are expected to coordinate the implementation of the shared achievement challenges.

Social network analysis provides a tool to help examine the relational patterns to determine if these goals are being met.

Methods

Sample and Data Collection

Communities of Learning are typically composed of a secondary school and several primary schools. The Pohutukawa CoL follows this structure with one secondary school and four primary schools, all of which were focused on improving student achievement in reading, writing, and mathematics. In total, 101 educators from early childhood education through secondary levels participated in an online survey that was administered at the start of the 2019 academic year. Of the seventy-eight respondents (response rate = 77 percent), 59 percent are from primary schools, 75 percent are full-time employees, 56 percent do *not* possess a formal leadership role in their school/CoL, and 76 percent are female. Educators had been working in the field on average ninteen years (SD = 11.60), had worked in their current school for about nine years (SD = 8.77), and in their current positions for approximately six years (SD = 5.53). The sample included the CoL leadership team members as well as principals, deputy (or associate, assistant) principals, syndicate or team leaders, and department heads as well as classroom teachers and classroom aides.

The social network survey included three sections based on instruments that had been validated in previous studies (see Daly, 2010): social networks, expertise, and demographic information. Social network questions focused on multiple relational dimensions including collaboration, advice seeking, go-to person, materials/resources, close relationship, and encouragement. Querying multiple relational dimensions provided opportunities for the research team to understand how relational spaces take on different shapes or forms depending on the type of social resource that is being exchanged. In this chapter, given the *Community of Learning-Kāhui Ako* policy's focus on collaboration, we focus solely on the patterns of collaboration.

Respondents were asked to answer the following question to elicit the names of colleagues with whom they have collaborated within their CoL: "How frequently do you **collaborate** with the following people to **analyse data on student learning**? By 'collaborate' we mean mutual work, sharing, and exchanging ideas." They were provided with a roster of the names of educators from each school within the Pohutukawa CoL, and for each identified collaborator, they were asked to indicate the frequency of collaboration for those individuals on a Likert-type scale ranging from 1 (yearly) to 4 (daily). Using a roster-based approach to sociometric data collection (as opposed to the free choice method) reduces memory bias and increases data validity (Scott, 2017).

Data Analysis

In order to examine the collaboration patterns among educators in the Pohutukawa CoL, we focus on describing the relational patterns in this chapter using descriptive network statistics. While there is a wide array of sophisticated SNA techniques, descriptive statistics are often undervalued and under-used; they can, in fact, provide us with useful information to understand how people are interacting with each other, which is the first step in building relational literacy in a network.

The research team focused the analysis on only those ties that happened on a least a monthly basis (i.e., those relationships identified at a monthly, weekly, or daily frequency) in order to focus on the explicit calls for the development of regular across-school collaboration in the national *Community of Learning-Kāhui Ako* policy. It also contributes to increased validity of the sociometric data as research shows that people are more accurately able to recall interactions that take place on a more frequent basis (Carolan, 2014).

To characterize the overall pattern of collaboration across this CoL, we focused on network cohesion measures to provide a general picture of the extent to which educators are collaborating with each other. Borgatti and colleagues (2018) describe *cohesion* as "knittedness" or the extent to which people are connected to each other in a network. We considered measures including *density* (the number of ties present in a network in relation to the total number of ties possible), *centralization* (the extent to which the network activity focuses on a specific set of people within the network), *fragmentation* (a measure of access that describes the extent to which people in the network can access the resources of others), and *reciprocity* (the proportion of mutual ties in the network) to query network cohesion.

At the level of the individual, we used *degree centrality*, a network measure that focuses on the total number of ties a person possesses within a network. The higher the degree centrality score, the more relationships they have with their colleagues. The average number of ties in the network is based on degree centrality.

The Structure of the Network

Collaboration *within* and *across* Schools in the Pohutukawa CoL

Collaboration patterns are very weak across the Pohutukawa CoL. Regardless of their role, educators possess on average 4.2 ties (SD = 6.09); in other words, they report collaborating with about four other colleagues. The density of the network is 4.2 percent, indicating a very sparse network where less than one out of every ten possible relationships is present. While the centralization measures indicate that the interactions are spread out across the community and not strongly focused on a particular subgroup (CD=0.347), only about one out of every five reported ties was reciprocal where both actors named each other as someone with whom they collaborate (R=20.6 percent). When considering inter-school collaboration ties—that is, ties where each educator in the relational pair works at a different school—the network becomes even less active with each person reporting zero ties on average (M=0.2, SD = 0.69). The across school collaboration network has a density of 0.2 percent, barely registering any activity at all. Of the twenty ties reported in this network, only 18 percent (about 3 ties) were identified as reciprocal ties. Figure 10.2 (graphs A and B) provides network illustrations for the CoL network including all network ties and across school ties only.

When focusing on collaboration at the school level, however, much more collaborative activity is evident. Within schools, educators are collaborating with each other with total reported ties ranging from 12 to 195 ties and network densities ranging from 11 percent to 60 percent. It is important to note that the total number of faculty within a school affects network density; the larger the school faculty, the more difficult it is to achieve higher network density. Take, for example, the smallest school in this CoL with five members where the maximum number of ties (i.e., everyone is collaborating with each other) would be twenty ties in contrast with the largest school in this CoL with forty-two members and a tie maximum quantity of 1722 ties.

A. All collaboration ties within the CoL (N=428 ties)

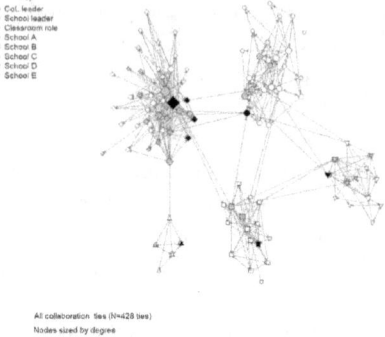

B. Across-school collaboration ties within the CoL (N=20 ties)

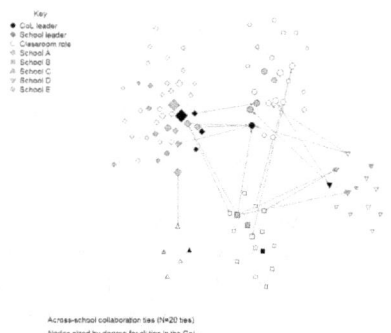

C. Collaboration ties among CoL leadership team members (N=5 ties)

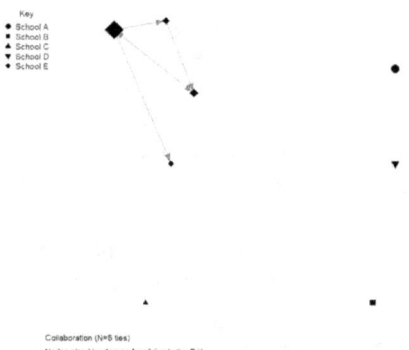

Figure 10.2 Collaboration patterns within the Pohutukawa CoL and among CoL leadership team members.

Note. Each shape identifies a separate school in the Pohutukawa CoL. Color refers to role in the school system: white = classroom teachers/teacher assistants, grey = school level leaders (e.g., principals, department heads), black = CoL leaders. The size of the shape represents indegree centrality score; the larger the node, the more often the individual was named as a collaborator. The node position is fixed in all graphs.

Table 10.1 Cohesion measures for school and CoL collaboration networks

Measure	All Monthly Ties	Across School Ties only	School 1	School 2	School 3	School 4	School 5
Number of Ties	428	20	89	64	12	48	195
Average Degree	4.2	0.2	3.6	4	2.4	3.7	4.6
Density	4.2 percent	0.2 percent	14.8 percent	26.7 percent	60 percent	30.8 percent	11.3 percent
Fragmentation	0.364	0.997	0.442	0.121	0.35	0.077	0.544
Centralization	0.347	0.048	0.339	0.400	0.167	0.341	0.843
Out-Centralization	0.361	0.028	0.366	0.498	0.500	0.389	0.883
In-Centralization	0.078	0.028	0.236	0.569	0.500	0.479	0.134
Reciprocity	20.6 percent	17.6 percent	29 percent	18.5 percent	33.3 percent	33.3 percent	14.7 percent

Regardless of these important contextual differences, in comparison with the levels of collaborative activity as a whole, it is quite evident that the most collaboration is taking place among educators within the same school, which is not unexpected given that there is greater opportunity for educators to connect within their home schools. Table 10.1 provides a summary of the network cohesion measures for the CoL as a whole, for across school ties only, and within each separate school for comparison. Thus, as evidenced here, while collaboration is happening within schools, across school collaboration is minimal—much less than we might hope given that the CoL had been operating for three years at the time of the study.

Collaboration among CoL Leaders

Networks are defined by where researchers decide to place the boundary (Borgatti et al., 2018). By shifting the boundary to include only the CoL leadership team, we are able to focus specifically on the collaboration ties among members of the leadership team. Graph C in Figure 10.2 provides an illustration of the CoL leadership team's collaboration network.

As shown, many of the CoL leadership team members did not identify each other as colleagues with whom they collaborate around issues of student achievement on at least a monthly basis; in fact, only those whose work is situated within the same school (i.e., CoL principal, ASL, and two WSLs) cited collaborating with each other. This finding is surprising given the specific nature of the roles of the CoL leads, and for the CoL principal and ASL in particular. The term "collaboration" was defined in the survey instrument in an effort to build a common understanding of what is meant by collaboration—a definition that included "mutual work"—and the absence of collaboration ties among the leadership team members is curious and worth further investigation.

Centrality of CoL Leadership Team in the Collaboration Network

Within the collaboration network, CoL leadership team members are among the most active participants (see Sinnema et al., 2020 for a more elaborated analysis of leader centrality in the advice and collaboration networks). Six out of the eight CoL leaders rank in the top quartile of activity within the collaboration network; however, an analysis of the relationship between role category (i.e., CoL leader, school leader, or classroom teacher/aide) was not significantly associated with degree centrality scores. Instead, individuals' perceived expertise in general teaching practice and in literacy practice is positively associated with indegree scores ($r = .24$, $p = .001$ and $r = .27$, $p < .01$, respectively), meaning that the people who are sought out as collaborators in this network are those people who report higher perceptions of expertise in these areas (Sinnema et al., 2020). Thus, while the CoL policy may identify specific roles to support the collaborative work of the CoL, an individual's named role (i.e., position in the formal organization) does not correlate with their

In Pursuit of Community of Learning 181

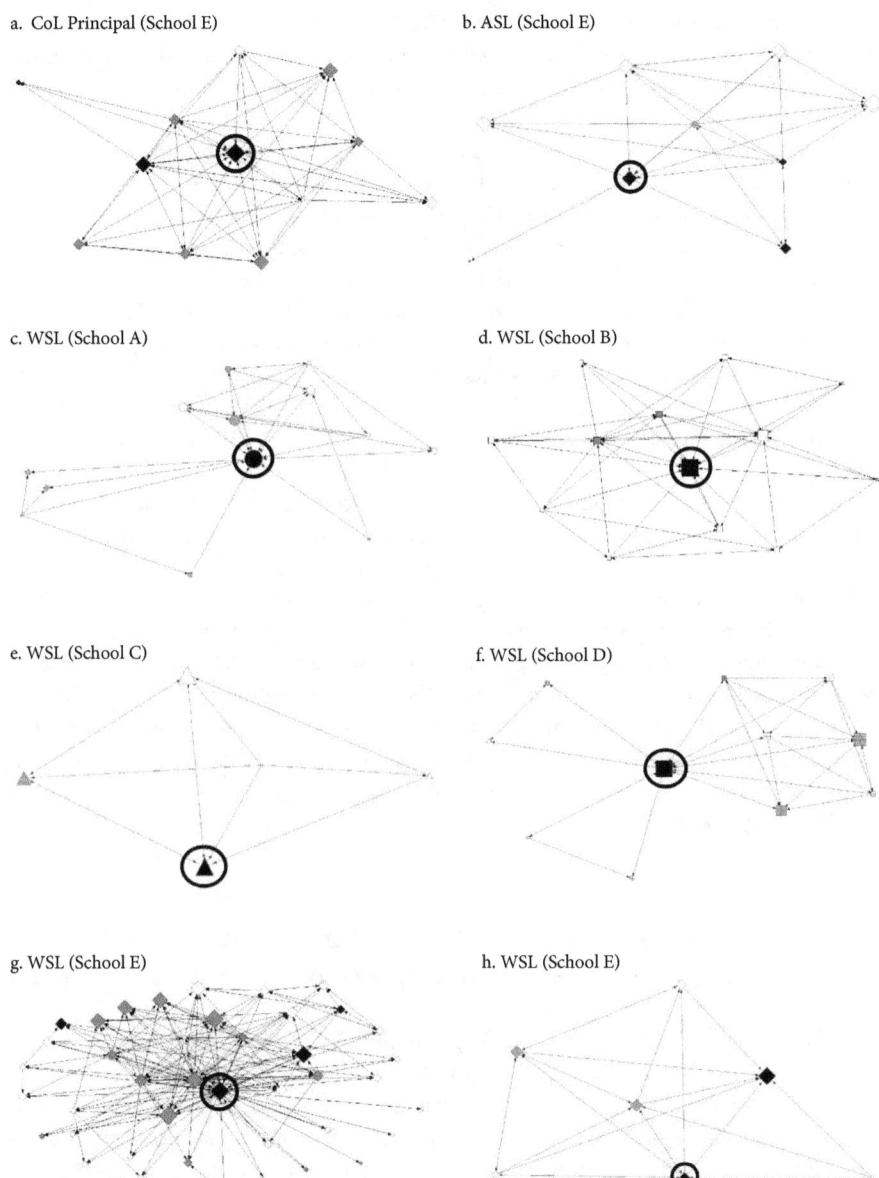

Figure 10.3 Collaboration ego networks for Pohutukawa CoL leadership team.

Note. Each shape identifies a separate school in the Pohutukawa CoL. The size of the shape represents indegree centrality score; the larger the node, the more often the individual was named as a collaborator. The focal node (i.e., ego) is circled.

levels of collaboration within the network itself. Yet, the collaborative activity of the CoL leaders does matter within this policy context, so we considered the individual ego networks for each CoL lead to understand what their collaborative work looks like across the CoL.

To better understand the social positions of the CoL leadership team within the collaboration network, we extracted the ego networks (i.e., networks that contain only the ties connected to ego) of the CoL principal, ASL, and each WSL. Recall from the *Communities of Learning-Kāhui Ako* policy that the CoL principal and ASL are expected to cultivate collaboration for the sharing of best practices across the CoL and the WSLs are expected to do the same within their schools. Furthermore, the CoL leadership team is expected to collaborate with each other to support this work within and across schools. As such, one would expect each leader's network to include ties with their colleagues within their schools and with the other CoL leaders. However, as the individual ego networks show us in Figure 10.3, this is not the case—for anyone.

As the ego network graphs illustrate, with the exception of the ASL and two WSLs in schools A and C, most CoL leads' collaborative work is restricted to colleagues within the same schools. Even for those people with across school ties, the connections are limited. For example, the WSL in school A is connected to three classroom teachers in three different schools while school C's WSL is connected to a school leader and classroom teacher in a neighboring school. Thus, while these WSLs are collaborating with other schools (albeit in limited ways), they did not identify their CoL leadership colleagues as collaborators. The Pohutukawa CoL's ASL, whose position explicitly states an expectation of cultivating across school ties, possesses a network that is predominantly composed of within school ties, with only one tie to a classroom teacher in another school.

Thinking through the Collaborative Space in the Pohutukawa CoL

The New Zealand Ministry of Education's *Community of Learning-Kāhui Ako* policy actively foregrounds the importance of relationships and collaborative work in developing sustainable school systems that are focused on student achievement. As described at the beginning of the chapter, the national Ministry of Education is supporting the implementation of the CoL policy with specific guidelines about the structure of the communities and the establishment and membership of CoL leadership teams (see Ministry of Education, 2016a). These guidelines are further supported with resources including release time to engage in this work (see Ministry of Education, 2016b, p. 17). Despite this elaborated policy infrastructure, our analyses suggest that the collaborative work within the Pohutukawa CoL is extremely limited (years after the establishment of the CoL), taking place most frequently *within schools* and *not across schools*. This greatly constrains the achievement of the policy's goals of leveraging the knowledge and skills of educators across the CoL to improve the learning environments in each school.

The value of social network methods is that they enable us to see the "invisible work" (Cross et al., 2002) that is (or is not) happening within a social space—in this case, a Community of Learning. New Zealand's education policies set forth a specific vision for what collaborative work will look like within each CoL, including the roles of the members of the leadership team. In considering the network maps for the Pohutukawa CoL in relation to these policies, these findings indicate that this learning community is struggling to meet the national goals of collaboration. Despite being CoL members for nearly three years at the time of this study, across school collaboration as imagined by the *Community of Learning-Kāhui Ako* policy was not happening across this collective of schools. While collaboration seems to be a practice that is somewhat established within schools (further research is required to understand the dynamics of what collaborative work looks like in each school context), a focus on developing capacity for improved student achievement through across school approaches to capacity building was not evident.

The question remains: why is collaboration so limited within this CoL despite being one of the first learning communities established under this national policy? We offer three approaches to consider our observations: 1) situating the CoL within a network of New Zealand education policies; 2) shifting toward an across school focus using systems thinking; and 3) building collaborative cultures with intentionality.

Situating the CoL within a Network of New Zealand Education Policies

It is important to understand that relationships are not limited to the space between people alone. Relational space encompasses the space between all available resources—that is, the relationships between human and social resources with other types of non-human resources (e.g., physical, financial, governance) also matter (Butler et al., 2015; Rodway & Farley-Ripple, 2020). As such, it is necessary to consider the ways in which the educators in the Pohutukawa CoL relate not only to each other and to the *Community of Learning-Kāhui Ako* policy, but also how they (i.e., the people and the policy) relate to other resources within the broader educational landscape. Notably, other policy dimensions within the educational governance infrastructure impact the implementation of the Community of Learning framework; therefore, it is essential to consider each CoL's history with various education policies in order to understand how the *Community of Learning-Kāhui Ako* policy factors into the policy narrative.

For example, there are several studies that consider the Community of Learning context that show the contradictory policy directives impede the willingness and ability of schools within a CoL to collaborate with each other (Highfield & Webber, 2021; Wylie, 2016). Within the Pohutukawa CoL, our colleagues identified that the history of competition among schools—particularly primary schools—has resulted in a lack of relational trust among educators, and for school leaders in particular (see

Sinnema et al., 2022). Historically, school choice policies have created a culture of competition among schools that is heavily influenced by the per student funding model that exists nationally. Schools are funded based on the student roll (see Ministry of Education, 2022)—the greater a school's enrollment, the higher the amount of funding provided to that school—thus, there is an incentive for schools to guard their practice with hopes of creating a "competitive advantage" in attracting students to increase school funding. Other studies of Kāhui Ako schools offer support that the competitive environment created by the school funding model is constraining collaboration (e.g., Highfield & Webber, 2021); the fear of school closures as a result of low enrollment negatively affects schools' willingness to work with each other (Witten et al., 2003). In short, many school leaders perceive greater risks than benefits from working with each other. Thus, despite the fulsome nature of the *Community of Learning-Kāhui Ako* policy and its supporting resources, the influence of the broader context in which these schools operate limit the enthusiasm and opportunities for this work to come to life in practice.

Shifting toward an across School Focus Using Systems Thinking

When new policies are announced, the tendency is to appoint a person (or group of people) with the formal responsibility of overseeing the implementation of that policy. Oftentimes, that responsibility falls on the shoulders of school administrators, but sometimes—as is the case with the Pohutukawa CoL—a separate group of people are given formal roles (i.e., role titles) and receive resources (e.g., release time) to support their work. However, research shows that the appointment of people in formal roles does not always result in them carrying out their work in the ways intended (Coburn & Russell, 2008; Moolenaar, 2012). This is what we observe in the Pohutukawa CoL where people with formal roles and responsibilities for cultivating collaboration across the CoL appear not to be doing so. Only the ASL and two WSLs reported across school collaboration ties, but even those ties were minimal. With a network density of less than 1 percent, the amount of across-school collaboration barely registers in the network measures. This observation is consistent with other network studies that found that people in formal positions often played peripheral roles in the informal organization of schools (e.g., Atteberry & Bryk, 2010; Kochan & Teddlie, 2005).

One might consider to what extent the "right people are in the right roles" (Collins, 2001) within the CoL leadership team. Strong relationships between administrators and educators are necessary antecedents to collaborative work and knowledge sharing (Reagans & McEvily, 2003; Rodway, 2019). In the context of policy implementation, relational patterns function as both enablers and constraints of moving policy into practice (Spillane et al., 2006) and without these relationships, CoL leaders will lack the opportunities necessary to generate shared understanding and purpose to guide the collaborative work (Grissom et al., 2021). In the Pohutukawa CoL, it could be argued that these relationships among the CoL leadership team—relationships that are necessary to carry out this work—are missing. Indeed, the network analysis supports that point of view. The Ministry of Education documentation includes in its definition of collaboration the shared responsibility for defining common goals and carrying out the work necessary to meet them through relationships imbued with trust, respect, and support (Ministry of Education, 2015). These goals appear not to be met, despite three years of working together in the Pohutukawa CoL. Thus, it is fair to question whether or not the people appointed to these roles are the "right people" to lead this work.

It is important to consider, however, that the work of the CoL leads is embedded in a broader social network; it is not just their relational patterns within the leadership group that define the success of the *Community of Learning-Kāhui Ako* policy. At the school level, the CoL leads are very active with collaboration networks that demonstrate within school conditions that are supportive of collaborative work. When considering their work within these domains, there is success: educators report collaborating with each other within their schools. However, at the systems level (i.e., across schools), a different story emerges and the CoL leads' work falls woefully short. As it has been argued in related work (see Sinnema et al., 2020), "the CoL leadership team face the challenge of redefining their roles to shift from more school centric to adopt a more systems view" (p. 13). Absent this systems-oriented view, the policy will not yield its intended results. Simply formalizing a leadership role without ensuring that the work is enacted at a systems level is insufficient. Leaders, including system, CoL and school leaders, must be intentional about cultivating collaborative cultures that engage educators across communities; otherwise the policy fails to achieve the goal of increased expertise and knowledge sharing across schools.

Building Collaborative Cultures with Intentionality

Building a collaborative culture within an organization, or in this case among a constellation of schools within a CoL, does not happen on its own; it takes time and intentionality. The extent to which a person will seek information from someone else in their network has been shown to depend on their *awareness* of the other person's knowledge and skills, and their *access* to the other person, in terms of the other person's availability, ability to effectively communicate the information needed, and resources to fulfill the requests made of them (Borgatti & Cross, 2003). Access to others may be due to unexpected interactions with others as a result of physical proximity (i.e., propinquity) in the workplace, for example, where people share the same spaces such as classroom, office, or photocopier location (Spillane et al., 2017). Propinquity increases interactions that can help to build awareness of other people's knowledge and skills (Borgatti & Cross, 2003) and increases the likelihood that educators talk to each other about their work (Spillane et al., 2017). Awareness and access may also be mediated by homophily, a social network concept that highlights the extent to which people tend to seek out like-minded others. The more similar two people are to each other, the more likely they are to have a connection (McPherson et al., 2001). Without intentional action people's networks are shaped by propinquity and homophily, whilst individuals who display high network intentionality tend to build more deliberate, rather than serendipitous, connections.

Network intentionality is defined as an individual's intentions to create, broker, maintain, and assess their ties with colleagues through actively seeking relationships, their belief in the benefits of having the right relationships, assessing their relationships, and, enjoying connecting with others (Moolenaar et al., 2014). Educators with high levels of network intentionality also show high levels of out-going relational activity (Moolenaar et al., 2014). In the Pohutukawa CoL, the predominance of within school ties over across school ties suggests that propinquity is an influential driver of connections; therefore, increasing educators' network intentionality may aid in increasing the number of across school ties. CoL leaders could help to grow educators' network intentionality by increasing their awareness of others' expertise in the CoL.

Given access to others is also a driver of connection (Borgatti & Cross, 2003), it can also be argued that more funding for CoLs could be allocated to creating space for educators to connect rather than funding a limited number of formalized roles. As "most teachers who are in schools in a CoL are not aware that they are in a CoL" (New Zealand Post Primary Teachers' Association, 2017, p. 9), this adds to the argument for funding space for more educators to collaborate on CoL work. The building and sharing of knowledge and expertise—key components of the collaborative work expected by the Ministry of Education—is, at its heart, a relational practice (Reeves, 2010); it can only happen through exchange, thereby insisting on the importance of relational space (Rodway & Farley-Ripple, 2020). Often educators stick to spaces that are familiar, such as within their own school, for example, never knowing about or having access to the knowledge and expertise available to them outside of their own schools. Providing that space is important as building connections with others takes time, and "people have only so much relational energy to expend" (Cross et al., 2002, p. 40).

Investing in providing space and time for educators to come together around shared problems of practice may be a more impactful way to cultivate cultures of collaboration. To some extent, this is occurring. Through the Communities of Learning initiative, schools are provided with multiple resources including inquiry time "to support kaiako/teachers to take time to undertake structured opportunities to access, observe, collaborate and reflect with [CoL] kaiako/teachers across Communities and within schools" (Ministry of Education, 2016b, p. 17). Yet despite having a minimum of 50 hours of inquiry time in addition to release time for formal leadership roles (see Ministry of Education, 2016b), the challenge of across-school collaboration remains. Network intentionality, particularly among the CoL leadership team, would be beneficial to cultivating the relational infrastructure necessary to do this work, especially when that intention is specifically focused on developing relationships across schools.

Limitations of the Study

This study offers a singular view of the Pohutukawa CoL collaboration network; it reflects data that were collected at a single point in time. Future studies should consider the use of longitudinal study designs to capture how the relational patterns change over time. Similarly, this work relies on quantitative social network analysis with data collected using a survey instrument. While qualitative data were collected, it has not been integrated here. Next steps in this study should include more work that incorporates both the quantitative and qualitative data together rather than treating them separately as has been the case to date. Evidently, this is a singular case that is unique to a particular context, so the findings are not generalizable on their own. That said, they add another empirical example of how a relational approach to understanding policy implementation highlights the importance of social space in achieving policy goals. Further studies of other communities will enable greater comparison of the influence of relationships in the implementation of the *Communities of Learning-Kāhui Ako* policy, which will be beneficial to policymakers, school and system leaders, and education researchers alike.

Implications for School and System Leaders

Considering the ways the enactment of the *Communities of Learning-Kāhui Ako* policy was limited, we suggest a number of implications to successfully enact policies focused on collaboration in multi-school networks. A lack of reciprocated collaboration ties in the Pohutukawa CoL calls into question educators' understanding of collaborative work. School and system leaders need to establish collaborative cultures through providing support and structures for collaboration—without associated professional learning in effective collaboration, improvement efforts are likely to fall short of aspirations (Carpenter, 2015). The preponderance of within-school collaboration ties over across school ties is likely influenced by homophily and propinquity (connecting with similar people who are in close proximity). To overcome this school and CoL leaders should aim to increase awareness and access (Borgatti & Cross, 2003). Leaders could increase awareness through strategies such as an expertise database, so that educators can identify people in other schools with relevant knowledge with whom they can collaborate. Access could be improved through providing regular time and space for teachers to collaborate. It is important that formal CoL leaders also apply these strategies to their own work to increase their own collaboration ties.

At the system level, leaders need to consider relational spaces in terms of the relationships between people and other existing policies, resources, and norms. The tension between the *Communities of Learning-Kāhui Ako* policy and other policies highlights the need for a greater consideration of complementarity—the degree to which the values espoused in different policies complement each other (Sinnema et al., 2022). Policies that encourage competition between schools undermine the values of the *Communities of Learning-Kāhui Ako* policy, and also link to educators existing norms of working predominantly with others in their own school. At the school level, leadership has been shown to influence the way teachers work together by encouraging them to deprivatize their practice (Vanblaere & Devos, 2016), and perhaps a corollary of this is that system leaders need to consider how they influence the deprivatization of practice across schools. Possibilities exist for system leaders to provide more professional learning and support for CoL leaders to develop their system level thinking around across school collaboration networks. Beyond support for formal CoL leaders, an important consideration for system leaders is how to provide relational space for *all* educators within a CoL to develop their across school networks.

Implications for Educational Research

In describing the patterns of collaboration observed in Pohutukawa CoL, it was surprising that only 20 percent were reciprocated, despite the collaboration being defined as "mutual work, sharing, and exchanging ideas." This raises the question of how the educators viewed collaboration and what was happening in the remaining "one-way" collaboration ties. This is where further qualitative research work would be helpful in uncovering educators' interpretation of collaboration and understanding the nature of the interactions that have been captured in the collaboration networks described here.

Given the low number of across school ties in the Pohutukawa CoL it would be useful to understand what factors lead to the development of across school ties that do exist. Further research could use longitudinal approaches to capture information on the development of multi-school networks, and compare successful networks (those that develop many across school ties) to less successful networks to uncover the drivers of across school tie formation.

Conclusion

Social network analysis provides a valuable way to assess collaboration networks and see the otherwise "invisible" patterns of interaction (Cross et al., 2002). What we see in the Pohutukawa CoL is a pattern of interaction that does not enact the intent of New Zealand's *Communities of Learning-Kāhui Ako* multi-school network policy. We uncover low levels of across-school collaboration, very few reciprocated collaboration ties, and a formal CoL leadership team that generally does not collaborate across schools. The idea of relational space provides a way of thinking about why this is the case. Beyond the relations between the people within the CoL we need to consider their relationship to existing policies, resources, and norms. By considering how to increase the complementarity of policies (Sinnema et al., 2022), and peoples' *awareness* and *access* to other peoples' knowledge (Borgatti & Cross, 2003) leaders can increase the effective implementation of multi-school collaboration policy.

References

Atteberry, A., & Bryk, A. S. (2010). Centrality, connection, and commitment: The role of social networks in a school-based literacy initiative. In Daly, A. J. (Ed.), *Social network theory and educational change* (pp. 51–75). Harvard Education Press.

Borgatti, S. P., & Cross, R. (2003). A relational view of information seeking and learning in social networks. *Management Science, 49*(4), 432–45. https://doi.org/10.1287/mnsc.49.4.432.14428

Borgatti, S. P., Everett, M. G., & Johnson, J. C. (2018). *Analyzing social networks* (2nd ed.). Sage Publications.

Butler, J. K., Kane, R. G., & Morshead, C. E. (2015). "It's my safe space": Student voice, teachers' education, and the relational space of an urban high school. *Urban Education, 52*(7), 889–916. https://doi.org/10.1177/0042085915574530

Carolan, B. V. (2014). *Social network analysis and education: Theory, methods, and applications*. Sage Publications.

Carpenter, D. (2015). School culture and leadership of professional learning communities. *International Journal of Educational Management, 29*(5), 682–94. https://doi.org/10.1108/IJEM-04-2014-0046

Coburn, C. E., & Russell, J. L. (2008). District policy and teachers' social networks. Educational *Evaluation & Policy Analysis, 30*(3), 203–35. https://doi.org/10.3102/0162373708321829

Coleman, J. S. (1988). Social capital in the creation of human capital. *American Journal of Sociology, 94*, S95–S120.

Collins, J. (2001). *Good to great: Why some companies make the leap and others don't.* Harper Business.

Cross, R., & Parker, A. (2004). *The hidden power of social networks: Understanding how work really gets done in organizations.* Harvard Business School Press.

Cross, R., Borgatti, S. P., & Parker, A. (2002). Making invisible work visible: Using social network analysis to support strategic collaboration. *California Management Review, 44*(2), 25–46.

Daly, A. J. (2010). *Social network theory and educational change.* Cambridge MA: Harvard Education Press.

Daly, A. J., Liou, Y.-H., Tran, N. A., Cornelissen, F., & Park, V. (2014). The rise of neurotics: Social networks, leadership, and efficacy in district reform. *Educational Administration Quarterly, 50*(2), 233. https://doi.org/10.1177/0013161X13492795

Datnow, A., & Park, V. (2018). *Professional collaboration with purpose: Teacher learning towards equitable and excellent schools.* Routledge.

Education Council (2017). *Our code our standards: Code of professional responsibility and standards for the teaching profession.* New Zealand: Education Council.

Education Council (2018). *The leadership strategy for the teaching profession of Aotearoa New Zealand: Enabling every teacher to develop their leadership capability.* New Zealand: Education Council.

Education Review Office. (2016). *School evaluation indicators.* Ministry of Education. Retrieved February 1, 2022 Available at: https://ero.govt.nz/how-ero-reviews/schoolskura-english-medium/school-evaluation-indicators

Goddard, Y., Goddard, R., & Tschannen-Moran, M. (2007). A theoretical and empirical investigation of teacher collaboration for school improvement and student achievement in public elementary schools. *Teachers College Record, 109*(4), 877–96.

Greany, T. (2021). Editorial for special issue-leadership in multi-school organisations. *School Leadership & Management*, *41*(4–5), 285–9. https://doi.org/10.1080/13632434.2021.1981110

Greany, T., & Kamp, A. (2022). *Leading educational networks: Theory, policy and practice*. Bloomsbury Publishing.

Grissom, J. A., Egalite, A. J., & Lindsay, C. A. (2021). *How principals affect students and schools: A systematic synthesis of two decades of research*. The Wallace Foundation. https://www.wallacefoundation.org/knowledge-center/Documents/How-Principals-Affect-Students-and-Schools.pdf

Hanneman, R. A., & Riddle, M. (2005). *Introduction to social network methods*. Riverside, CA: University of California, Riverside (published in digital form at http://faculty.ucr.edu/~hanneman/)

Hargreaves, A., & O'Connor, M. T. (2018). *Collaborative professionalism: When teaching together means learning for all*. Corwin Press.

Highfield, C., & Webber, M. (2021). Mana Ūkaipō: Māori student connection, belonging and engagement at school. *New Zealand Journal of Educational Studies*, *56*(2), 145–64. https://doi.org/10.1007/s408411-021-00226-z

Hopkins, M., Ozimek, D., & Sweet, T. M. (2017). Mathematics coaching and instructional reform: individual and collective change. *Journal of Mathematical Behavior*, *46*, 215–30. https://doi.org/10.1016/j.jmathb.2016.11.003

Kochan, S., & Teddlie, C. (2005). An evaluation of communication among high school faculty using network analysis. *New Directions for Evaluation*, *107*, 41–53. https://doi.org/10.1002/ev.160

Liou, Y.-H., & Daly, A. J. (2018). Broken bridges: A social network perspective on urban high school leadership. *Journal of Educational Administration*, *56*(5), 562–84. https://doi.org/10.1108/JEA-01-2018-0010

McPherson, M., Smith-Lovin, L., & Cook, J. M. (2001). Birds of a feather: Homophily in social networks. *Annual Review of Sociology*, *27*(1), 415–44. https://doi.org/10.1146/annurev.soc.27.1.415

Ministry of Education. (2022, March 28). *Operational funding*. Ministry of Education. https://www.education.govt.nz/school/funding-and-financials/resourcing/operational-funding/

Ministry of Education. (2015). *Community of schools: Tips and starters: Working together*. New Zealand Government. https://assets.education.govt.nz/public/Documents/Ministry/Investing-in-Educational-Success/Communities-of-Schools/IESCommunitiesOfSchoolsTipsAndStarters-web-enabledV3.pdf

Ministry of Education (2016a). *Community of Learning: Role selection and appointment information*. New Zealand Government. https://www.education.govt.nz/assets/Documents/Ministry/Investing-in-Educational-Success/Communities-of-Schools/Community-of-Learning-Role-Selection-and-Appointment-Information-web-enabled.pdf

Ministry of Education. (2016b). *Community of learning: Guide for schools and kura*. New Zealand Government. https://www.education.govt.nz/assets/Documents/col/Communities-of-Learning-Guide-for-Schools-and-Kura-web-enabled.pdf

Ministry of Education. (2021). *Communities of learning | Kāhui ako: Evidence and data*. Ministry of Education. https://www.education.govt.nz/communities-of-learning/evidence-and-data/

Moolenaar, N. M. (2012). A social network perspective on teacher collaboration in schools: Theory, methodology, and applications. *American Journal of Education*, *119*(1), 7–39. https://doi.org/10.1086/667715

Moolenaar, N. M., Daly, A. J., Cornelissen, F., Liou, Y.-H., Caillier, S., Riordan, R., Wilson, K., Cohen, N. A. (2014). Linked to innovation: Shaping an innovative climate through network intentionality and educators' social network position. *Journal of Educational Change, 15*(2), 99–123. https://doi.org/10.1007/s10833-014-9230-4

New Zealand Post Primary Teachers' Association. (2017). *Communities of Learning: The slippage between planning and implementation.* Available at: https://www.ppta.org.nz/advice-and-issues/communities-of-learning-cols/document/545

Perry, B. L., Pescosolido, B. A., & Borgatti, S. P. (2018). *Egocentric network analysis: Foundations, methods, and models.* Cambridge university press.

Reagans, R., & McEvily, B. (2003). Network structure and knowledge transfer: The effects of cohesion and range. *Administrative Science Quarterly, 48*(2), 240–67. https://doi.org/10.2307/3556658

Reeves, J. (2010). *Professional learning as relational practice.* Springer.

Rodway, J. (2019). Coaching as a knowledge mobilization strategy: Coaches' centrality in a provincial research brokering network. *International Journal of Education Policy and Leadership, 14*(5), 1–18. http://journals.sfu.ca/ijepl/index.php/ijepl/article/view/864

Rodway, J., & Farley-Ripple, E. N. (2020). Shifting our gaze: Relational space in professional learning network research. In Schnellert, L. (Ed.), *Professional learning networks: Facilitating transformation in diverse contexts with equity-seeking communities.* Emerald Publishing Limited.

Rosenholtz, S. J. (1989). Workplace conditions that affect teacher quality and commitment: Implications for teacher induction programs. *The Elementary School Journal, 89*(4), 421–39.

Scott, J. (2000). *Social network analysis.* London, UK: Sage Publications.

Scott, J. (2017). *Social network analysis* (4th ed.). Sage Publications.

Sinnema, C., Daly, A. J., Liou, Y. H., & Rodway, J. (2020). Exploring the communities of learning policy in New Zealand using social network analysis: A case study of leadership, expertise, and networks. *International Journal of Educational Research, 99*, 1–16. https://doi.org/10.1016/j.ijer.2019.10.002

Sinnema, C., Liou, Y. H., Daly, A., Cann, R., & Rodway, J. (2021). When seekers reap rewards and providers pay a price: The role of relationships and discussion in improving practice in a community of learning. *Teaching and Teacher Education, 107*, 1–14. https://doi.org/10.1016/j.tate.2021.103474

Sinnema, C., Hannah, D., Finnerty, A., & Daly, A. J. (2022). A theory of action account of an across-school collaboration policy in practice. *Journal of Educational Change, 23*(1), 33–60. https://doi.org/10.1007/s10833-020-09408-w

Spillane, J. P., Reiser, B., & Gomez, L. (2006). Policy implementation and cognition: The role of human, social, and distributed cognition in framing policy implementation. In Honig, M. (Ed.), *New directions in education policy implementation* (pp. 47–64). State University of New York Press.

Spillane, J. P., Healey, K., & Kim, C. M. (2010). Leading and managing instruction: Formal and informal aspects of the elementary school organization. In Daly, A. J. (Ed.), *Social network theory and educational change* (pp. 127–58). Harvard Education Press.

Spillane, J. P., Shirrell, M., & Sweet, T. M. (2017). The elephant in the schoolhouse: The role of propinquity in school staff interactions about teaching. *Sociology of Education, 90*(2), 149–71. https://doi.org/10.1177/0038040717696151

Stoll, L., & Louis, K. S. (2007). *Professional learning communities: Divergence, depth and dilemmas.* UK: McGraw-Hill Education.

Vanblaere, B., & Devos, G. (2016). Relating school leadership to perceived professional learning community characteristics: A multilevel analysis. *Teaching & Teacher Education, 57*, 26–38. http://dx.doi.org/10.1016/j.tate.2016.03.003

Wasserman, S., & Faust, K. (1994). *Social network analysis: Methods and applications.* Cambridge University Press.

Witten, K., Kearns, R., Lewis, N., Coster, H., & McCreanor, T. (2003). Educational restructuring from a community viewpoint: A case study of school closure from Invercargill, New Zealand. *Environment and Planning C: Government and Policy, 21*(2), 20–223. https://doi.org/10.1068/c05r

Wylie, C. (2016). *Communities of Learning | Kāhui Ako: The Emergent Stage.* New Zealand Council for Educational Research. Available at: https://www.nzcer.org.nz/research/publications/communities-learning-emergent-stage

11

The Role of Relationships: Illustrating System-Wide Disruption on Leadership Networks

David Trautman, Anita Caduff, and Alan J. Daly

Introduction

By and large, practitioner literature on school leadership is written with the underlying assumption, and often the explicit acknowledgment, that the role of leaders is not to *maintain* systems, but rather to *change* them. One would be hard-pressed to find a piece of literature on education—practitioner-focused or otherwise—which states that schools are good as they currently stand. Paradoxically, while leaders are being told they need to change schools, they operate within an organizational system that is very traditional, in the sense that it is highly bureaucratic, regulated, and hierarchical. Typically, responsibility for this rigidity is directed up the ladder toward district leadership. At the same time, even in the face of disruption aimed at organizational shift, for example, through personnel changes during restructuring, the "grammar" of the organization rarely changes; the typical ways of doing business seem to maintain themselves (Tyack & Tobin, 1993).

Disruptions in the form of turnover, churn, and restructuring are frequent among school and district leaders (Goldring & Taie, 2018; Grissom & Andersen, 2012; Snodgrass Rangel, 2018). On the one hand, these system-wide disruptions may have positive localized effects if less-performing and disconnected individuals leave. On the other hand, they might impact systems negatively when they result in the loss of leaders who are central in leading improvement efforts, creating an environment for positive change, and building positive social structures imperative to the transformation of their institution (Björk et al., 2014; Louis et al., 2010). While research sheds light on reasons for leadership churn and its effects on teacher and student outcomes (see Snodgrass Rangel, 2018), less is known about the turnover's link to the leaders' social networks (Finnigan & Daly, 2016). Therefore, this exploratory longitudinal multiple case study examines the connection between district restructuring and the implications for leaders' social networks in four case-areas that were part of a large urban US school district.

The networks we examine are formed around professional interactions between leaders, and in particular, on the extent to which they regularly bring useful, new ideas from research to their colleagues. Asen et al. (2013) defined research evidence as "empirical findings derived from systematic analysis of information, guided by purposeful research questions and method" (p. 40). However, respondents might have a different understanding of research, and might consult school evaluations, student performance data, leadership books, or publications from professional organizations instead (Asen et al., 2013; Farley-Ripple, 2012). Because research evidence use is not habitually embedded in interactions within the district, these networks provide portraits of how developing leadership practices may be impacted by churn.

We situate these cases in a theoretical framework around structure and agency informed by a social network perspective to further explore the opportunities and implications for transformation to occur during such shifts. In doing so, we invite readers to consider the role of relationships in systems change. We begin by sketching out our theoretical grounding. We then apply this framework as an interpretive lens through which to view a longitudinal portrait of change in leadership networks in a district experiencing restructuring. Our empirical analysis is not designed to be demonstrative, but rather illustrative of the theoretical model. We then close with a discussion highlighting both the possibilities for agency in change efforts and opportunities for further research.

Theoretical Framing—Structure and Agency from a Social Network Perspective

Social Networks

The social network perspective centers relationships between individuals over the individual attributes of actors (Borgatti et al., 2018; Wasserman & Faust, 1994). Individuals' access to resources and influence is considered in light of their position within the larger network's structure in which they are embedded (Coleman, 1988; Gould, 1989; Granovetter, 1973; Lin, 2001). Indeed, educator social network structures have been found to facilitate and constrain, *inter alia*, collective efficacy (Berebitsky & Salloum, 2017; Daly et al., 2010), innovative climate (Moolenaar et al., 2010), retention of teachers (Hopkins et al., 2019), and exchange of best practices (Daly & Finnigan, 2012). Social networks were even associated with student outcomes (Daly et al., 2014; Pil & Leana, 2009). Furthermore, individual educators' access to expertise (Frank et al., 2004), commitment (Thomas et al., 2020), and research use (Brown et al., 2016) were determined by the organizations' social structure and educators' position in the social network. These empirical findings point not just to the importance of social networks in research, but also to the importance of understanding more broadly the role of relationships structuring social life.

Structures

A relational approach to structures views them as composed of and dependent upon relationships. This perspective is a departure from how people often think about structures as things external to, or imposed upon, social life. Despite their *appearance* as independent, exogenous "things" outside of relationships, structures are, in their origin, an aggregated, collective result of individual interactions (Emirbayer, 1997; Martin, 2009; Crossley, 2022). The relational position we thus embrace is that social relationships, schemas,[1] and resources make up structure (Crossley, 2022; Martin, 2009). This theoretical stance traces back to conceptualizations of structure developed over the last half-century. Sewell (1992), for example, defines structures as "constituted by mutually sustaining cultural schemas and sets of resources that empower and constrain social action and tend to be reproduced by that action" (p. 27). Schemas (or "rules") encompass the tacit, generalizable procedures which guide and pattern social life, or, more basically, the way we do things, while resources tend to have a physical existence (Giddens, 1984). However, it is only within the context of social relationships that schemas and resources constitute a structure; Crossley (2022) emphasizes this by explicitly including "relationships" as a "third R" (p. 172) to the rules and resources shorthand for structure. He emphasizes a social network perspective and that schemas and resources do not exist *within* individuals, but *between* them. In other words, the relationship between two individuals is the basic building blocks of structure because that is the site of where schema and resources are developed, acquire meaning, and are reproduced. Because social network analysis allows us to view how specific relationships are organized within a network, methodologically, social network analysis allows us to empirically examine small "slices" of these larger structures (Crossley, 2022).

Concretizing this theoretical explanation, let us apply it to an example within the context of a school district. Within these organizations there are a number of structures which pattern and shape social behavior, such as hierarchy. Conceivably, all employees within the school district accept that there is an organizational hierarchy and expect to follow the orders that are issued by those above them. No one needs to tell principals that they have to follow the directives of the superintendent; it is a habitual expectation. This is a cultural schema that is also reinforced by concrete resources, such as collective bargaining agreements and the organization of physical space (e.g., the meaning held by an office with an imposing desk). As a structure, hierarchy in district organizations exists because we allow and expect our social and professional relationships to be structured as such. It also has the appearance of being a fixed entity, something that just *is*. While it may be inconceivable to abandon all notions of hierarchy—as it is a structure that extends far beyond the district organization and permeates virtually all social life—district leaders *can* develop horizontal relationships with others in vertically distinct positions. That this departure from the type of relationship is implicitly reinforced by the hierarchical structure, in essence, is agency. While social network analysis cannot provide evidence of agency *per se,* it can be used to show when, where, and how new patterns of interaction develop and collapse. This, in turn, enables us to visualize and describe how these relationships take shape over time within an organization.

Agency

Because the fundamental building blocks of structures are individual relationships, there exists the possibility for actors to transform structures within those very relationships. As we noted, it is possible to depart from structural expectations within our dyadic interactions. In other words, innovatively engaging different schema or resources within a context, going "against the grain," or working to establish a new routine for interactions are all ways in which actors actively shape the nature of their relationships. From this perspective, agency is a dynamic, transactional process (Emirbayer, 1997; Emirbayer & Mische, 1998).

At the organizational level, there exists the possibility that we can within a network develop new, localized patterns of behavior (e.g., "organizational culture"). Leaders can, for example, establish patterns of relationships that are more horizontal (e.g., a culture in which subordinates feel comfortable critiquing the ideas of their superiors). We can also develop practices that are not structurally reinforced. School districts, for example, set up such that use of research evidence regularly is *not* embedded in practice via structural mechanisms (i.e., it is not naturally reproductive to the extent that it is unconsciously embedded in the way educators go about their work). However, it *is* possible for leaders to intentionally and regularly embed the use of research evidence into their various interactions such that it becomes standard for this to become a staple practice throughout the organization. While social network analysis alone cannot provide us with insight on the intentionality and causality behind these shifts, slices represented by sociograms illustrate the extent to which these particular relationships occur and how they are organized.

Methods

In this exploratory longitudinal multiple case study, we offer four portraits of social network change within a school system, in which we observe how interactions around research evidence within their networks are enhanced or diminished over time in the midst of leadership churn. We consider efforts toward integrating research evidence into educator practice as part of the larger national policy movement and framework of No Child Left Behind beginning in the late aughts. As we have mentioned, however, dependency on research evidence in educator practice was very much not a structural element of schools and districts. If it were, then we would see systemic, regularized patterns of these interactions regardless of the individuals involved.

Social network analysis (SNA) provides formal methods to empirically study social processes. A fundamental tenet of social network analysis is that the unit of analysis is the dyadic relationship, not the individual (Wasserman & Faust, 1994). This is important to note because what is being measured is not the degree to which individuals use research in their practice, but rather the degree to which they perceive others and are perceived by others to have brought innovative, relevant, and empirically grounded ideas into their interactions. Research evidence may be regularly offered up in conversation by an actor, but may not actually be registered as such or acted upon by their listeners, limiting its diffusion into practice.

A social network consists of actors that are connected through relationships (also called ties) (Wasserman & Faust, 1994). Longitudinal descriptive social network analysis allows us to visualize how particular aspects of localized interactions develop over time within an organization. A slice is not a comprehensive portrait of the structures in the network, but rather one specific way in which actors are organized around a particular schema. In the context of our portraits, we look at how four district leaders engaged with research evidence at two points in time in their networks. We also examine interactions around research evidence in three of the areas they led. The sociograms produced by this process provide us with the opportunity to see how networks of dyadic relationships developed over time around research evidence.

Research Site

The cases in this study come from Bern City Unified School District (BCUSD), a large school district in the Western United States spanning an area of over 200 square miles. At the time of the study, the district served over 130,000 students in preschool through grade 12. It was composed of more than 100 elementary and K-8 schools, over 40 middle and high schools, in addition to charter schools and other non-traditional variants. With more than 200 educational facilities, the district had 14,000 employees, close to half of whom (6,500) were teachers. There were a wide range of administrator positions overseeing the district, including district superintendents, area superintendents, central office directors and managers, and principals.

Given its large size, the district was divided into nine areas which were each led by an area superintendent. These areas consisted of up to three high school clusters (an elementary and middle school that feed into the high school) and were roughly the size of many mid-size districts in the United States. They were loosely organized by geographic location. During the study, in an effort to improve schools, increase alignment across the district, and improve communication and collaboration, the district restructured itself, reducing the number of areas from nine to seven. In doing so, each area was restructured such that it was only tangentially similar to its previous organization. It should be noted that the need for restructuring was driven by a number of factors external to district-level employees, including the governing board's directives and state mandates due to the district's underperformance on Adequate Yearly Performance. Not insignificantly, the district was also facing a significant budget shortfall, which meant that at the time of restructuring, there were a number of teacher "pink slip" layoffs which, according to participants, was strongly felt at the sites. On top of this, during this restructuring process, approximately 20 percent of BCUSD's leaders left the district.

Participants and Data Collection

Over a three-year period, data were collected from the district and area superintendents, central office staff, and principals at the school sites regarding the organizational climate, organizational learning, and social interactions around research use. In this chapter we examine social network data produced by participant responses to the question, "Which site administrators/district office administrators regularly bring new ideas from research that you use (by regular we mean at least twice a month and by research we mean empirical studies)?" Participants responded to this prompt using a full leadership roster, known as saturation sampling (Carolan, 2014). This produced binary data in which participants were either nominated or not.

In year 1, there were 257 leaders represented in the data collection, of which we knew the positions of 94.2 percent of the district leadership team. The majority of these positions were site principals (185 or 71.9 percent), followed by central office administrators (44 or 17.1 percent) and area as well as superintendents (13 or 5.1 percent). In year 3, there were 248 leaders represented in the data collection, of which we knew the positions of 96.4 percent. The majority of these positions continued to be site principals (173 or 69.8 percent), followed by central office administrators (57 or 23.0 percent) and area as well as superintendents (9 or 3.6 percent). As many as 203 participants belonged to the leadership team in both years 1 and 3. Response rates for social network questions in year 1 were 91.4 percent and 76.2 percent in year 3. Generally, in social network analysis a response rate of above 70 percent is required (Kossinets, 2006).

Data Analysis

Sociograms were drawn using Netdraw software (Borgatti, 2002) and network analyses conducted in UCINET (Borgatti et al., 2002). Each actor is represented by a node on the sociogram. The arrows indicate the number of ties, or nominations, between nodes. Arrows pointing to a node represent a tie in which that individual was nominated by another (located at the other end of the arrow). Nodes are sized according to indegree; the more nominations someone receives, the larger their node appears on the sociogram. Double-sided arrows indicate reciprocal nominations, in which two individuals nominated each other in response to the research evidence prompt. In addition to indegree, individual measures also include outdegree, which grows in proportion to the number of nominations issued by each participant. Whole-network measures include density (the number of actual ties divided by the number of possible ties), centralization (the extent to which individual nodes dominate the network), and average degree (the average degree of all the nodes) (Borgatti et al., 2018; Wasserman & Faust, 1994).

The egocentric network maps were drawn from the whole social network, and include the ego, alters one step away from the ego (i.e., one-step ego networks), and ties among the ego and alters. With alters, we refer to actors who are directly connected to the ego.

Findings

Case 1: The Promotion of an Area Superintendent Enhances the Social Infrastructure around the Diffusion of Research Evidence

We begin by looking at a case where the *promotion* of a particular leader within a particular network led to an enhanced social infrastructure around research evidence around this individual. The area superintendent in this area, "A," remained in the district throughout the study. In year 1, the experienced administrator, who had worked for more than twenty years in education, had been in the position of the area superintendent for one year and had worked in the district for three years. They had a research evidence indegree of 16 and outdegree of 5. Their direct alters (i.e., actors who were connected to them through a tie) included principals, instructional leaders, and other support staff (see Figure 11.1, graphs 1 and 2). Additionally, they were connected not only to principals from their area but had ties to principals from other areas too. In year 3, area superintendent A was promoted to the position of district superintendent. They were sought out for ideas based on research evidence by fifteen leaders (i.e., indegree); in turn, they sought out twenty colleagues for research evidence (i.e., outdegree). Overall, two years after the first data collection, Superintendent A had a more extensive ego network; they were better connected within the district and had more capacity to broker research evidence to principals. Figure 11.1 (graphs 1 and 2) shows the ego network of area superintendent A in years 1 and 3.

1. Area Superintendent A, Year 1

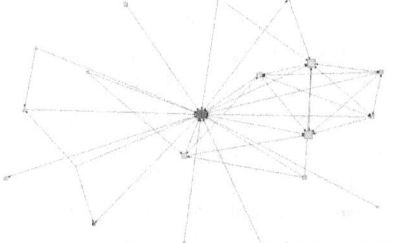

2. Area Superintendent A, Year 3

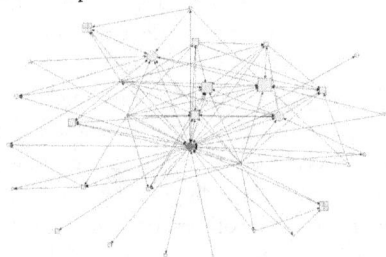

3. Area Superintendent B1 in Year 1

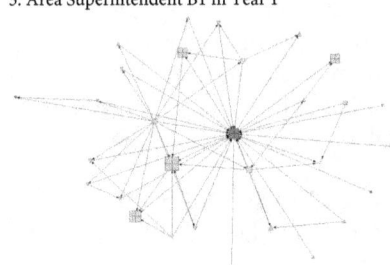

4. Area Superintendent B2 in Year 3

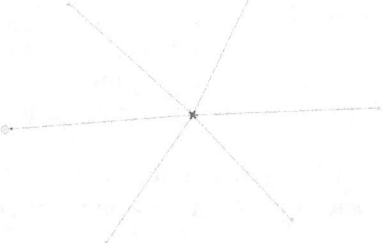

5. Area Superintendent C in Year 1

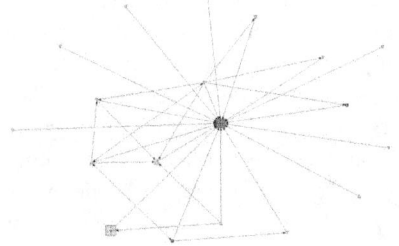

6. Area Superintendent C in Year 3

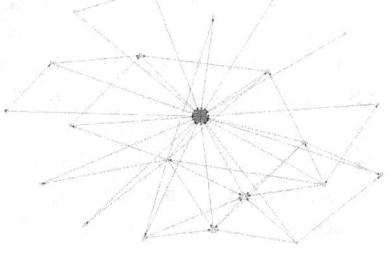

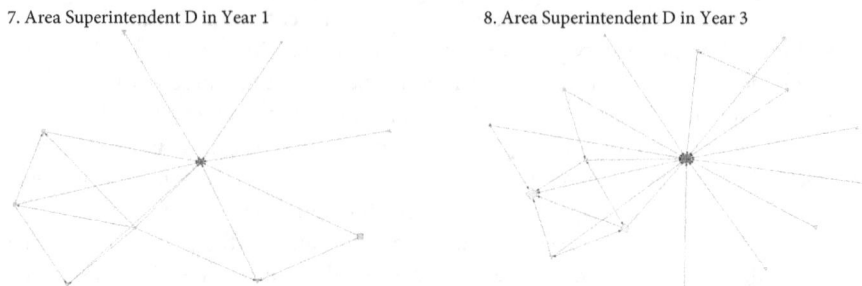

7. Area Superintendent D in Year 1

8. Area Superintendent D in Year 3

Figure 11.1 Ego network "research evidence" of area superintendents over time.

Note. Light gray = alters; dark gray = ego (i.e., area superintendent); squares = instructional leaders; circles = other support staff; down-triangle = principals from lower-performing schools; up-triangles = principals from higher-performing schools; diamond = district superintendent; boxes = area superintendents; circle-in-box = other; plus = not identified. Node size indicates the indegree in the district network. Some actors changed their position between years 1 and 3; thus, their node's shape changed too.

In the case of area superintendent A, we see that their repositioning led to a development of a stronger network of interactions around research evidence use. In these ego networks, we see that a previously well-connected leader was placed in a role that amplified their need to be central in interactions in general, which appeared to fuel a more robust set of interactions that facilitated diffusion of and access to research evidence. In other words, in their new role, they both recognized more individuals for providing useful research evidence and were exposed to more individuals who were highly rated by others for bringing research evidence to the table. As a central leader in the district, the development of these interactions around research evidence not only has the potential to influence decision-making from an evidence-based perspective, but also presents the potential for research evidence use to become embedded within the network to an extent that it becomes an expected part of engagement in leadership work (i.e., an expected way of doing things). While more data need to be collected on how this is sustained over time, it presents a promising picture of how the regularity of interactions around research evidence can expand.

Case 2: The Positioning of a New Area Superintendent Diminishes the Social Infrastructure around the Diffusion of Research Evidence

We now look at how the *replacement* of a particular leader within a particular network diminished the social infrastructure around research evidence. The area superintendent in this area, "B," changed between years 1 and 3. The first area superintendent, B1, had more than twenty years of experience in education and as an administrator. Despite them having been the area superintendent for only one year, they were well-connected in the district. They were sought out for research ideas by twenty-one respondents (i.e., indegree), and they reached out to eight leaders for research ideas (i.e., outdegree). Their direct alters included eleven principals of area B, instructional leaders, other support staff, and other area superintendents (see Figure 11.1, graph 3). They were succeeded by area superintendent B2 who, as well, had more than twenty years of experience as an educator and had worked in the district for more than twenty years. Compared to area superintendent B1, in year 3, the new area superintendent, B2, was sought out less often for research ideas (indegree = 5), and they did not seek out others for research ideas often (outdegree = 1). Their ego network (see Figure 11.1, graph 4) shows that they were sought out by only four principals, and other principals in area B had to seek research ideas from someone else. At the same time, this area also faced a significant degree of turnover, with only three principals of twenty remaining in the area between years 1 and 3.

In the case of area superintendent B2, we see that the leadership transition led to a diminishment of research evidence use in interactions. In these ego networks, we see that a previously well-connected leader was replaced by someone who, though they were also an experienced educator with a longer tenure in the district, did not engage in interactions that facilitated the diffusion of and access to research evidence.

The corresponding change in the area network was also noticeable (see Figure 11.2, graphs 1 and 2); between year 1 and 3, the density, connectedness, and average degree of the area B's network decreased, meaning that leaders had fewer ties through which they could access ideas originating from research evidence. While the area network data could be a function of turnover (and fewer interactions and ties in general, regardless of whether the content was research based or not), the egonet evidence suggests that the new leader also did not engage in regularized interactions around research evidence use. Though there was an increase in the possible number of ties due to an increase in the number of leaders in the area due to restructuring, there was a decrease in the actual number of ties identified around research evidence use. Despite their experience as an educator, area superintendent B2 did not appear to engage in the types of relationships which would foster a patterned, expected use of research to inform practice in their network. Instead, during this leadership transition a large capacity to diffuse and broker research evidence was lost. Note that this occurred at the same time that the district superintendent developed a more robust network around research evidence, suggesting that the growth experienced by Superintendent A was neither uniform across the district nor a function of external pressures dictating evidence use. This case highlights the influence particular individuals may play in shaping the nature of interactions within their networks.

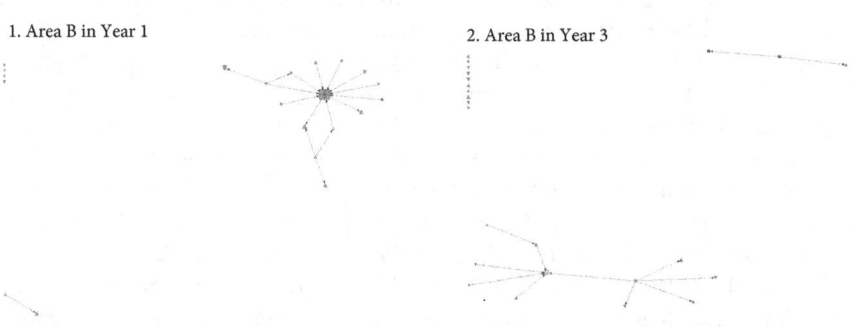

1. Area B in Year 1

2. Area B in Year 3

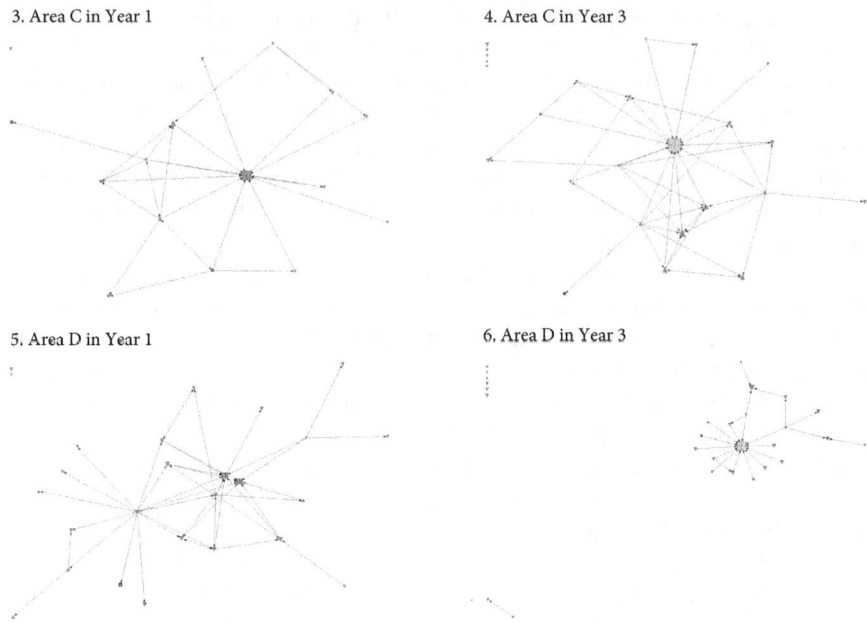

Figure 11.2 Area network "research evidence" over time.

Note. diamond = district superintendent; boxes = area superintendents; squares = instructional leaders; circles = other support staff; down-triangle = primary school principals; up-triangles = secondary school principals; circle-in-box = other principals; plus = not identified. Node size indicates the indegree in the district network. Some actors changed their position between years 1 and 3; thus, their node's shape changed too.

Case 3: The Retention of an Area Superintendent in a Restructured Area Enhanced the Social Infrastructure around the Diffusion of Research Evidence

We now look at how the *retention* of a particular leader within a particular network enhanced the social infrastructure around research evidence. The restructuring of area C resulted in the number of area members increasing from sixteen to twenty-five between years 1 and 3. From the initial sixteen members, ten remained in the area (62.5 percent), while three left the district and three leaders moved to another area. Of the new members in the area, fourteen moved from other areas and positions while one was newly hired. Despite the majority (60 percent) of leaders being new to the area, both the ego network (Figure 11.1, graphs 5 and 6) and area network (Figure 11.2, graphs 3 and 4) for research evidence developed over the three years, particularly in relation to the number of ties. Through this process, the centrality of the area superintendent in the area network increased. The density of their egonet also increased, indicating their alters reaching out to each other for ideas originating from research evidence more often than they did in year 1. However, the area superintendent did not reach out to anyone for ideas from research evidence either in year 1 or in year 3.

This unidirectional nature of the area C superintendent's interactions around research evidence highlights an important feature of relationships; though they were highly recognized for bringing research into the conversation of peers, they did not indicate receiving it from other peers. This highlights the relational nature of a dyad, which, even in unidirectional ties, is dependent upon action on both ends; in this case, someone must both provide research evidence and have this acknowledged by someone else. Even though Superintendent C had an outdegree of 0, other individuals in their network recognized colleagues in the network who provided them with relevant, useful research evidence. Regardless, this case illustrates that, despite disruption to their area, leaders within this network did not just maintain the use of research evidence in their interactions, but further developed it. In other words, despite the restructuring and churn, the area's social infrastructure did not seem to be damaged. It also highlights the potential for research evidence use to become further embedded within the network even in the absence of key members *receiving* it from others.

Case 4: The Retention of an Area Superintendent in A Restructured Area Diminished the Social Infrastructure around the Diffusion of Research Evidence

Next we see how the *retention* of a particular leader within a particular network diminished the social infrastructure around research evidence. While the increase in members for area D—an increase from twenty-six to twenty-eight—was not as large as that of area C, their new sizes were comparable. They also faced similar levels of churn; from the twenty-six members in year 1, thirteen remained in the area (50 percent). Ten leaders left the district, three leaders changed to another area, seven leaders moved from other areas and positions to area D, and eight principals were newly hired. The area network map (Figure 11.2, graphs 5 and 6) and whole network measures suggest that there was damage to the capacity to disseminate and access research evidence through restructuring. While area C increased its ties over the three years, in Area D, the number of ties decreased from forty-four to twenty-three, even with an increase in the number of nodes.

Despite the similarities to the situation in area C, in the case of area superintendent D, we see that their continued leadership was met with a diminishment of research evidence use in interactions within the area. Interestingly, within the four cases, this area superintendent had the least-developed research evidence egonet (Figure 11.1, graphs 7 and 8) in year 1. While their egonet had developed by year 3, it still remained less developed than the other area superintendents starting points in year 1. Though this area superintendent expanded their centrality and was a constant throughout the restructuring process, the capacity to access and distribute research evidence in the area was lost through the restructuring.

Discussion

In each of the four cases, despite experiencing similar levels of churn, we see vastly different outcomes within leadership networks. Some leaders and networks further developed their interactions around research evidence, while in other areas these networks were diminished. We saw, for example, in area B that the network relationships around research evidence did not sustain themselves given other structural pressures once Superintendent B1 left. In areas C and D, despite similar levels of churn and stability in the area superintendent role, we saw contrasting development in the research evidence networks; in area C capacity was gained while in area D it was diminished.

As illustrations, these sociograms cannot alone explain the causality behind the shifts. What they can do is show what happens to leaders' networks around research evidence use during a period of system-wide disruption and restructuring. We suggest that the development and inhibition of these networks were related on some level to the individual leaders' behavior around research evidence use within the network. However, methodologically, the social network perspective requires that the actor must both *engage* in a particular way that is correspondingly *received* by another. In this sense, behavior cannot be disconnected from the relationships in which it occurs, even while it retains elements of individual choice. For example, the growth in the egonet for Superintendent A suggests at least some degree of intentionality on their part in accessing the research evidence provided by others. That is, the increase in their outgoing nominations indicates not just that others in their network were proffering research evidence, but also that Superintendent A acknowledged and internalized these offerings as relevant and useful research to their practice.

Other area superintendents appeared to engage in different ways which may have impacted their area networks. For example, Superintendent C had a large number of indegree nominations, but no outdegree nominations. Despite the unidirectionality, the network around them experienced an increase in the capacity for research evidence diffusion. One possible explanation could be that their modeling of research evidence-based conversations in relationships resulted in a spread of research evidence-based conversations as a practice. By contrast, the area D superintendent developed their own network but their area network's capacity diminished. As we noted, in both year 1 and year 3 they had a less-developed egonet in comparison to the other area superintendents. While the expansion of their role positively influenced their own network, their leadership did not develop capacity with their network. In other words, it appears their influence was not leveraged to develop a more robust, research-informed environment in their area.

All of these cases indicate that change efforts, including those induced by disruption, must take into account the role of relationships in shaping outcomes. That is, even when operating within the same context, role, and policy framework, we see that the ways in which individuals form relationships vary. When district leaders are promoted, repositioned, or retained, decision-makers need to consider the potential impact on the network as a whole. Policies and procedures are limited in their ability to effect change because they are dependent on how they take shape within the context of social interactions (i.e., how they are enacted within the social realm). For example, while research evidence use was part of the formal No Child Left Behind policy framework, there was not a homogeneous impact on research evidence use in practice in BCUSD. While a number of factors may explain why different areas developed varied levels of research evidence engagement within leader networks, we argue that relationships, as an expression of agency, are one factor that should not be overlooked.

By taking into account the role of relationships, systems leaders can lean into their own opportunity for agency. Like anyone else in the organization, of course, they can mobilize diverse schemas and resources in innovative ways grounded in knowledgeable reflexivity (Emirbayer & Mische, 1998; Sewell, 1992) in order to shape the nature of their interactions. In other words, they can work to transform their relationships in terms of content, directionality, emotion, trust, content, and a host of other factors. Because leadership positions often demand a greater need to be central in interactions in general, they have access to a broader network of individuals through which they can express this agency. In our first case, Superintendent A's central role, both in the formal hierarchy and network, positions them to influence the relationships built by others. One area for future research is the degree to which a deepening of relationships based on evidence use from the leader strengthens relationships based on evidence use in the network they lead.

Another key space for agency among leaders is the openings created by the unpredictability of resources (Sewell, 1992) and moments of systemic disruption (Emirbayer & Mische, 1998). Moments of crisis or disruption, for example, can provide leaders with greater latitude to hire, fire, or reposition individuals within the formal organizational structure. As we saw, the (re)positioning of individuals within the hierarchy can lead to vastly different outcomes within networks. One role of the systems leader, therefore, is to strategically manipulate professional relationships in such a way that they move the organization in a particular direction (and develop a corresponding, mutually reinforcing policy framework). It should be noted that while the system leader has the ability to dictate the professional relationships which exist by placing individuals in a structured relationship with each other and insisting that they communicate with one another (e.g., through meetings, agendas, or directives), they are limited in their ability to shape the *nature of that interaction* (e.g., prevent people from simply "checking the boxes" to ensure compliance).

Limitations and Future Research

What we cannot conclusively say based on these data is whether the changes in the area networks and egonets are occurring *because* of one another, we do suggest the changes in the area networks may be related to the individual leadership of the area superintendents. Given the variation despite similar contexts for the cases, we know that there are factors beyond the policy context and churn which are shaping the interactions within each area. However, future research that combines qualitative and quantitative methods could shed further light on the processes driving these shifts, which, with the current data, we can only descriptively observe.

In particular, we suggested that there is a certain degree of intentionality behind research evidence use in these networks and that it is thus an expression of agency; even though it may be encouraged through policy frameworks, it is up to individuals to choose to incorporate it in practice. Qualitative data collection could further shed light on the degree to which leaders are intentional about shaping their interactions around specific practices, such as research evidence use, and the extent to which this shows up within their social networks.

Because social network analysis examines dyadic relationships, it is important to consider how dynamics of race, class, and gender, among other categories, mediate relationship formation. This may be show up both through homophily, in that individuals are more likely to form relationships with those similar to themselves (McPherson et al., 2001), and through cognitive bias, in which stereotypes influence how we judge and form impressions of others (Amodio & Devine, 2006). Interpretations of who bring useful ideas from research to the table may be particularly shaped by biases. Further research should thus consider the ways in which shifts in leaders' social networks are influenced by the intersectional identities of participants.

Conclusion

Even in the same organizational role, people perform differently in terms of the nature and content of the relationships they develop. Formal positions, organizational structure, and resources alone do not in and of themselves determine how individuals will engage with one another. In other words, policies, procedures, mandates, and even job descriptions do not alone determine how practices are enacted in social spaces. Taking a relational perspective on structures and visualizing them through social network analysis enable us to observe slices of how social practices take shape. We believe that these observations highlight the possibility for individuals to actively shape and transform the network of interactions around them in the face of system-wide disruption. This also means that leaders need to take into account the role of relationships when making decisions about individuals in *particular* roles and how they will, or will not, encourage the enhancement of particular patterns of interactions within their networks. Of course, as successful interactional processes are replicated with the same individual and with other individuals, all of whom may be in communication with one another, larger interactional patterns within the organization may shift and become embedded in practice as a systems change.

Note

1   We use the terms schemas and rules interchangeably.

References

Amodio, D. M., & Devine, P. G. (2006). Stereotyping and evaluation in implicit race bias: Evidence for independent constructs and unique effects on behavior. *Journal of Personality and Social Psychology, 91*(4), 652–61. doi: https://doi.org/10.1037/0022-3514.91.4.652

Asen, R., Gurke, D., Conners, P., Solomon, R., & Gumm, E. (2013). Research evidence and school board deliberations: Lessons from three Wisconsin school districts. *Educational Policy, 27*(1), 33–63. https://doi.org/10.1177/0895904811429291

Berebitsky, D., & Salloum, S. J. (2017). The relationship between collective efficacy and teachers' social networks in urban middle schools. *AERA Open*. https://doi.org/10.1177/2332858417743927

Björk, L. G., Browne-Ferrigno, T., & Kowalski, T. J. (2014). The superintendent and educational reform in the United States of America. *Leadership and Policy in Schools*, *13*(4), 444–65. https://doi.org/10.1080/15700763.2014.945656

Borgatti, S. P. (2002). *NetDraw software for network visualization*. Analytic Technologies.

Borgatti, S. P., Everett, M. G., & Freeman, L. C. (2002). *Ucinet for Windows: Software for social network analysis*. Analytic Technologies.

Borgatti, S. P., Everett, M. G., & Johnson, J. C. (2018). *Analyzing social networks* (2nd ed.). Sage Publications.

Brown, C., Daly, A., & Liou, Y.-H. (2016). Improving trust, improving schools: Findings from a social network analysis of 43 primary schools in England. *Journal of Professional Capital and Community*, *1*(1), 69–91. https://doi.org/10.1108/JPCC-09-2015-0004

Carolan, B. V. (2014). *Social network analysis and education: Theory, methods & applications*. Sage Publications.

Coleman, J. S. (1988). Social capital in the creation of human capital. *American Journal of Sociology*, *94*, S95–S120.

Crossley, N. (2022). A dependent structure of interdependence: Structure and agency in relational perspective. *Sociology*, *56*(1), 166–82.

Daly, A. J., & Finnigan, K. S. (2012). Exploring the space between: Social networks, trust, and urban school district leaders. *Journal of School Leadership*, *22*(3), 493–530. https://doi.org/10.1177/105268461202200304

Daly, A. J., Moolenaar, N. M., Bolivar, J. M., & Burke, P. (2010). Relationships in reform: The role of teachers' social networks. *Journal of Educational Administration*, *48*(3), 359–91. https://doi.org/10.1108/09578231011041062

Daly, A. J., Moolenaar, N. M., Der-Martirosian, C., & Liou, Y.-H. (2014). Accessing capital resources: Investigating the effects of teacher human and social capital on student achievement. *Teachers College Record*, *116*(7), 1–42. https://doi.org/10.1177/016146811411600702

Emirbayer, M. (1997). Manifesto for a relational sociology. *American Journal of Sociology*, *103*(2), 281–317. https://doi.org/10.1086/231209

Emirbayer, M., & Mische, A. (1998). What is agency? *American Journal of Sociology*, *103*(4), 962–1023. https://doi.org/10.1086/231294

Farley-Ripple, E. N. (2012). Research use in school district central office decision making: A case study. *Educational Management Administration & Leadership*, *40*(6), 786–806. https://doi.org/10.1177/1741143212456912

Finnigan, K., & Daly, A. J. (2016). How leadership churn undermines learning and improvement in low-performing school districts. In Daly, A. J., & Finnigan, K. (Eds.), *Thinking systemically: Improving districts under pressure*. American Educational Research Association Publishing Group.

Frank, K. A., Zhao, Y., & Borman, K. (2004). Social capital and the diffusion of innovations within organizations: The case of computer technology in schools. *Sociology of Education*, *77*(2), 148–71. https://doi.org/10.1177/003804070407700203

Giddens, A. (1984). *The constitution of society: Outline of the theory of structuration*. University of California Press.

Goldring, R., & Taie, S. (2018). *Principal Attrition and Mobility: Results from the 2016-7 Principal Follow-Up Survey: First look (NCES 2018-66)*. U.S. Department of Education, National Center of Education Statistics. https://files.eric.ed.gov/fulltext/ED585933.pdf

Gould, R. V. (1989). Power and social structure in community elites. *Social Forces, 68*(2), 531. https://doi.org/10.2307/2579259

Granovetter, M. S. (1973). The strength of weak ties. *American Journal of Sociology, 78*(6), 1360–80.

Grissom, J. A., & Andersen, S. (2012). Why superintendents turn over. *American Educational Research Journal, 49*(6), 1146–80. https://doi.org/10.3102/0002831212462622

Hopkins, M., Bjorklund, P., & Spillane, J. P. (2019). The social side of teacher turnover: Closeness and trust among general and special education teachers in the United States. *International Journal of Educational Research, 98*, 292–302. https://doi.org/10.1016/j.ijer.2019.08.020

Kossinets, G. (2006). Effects of missing data in social networks. *Social Networks, 28*(3), 247–68. https://doi.org/10.1016/j.socnet.2005.07.002

Lin, N. (2001). *Social capital: A theory of social structure and action.* Cambridge University Press.

Louis, K. S., Dretzke, B., & Wahlstrom, K. (2010). How does leadership affect student achievement? Results from a national US survey. *School Effectiveness and School Improvement, 21*(3), 315–36. https://doi.org/10.1080/09243453.2010.486586

Martin, J. L. (2009). *Social structures.* Princeton University Press.

McPherson, M., Smith-Lovin, L., & Cook, J. M. (2001). Birds of a feather: Homophily in social networks. *Annual Review of Sociology, 27*, 415–44. http://doi.org/10.3410/f.725356294.793504070

Moolenaar, N. M., Daly, A. J., & Sleegers, P. J. C. (2010). Occupying the principal position: Examining relationships between transformational leadership, social network position, and schools' innovative climate. *Educational Administration Quarterly, 46*(5), 623–70. https://doi.org/10.1177/0013161X10378689

Pil, F. K., & Leana, C. (2009). Applying organizational research to public school reform: The effects of teacher human and social capital on performance. *Academy of Management Journal, 52*(6). https://doi.org/10.5465/amj.2009.47084647

Sewell, W. H. (1992). A theory of structure: Duality, agency, and transformation. *The American Journal of Sociology, 98*(1), 1–29. https://doi.org/10.1086/229967

Snodgrass Rangel, V. (2018). A review of the literature on principal turnover. *Review of Educational Research, 88*(1), 87–124. https://doi.org/10.3102/0034654317743197

Thomas, L., Tuytens, M., Devos, G., Kelchtermans, G., & Vanderlinde, R. (2020). Transformational school leadership as a key factor for teachers' job attitudes during their first year in the profession. *Educational Management Administration & Leadership, 48*(1), 106–32. https://doi.org/10.1177/1741143218781064

Tyack, D., & Tobin, W. (1993). The "grammar" of schooling: Why has it been so hard to change? *American Educational Research Journal, 31*(3), 453–79.

Wasserman, S., & Faust, K. (1994). *Social network analysis: Methods and applications.* Cambridge University Press.

12

Knowledge Brokers as Informal Leaders in a Multi-District Learning Network

Joelle Rodway, Yi-Hwa Liou, Alan J. Daly, Mica Pollock,
and Susan Yonezawa

Education systems around the world embrace professional learning and development as an important capacity-building strategy for increasing human capital (Bryk et al., 2015; Stoll, 2020). Since the 1990s, professional learning communities (PLCs) have been an example of a system reform approach that considers the social side of professional learning, recognizing the importance of the collective efforts of educators supporting each other in their professional learning in order to improve school effectiveness in their local context (e.g., Harris & Jones, 2010). Despite decades of experience, there remains no common definition of PLCs (Stoll et al., 2006), and in recent years, the concept has evolved into "professional learning networks" (PLNs, see Brown & Poortman, 2018). Where PLCs focus on learning within a school (DuFour, 2007; Vanblaere & Devos, 2018), PLNs emphasize the interconnectedness of people coming from multiple spaces (i.e., not only within the same school) to learn together (Brown & Poortman, 2018; Schnellert, 2020).

Regardless of the terminology, the common point across these approaches is the foregrounding of learning as a communal activity, something that occurs in relationship with others. Each approach highlights the importance of interconnectedness among people in the pursuit of learning. This makes sense given that learning has long been regarded as a social activity (Bandura, 1977; Vygotsky, 1978). Beginning around the mid-2000s/early 2010s, education researchers joined other social scientists in using social network analysis (and related theories) to better understand the influence and impact of relational patterns on educational outcomes (e.g., Frank et al., 2004; Daly, 2010). Similar to their colleagues in other fields such as management and political science, educationalists with an interest in social dynamics began focusing on what is happening in the space in-between, emphasizing the importance of social space (Rodway & Daly, 2019).

Over the years, there has been a steady increase in the volume of education research that takes a network perspective (e.g., Yoon & Baker-Doyle, 2018; Daly, 2010). Many network studies to date focus on patterns of direct interactions—that is, the direct exchange of social resources (e.g., information, advice). Fewer studies have focused on the patterns of indirect interactions and how they influence the exchange of resources within a learning network. In this chapter, we demonstrate the importance for education leaders to understand not only that the patterns of direct interaction matter within a network, but as importantly, the patterns of indirect interaction matter as well. Using the example of the California Math Network (CMN) in the United States, we show how understanding the role of knowledge brokers—individuals who connect otherwise unconnected peers through knowledge exchange—provides a much richer understanding of the relational depth among educators within a system.

We begin this chapter with a description of the context of the study, providing the research questions that guided our work. From there, we review the literature on what is known about knowledge brokering with an emphasis on educational settings, and present a conceptual framework rooted in social network theory offering an entry point to understanding knowledge brokering as an act of informal leadership within a social ecosystem.

The California Math Network

The CMN is a collective of school districts in California that have partnered with a local university to provide a variety of professional learning opportunities (e.g., teacher-led talks, formal professional development sessions, informal network meet-ups) to upper elementary educators (i.e., fifth grade) and lower secondary educators (i.e., sixth grade) with opportunities to improve mathematics instruction. Each academic year, university faculty and staff work with school district personnel to offer a wide variety of learning opportunities where educators both within and across member school districts can engage in instructional development and share resources with each other. The CMN leadership team focused on developing stronger connections among and between educators that span the transition years from elementary to secondary schools within the math network—an important, yet understudied, dimension of school systems. While the math network continues its works at present, our study focused on its early development from 2016 to 2018.

Given the group's explicit focus on cultivating relationships between groups of educators who typically do not interact, our research team focused attention on the role of knowledge brokering within and across schools and school districts to examine more robustly the extent to which the CMN was achieving its goal of building across school and district relationships. Thus, the research questions guiding this research included the following:

1. What are the patterns of knowledge exchange within this network?
2. Who are the knowledge brokers in this network? To what extent do they align with the formal organization of the school districts?

What Is Knowledge Brokering?

The idea of "linking agents" (Louis, 1977) has been around for decades as has the presence of scholars interested in knowledge dissemination and knowledge utilization (e.g., Louis, 1998, 2010; Weiss, 1979). In more recent times, the term "knowledge mobilization" (KMb) has evolved in the field of education research, focusing specifically on the connections between research, policy, and practice (Cooper et al., 2009). Drawing on the early work of linking agents within the KMb context, the term "knowledge broker" has come to refer to those individuals that facilitate connections between otherwise disconnected people that mobilize resources within a defined group (Bornbaum et al., 2015). There are many other terms used in the field of educational administration that also refer to knowledge brokers, including "intermediaries" (Honig, 2004) and boundary spanners (Malin & Brown, 2020). Despite its growing popularity, the concept of a knowledge broker is often not clearly articulated in education research (Neal et al., 2022), yet there is some work that focuses on the characteristics of the people and agencies that are engaged in knowledge brokering work (see Cooper, 2014).

Much of the education research that considers the role of knowledge brokers focuses on research and evidence use (e.g., Daly et al., 2014; Farley-Ripple et al., 2018). However, some studies (e.g., Jusinski, 2021; Macdonald, 2015) take a broader approach considering what types of education knowledge are mobilized more broadly. There is wide variation in how knowledge brokering activity manifests itself across different contexts. Social activity is highly dependent on context, which brings a multitude of challenges to generalizing about knowledge brokering activity. For example, formal organizational hierarchies can influence patterns of brokering activity in some contexts (e.g., Farley-Ripple & Buttram, 2015; Hopkins et al., 2018) but not in others (e.g., Daly et al., 2014; Rodway, 2019). Similarly, while some research focuses on the importance of external organizations knowledge intermediaries or brokers (Honig, 2004; Malin et al., 2018), other research demonstrates how individuals from inside educational organizations are integral to knowledge brokering activity (van den Boom-Muilenburg et al., 2022), even highlighting how school-level practitioners are often overlooked in this space (Farley-Ripple & Grajeda, 2019).

Wenger (1998) defined [knowledge] brokering as "connections provided by people who can introduce elements of one practice into another" (p. 105). This view emphasizes the connection between the known and the unknown where socially situated individuals bridge the knowledge gap. While there is no universally accepted definition of a broker (Neal et al., 2022), there are some common elements of knowledge brokering work that have been identified in the literature. Knowledge brokering is predicated on trust (Van Kammen et al., 2006). Knowledge brokers tend to be either internally or externally situated (Beibel et al., 2013; Wenger 1998) and support collaboration and knowledge sharing by facilitating processes that identify common goals (Bornbaum et al., 2015). They identify and coordinate opportunities through communicating and sharing the knowledge needed to build capacity to carry out complex work (van Kammen et al., 2006; Ward et al., 2012). What this work looks like in practice, particularly in education, remains an area for further research (Ward, 2020).

Knowledge Brokering from a Social Network Perspective: A Conceptual Framework

Social network theory and analysis offers a particular view of knowledge brokering and the people who carry out the work of connecting others with the resources they need. From a social network perspective, knowledge brokers are identified by focusing on "one's position within the social space" (Rodway et al., 2021, p. 150); that is, they are identified by measuring the extent to which they are facilitating connections between people who, in the absence of their relationship with the knowledge broker, would not be connected at all. Social network analysis (SNA) allows researchers to identify who is facilitating knowledge brokerage by focusing on the patterns of interaction among and between the people within a group such as a school, a professional learning community or network, and so forth (Borgatti et al., 2018; Rodway, 2019; Rodway & Daly, 2019). Using theoretical concepts such as *cohesion* and *centrality*, SNA describes social ecosystems in terms of the extent that relational patterns in the network facilitate and/or constrain resource exchange (i.e., cohesion) and it highlights actors who are influencing the flow of resources within a network (i.e., centrality).

Connectedness: The Relational Foundation of Knowledge Brokering

Connection is the relational foundation of knowledge brokering given that it is an inherently social task. The more cohesive a network—that is, the more connected the network (Borgatti et al., 2018)—the easier it is for resources to be mobilized within it as pathways for resource exchange are more plentiful. SNA offers many measures that can be used to characterize the degree of connectedness within a network. *Density* is the most common measure; it identifies the number of ties present in a network as a proportion of the total number of possible ties (Wasserman & Faust, 1994). *Centralization* is another cohesion measure that identifies the extent to which relational activity focuses on a specific set of actors in the network (Carolan, 2014). In highly centralized networks, a small number of people are more active than others. It results in core-periphery structures where the network "core" is composed of an active group of members, who have greater access to network resources. Accompanying the core is the network "periphery" where less active network members have less access to resources. *Fragmentation* is a complementary measure that provides an understanding of the extent to which, given the patterns of interaction within a group, members can access the resources from others. It is the opposite of connectedness (Borgatti et al., 2018). When fragmentation scores are high (i.e., close to 1.0), many actors in the network are unable to connect with others, thereby restricting resource flow. *Reciprocity* measures the number of relationships where resources flow in both directions—that is, the actors sharing the relationship both provide and receive resources from each other. Collectively, these measures (along with others not mentioned here) provide an overall understanding of the degree of connectedness within a network. This is an important starting point when thinking about knowledge brokering. It theoretically stands that, in more cohesive networks (i.e., networks with a high degree of connectedness), there is greater opportunity for knowledge brokering. Network centrality measures help us to focus on this individual level of activity.

Centrality: Measuring Direct versus Indirect Knowledge Brokering Activity

Although not often presented in this way in academic literature, from our view, knowledge brokering can be conceived of as both a direct and indirect activity. Take for example the exchange of advice (or other forms of information). In a network context, actor A—let's call them Dale—might reach out to Taylor (actor B) asking for advice. In this context, Dale is directly providing Taylor with advice; they are directly brokering knowledge to another individual who, in the absence of this relationship, may not have access to that advice. Network measures of *degree centrality* provide details on direct resource brokering (i.e., knowledge brokering) activity. Degree centrality describes an individual's position in the network (Wasserman & Faust, 1994). The higher one's degree centrality score, the more connections they maintain within the network. It can be interpreted in many ways in terms of consequence (Borgatti et al., 2018). For example, individuals with high levels of degree centrality are often thought of as prominent or prestigious actors in a network (Prell, 2011).

Degree centrality can be considered in two ways: in terms of who is seeking a resource and who is providing a resource. *Outdegree centrality* is a measure that can be used to identify resource seekers. The more times a person asks someone else for advice (or another social resource), the higher their outdegree score. Similarly, *indegree centrality* is a measure that identifies resource providers. The more times an individual has been named as the source of advice, for example, the higher their indegree score. It is these individuals—the resource providers—who are functioning in the capacity of knowledge brokers. As such, indegree centrality can be taken as a measure of direct knowledge brokering activity.

However, social resources are not only accessible through direct ties (i.e., our direct relationships with others). SNA also provides us with tools to consider *indirect* forms of knowledge brokering. *Betweenness centrality* identifies the extent to which a person mediates connections between others who are not directly connected in the network (Carolan, 2014). Recall from the earlier example where Dale (Actor A) reached out to Taylor (Actor B) for advice—an example of direct knowledge exchange—think about what happens if Taylor had previously received advice from Morgan (Actor C). In this case, Dale and Morgan have an indirect connection mediated by Taylor through which forms of knowledge (i.e., advice) may flow. As a result, Taylor would have a higher betweenness centrality score because they are the mediator. These two scenarios provide an illustration of the conceptual framework focusing on direct and indirect knowledge brokering activity used in this study. Figure 12.1 provides an illustration of these two approaches to knowledge brokering through direct and indirect activity.

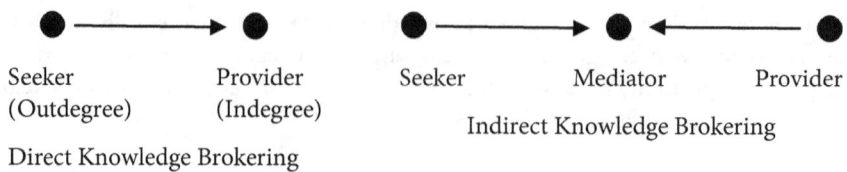

Figure 12.1 Conceptual Framework: Direct versus Indirect Knowledge Brokering.

Methods

In this study, we focused on data collected from two school districts that participated in the CMN in 2016–2018. These two districts shared a common commitment to improving mathematics instruction within their schools. Uniquely, these two districts were feeder school districts—that is, one district served elementary school-aged children in the community (i.e., Kindergarten through fifth grade) while the other served youth in the middle and secondary school system (i.e., sixth through twelfth grades). This is an important aspect of this work as there is scant research that focuses on the elementary to middle school transition. Because data were collected across two academic years, we were able to map the network dynamics and evolution within and across the school districts. As a result of this longitudinal design, the research team was able to examine the patterns of social change within the network, providing insight into the influence of the math network's reform efforts (Borgatti et al., 2018).

Sample

Our sample included teachers, instructional coaches (i.e., individuals whose work focused on working with teachers on matters related to numeracy and mathematics), and school administrators. Over time, the people involved in a network will change; this is called *network churn* (Sasovova et al., 2010). To address this phenomenon, in our analyses, the team focused on what we called the network "stable core"—that is, those individuals who were present in the network (i.e., maintained employment in their district) throughout the duration of the study. Research shows that an individual's centrality (or prominence) in a network tends to be related to the length of time they have been involved in a school or district's reform efforts (e.g., Liou et al., 2022). Thus, the final sample included a total of fifty-eight educators (N=29 from each school district) in the stable core that included fifth and sixth grade teachers (n=36), school principals and assistant principals (n=10), and instructional coaches (n=12). At the time of the first survey administration in October 2016, participants reported being an educator for an average of 17.4 years (SD = 7.6), working in their district for an average 14.7 years (SD = 8.1 years), and in their school for an average of 7.6 years (SD = 6.8). At the time of our final survey administration in May 2018, two teachers had transitioned into instructional coach positions, and one instructional coach had returned to a teaching role.

Data Collection

A social network survey was administered to all participants that contained social network questions that asked about different types of social resources exchanged with their colleagues as well as basic demographic data (e.g., gender, number of years in the profession, in their school, and so forth). In this analysis, we focus on two instrumental relations: advice and materials. These types of relationships are investigated frequently in education research (e.g., Daly, 2010; Farley-Ripple & Buttram, 2015). Network questions were phrased intentionally to collect directed network data; responses to these questions enabled researchers to understand patterns of resource seeking behavior (from whom is the respondent seeking advice, for example) and resource provision (how frequently the participant was identified as someone who gave advice).

The survey was constructed using the roster method approach: for each question, the respondent was provided with a roster listing all staff members included in the sampling frame. This strategy is frequently used to guard against recall error (Borgatti et al., 2018). Respondents were not limited in the number of colleagues they could nominate in their responses (i.e., they could nominate as many people as they liked), and for each colleague they identified, they were asked to identify the frequency of their interaction on a four-point scale ranging from yearly (1) to daily (4).

Data Analysis

Our team analyzed the data using UCINet (Borgatti et al., 2002) using relational datasets that included only interactions that were reported on at least a monthly basis in order to improve the reliability of the network data (Daly, 2010). A sociometric matrix was created for each relational dimension for use in the network analyses and to draw the network maps using NetDraw (Borgatti et al., 2002), a network illustration software program.

Network cohesion measures were used to characterize each relationship dimension at the whole network level. These measures included network *density* (the number of ties reported as a proportion of the total number of possible ties), *centralization* (the extent to which the network activity focused on a particular set of network actors), *fragmentation* (a measure of connectedness among network members), and *reciprocity* (the proportion of mutual ties). Together, these measures provide a robust description of the extent to which social resources such as advice, ideas, and materials can circulate throughout a network (Carolan, 2014). They provide insight into the extent to which the patterns of interaction within a group facilitate and/or constrain resource exchange (Wasserman & Faust, 1994).

Given the emphasis on knowledge brokering in this study, social network measures focused on centrality, measuring each individual network member's activity (i.e., node-level). Centrality encompasses a family of measures that seek to elaborate the different ways that individuals occupy positions of prominence and prestige within a network (Carolan, 2014; Prell, 2011). In this study, we used two centrality measures.

To understand the direct connection of a resource between two educators, we used degree centrality—the most widely used of the centrality measures (Borgatti et al., 2018)—to provide an index of activity within the network. Measures of *outdegree* provided information on the number of times a CMN educator sought out a particular resource (i.e., resource seeking behavior) and measures of *indegree* identified the frequency within which an educator provided a resource to another (i.e., resource provision). In addition, our team used betweenness centrality to illuminate those individuals who were brokering relationships between two otherwise unconnected individuals within the CMN. Combined, these measures provide us with a rich description of the different paths through which participants within the CMN have access to the resources—in this case, advice and materials—within the multi-district network.

We also used descriptive statistics to query the relationship between the demographic characteristics of the CMN educators and their centrality scores. Because these data are not independent, we used the quadratic assignment procedure (QAP) to ascertain measures of significance during means testing (Borgatti et al., 2018). The QAP is a permutation-based procedure that considers the number of times a network pattern randomly yields a particular result in order to estimate statistical significance, thereby accounting for the interdependent nature of these data.

Results

Overall Patterns of Knowledge Exchange

It is important to consider the overall patterns of interaction across the whole network to understand how forms of knowledge such as advice and materials are mobilized within a network. Table 1 presents the network cohesion measures for the advice and materials dimensions of the CMN for each time point, providing an indication of the levels of activity and details on the general characteristics of the patterns of exchange within advice and materials relationships.

Network cohesion measures provide overall metrics that can be used to understand the extent to which the observed network efficiently mobilizes the resources within it. For the advice network, we see statistically significant growth in density over the two years of the project for both advice ($t = -4.243$, $p < .001$) and materials ($t = -1.977$, $p < .05$). Although the network remains sparse—fewer than one out of every possible ten connections are present in either relational dimension—the rise in activity provides increased opportunity for advice and materials to move much more efficiently through the network by the end of the second year of the districts' involvement in the network.

In the advice network, centralization scores indicate that resource exchange is spread out across the network in terms of both resource seeking and provision. Many people are seeking and providing advice within this group. However, in the materials network, there was an increase in centralization in network activity over time. The directional centralization scores further elaborate that it is the resource-seeking behavior that is focused on a subgroup of people ($CD_{out} = 0.96$), whereas the provision of materials is a responsibility that is shared across the network ($CD_{in} = 0.192$). In other words, there is

Table 12.1 Cohesion measures for advice and materials networks

Measure	Advice (T1)	Advice (T2)	Materials (T1)	Materials (T2)
Average degree	2.02	4.14	1.62	3.22
Density[1]	0.035	0.073	0.028	0.057
Centralization[1]	0.209	0.231	0.419	0.932
Out-centralization[1]	0.160	0.230	0.382	0.960
In-centralization[1]	0.107	0.158	0.185	0.192
Fragmentation[1]	0.917	0.613	0.882	0.743
Reciprocity[1]	0.158	0.311	0.093	0.133

Note. [1] The cohesion measures can be interpreted in percentage.

a select group of people who are more frequently seeking materials within the CMN, but they are receiving these resources from a variety of people across the network.

The fragmentation scores also indicate that, over time, educators in the CMN are gaining greater access to advice and materials as the people within the network become more connected (although the change in score in the materials network is much less than the reduction in the advice network). The reciprocity scores—which indicate what proportion of the ties in the network are mutual ties (i.e., both actors named the other as a source of advice or materials)—show a strengthening of relationships over time. The proportion of reciprocal advice ties more than doubled over this time period while there was also an approximately 50 percent increase in the number of reciprocal materials ties. Overall, this network is developing in ways that enable greater mobilization of and access to advice and materials among the educators participating in the CMN. As such, there is greater opportunity for knowledge brokering in this context as the CMN evolves.

Direct Knowledge Brokering Activity

At the level of the individual actors in the network, one can conceptualize knowledge exchange through both direct and indirect activity as measured by direct and indirect ties. Measures of degree centrality focus on the direct ties that exist among pairs in a network (Borgatti et al., 2018). Recall that outdegree identifies the resource seekers in a social network and indegree identifies the resource providers. Figure 12.2 (graphs a, b, c, and d) presents the social network maps for each network at time 1 and time 2. In keeping with the focus on knowledge brokering (i.e., who is connecting whom with identified resources), the size of each node (i.e., each shape that represents a person in the CMN) corresponds with its indegree centrality score thereby identifying who are the people who are most frequently providing advice and/or materials to colleagues in the math network.

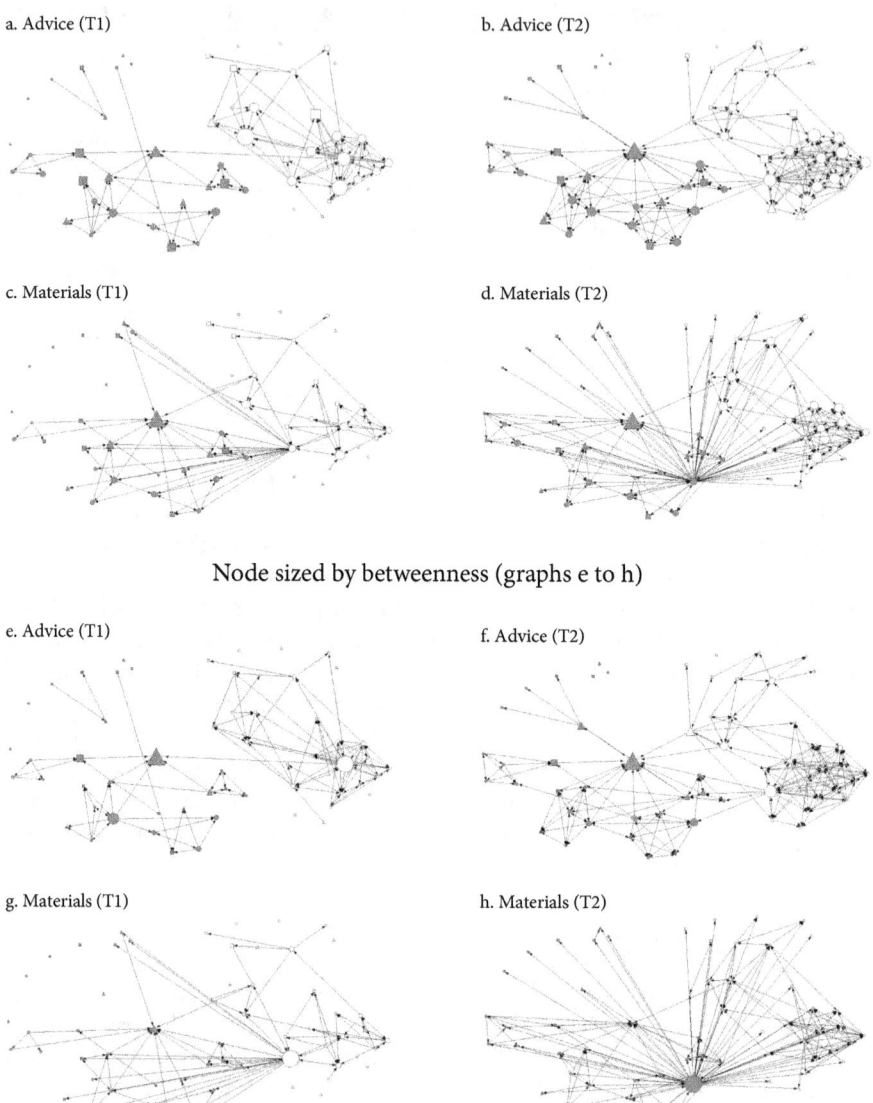

Figure 12.2 Network maps for advice and materials relations at time 1 and time 2 sized by indegree or betweenness.

Note. Gray = primary/elementary school district; white = secondary school district; circles = classroom teachers; triangles = instructional coaches; squares = principals. Outgoing arrows indicate resource seeking behavior, whereas incoming arrows identify the providers of resources.

From a knowledge-brokering perspective, recall that degree centrality can be conceptualized as a direct pathway between an individual and sought out information mediated through a direct relationship with another person (A → resource → B). Some roles within a school district—an instructional coach or school leader, for example—may be perceived as key knowledge brokers within a system because the responsibilities of their position require them to provide educators with the resources they need to develop effective learning environments. These organizationally defined positions, however, do not always accurately portray the patterns of interaction within a group (e.g., a school or a district). During the initial months of the CMN (time 1), participants averaged 2.02 advice ties (SD_{out} = 2.59, SD_{in} = 1.8) increasing by over 200 percent to an average of 4.14 ties (SD_{out} = 4.11, SD_{in} = 2.79) by the end of the second year (time 2). Similarly, the average number of ties in the materials network increased about 175 percent, rising from 1.6 ties (SD_{out} = 3.27, SD_{in} = 1.99) at time 1 to 3.22 ties (SD_{out} = 7.23, SD_{in} = 2.41) at time 2. When role type is considered in an analysis of variance between the different role groups in the math network, no significant differences are identified at either time points in either relationship domain. Similarly, there were no significant differences found based on gender, years of service in the district, school, current position, or total number of years as an educator. Differences in centrality scores appear to occur at random with none of the queried variables showing any relationship (positive or negative) with levels of direct activity within the CMN.

Indirect Knowledge Brokering Activity

Social network theory helps us to understand that our access to resources within social networks is not only mediated by our direct relationships with others in the network, but also through our *indirect* relationships with others. Betweenness centrality is a useful social network measure that identifies the people within a network who are facilitating connections among otherwise unconnected people. In other words, person A can access person C's resources indirectly through their relationship with person B (A ↔ B ↔ C). It is a common measure of brokerage. Figure 12.2 (graphs e, f, g, and h) presents the advice and materials network maps for the CMN with the size of the nodes determined by betweenness centrality score, illustrating the informal knowledge brokering that is occurring within the network.

The average betweenness scores in the advice network at time 1 and time 2 were 3.76 (SD = 9.83) and 44.35 (SD = 83.93), respectively. The higher the betweenness score, the more often that individual facilitated connections between otherwise disconnected actors in the network. In the materials network, betweenness scores averaged 8.86 (SD = 34.2) at time 1 and 19.38 (SD = 68.49) at time 2. This growth in indirect knowledge brokering activity is expected given that betweenness is a function of direct network activity. A close examination of these scores mirrors the analyses of direct patterns of interaction (i.e., indegree centrality): none of the queried participant attributes (i.e., gender, role, and various dimensions of years of service) were significantly associated with betweenness.

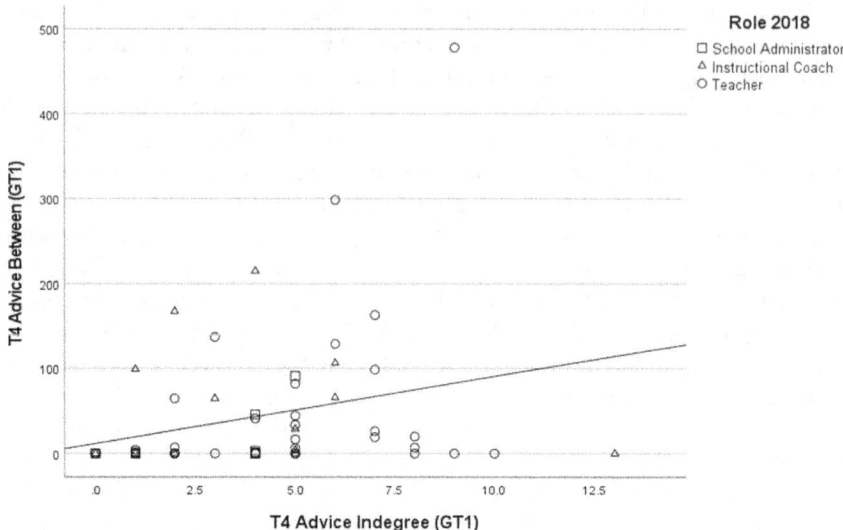

Figure 12.3 Relationship between indegree centrality (direct brokering) and betweenness centrality (indirect brokering).

While the individual attributes tested in these analyses did not reveal any significant correlations with centrality scores (i.e., role type is not significantly associated with betweenness centrality score), when time 2 indegree and betweenness scores are plotted in the same graph (see Figure 12.3), it is evident that classroom teachers play an important role in mobilizing resources within this group. While they may not often be thought of in terms of being important knowledge brokers in a learning network, it is important to acknowledge that the individuals with the most influence within a learning network do not always hold formal positions of responsibility (i.e., formal leadership roles).

Making Sense of the Data in Practical Terms

The network cohesion results, supported by a closer look at individual levels of direct and indirect activity (i.e., degree and betweenness centrality), describe a network that is strengthening over time, generating multiple new pathways for advice and materials to be mobilized among CMN participants as educators increasingly engage with each other. However, individual characteristics (e.g., role type, years of service) do not explain any of the variance in number of direct and indirect relationships for each network participant, leaving the question of what factors predict advice relationships in this analysis unanswered (an important area for future study). These findings emphasize, however, that policymakers and decision-makers cannot simply assume that the people whose formal role duties explicitly include supporting educators with resources to support their work are the most active or most central people in the network. As this analysis shows, this is not always the case. As such, we draw attention to three key points to make connections between these network analyses and their relevance for educational practice: (1) knowledge brokering is not a hierarchically defined position; (2) knowledge brokering is not a static position; and (3) relational literacy is essential to effective leadership.

Knowledge Brokering Is Not a Hierarchically Defined Position

School-based practitioners are knowledge brokers (Farley-Ripple & Grajeda, 2020). The task of ensuring that educators, particularly classroom teachers, have the resources they need for effective classroom instruction is often represented in specific roles within a school system, both inside and outside schools and district offices. Take, for example, the idea of instructional leadership, which refers to the specific practices of school administrators that build the capacity of their staff in developing teaching and learning environments that meet the needs of the learners in their schools (Hallinger, 2010). The work of instructional leadership—typically ascribed to school principals, while also extending to instructional coaches and other district office staff—is predicated on mobilizing knowledge. Connecting teachers and other education (para)professionals to knowledge that supports their learning and professional growth is a direct form of knowledge brokerage; new connections are formed where they did not previously exist between forms of knowledge and their users. However, oftentimes, people holding positions in the formal hierarchy are privileged as the assumed knowledge keepers—the higher up one's position, the more influential they are in terms of knowledge exchange. In practice, however, this assumption does not always hold as demonstrated in this case and in others (e.g., Farley-Ripple & Grajeda, 2020; van den Boom-Muilenberg et al., 2022).

Classroom teachers know their value in terms of supporting their own and their colleagues' professional learning. Professional learning "for and by teachers" (Lieberman et al., 2015) and other forms of teacher leadership have been shown to foster effective forms of knowledge exchange (Campbell et al., 2015). As this study shows, classroom teachers are often key actors in mobilizing knowledge within a learning ecosystem. They are often the informal knowledge brokers who are doing the heavy lifting of connecting colleagues with the resources required to meet their goals. This is evident in the CMN where, among the diverse participants in the learning network (many of whom had positions of responsibility that included knowledge brokering responsibilities), classroom teachers emerged as influential knowledge brokers through their direct and indirect ties with colleagues. Yet, while exceptions exist, many education systems do not intentionally maximize the benefits of the knowledge and expertise of teachers within the system in terms of leading their own professional learning.

Knowledge Brokering Is Not a Static Position

Social spaces are dynamic; they are ever changing. What exists one day might not be there the next. Meyer (2010) rightfully acknowledged, "Knowledge brokers produce, enable, and facilitate movement, and *they themselves are in movement*" (p. 123, emphasis added). The benefit of longitudinal approaches to research—and especially social network research—is that researchers are able to demonstrate the shifts in relational space over time. Initially, CMN members were restricted by the limited pathways provided by the patterns of interaction within the network. Over time, as the social network grew and relationships strengthened (i.e., increased network cohesion), opportunities for resource exchange increased through increased connectivity. As evidenced in the network illustrations, prominent individuals in terms of both direct and indirect knowledge brokering activity changed over time. While some individuals held on to their positions as knowledge brokers, others who may have found themselves in prominent positions at time 1 found themselves to be in less influential positions as the network grew (see Rodway et al., 2021 for an elaboration on this point). Increases in knowledge brokering activity cannot be assumed as groups work together over time, however. Some research studies provide examples where knowledge brokering activity decreases as relational patterns (d)evolve within a given time frame (e.g., Hubers et al., 2018).

There are many calls in the research on knowledge mobilization to focus on *the processes* that facilitate and constrain knowledge exchange (e.g., Lomas, 2007). It is important to recognize the function and influence of social space on how people become aware of, access, and use various types of knowledge in support of their work. Context is an important factor to consider when seeking to understand knowledge exchange (Ward et al., 2012). Often, attention is focused on the conditions that exist within organizational or local contexts, such as characteristics of the institution, demographic descriptions of populations, and so forth. How people interact with others and other dimensions of social spaces are often overlooked in these considerations. Building a social understanding of knowledge brokering in addition to the prevailing focus on technical understandings is essential (Lomas, 2007) to understanding the complexity of knowledge brokering work (Wenger, 1998).

Relational Literacy Is Essential to Effective Leadership

Organizational hierarchies assert power; they identify who has the authority to make decisions in identified contexts impacting defined groups of people. However, knowledge brokering is about influence—who is creating connections where they did not previously exist. As such, there needs to be a shift from thinking about knowledge brokering as a role toward a skill set (Conklin et al., 2013). Building and maintaining relationships as well as understanding how relationships influence knowledge exchange is a key function of effective knowledge brokering that requires a relational skillset. There is recognition of the importance of interpersonal relationships in the knowledge mobilization literature (e.g., Bornbaum et al., 2015; Conklin et al., 2013), but to date, there is very little research that explicitly foregrounds the relational dimensions of knowledge exchange processes.

In education contexts, there is a growing understanding of social and emotional learning that emphasizes the importance of relationships to student learning (Humphrey et al., 2020) and relational literacy is a concept that has emerged in the curriculum literature (e.g., Salmon & Freedman, 2001) as it relates to the social-emotional development of children. However, relational literacy has yet to become an area of explicit focus for teacher or leadership development despite its noted importance (see Dyer, 2001; Lasater, 2016). Given that effective professional learning networks are rooted in strong relational foundations, this needs to change if we want networked learning strategies to be successful.

Collaborative strategies for knowledge sharing and joint work in schools are gaining traction globally (e.g., Hargreaves & O'Connor, 2018). Policies such as the Communities of Learning strategy in NZ (see Chapter 10 in this volume, for example) call for schools to work with each other, directly naming knowledge sharing within and across schools as an important element of school improvement strategies. These calls for greater collaboration within systems inherently bring educators' capacity—and school leaders, in particular—to build and maintain positive school cultures through cultivating networked relationships imbued with trust and respect (Bryk et al., 2015). A key lesson of this research for school and system administrators lies in the understanding that this work (including, but not limited to, knowledge exchange and brokering) is both a direct and indirect activity. It is embedded in the patterns of interaction among and between the schools that comprise the larger learning ecosystem.

Social networks are complex and often invisible, yet they can yield significant outcomes (both positive and negative) in schools and school systems. Strong leaders recognize the importance of relational space; they deliberately develop their own relational literacy skills allowing them to better engage in and understand how social dynamics contribute to the success or demise of school and system improvement efforts. Many leaders often have a sense of what is happening in their schools in terms of direct activity, but this chapter endeavors to provoke thinking about how these direct patterns of interaction also implicate patterns of indirect activity, which are as—if not more—important in terms of mobilizing knowledge within and across organizations.

Limitations and Next Steps

As is the case with social network studies in general, these findings are applicable only to the context of the CMN. While one cannot generalize from these findings, this case does provide another example of how SNA can be applied to the study of knowledge brokering as an approach to understanding the effects of social spaces. Collectively, this body of work allows for more nuanced models of knowledge brokerage that take relational dimensions into account. As we have acknowledged elsewhere (Rodway et al., 2021), this work continues to focus on the role of the individual as knowledge brokers. This work would benefit from an extended analysis that applies frameworks such as Gould and Fernandez (1989) to consider triadic structures, better elaborating on how knowledge is being brokered within and across groups.

This study focused on the patterns of interaction as they were reported among the group of individuals who participated in the CMN over a two-year period. Other people came into and left the network over this timeframe whose presence in the network undoubtedly contributed to the social space. In this way, this work is limited and presents a partial view of knowledge brokering activity. Furthermore, people operate in multiple social networks simultaneously—a factor that must be considered when interpreting this work. This research describes only one side of a multidimensional relational space. Similarly, in this work, the focus remained within the math network, failing to consider the differing contextual differences that may affect individuals' work. In this case, the network was tightly bound; emphasis was placed on a specific subgroup of people. Future research designs should use complementary strategies that enable a more robust view of the who, what, why, and how of knowledge brokering (Ward, 2020).

Developing Relational Leaders

Enhancing relational literacy through engaging a network mindset when cultivating a learning ecosystem is the work of relational leaders. Recent research in neurosciences demonstrates how important the quality of relationships is to learning (Immordino-Yang et al., 2019). Knowledge exchange is an essential activity when learning is the goal; it undergirds the work of all professional learning and development in education. The role of knowledge brokering in this space cannot be undervalued if providing widespread access to knowledge to build capacity in schools and school systems is the goal. While the importance of connecting people to the human and social resources they need to learn and perform is generally accepted in practice, little is known about how the social dimensions of knowledge brokerage influence the outcomes of this activity. People's use of various forms of knowledge (e.g., advice and materials) is dependent on the extent to which they are connected to resources and social networks mediate the distribution of these resources through direct and indirect patterns of knowledge exchange.

Leadership is about influence, and as such, it cannot solely be acclaimed by a role defined by an organizational hierarchy. To be influential, one must invest in relationships. Given this perspective, relational leaders will come to understand that, through both their direct and indirect activity in a learning network, knowledge brokers exert their influence becoming leaders themselves whether formally recognized or not.

References

Bandura, A. (1977). *Social learning theory*. Englewood Cliffs, NJ: Prentice-Hall.
Borgatti, S. P., Everett, M. G., & Freeman, L. C. (2002). *Ucinet for windows: Software for social network analysis*.
Borgatti, S. P., Everett, M. G., & Johnson, J. C. (2018). *Analyzing social networks* (2nd ed.). Sage Publishing.

Bornbaum, C. C., Kornas, K., Peirson, L., & Rosella, L. C. (2015). Exploring the function and effectiveness of knowledge brokers as facilitators of knowledge translation in health-related settings: A systematic review and thematic analysis. *Implementation Science*, *10*(1), 1–12. https://doi.org/10.1186/s13012-015-0351-9.

Brown, C., & Poortman, C. L. (Eds.). (2018). *Networks for learning: Effective collaboration for teacher, school and system improvement*. Routledge.

Bryk, A. S., Gomez, L. M., Grunow, A., & LeMahieu, P. G. (2015). *Learning to improve: How America's schools can get better at getting better*. Harvard Education Press.

Campbell, C., Lieberman, A., & Yashkina, A. (2015). Teachers leading educational improvements: Developing teachers' leadership, improving practices, and collaborating to share knowledge. *Leading and Managing*, *21*(2), 90–105.

Carolan, B. V. (2014). *Social network analysis and education: Theory, methods, and applications*. Sage Publications.

Conklin, J., Lusk, E., Harris, M., & Stolee, P. (2013). Knowledge brokers in a knowledge network: The case of seniors health research transfer network knowledge brokers. *Implementation Science*, *8*(1), 1–10. https://doi.org/10.1186/1748-5908-8-7

Cooper, A., Levin, B., & Campbell, C. (2009). The growing (but still limited) importance of evidence in education policy and practice. *Journal of Educational Change*, *10*(2), 159–71.

Cooper, A. (2014). Knowledge mobilisation in education across Canada: A cross-case analysis of 44 research brokering organisations. *Evidence & Policy*, *10*(1), 29–59.

Cooper, A., Rodway, J., MacGregor, S., Shewchuk, S., & Searle, M. (2020). Knowledge brokering: "Not a place for novices or new conscripts." In Malin, J., & Brown, C. (Eds.) The *role of knowledge brokers in education: Connecting the dots between research and practice* (pp. 90–107). Routledge.

Daly, A. J. (2010). *Social network theory and educational change*. Harvard Education Press.

Daly, A. J., Finnigan, K. S., Jordan, S., Moolenaar, N. M., & Che, J. (2014). Misalignment and perverse incentives: Examining the politics of district leaders as brokers in the use of research evidence. *Educational Policy*, *28*(2), 145–74. https://doi.org/10.1177/0895904813513149

Dufour, R. (2007). Professional learning communities: A bandwagon, an idea worth considering, or our best hope for high levels of learning? *Middle School Journal*, *39*(1), 4–8. https://doi.org/10.1080/00940771.2007.11461607

Dyer, K. M. (2001). Relational leadership. *School Administrator*, *58*(10), 28–30.

Farley-Ripple, E. N. & Buttram, J. (2015). The development of capacity for data use: The role of teacher networks in an elementary school. *Teachers College Record*, *117*(4), 1–34.

Farley-Ripple, E., & Grajeda, S. (2019). Avenues of influence: An exploration of school-based practitioners as knowledge brokers and mobilizers. InMalin, J., & Brown, C. (Eds.), *The role of knowledge brokers in education* (pp. 65–89). Routledge.

Farley-Ripple, E. N., & Grajeda, S. (2020). Avenues of influence: An exploration of school-based practitioners as knowledge brokers and mobilizers. In Malin, J., & Brown, C. (Eds.), *The role of knowledge brokers in education: Connecting the dots between research and practice* (pp. 65–89). Routledge.

Farley-Ripple, E., May, H., Karpyn, A., Tilley, K., & McDonough, K. (2018). Rethinking connections between research and practice in education: A conceptual framework. *Educational Researcher*, *47*(4), 235–45. https://doi.org/10.3102/0013189X18761042

Frank, K. A., Zhao, Y., & Borman, K. (2004). Social capital and the diffusion of innovations within organizations: The case of computer technology in schools. *Sociology of Education*, *77*(2), 148–71.

Gould, R. V., & Fernandez, R. M. (1989). Structures of mediation: A formal approach to brokerage in transaction networks. *Sociological Methodology, 19*, 89–126. https://doi.org/10.2307/270949

Hallinger, P. (2010). Developing instructional leadership. In Davies, B., & Brundrett, M. (Eds.), *Developing successful leadership* (pp. 61–76). Springer.

Hargreaves, A., & O'Connor, M. T. (2018). *Collaborative professionalism: When teaching together means learning for all*. Corwin Press.

Harris, A., & Jones, M. (2010). Professional learning communities and system improvement. *Improving Schools, 13*(2), 172–81.

Honig, M. I. (2004). The new middle management: Intermediary organizations in education policy implementation. *Educational Evaluation and Policy Analysis, 26*(1), 65–87.

Hopkins, M., Wiley, K. E., Penuel, W. R., & Farrell, C. C. (2018). Brokering research in science education policy implementation: The case of a professional association. *Evidence & Policy: A Journal of Research, Debate and Practice, 14*(3), 459–76. https://doi.org/10.1332/174426418X152

Hubers, M. D., Moolenaar, N. M., Schildkamp, K., Daly, A. J., Handelzalts, A., & Pieters, J. M. (2018). Share and succeed: The development of knowledge sharing and brokerage in data teams' network structures. *Research Papers in Education, 33*(2), 216–38. https://doi.org/10.1080/02671522.2017.1286682

Humphrey, N., Lendrum, A., Wigelsworth, M., & Greenberg, M. T. (Eds.). (2020). *Social and emotional learning*. Routledge.

Immordino-Yang, M. H., Darling-Hammond, L., & Krone, C. R. (2019). Nurturing nature: How brain development is inherently social and emotional, and what this means for education. *Educational Psychologist, 54*(3), 185–204. https://doi.org/10.1080/00461520.2019.1633924

Jusinski, M. M. (2021). Knowledge broker teachers and professional development. *Teacher Development, 25*(2), 178–95.

Lasater, K. (2016). School leader relationships: The need for explicit training on rapport, trust, and communication. *Journal of School Administration Research and Development, 1*(2), 19–26.

Lieberman, A., Campbell, C., & Yashkina, A. (2015). Teacher learning and leadership program: Professional development for and by teachers. In Evers,, J., & Kneyber, R. (Eds.), *Flip the system: Changing education from the ground up* (pp. 230–49). Routledge.

Liou, Y.-H., Lee, Y. S., Chiang-Lin, T. J., & Daly, A. J. (2022). Leaders' advice networks over time: The role of beliefs and organizational learning during change implementation. *Journal of Educational Administration, 60*(6), 579–96. https://doi.org/10.1108/JEA-02-2022-0032

Louis, K. S. (1977). Dissemination of information from centralized bureaucracies to local schools: The role of the linking agent. *Human Relations, 30*(1), 25–42.

Louis, K. S. (1998). Reconnecting knowledge utilization and school improvement: Two steps forward, one step back. In Hargreaves, A., Lieberman, A., Fullan, M., & Hopkins, D. (Eds.), *International Handbook of Educational Change* (pp. 1074–95). Springer.

Louis, K. S. (2010). Better schools through better knowledge? New understanding, new uncertainty. In Hargreaves, A., Lieberman, A., Fullan, M., & Hopkins, D. (Eds.), *Second International Handbook of Educational Change* (pp. 3–27). Springer.

Lomas, J. (2007). The in-between world of knowledge brokering. *The BMJ, 334*(7585), 129–132.

Macdonald, D. (2015). Teacher-as-knowledge-broker in a futures-oriented health and physical education. *Sport, Education and Society, 20*(1), 27–41.

Malin, J., & Brown, C. (2020). *The role of knowledge brokers in education: Connecting the dots between research and practice*. Routledge.

Malin, J. R., Brown, C., & Trubceac, A. S. (2018). Going for broke: A multiple-case study of brokerage in education. *AERA Open, 4*(2), 1–14. https://doi.org/10.1177/2332858418769297

Meyer, M. (2010). The rise of the knowledge broker. *Science Communication, 32*(1), 118–27.

Neal, J. W., Neal, Z. P., & Brutzman, B. (2022). Defining brokers, intermediaries, and boundary spanners: A systematic review. *Evidence & Policy: A Journal of Research, Debate and Practice, 18*(1), 7–24. https://doi.org/10.1332/174426420X16083745764324

Prell, C. (2011). *Social network analysis: History, theory and methodology*. Sage Publications.

Rodway, J. (2019). Coaching as a knowledge mobilization strategy: Coaches' centrality in a provincial research brokering network. *International Journal of Education Policy and Leadership, 14*(5), 1–18.

Rodway, J., & Daly, A. J. (2019). Defining schools as social spaces: A social network approach to researching schools as organizations. In James, C., Spicer, D. E., Connolly, M., & Kruse, S. D. (Eds.), *The SAGE International Handbook on School Organization* (Ch. 35). Thousand Oaks, CA: Sage Publications.

Rodway, J., MacGregor, S., Daly, A., Liou, Y.-H., Yonezawa, S., & Pollock, M. (2021). A network case of knowledge brokering. *Journal of Professional Capital and Community, 6*(2), 148–63. https://doi.org/10.1108/JPCC-11-2020-0089

Salmon, D., & Freedman, R. A. (2001). *Facilitating interpersonal relationships in the classroom: The relational literacy curriculum*. Routledge.

Sasovova, Z., Mehra, A., Borgatti, S. P., & Schippers, M. C. (2010). Network churn: The effects of self-monitoring personality on brokerage dynamics. *Administrative Science Quarterly, 55*(4), 639–70. https://doi.org/10.2189/asqu.2010.55.4.639

Schnellert, L. (Ed.). (2020). *Professional learning networks: Facilitating transformation in diverse contexts with equity-seeking communities*. Emerald Group Publishing.

Stoll, L. (2020). Creating capacity for learning: Are we there yet? *Journal of Educational Change, 21*(3), 421–30. https://doi.org/10.1007/s10833-020-09394-z

Stoll, L., Bolam, R., McMahon, A., Wallace, M., & Thomas, S. (2006). Professional learning communities: A review of the literature. *Journal of Educational Change, 7*(4), 221–58.

Vanblaere, B., & Devos, G. (2018). The role of departmental leadership for professional learning communities. *Educational Administration Quarterly, 54*(1), 85–114. https://doi.org/10.1177/0013161X17718023

van den Boom-Muilenburg, S. N., Poortman, C. L., Daly, A. J., Schildkamp, K., De vries, S., Rodway, J., & Van veen, K. (2022). Key actors leading knowledge brokerage for sustainable school improvement with PLCs: Who brokers what? *Teaching and Teacher Education, 110*, 1–17. https://doi.org/10.1016/j.tate.2021.103577

Van Kammen, J., De savigny, D., & Sewankambo, N. (2006). Using knowledge brokering to promote evidence-based policy-making: The need for support structures. *Bulletin of the World Health Organization, 84*, 608–12.

Vygotsky, L. S. (1978). *Mind in society: The development of higher psychological processes*. Harvard University Press.

Ward, V. (2020). Using frameworks and models to support knowledge mobilization. In Malin, J., & Brown, C. (Eds.), *The role of knowledge brokers in education: Connecting the dots between research and practice* (pp. 168–81). Routledge.

Ward, V., Smith, S., House, A., & Hamer, S. (2012). Exploring knowledge exchange: A useful framework for practice and policy. *Social Science & Medicine, 74*(3), 297–304. https://doi.org/10.1016/j.socscimed.2011.09.021

Wasserman, S., & Faust, K. (1994). *Social network analysis: Methods and applications.* Cambridge, NY: Cambridge University Press.

Weiss, C. H. (1979). The many meanings of research utilization. *Public Administration Review, 39*(5), 426–31.

Wenger, E. (1998). *Communities of practice: Learning, meaning, and identity.* Cambridge University Press.

Yoon, S. A., & Baker-Doyle, K. J. (Eds.). (2018). *Networked by design: Interventions for teachers to develop social capital.* Routledge.

Part 5

Educational Leadership beyond Traditional Boundaries

13

An Investigation of the Northeast Big Data Innovation Hub through Social Network Analysis

René Bastón, Catherine Cramer, Alan J. Daly, Florence D. Hudson,
Yi-Hwa Liou, Kathryn Naum, Wren Thompson, Laycca Umer,
and Stephen Uzzo

Introduction

While academic networks intended to organize and purvey knowledge have explicit content and process goals, academic institutions collaborate with other institutions in a variety of ways. Research in general is a collaborative, cross-functional enterprise: open science and open data allow rapid sharing; validating and growing research, translational science and research to practice partnerships allow scientific ideas to be effectively put to practical use; and open knowledge networks, knowledge sharing and management, and convergent science allow intelligent interdisciplinary science to accelerate discovery (Börner et al., 2009; Bücheler & Sieg, 2011; Burgelman et al., 2019; Ledford, 2015; McKiernan et al., 2016; Stokols et al., 2008). While all of these facets of academic collaboration help "grease the wheels" of innovation, it is understanding the challenges and opportunities that the structure of those interactions affords that lead to the kinds of learning and leadership that accelerate innovation. It is our purpose here to elucidate some of those structures through a small-scale pilot study of the evolution of an innovation network, which suggests ways that academic leadership can leverage this kind of study in order to learn to more deeply understand the effect of this evolution on building innovative partnerships within the network, and to effectively respond to how the network changes over time.

Over the past two decades, interest in the formation and evolution of innovation networks has grown (Ahrweiler & Keane, 2013; Campbell, 2006; Levén, et al., 2014; Walshok, et al., 2014; Zander, 2002). While growth in innovation networks is rarely a highly controlled process (Silva & Guerrini, 2018), hub leads (central players that act as organizing and communication structures within the network) can provide essential leadership and serve as important catalysts for innovation (Gloor, 2006; Hallenga-Brink & Vervoort, 2015; Prince, et al., 2014). Dhanaraj and Parkhe (2006) indicate that orchestration of network activities by hub lead organizations can elicit effective knowledge mobility, innovation appropriability, and stability that is essential to maintaining an effective innovation network.

In 2015, the National Science Foundation's (NSF) Directorate for Computer and Information Science and Engineering established a national network of innovation hubs for big data, one in each of the four US Census Regions. Each Hub is coordinated by a lead university with the intent for them to engage stakeholders in each region (local, county and state governments, private industry, other universities, and non-profit institutions) to focus on regional needs and issues. Partnerships, collaborations and coordinated activities initiated by each Hub create and sustain a greater innovation ecosystem for big data (and data science, in general) across the United States (NSF, 2015), and eventually around the world. One of these four regional hubs—the Northeast Big Data Innovation Hub (NEBDIH, also referred to herein as "the Hub")—is the subject of this study. The NEBDIH is managed by Columbia University's Data Science Institute. As of this writing, the NEBDIH represents the most densely populated region of the United States and has grown to include a network of 6,038 individuals at 1,181 organizations across fifty states (plus Puerto Rico, Washington, DC) and thirty-seven countries.

Social network analysis (SNA) can be used to understand the structure and evolution of such innovation networks and can help elucidate the role of hubs in network evolution and the value members bring to the network as well as the capacity of the network to thrive (Cinelli, et al., 2019; Gloor, et al., 2008; Kolleck, 2013; Xiaotian, 2018). The goal of this quasi-experimental pilot study was to use a social network analysis lens to look at the growth of the NEBDIH network and to reveal the needs of the community of institutions comprising the Hub through posing the following questions:

- How have the structure, partnerships, and participants of the NEBDIH network evolved as a result of the formation of the Hub?
- What is the impact of collaborations within the Hub network?
- What intellectual growth can be revealed through identifying key characteristics of sustainable partnerships and determining relative resiliency of these relationships?
- How can the Big Data Hub leadership leverage the outcomes of SNA studies of this kind to advance their mission and goals?

Our theory of action posited that network analysis, when correlated to the activities, plans, internal community structure, goals and objectives of the Hub network, as well as to other evaluative work, will inform leadership and practice in a way that enhances the achievements of participants in the network and the effectiveness of the NEBDIH itself.

This analytical approach uses SNA metrics to: reveal patterns and structures in the NEBDIH network, deepen understanding of the impact of tactics and strategies employed in leading and managing the NEBDIH, and may be generalizable to other Big Data Hubs. This study is intended to reveal practices and useful information to guide Hub principal investigators and executive directors to be more successful in generating and maintaining collaborations. SNA can support a variety of evaluation approaches and helps to corroborate ethnographic data and conclusions about behaviors and interactions in management structures, workflow, and interpersonal relationships that enhance intellectual knowledge-building and innovation. Importantly, this kind of study can help reveal the degree to which partnerships are dependent on external funding, are sustainable after funding ceases, and can reveal network relationships that effectively leverage non-NSF sources of funding through current and potential national and international collaborations. Finally, this kind of work can provide specific concrete measures of the success of the NEBDIH and address near-term strategic priorities of engagement and financial sustainability. Further, it can guide cycles of evaluating success and managing change in ways that drive toward institutional and network goals.

Methods

A two-part survey instrument was developed and administered to participants (at the institutional and individual level) in the NEBDIH. The survey was distributed to 231 organizations and 651 individuals. The first part included a set of attitudinal statements for which a level of agreement (Likert scale) was sought to characterize each partner's relationship with the Hub. The attitudinal statements were as follows:

- The Northeast Big Data Innovation Hub (NEBDIH) is accelerating data-driven innovation/solutions through its work.
- The NEBDIH is making an impact on Big Data.
- The NEBDIH creates partnerships that would not exist otherwise.
- Projects developed and/or supported by the NEBDIH are relevant to the field that I work in.
- Since I've been engaged with the Hub, it has evolved in ways that are more impactful to my organization/work.
- I advocate for the NEBDIH among my colleagues/partners who may not be familiar with it.

The second part focused on the structure of relationships among members, both prior to the formation of the NEBDIH in 2015, and at the end of the first grant-funded period in 2018. Structure of relationships prior to the formation of the Hub used a retrospective survey. Retrospective analysis is a commonly used approach in quasi-experimental design to understand previous behaviors for comparison purposes, and while it relies on subjects to recall a prior condition, it is a valuable and accepted method for understanding change over time (Bernard, et al., 1984; Faulkner & Nkwake, 2017; Monaghan, et al., 2020). The survey questions about the end of the first grant-funded period (2020) would also serve to establish a baseline that could be used to further examine the evolution of the Hub during its second period of NSF support (2019–2023) and reveal the effect of the recommendations of this study on the structure and sustainability of the network at that time point. We examined five distinct inter-organizational relationships that are key to the promotion of the NEBDIH's network efforts among sectors of organizations, including:

- *Pre-existing Collaboration*: who the members collaborated with prior to joining the NEBDIH. Pre-existing collaboration asks the actor (person being surveyed) to retrospectively provide information about their affiliation to others in the network

before the formation of the network. This information helps identify the change over time in the formation of the network and how effectively that formation took place.
- *Go-to Organizations*: organizations that a member goes to as a reliable source of information and that influence their work. Go-to organizations ask actors to identify those in the network who are brokers of information and activities at either the individual or organizational level. It identifies who are the ones that get things done, are more likely to be receptive to new connections, and are able to help others in the network.
- *Advice*: frequency with which a member organization goes to colleagues of another NEBDIH member for advice about questions and decisions related to its efforts.
- *Collaboration*: the frequency with which a member of the NEBDIH collaborates with another member on projects or other activities. Collaboration indicates cooperative work that is carried out mutually between two organizations, which means that they have mutual interests and pursue work according to those interests.
- *Strategic Planning* (binary): frequency with which a member of the NEBDIH engages in strategic planning with the Hub and other organizations that are part of the NEBDIH network. Strategic planning means that the two nodes plan together about future activities. The term "binary" indicates only whether one organization connects with another, not the nature, quality or frequency of that connection. Yearly, monthly, weekly, and daily indicate interest in the frequency of the connections, which is an indicator of the strength of ties.

The purpose of looking at these questions is to help determine not only whether individuals and organizations are connected, but also the nature of those connections. The survey process was closed by the end of 2018. Of the surveys distributed, 36 organizations (16 percent) and 129 individuals (20 percent) responded. Data collected was tabulated and cleaned in Excel and analysis and visualization was performed using UCINET.

Results

Results reveal attitudes, quality of relationships, and network characteristics of the partner's participation in the NEBDIH. Here we show the participant level attributes from the first part of the survey, followed by the network characteristics from the second part of the survey, utilizing such attributes as betweenness centrality and ego network degree distribution of participants. The results also reveal the nature of interdisciplinary relationships among NEBDIH Spokes (funded projects under the auspices of the main Hub) and patterns of exogenous ties with other Hubs and with institutions outside the Northeast Hub's region at the time of the survey.

Participant Level Attributes

This outlines the level of participation in the survey along with attitudes toward the NEBDIH by its participating organizations. The level of participation in the survey is broken out at the sector and organizational level, which indicates that 38 percent of the participants in the survey were from academia, 36 percent from industry, 16 percent from non-profit, and 10 percent from government. We use this organizational type (non-profit, academia, industry, and government) as the demographic data.

We then used a series of six Likert scale agreement items to gather participant perceptions of the NEBDIH in terms of the innovative climate of the network and perceived value of the NEBDIH. In summary, the results of this part of the survey indicate that the NEBDIH:

- is accelerating data-driven innovation and solutions through its work;
- is making an impact on Big Data;
- creates partnerships that would not exist otherwise;
- is developing and/or supporting projects that are relevant to the field that participants work in;
- has evolved in ways that are more impactful to participants' organizations and work; and
- is advocated by participants among their colleagues/partners who may not be familiar with it.

Table 13.1 Scale-level descriptive statistics of perceived innovative climate scale

6 Items	min	max	mean	Std. deviation
1. The Northeast Big Data Innovation Hub (NEBDIH) is accelerating data-driven innovation/solutions through its work.	2	6	4.37	0.97
2. The NEBDIH is making an impact on Big Data.	2	6	4.23	1.00
3. The NEBDIH creates partnerships that would not exist otherwise.	2	6	4.44	1.03
4. Projects developed and/or supported by the NEBDIH are relevant to the field that I work in.	2	6	4.43	1.09
5. Since I've been engaged with the Hub, it has evolved in ways that are more impactful to my organization/work.	1	6	3.74	1.29
6. I advocate the NEBDIH among my colleagues/partners who may not be familiar with it.	2	6	4.19	1.24
Scale-level statistics: overall innovative climate (IC)	2	6	4.19	0.95

Stacked bar chart of each item:

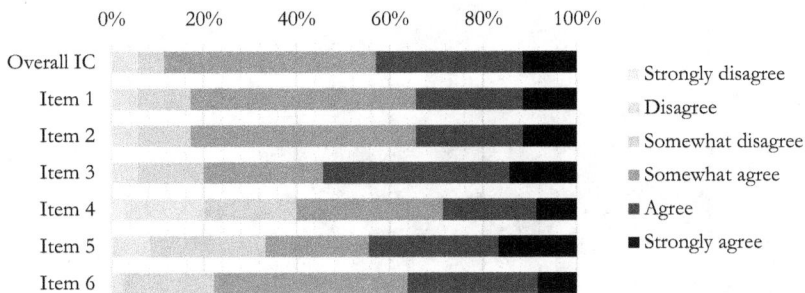

In Table 13.1 we show the scale-level statistics for six attitudinal items from the survey. In this table we calculate the standard deviation to understand whether there is general agreement among responses. A standard deviation (σ) of <1.0 (in this case 0.95) means there is good general agreement. The stacked bar chart in Table 13.1 shows responses for these six items and the overall climate of innovation. Note that in all cases there was approximately 60 percent or better agreement with the question among respondents.

Analysis of Overall Network Structure

It is beneficial to look at the network's overall structuring in order to identify the strength of relationships across the many members of the NEBDIH and the patterns of these ties among and within sectors. This aspect of the research reveals these patterns before and after the formation of the NEBDIH. Here we provide observations and interpretations of these sets of connections, patterns, and trends. To interpret the graphs, note that the dots are individual organizations that are members of the NEBDIH and the lines are connections that indicate that the interacting organizations collaborate on a regular basis. Arrows at the ends of the lines indicate the direction of relationship (sending, receiving, or both). The size of each dot indicates the relative degree distribution (how many lines they have connecting to other dots). The shape and shade of the dot indicate what sector they come from: circles indicate academia, squares indicate government, triangles indicate industry, and diamonds indicate nonprofit. Each network relationship is shown as a set of graphs that include outdegree (direction of relationships outward from an organization to others), indegree (direction of relationships inward to an organization), and Hub's Ego Neighborhood (direct connections [1-step] from the Hub itself). Core groups are indicated by the cluster of large dots in the center of the graphs. The dots lined up against the left margin of the figure are nodes that have no connections (isolates).

Pre-Existing Collaboration Relationships

Figure 1 is generated through participants identifying the relationships which they had prior to the existence of the NEBDIH. Participants were posed with the question: *Please select the academic organizations with which you have collaborated prior to joining the Big Data Hub network.*

a. Outdegree. Note the significantly large core group around the NEBDIH.

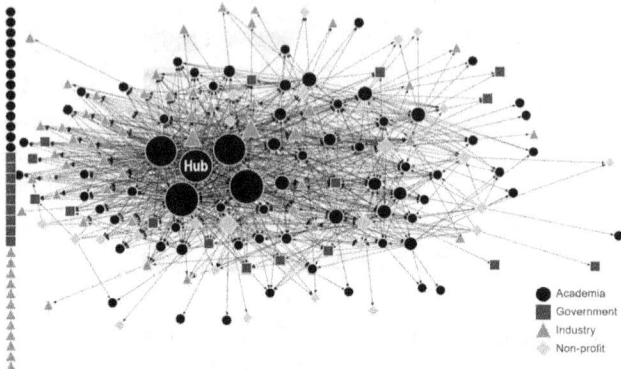

b. Indegree. Notice the strength of relationships is now more spread out. Less respondents indicated a preexisting relationship with the NEBDIH, which is expected.

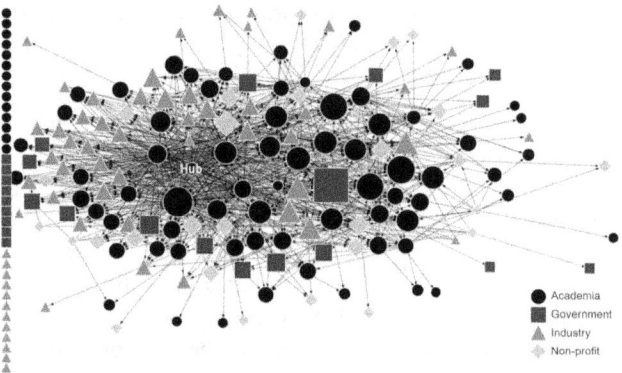

c. Indegree; Hub's Ego Neighborhood (1-step). Shows just the connections within a single link from the NEBDIH. Secondary connections are grayed out.

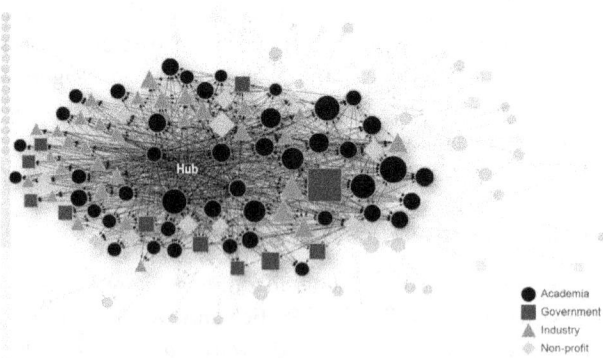

Figure 13.1 Pre-existing collaboration networks (Binary).

Relationships Formed after the Creation of the Northeast Big Data Innovation Hub

This section includes the network graphs representing the Hub relationships toward the end of the first funding period (2015–2018). It includes network representations based on the four following criteria:

1. **Collaboration**: frequency with which a member of the NEBDIH collaborates with colleagues from another member on projects or other activities.
2. **Go-to Organizations**: organizations that a member goes to as a reliable source of information and influences their work.
3. **Advice**: frequency with which a member organization goes to colleagues of another NEBDIH member for advice about questions and decisions related to its efforts.
4. **Strategic Planning**: frequency with which a member of the NEBDIH engages in strategic planning with colleagues from another member organization.

All graphs presented in this section are the same views as in Figure 13.1 including outdegree, indegree, and one-step ego network.

Collaboration Relationship

When we use the term "collaboration" we mean mutual partnership work that includes the sharing of important information, exchanging of ideas, and joint effort. This defines a relationship that goes beyond information exchange, to engagement in mutually reciprocated action. The data used to configure the network graphs are based on the question: *How frequently do you collaborate with colleagues from the following organizations (yearly, monthly, weekly, and daily)?* Figure 13.2 shows Collaboration Relationship on two frequency bases: monthly, weekly, and daily and weekly and daily.

Monthly, weekly, and daily interaction

Weekly and daily interaction

a. Outdegree. Two clusters are visible, with the dense cluster on the right containing the NEBDIH.

d. Outdegree. The Hub's connectivity in this view is greatly diminished compared to neighbors in the cluster.

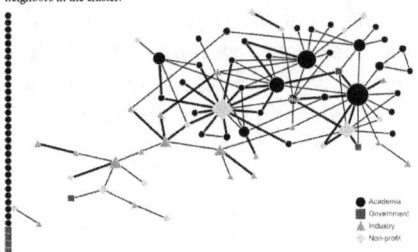

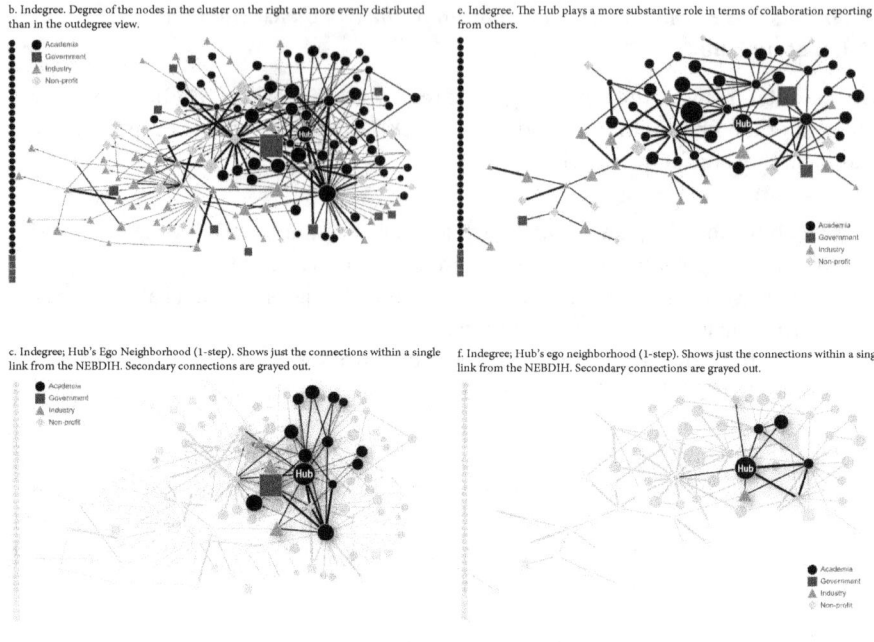

Figure 13.2 Collaboration networks.

Go-to Organization/s

The term "go-to organization" indicates one or more organizations that the member contacts and considers a reliable source of information and that influences their work. For this part of the study, we posed the question: *Which organization(s) is/are your "go-to" organization(s) in the Northeast Big Data Innovation Hub network?* The Go-to Organization networks are shown in Figure 3.

Advice Relationship

The term "advice" means genuinely seeking guidance about meaningful questions or important decisions related to the member organization's efforts. We asked the question: *How frequently do you turn to colleagues from the following Hub-affiliated organization(s) for advice about questions and decisions related to your organization's efforts (monthly, weekly, daily)?* Figure 4 shows Advice Relationship on two frequency bases: monthly, weekly, and daily and weekly and daily.

a. Outdegree. This is much denser network and the Hub's partners play a significant role, but the cluster on the right (which is Columbia University itself) is equivalent.

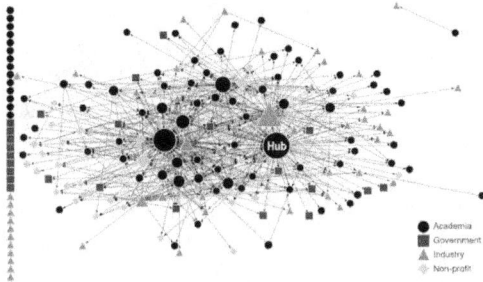

b. Indegree. When compared to outdegree, the Hub garners a smaller number of links than Columbia University itself.

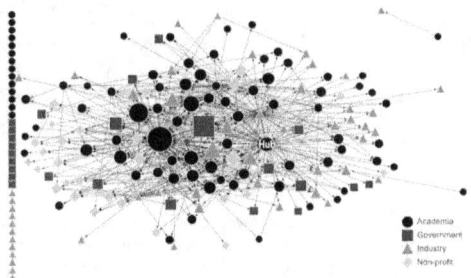

c. Indegree; Hub's ego neighborhood (1-step). Shows just the connections within a single link from the NEBDIH. Secondary connections are grayed out.

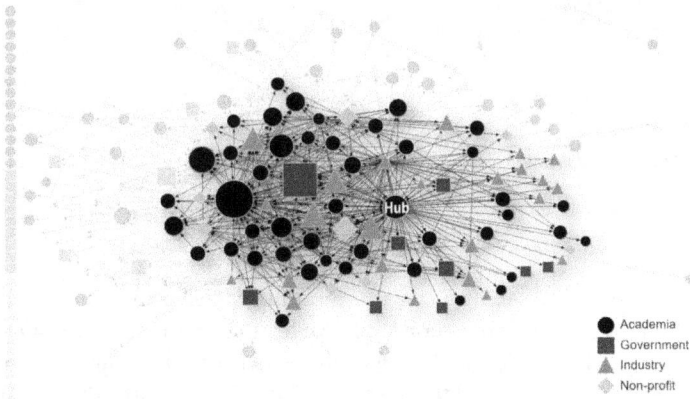

Figure 13.3 Go-to organization/s networks (Binary).

Monthly, weekly, and daily interaction

Weekly and daily interaction

a. Outdegree. Shows less clustering across respondents than in collaboration measures.

d. Outdegree. Note the most connected node here is Columbia University itself.

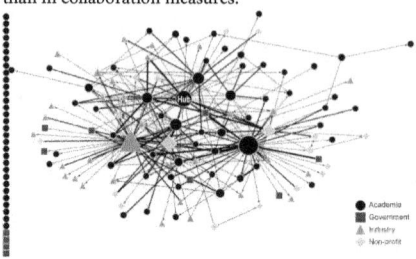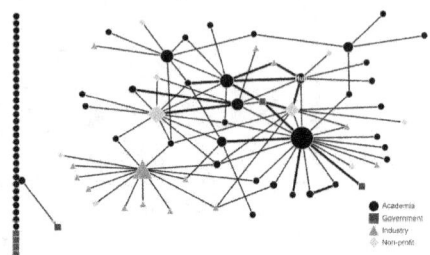

b. Indegree. Shows less clustering consistent with the outdegree view.

e. Indegree. Shows significantly more evenly distributed degree distribution.

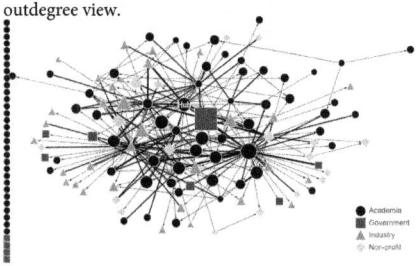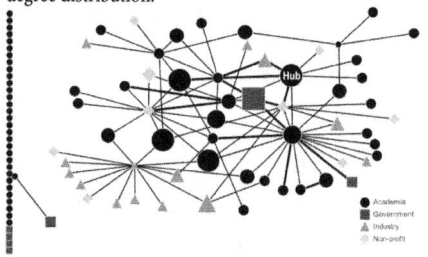

c. Indegree; Hub's ego neighborhood (1-step). Shows just the connections within a single link from the NEBDIH. Secondary connections are grayed out.

f. Indegree; Hub's ego neighborhood (1-step). Shows just the connections within a single link from the NEBDIH. Secondary connections are grayed out.

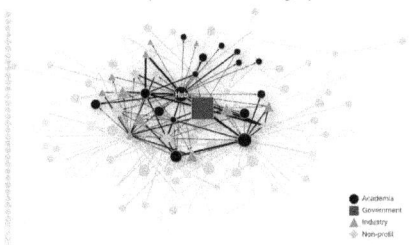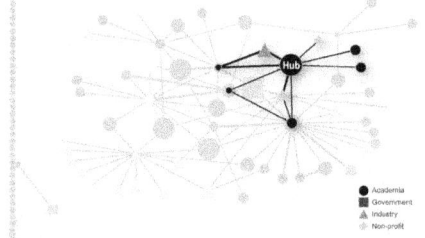

Figure 13.4 Advice networks.

Strategic Planning Relationship

The term "strategic planning" means coordinated plans and efforts that create a foundation for initiatives or actions to move forward in the future. Strategic planning may include collaboration and implies longer-term partnership work based on an articulated strategy. We asked the question: *Please select the organization(s) with which you engage in strategic planning (binary)*. The Strategic Planning networks are shown in Figure 13.5.

a. Outdegree. Here, the Hub has an opportunity for growth.

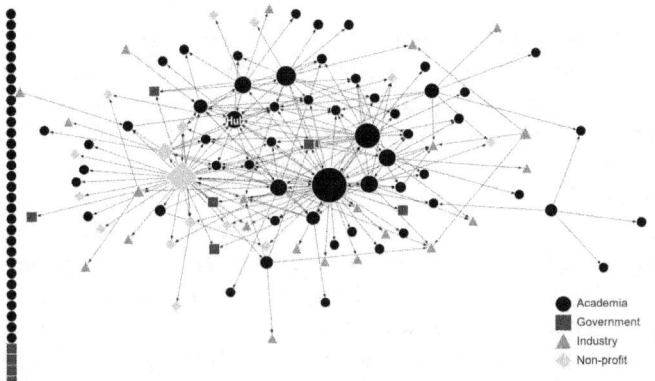

b. Indegree. Here more evenly distributed connections indicate more effective communication.

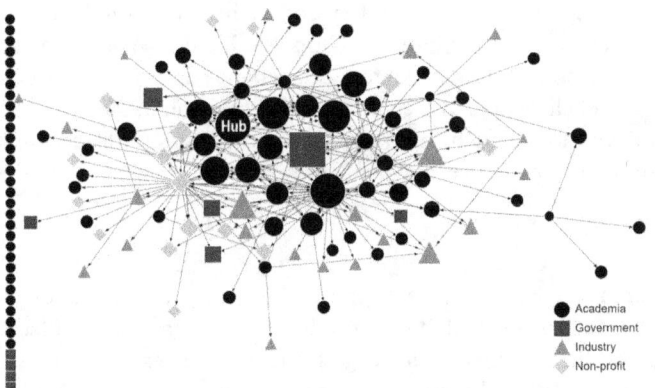

c. Indegree; Hub's ego neighborhood (1-step). Shows just the connections within a single link from the NEBDIH. Secondary connections are grayed out. Shows a fairly well-connected core cluster.

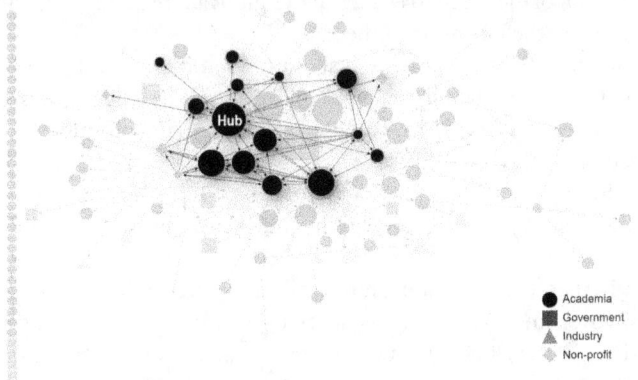

Figure 13.5 Strategic planning networks (Binary).

Discussion

Here we provide useful findings from the results that can inform leadership and policies for the NEBDIH, and some that have implications for the other three Big Data Innovation Hubs. While we acknowledge that the scale of this study was small and response rate was low, it provides evidence of the kinds of parameters that can inform policymaking for the Hub and can lead to deepening reflection on practice and adaptive approaches to management. In some ways the BDHubs are tantamount to Network Improvement Communities (Russell, et al., 2017), as they are in continual states of building and assessing the formation, health and sustainability of partnerships and networks resulting from targeting needs in overall big data research, knowledge, and practice. For instance, the NEBDIH launched the COVID Information Commons in July of 2020 for knowledge-sharing about Covid-19 across all of the BD Hubs and globally. As a sustainable and freely available database of Covid-19 information and data, it builds a framework for orienting ideas toward addressing a specific problem; designs tools, as a community, to use the data to accelerate research; and functions as a learning community to adapt the structure and function of the network to best serve the goals and essential outcomes for the initiative (Bryk, et al, 2011). As this small-scale study suggests, the use of SNA in this context can serve as an evaluative tool to identify opportunities and challenges in the structure and function of the network, which are otherwise difficult to ascertain, and provides opportunities for leadership to develop strategies for improvement that can be further assessed through SNA processes.

General

"Prior to" joining the NEBDIH, there appear to be dense ties that are connected to the Hub; approximately 69 percent of organizations were connected to at least one other organization within the system. This suggests that existing resources and support were to some extent at play in the system. However, such resources were not distributed across the entire system, as these ties mostly existed among and between academic (circle nodes) and industry (triangle nodes) sectors. It means that the Data Science Institute at Columbia University in the City of New York and/or its employees (the parent organization of the NEBDIH) likely had significant relationships with industrial organizations before the inception of the Hub.

In addition, the pattern of "prior" collaboration indicates that the academic sector had the largest number of outgoing ties in collaborating with others before they joined the NEBDIH network. These outgoing ties went to organizations from multiple sectors, reflecting relatively well-distributed resources across the system. However, the role of the NEBDIH in this early phase did not appear to be central in the pre-existing network, as indicated by lower indegree (incoming ties) for the NEBDIH than might be expected.

Significantly, ties between and among the four sectors (non-profit, academia, industry, and government) are twice as dense in the information sharing relationship (Go-to density = 0.011) than in the frequent collaboration relationship (density = 0.005), advice-seeking relationship (Advice density = 0.005), and strategic planning relationship (density = 0.004). This indicates that partners are accustomed to going to each other for information (which may be considered a more surface set of interactions), but relationships that are considered to be deeper and perhaps more intense for frequent collaboration (advice seeking or strategic planning) are infrequent. This finding reflects areas for potential future growth for the NEBDIH. There is an opportunity for the Hub to identify the nature of the more superficial relationships and determine where to strategically put effort into deepening them. The risk of leaving this structure in the status quo is that it may impede the development of longer-term relationships for building the collaborative capacity of the system as a whole.

There appears to be a tendency for cross-sector interactions to be surface level relationships (i.e., go-to organizations and advice seeking), in comparison to deeper and more intense relations such as collaboration and strategic planning. This is supported by the calculation of the ratio of external to internal ties (E-I Index), a measure of outward tendency versus inward tendency for each sector. For instance, the Go-to and Advice-Seeking relationships are more outward oriented (E-I index = 0.263 and 0.120), meaning that organizational sectors tend to be reaching out to others from different sectors. In contrast, frequent collaboration (monthly, weekly and daily) and strategic planning relationships tend to be more inward focused (E-I index = 0.004 and −0.093), suggesting that organizations are more likely to collaborate with others within the same sector for strategic planning and joint efforts.

The cross-sector interactions existing in surface level relationships suggest the likelihood of boundary crossing and potential for brokering activity and resources at the initial formation stage of the Hub's network. However, these boundary-crossing ties are not yet converted to the development of deeper and more intense relationships necessary for long-term joint efforts (e.g., strategic alliances, partnerships, coalitions, cooperative/collaborative arrangements). This suggests that the NEBDIH network may need to facilitate linkages between sectors of organizations, stimulating and coordinating knowledge sharing, and brokering and providing opportunities to deepen relationships. An organization's brokerage behavior refers to occupying a structural position that connects pairs of otherwise disconnected actors.

There are a large number of *isolates* within the Hub's network that are nodes that do not appear to be connected with anyone, either through their own reporting or that of other partners. That is, approximately 87–97 percent of pairs are ***disconnected*** in Go-to, Advice, Collaboration, and Strategic Planning relationships. This reflects a high degree of disconnected pairs of organizations in all the networks regardless of types of ties. This is also a good growth opportunity. Finding ways to bring these disconnected institutions into better collaboration will contribute to diversity of voices and expertise, and could potentially bring more innovation to the network overall through exogenous ties.

The Core Group(s)

Through each of the network measures, we identified a core group of actors in the graph figures above. They are shown as the large-size nodes in the central and dense part of the network graph.

1. There appears to be a tendency to form a core structure for Go-to, Advice, Collaboration, and Strategic Planning relationships, suggesting the underlying network structure reflects a formation of core versus periphery groups in the initial developmental phase of the NEBDIH network. This means that the core group has more dense ties than those in the periphery group. This also means that the core group within the network has a greater influence on the flow and dissemination of resources and information across the network, and thus may play a leadership role in leveraging systems change.

2. In addition, the core group only represents 6–10 percent of the whole system. While organizations in the core group can be points of leverage as they can all act to bring in people from the periphery, the core members are made up of a less diverse cross-sector of organizations. For instance, approximately 50–80 percent of the core members are from the academic sector, with the remaining members from industry and non-profit sectors and only one government agency. The core group is less representative of cross-sector organizations for higher-level relationships, i.e., frequent collaboration and strategic planning. That is, the core members within both Collaboration and Strategic Planning networks include organizations from all sectors except industry, whereas those in Go-to and Advice relationships include representatives of all sectors. This suggests more influential ties need to be catalyzed for organizations to develop more diverse partnership relationships in order to scale knowledge and practice.

Role of Individual Sectors in the System

Here we discuss the relationship among different sectors.

1. The academic sector tends to seek a great deal of resources and is often sought for resources such as information (Go-To), advice, frequent collaboration, and strategic planning. As would be expected, academic institutions emphasize external support to accomplish their goals, while they are considered important resources for knowledge and expertise.
2. Only a few government partners participate significantly in the network. Many government partners exist on the periphery and are not yet as involved, suggesting a potential point for growth. This is particularly important if the NEBDIH and its partnerships are pursuing a policy agenda and want to be involved in decision- and policymaking.
3. Industry partners tend to "collaborate" with other industry partners, but are less connected with other sectors for strategic planning or sharing information or advice. Homophily ("birds of a feather" or the tendency to affiliate with those who have like characteristics and interests) is a common problem in cross-sector collaboration. Developing strategies to strengthen connections across sectors is an area for the Hub to explore, particularly to make the NEBDIH and its partnerships more sustainable and innovative.
4. Non-profit organizations are less considered as being a source of information by other participating organizations (periphery in Go-to network), but a few

of them are playing a larger role in being connectors of the different sectors for collaboration and strategic planning relationships. This represents an opportunity to leverage non-profit institutions as possible brokers of relationships among sectors. This is potentially an area for the Hub to explore.

Conclusions

This project is one of the first of its kind to map the patterns of the social landscape of a regional, cross-sector research and innovation hub system. We examined four important and distinct inter-organizational relationships that are key to the promotion of the NEBDIH networking efforts among sectors of organizations, including Go-to, Advice, Collaboration, and Strategic Planning relationships. The social network analysis revealed strengths of the regional ecosystem, and identified ways for leadership of the hub to catalyze and enable strategies for future growth. It provided evidence of the important role that ego networks can play in understanding the role that hub organizations can play as arbiters of change in innovation networks. We come away from this pilot study with three main conclusions.

First, as each type of relationship measures a distinct way that participants connect, the network density or degree of connectedness varies by relationship. Overall, there was a relatively high amount of interaction among sectors of organizations in the surface level network (Go-to and Advice), indicating that the "pipes" for resources and support are in place and are being activated by almost all sectors for exchanging/sharing reliable sources of information. However, these same existing relationships were not converted to the deeper collaborative and strategic ties that are needed to promote, develop, and enhance effectiveness of the kinds of partnerships that are key to the mission of the NEBDIH. Density is a key feature in the initial phase of network formation in order to facilitate faster movement of information and resources (Popp et al., 2013). The NEBDIH may use existing "pipes" for flows of resources/support and convert them into longer-term partnerships to form a more cohesive system for all sectors.

Second, the Hub's system contains the well-established tendency for cross-sector interactions to have surface level relationships, suggesting the likelihood of boundary crossing and potential for brokering activity in the initial developmental phase of a system. However, such boundary-crossing patterns are relatively weak for both collaboration and strategic planning relationships. Our results suggest that those higher-level connections are limited and indicate a growth area for organizational leaders to explore. From a systems-thinking perspective, leadership of the NEBDIH will benefit from focusing on the structure of the subsystems and clusters of relationships within the greater Hub system. This will provide insights into the kinds of mutual influence present in the system and may provide leverage points for developing additional capacity for leading and collaborating at a full systems level of the NEBDIH (Daly & Finnigan, 2016; Shaked & Schechter, 2019).

Third, while there appears to be a central core structure within each of the four network relationships (Go-to, Advice, Collaboration, and Strategic Planning), the core group of nodes does not appear to be well-represented, nor does it play a leading role in creating mechanisms necessary to accelerate collaboration and learning, as will be needed to strengthen the network (Russell et al., 2017). Less than 10 percent of the organizations represent the core members in the system, and these organizations did not represent a diverse set of sectors. Most connections to the core organizations exist within a relatively narrow band of sectors, i.e., academic institutions. Although core members are highly connected and as such can readily share resources with one another, ultimately this may come at the expense of the entire system given the overreliance on a few core organizations reflecting a narrow band of sectors. What this means is that the network can be strengthened through leadership calling on partnerships to be more inclusive and working to bridge sectors of participating organizations.

These conclusions suggest that there is a great deal of room for growth in the Hub network and that there is a significant role for leadership to help facilitate and manage the growth of the network. In this study we found that although individuals and organizations may appear to act independently, they are, in fact, embedded in complex networks of relationships and wider sets of interactions. Many of the relationships observed in this study are likely to still be at an organization level (i.e., among the few core organizations) and not at a subgroup or systems level. Increasing the connectedness of these collaborations and integrating them into more organizations and existing networks will be crucial to expanding collaboration and strengthening the network. By identifying strategies to strengthen the partnerships and networks, the Hub can lead the network's growth, expand diversity, and accelerate innovation.

This project represents a new area of study in large-scale systems improvement that provides a holistic picture of cross-sector interactions within a regional innovation hub system. The act of collecting this data alone has changed the way partners think about the work they are doing together. This type of network data allows us to systematically examine the pattern of core relationships and to identify strengths and weaknesses and areas for growth. By examining structural characteristics of the system and its subsystems (i.e., sectors), this analysis offers insights into the extent to which different structures may potentially constrain or support the opportunities necessary for systemic improvement efforts across the region and beyond.

One major takeaway from this project is the strategy of "catalyzing" a systems-level approach to the development and sustainability of a regional hub network using a social network perspective. Network structures can reveal and address systemic issues that inhibit the system from achieving scale in innovation and improvement. Identifying the constraints and opportunities of the system as described herein will assist the NEBDIH in identifying approaches to lead and manage the creation of a catalyzing network structure that has the potential for large-scale change. Bringing together key stakeholders/sectors to support collective efforts and build deeper partnerships is central to this strategy. It is equally important to develop capacity for systemically accessing and mobilizing resources for change. Developing and strengthening such capacity, leveraging existing ties, involving diverse partners, and increasing ability to broker useful resources represent first steps, but developing a systems-level leadership approach holds the most promise in confronting barriers that interfere with inter-organizational (institutional) cooperation. This will enable support for different sectors and organizations to better distribute the leadership necessary for networked practices to take hold. Network practices include increased cooperation and communication across members, increased understanding of the value that members bring to other organizations and the network as a whole, and the capacity for the NEBDIH to activate and achieve consensus on policy goals.

A small-scale investigation of this type may also be of interest to NSF as a model for other research, innovation, and education networks throughout and across the Directorates to better understand their effectiveness and sustainability. Sharing these findings with NSF could stimulate interest in leveraging these kinds of studies in the future. Correlated to other evaluation efforts related to the Big Data Innovation Hubs, this study can inform management of the Big Data Hubs program and the degree to which they are successful in their primary goal of building public-private, multi-sector partnerships and consortia to address high-priority societal needs. There may also be merit in correlating conclusions from this study with results from other ethnographic and process evaluation studies being done by individual Hubs, or the program overall. One such study is headed by Dr. Geoffrey Bowker (University of California Irvine), who was engaged by NSF to "investigate the ongoing activities at the BDHubs and their partner institutions, their emerging plans for the future, and tie these to the long history of developing research infrastructures (50+ years) to understand the changes we can expect BDHubs to encounter over time." There is increasing interest in the field of *network ethnography* (Berthod, et al., 2017; De Paula, 2013) in which examining both micro-practices and network level patterns is especially useful in characterizing complex and dynamic interorganizational networks like the NEBDIH. These techniques can be deployed in parallel and the results integrated. Thus, even though the work is being done separately, a "convergent-parallel" design may yield useful information.

This investigation contributes to understanding how the evolving strength of relationships in networks affects strategies, techniques, and organizational innovation. It demonstrates the utility of a network framing of management structures, communication, and program and policy development that can be used by leaders in education and research innovation networks to develop effective strategies and manage change. It also provides a more detailed understanding of the emergence of communities within the Hub than is possible using conventional phenomenological approaches. It accomplishes this through a general organizational understanding of the development and evolution of relationships in the data science and data science education fields, with particular focus on community formation. This project contributes to advancing NSF's Big Data Innovation Hubs initiative and other efforts to build more open, effective, and sustainable knowledge and innovation communities across the sciences, industry, and government. Improving understanding of the long-term evolution of collaborations, partnerships, and other relationships will lead to more effective and sustainable investment and design choices on the part of project leaders, community builders, participants, and funders.

Limitations

We acknowledge that this study is limited in the kinds of generalizable conclusions it can draw based on the low rate of participation (De Lima, 2010). Reasons for the low response rate are not completely clear. In hindsight, one possible strategy would have been to better anticipate the need for this study and promote it from the inception of the Hub as an essential tool for hub governance. A frequent problem in developing large-scale collaborative activities is identifying the utility of SNA well after the formation of the collaborations and partnerships. Thus, we see this study more as a step toward an approach to analyze hub-network relationships in order to achieve the goal of network improvement, increased innovation, effective knowledge management and creation, and efficient and intelligent growth. Further, this study is based purely on self-reporting, which the authors acknowledge, particularly for reports representing an entire institution, as being the point of view of the individual reporting. Also, some risk in interpreting the retrospective aspect of the study falls in the area of the reliability of the memory of the respondent. While it seems like a simple matter to know whether there was a pre-existing relationship, there is room for error.

The utility of conclusions drawn from this study and its ability to be predictive about the course of action implied by those conclusions for the future would be strengthened through a companion study that would take place at the end of the second funding period. Generalizability of conclusions would also be strengthened through conducting comparative studies of other Big Data Hub networks to help understand the degree to which conclusions might be transferrable to other contexts, or whether it is peculiar to the structure and evolution of the NEBDIH. Note that to protect the privacy of the participants in the study, individual nodes (with the exception of the Hub itself) have been deidentified, but the researchers have retained that information for the sake of informing future strategies to advance the work of the NEBDIH.

Future Work

We have collected sets of social network data of the Hub system both retrospectively before the Hub's formation and a snapshot at the end of the first funding period. This is an effective tool for measuring and diagnosing key aspects of collaboration and structures that enable or impede progress. We would hope to see some growth in the level of long-term partnership work for collaboration and strategic planning as we continue to work together. We will focus our efforts in building out existing networks and strategize community engagement for more robust networks designed to strengthen some core aspects of the work.

A number of strategies and professional activities can help promote the partner connectivity of the Hub network. For instance, activating existing Go-to ties and converting them into more strategic collaborative relationships will be critical in supporting the system to reach its goals around collaborative partnerships. Efforts around networked practices for systems change and improvement (Russell et al., 2017) may strengthen the existing structure of the system and initiate strategies to encourage greater engagement and collaboration for sectors in the system. Such efforts may include building networks for communities of network engagement, which is one way to increase cross-sector and systemic collaboration.

If support becomes available to advance this work, we would suggest using this study as a point of departure for a systems-level initiative to develop practices and gauge their effectiveness in strengthening the system, as recommended in this chapter. Supporting the creation of a network initiation team (Bryk et al., 2015) is an important first step. The role of such a leadership team is to spur organizational engagement, and prototype and refine practices that focus on learning and developing relationships in a few regions around the larger network community. Such teams can be part of network improvement communities in which the central task is building, evaluating, and growing the network (Cannata, et al., 2017; Kallio & Halverson, 2019).

Ongoing development such as facilitating linkages between academic institutions and other partners, stimulating and coordinating knowledge sharing and brokering, and translating knowledge (sources), information, and perspectives into practices of other organizations will be necessary leadership activities to support the wider system (Russell et al., 2017). These ongoing events are actionable entry points for all partners in the system and demand the functioning of a central, diverse network hub (set of core members that routinely work on improving systems-level practices) to lead and initiate partnership collaboration (Bryk et al., 2015). These practices require informal leaders (central core members) and institutional leaders to adopt a multidimensional approach to systems thinking (Shaked and Schechter, 2019), which involves connecting diverse components of a system to address goals important to both the NEBDIH and its stakeholders. Taken together, this would allow the system to scale and become more effective at building more collaborative partnerships. An important way to balance the network, remove barriers, and strengthen collaboration within and across sectors may lie in strategies relating to helping make cross-sector thematic connections to members, assessing needs of less connected members and sectors, and more intentionally brokering relationships across and within sectors. Also potentially beneficial is identifying and leveraging existing brokers (go-to organizations) to increase the strength of ties.

While this study is not exhaustive, it provides an innovative perspective on the whole system of the NEBDIH and a high-level examination of its structure and patterns. But there is much more to be learned, even from the existing data. For instance, with additional support, research into the data could reveal ego networks for some of the other organizations or sectors in the Hub, and there is room for doing community detection (Fortunato & Hric, 2016), in which we look more deeply at communities that form smaller networks within the overall network (multiple connection points to one organization's dot, more often located near the periphery). Identifying and connecting more deeply with those sub-communities could prove powerful in identifying where effective interventions and supports could be provided to cultivate stronger and more innovative partnerships. With this proposed future additional work we would anticipate seeing some growth in the level of true, longer-term collaboration and even some in strategic planning relationships as the NEBDIH evolves.

Acknowledgments

The authors would like to acknowledge Kathleen McKeown, former Principal Investigator, and Jeanette Wing, Current Principal Investigator of the NEBDIH under whose auspices this work was conducted. This study is based upon work supported by the National Science Foundation under Award no. 1550284. Any opinions, findings, and conclusions or recommendations expressed in this material are those of the author(s) and do not necessarily reflect the views of the National Science Foundation.

References

Ahrweiler, P., & Keane, M. T. (2013). Innovation networks. *Mind & Society*, *12*(1), 73–90.

Bernard, H. R., Killworth, P., Kronenfeld, D., & Sailer, L. (1984). The problem of informant accuracy: The validity of retrospective data. *Annual Review of Anthropology*, *13*(1), 495–517.

Berthod, O., Grothe-Hammer, M., & Sydow, J. (2017). Network ethnography: A mixed-method approach for the study of practices in interorganizational settings. *Organizational Research Methods*, *20*(2), 299–323.

Börner, K., Bettencourt, L. M., Gerstein, M., & Uzzo, S. M. (2009). Knowledge management and visualization tools in support of discovery. In *NSF Workshop Report, Indiana University, Los Alamos National Laboratory, Yale University, and New York Hall of Science*.

Bryk, A. S., Gomez, L. M., & Grunow, A. (2011). Getting ideas into action: Building networked improvement communities in education. In Hallinan, M. T. (Ed.), *Frontiers in Sociology of Education* (pp. 127–62). Berlin, Germany: Springer Dordrecht.

Bryk, A. S., Gomez, L. M., Grunow, A., & LeMahieu, P. G. (2015). *Learning to improve: How America's schools can get better at getting better*. Harvard Education Press.

Bücheler, T., & Sieg, J. H. (2011). Understanding science 2.0: Crowdsourcing and open innovation in the scientific method. *Procedia Computer Science*, *7*, 327–9.

Burgelman, J. C., Pascu, C., Szkuta, K., Von Schomberg, R., Karalopoulos, A., Repanas, K., & Schouppe, M. (2019). Open science, open data, and open scholarship: European policies to make science fit for the twenty-first century. *Frontiers in Big Data*, *2*, 43.

Campbell, D. F. (2006). The university/business research networks in science and technology: Knowledge production trends in the United States, European Union and Japan. In Carayannis, E. G. & Campbell, D. F. (Eds.). *Knowledge creation, diffusion, and use in innovation networks and knowledge clusters: A comparative systems approach across the United States, Europe, and Asia* (pp. 67–100). Greenwood Publishing Group.

Cannata, M., Redding, C., Brown, S., Joshi, E., Rutledge, S., & Joshi, E. (2017, April). How ideas spread: Establishing a networked improvement community. *In annual meeting of the American Educational Research Association in San Antonio, TX*.

Cinelli, M., Ferraro, G., & Iovanella, A. (2019). Network processes for collaborative innovation. *International Journal of Entrepreneurship and Small Business*, *36*(4), 430–52.

Daly, A. J., & Finnigan, K. S. (Eds.). (2016). *Thinking and acting systemically: Improving school districts under pressure*. American Educational Research Association.

De Lima, J. Á. (2010). Thinking more deeply about networks in education. *Journal of Educational Change, 11*(1), 1–21.

De Paula, R. (2013, May). The social meanings of social networks: Integrating SNA and ethnography of social networking. In Schwabe, D., Almeida, V. A. F., Glaser, H., Baeza-Yates, R., & Moon, S. (Eds.), *Proceedings of the 22nd International Conference on World Wide Web* (pp. 493–4). Proceedings of the 22nd international conference on World Wide Web. DOI:10.1145/2488388

Dhanaraj, C., & Parkhe, A. (2006). Orchestrating innovation networks. *Academy of Management Review, 31*(3), 659–69.

Faulkner, W. N., & Nkwake, A. M. (2017). The potential of social network analysis as a tool for monitoring and evaluation of capacity building interventions. *Journal of Gender, Agriculture and Food Security (Agri-Gender), 2*(302–1466), 125–48.

Fortunato, S., & Hric, D. (2016). Community detection in networks: A user guide. *Physics Reports, 659*, 1–44.

Gloor, P. A. (2006). *Swarm creativity: Competitive advantage through collaborative innovation networks*. Oxford University Press.

Gloor, P. A., Paasivaara, M., Schoder, D., & Willems, P. (2008). Finding collaborative innovation networks through correlating performance with social network structure. *International Journal of Production Research, 46*(5), 1357–71.

Hallenga-Brink, S., & Vervoort, I. (2015, June). Higher education institutions as international hubs in community service engineering innovation networks a European Lifelong Learning Program project. In proceedings, *2015 Conference on Raising Awareness for the Societal and Environmental Role of Engineering and (Re) Training Engineers for Participatory Design* (Engineering4Society) (pp. 34–40). IEEE.

Kallio, J. M., & Halverson, R. R. (2019). Designing for trust-building interactions in the initiation of a networked improvement community. *Frontiers in Education, 4*, 154. https://doi.org/10.3389/feduc.2019.00154

Kolleck, N. (2013). Social network analysis in innovation research: Using a mixed methods approach to analyze social innovations. *European Journal of Futures Research, 1*(1), 1–9.

Ledford, H. (2015). Team science. *Nature, 525*(7569), 308.

Levén, P., Holmström, J., & Mathiassen, L. (2014). Managing research and innovation networks: Evidence from a government sponsored cross-industry program. *Research Policy, 43*(1), 156–68.

McKiernan, E. C., Bourne, P. E., Brown, C. T., Buck, S., Kenall, A., Lin, J., ... & Yarkoni, T. (2016). How open science helps researchers succeed. *elife, 5*.

Monahan, R. C., Fronczek, R., Eikenboom, J., Middelkoop, H. A., Beaart-van de Voorde, L. J., Terwindt, G. M., & Steup-Beekman, G. M. (2020). Mortality in patients with systemic lupus erythematosus and neuropsychiatric involvement: A retrospective analysis from a tertiary referral center in the Netherlands. *Lupus, 29*(14), 1892–901.

Monaghan, S., Lavelle, J., & Gunnigle, P. (2017). Mapping networks: Exploring the utility of social network analysis in management research and practice. *Journal of Business Research, 76*, 136–44.

NSF (2015) *Big Data Regional Innovation Hubs (BD Hubs): Accelerating the Big Data Innovation Ecosystem*. National Science Foundation. https://www.nsf.gov/publications/pub_summ.jsp?ods_key=nsf15562&org=NSF. Accessed June 3, 2022.

Popp, J., MacKean, G., Casebeer, A., Milward, H. B., & Lindstrom, R. (2013). *Inter-organizational networks: A critical review of the literature to Inform practice*. Networks Leadership Summit Series IV.

Prince, K., Barrett, M., & Oborn, E. (2014). Dialogical strategies for orchestrating strategic innovation networks: The case of the Internet of Things. *Information and Organization, 24*(2), 106–27.

Russell, J. L., Bryk, A. S., Dolle, J., Gomez, L. M., LeMahieu, P., & Grunow, A. (2017). A framework for the initiation of networked improvement communities. *Teachers College Record, 119*(7), 1–36.

Shaked, H., and Schechter, C. (2019). Exploring systems thinking in school principals' "decision-making." *International Journal of Leadership in Education, 22*(5), 573–96.

Silva, A. L., & Guerrini, F. M. (2018). Self-organized innovation networks from the perspective of complex systems: A comprehensive conceptual review. *Journal of Organizational Change Management, 31*(5), 962–83. https://doi.org/10.1108/JOCM-10 2016 0210

Stokols, D., Hall, K. L., Taylor, B. K., & Moser, R. P. (2008). The science of team science: Overview of the field and introduction to the supplement. *American Journal of Preventive Medicine, 35*(2), S77–S89.

Walshok, M. L., Shapiro, J. D., & Owens, N. (2014). Transnational innovation networks aren't all created equal: Towards a classification system. *The Journal of Technology Transfer, 39*(3), 345–57.

Xiaotian, Y. (2018) *A Review of Innovation Networks*. Waseda University Repository.

Zander, I. (2002). The formation of international innovation networks in the multinational corporation: An evolutionary perspective. *Industrial and Corporate Change, 11*(2), 327–53.

14

Bridging the Divide—How Principals Can Broker Information and Resources between Off- and Online Spaces

Martin Rehm, Alan J. Daly, Peter Bjorklund Jr., Yi-Hwa Liou, and Miguel del Fresno

Educational Leadership and Social Side of the Principalship

Principals are facing a growing number of interconnected challenges. More specifically, they are asked to foster the introduction and implementation of educational innovations, while contextualizing these developments in their local frameworks and providing guidance and support for their teachers (Daly et al., 2019). As a result, they are increasingly reaching out to each other in order to find workable solutions. In this context, Reimers and Schleicher (2020) argue that it is increasingly important to better understand how principals engage in communities through communication and collaboration which involves accessing just-in-time information (e.g., news, ideas, approaches) and the exchange of knowledge, and strategies to face the challenges. Similarly, principals are becoming increasingly important (Valli et al., 2014) based on their contextual expertise in applying and translating information, resources, and experiences to their local circumstances (DeMatthews, 2018). Moreover, a common thread that cuts across studies in this space is the role of interpersonal relationships and the social processes in which principals go about shaping their personal and professional networks (Francera & Bliss, 2011; Heck & Hallinger, 2009; Leithwood et al., 2020). This in turn cannot only support them in achieving their own individual but also more broadly defined collective outcomes (Daly et al., 2013; Duguid, 2005; Hislop, 2002; Panahi et al., 2013). Such a social network perspective brings to the fore the dependencies of actors within a social system and offers insights into the affordances and constraints related to the flow of relational resources (e.g., expertise, knowledge). This perspective shifts the focus away from individual attributes toward an examination of the ties between individuals, thereby placing leadership directly in the role of a social undertaking (Cornelissen et al., 2015).

Yet, despite a growing amount of research investigating social networks in the educational space, the social networks of educational leaders, such as principals, particularly in online spaces, remain largely neglected (Daly et al., 2010; Rehm, 2016; Rehm & Notten, 2016). Furthermore, the intersection between leadership and social networks (both online and offline) has also received limited attention (Rehm et al., 2019). While previous research on leadership traits and styles (e.g., Cross et al., 2008; Jehn, 1997; Owens & Sutton, 1999) provides valuable insights, this dominant view of leadership behaviors and attributes underestimates the impact of social networks in both online and offline spaces (Knake et al., 2021). Here, we argue that the social processes of principals involve the interplay between and the continuum of their offline and online networking activities. In addressing this research gap, this study stipulates that principals are increasingly turning to online spaces, such as social media, in order to access and share relevant resources that they might be lacking in their immediate environments.

Boundary Crossing and the Social Side of Networks

The role of interpersonal relationships and the social processes in which principals go about shaping their personal and professional networks for improved outcomes have been increasingly investigated (Francera & Bliss, 2011; Heck & Hallinger, 2009). Social processes of leaders, in general, are not only an important mechanism that drives leadership (Daly et al., 2010). They also allow leaders to gain access to resources and information necessary to achieve individual and collective outcomes (Daly et al., 2013; Panahi et al., 2013). Furthermore, whether and to what extent resources are accessible and transferred within social networks may depend on the quantity and quality of ties an individual has. For example, a principal might be very well connected within her school and be able to get and share advice with a wide range of colleagues. However, information and practical experiences in the context of educational innovation might not always be easily accessible within principals' regular, within-school, offline networks (e.g., Boahin & Hofman, 2012; Ketelaar et al., 2012; Machado et al., 2016). Instead, one of the most commonly used and simplest strategies to introduce innovation in schools is for principals to engage in communities through communication and collaboration, involving accessing just in time information (e.g., news, ideas, approaches) and the exchange of information, knowledge, and strategies regarding the best practices from schools and communities (OECD, 2013). Similarly, and on a more general level, some scholars have argued that content determines the purpose of the network, which in turn affects a network's structure (D. Froehlich et al., 2020; Rehm et al., 2020). For instance, studies have shown that ties across systems—e.g., online and offline—have contributed to a better transfer of tacit, non-routine, or complex knowledge, which in turn may be associated with better outcomes (Van Waes et al., 2016). Even more so, other research has shown that *"boundary crossing"* (Akkerman & Bakker, 2011, p. 133) can indeed benefit individuals by enabling them to expand their horizon and look outside of their *"narrow daily existence"* (Williams, 2006, p. 600). This refers to instances where a principal might turn to colleagues from another school district or type of school that share a topical interest or already have been able to acquire relevant practical experience in a certain area. Similarly, a principal might turn to social media to gather information or share experiences with colleagues that they otherwise would not have immediate access to (Tynjälä, 2012; Van Waes et al., 2016).

Social Networks in Principal Leadership

Social network analysis is commonly used to investigate complex social and organizational behaviors of leaders such as instructional practice (Supovitz et al., 2010) and leadership (Rehm, 2016; Rehm & Notten, 2016; Rigby, 2016). Many of these studies have also examined informal network positions of educational leaders and their capacity to broker between otherwise less connected parts of the underlying networks (Daly et al., 2013). This later issue is gaining considerable attention as such a network position may provide educational leaders with better access and monitoring of resources, including tools and practices (Daly et al., 2019; Rehm, Cornelissen, Notten, et al., 2020). For example, network research on educational leaders indicates that principals who occupy central and influential positions in their leadership network tend to be more efficacious about their leadership practice (Daly et al., 2019; Rehm, Cornelissen, Notten, et al., 2020). Another social network study examined the social position of principals, indicating the importance of central roles in the districtwide leadership networks in accessing and exchanging advice around reform implementation (Daly et al., 2019). Similarly, the role of educational leadership has also become increasingly important in the process of educational improvement and change and is often suggested as critical in the work of networked improvement communities (Penuel et al., 2009; Pitts & Spillane, 2009). In this context, scholars like Cho and Jimerson (2017) have called for more research that examines the role of principals, particularly in terms of accessing and leveraging online and offline (e.g., face-to-face) networks around high-quality resources and practices. In the face of the aforementioned growing number of interconnected challenges, this appears to have a sense of urgency, as principals need to continuously adapt and update their knowledge and skills to meet new challenges and demands from their surroundings (Finsterwald et al., 2013).

In order to achieve this goal, principals may find it difficult to depend on formal, often short-term, interventions (Bidwell, 2001). Instead, informal learning networks have been suggested to possibly provide a viable, additional option to contribute to this development (e.g., Richter et al., 2011). These types of informal networks can provide principals with an opportunity to continuously share and update their practice (e.g., Hopkins, 2000), while offering greater flexibility (e.g., D. E. Froehlich et al., 2014), and providing a very practice-oriented context (Eraut, 2004). Instead of relying on top-down information portals from formal institutions, principals then become proactive by participating in personal and professional online networks and communities, reading blogs and Tweets, and accessing other online resources (Rodriguez-Gomez et al., 2020). Yet, although important to principals' learning, these types of activities are only very occasionally conducted by them (Rodriguez-Gomez et al., 2020). Given this perceived importance of informal online learning networks, the growing demand to introduce higher levels of educational innovation in schools, and a better understanding of principals' professional development efforts, an increasing number of studies have begun to look into these spaces (Greenhow et al., 2019; Karimi et al., 2019; Rehm et al., 2019).

Social Media and the Flow of information and Resources

Social media platforms, such as Facebook, LinkedIn, and Twitter, have significantly enhanced the opportunity to engage in informal learning with others irrespective of time and place (Owen et al., 2016; Rehm, 2021; Yu, Liu, Huang, & Cao, 2021). Furthermore, a variety of studies have already shown educational professionals, such as principals, use social media portals to access and share information that helps them and others to face their everyday challenges (Rehm, Cornelissen, Notten, et al., 2020; Risser, 2013). Consequently, these informal online networks have also been labeled *social opportunity spaces* (Rehm, 2018; Rehm et al., 2020; Rehm & Notten, 2016), as they enable individuals to engage in collaborative activities with a wide variety of other individuals and stimulate a process of critical reflection. However, these types of valuable and beneficial processes are not guaranteed when entering a social opportunity space. Instead, they effectively provide principals with access to a wide variety of information and resources that can aid them in facing new challenges, introduce educational innovation, and generally foster high-quality practice. To this end, social opportunity spaces, such as Twitter, provide a collaborative memory aid (Aramo-Immonen et al., 2016), which principals can use to jointly add to a common pool of information and resources that can be searched and accessed. As a result, potentially isolated information and expertise from individuals, possibly confined to their immediate offline, face-to-face networks, can be made available to others, thereby also contributing to their (informal) professional development (Tseng & Kuo, 2010). Similarly, Rudat and Buder (2015) suggest that Twitter contributes to so-called "*awareness information*" (p. 76), which can be subdivided into "*agent awareness*" (p. 76) and "*informational value*" (p. 76). *Agent awareness* entails the acknowledgment of other individuals within a network and one's position in relation to them. This information can be used to more effectively engage with others in collaborative activities, such as sharing information and elaborating how certain educational innovations might be practically implemented in classrooms (Lefebvre et al., 2016). Furthermore, being able to identify others and their information value in social opportunity spaces can also be instrumental in finding insights and resources that might be lacking in leaders' immediate face-to-face environments. For example, a principal might have heard about an interesting new approach to teaching STEM in a more equity-minded setting. However, while generally being interested and supportive of the idea of applying this approach at a local school, the applicable colleagues might not necessarily know how and which curricular activities and materials might be required. Building upon their online social media networks, a principal might then be able to get in touch not only with the experts who are at the forefront of designing and conceptualizing this approach. Additionally, principals might then also be able to get in touch with other principals and teachers that have already started to use this approach in their schools and classrooms, enabling them to possibly share and provide first-hand as well as practitioner-oriented insights about the dos and don'ts of introducing this in different circumstances. Departing from this notion and the applicable underlying considerations, this, in turn, underlines again the need to attain a better understanding of the offline and online network structures and resources being shared in these social opportunity spaces.

Moreover, this notion also ties in with the considerations of scholars like McPherson and colleagues (2015), who suggested that online networks constitute a combination of personal spaces that are socially connected, supporting social interactions and contributing to a complex interplay of communication, social practices, and technology infrastructure. Following this analogy, Daly and colleagues (Daly et al., 2019) have referred to the spaces as depicting a *social continuum*, reflecting a "*complex labyrinth of networks of connections that link people who share information, ideas, resources, perceptions, beliefs, myths, rumors, etc. in a real-time, immense, networked communication system*" (p. 14). The constellation of ties that surround actors can occur in both offline and online contexts, as part of the same *social continuum*. Here, social network analysis (SNA) can capture, describe and assess underlying communication processes, and it becomes possible to make the invisible visible (Daly et al., 2019). However, current research has either focused on Facebook (e.g., Sibona & Walczak, 2011; Tang et al., 2016) or largely neglected a professional (educational) setting (e.g., Antheunis et al., 2012; Chung, 2013). This research will focus on the potential overlap between offline and online networks, the type of individuals that can potentially be instrumental in bridging the divide between them, and the information that principals share and access in an exemplary informal online network, namely Twitter. In order to contextualize the information, we begin by briefly introducing some more detail about the immediate interplay between off- and online leadership networks, before then turning to the online realm. For a more detailed description and the applicable analyses of the underlying offline networks, we would like to kindly refer to previous research that has been published on this topic elsewhere (Rehm et al., 2021).

In the context of this contribution, the work is guided by the following research questions:

1. To what extent are principals able to bridge the divide between offline (face-to-face) and online (social media) networks?
2. Who are the central principals that actively broker between off- and online spaces?
3. What type of information and resources are these brokers able to access and then share with their offline networks?

Methods

This research is based on data from a project that was working with one urban mid-size public school district in the United States that serves approximately 76,000 diverse students from a variety of socioeconomic backgrounds. In this work, we present a case study about a districtwide leadership team of ninety-seven leaders, described below. The leadership team comprises all central office administrators (i.e., superintendent, director, supervisor, coordinator, etc.), secondary, and elementary school principals.

Context and Demographics

This study takes place in one of the most diverse school systems across the nation in terms of race and ethnicity, students' socioeconomic status, and language learning ability. Approximately 20 percent of the students were enrolled in bilingual and English language learning programs; 28 percent of students are African American, 27 percent Hispanic, 27 percent Asian, and 17 percent White; and almost 45 percent of students enrolled in free and reduced-price lunch. This district reflects a typical public PK-12 school district that serves diverse student populations in the United States. We selected this district as a case study because it has had a long history of creating a sense of community that involves students, their families, and its broader communities to address the diverse needs of learners.

Data Collection and Analysis

Offline Data Collection

The offline network data were collected from leaders via a social network survey in February/March 2020. Overall, ninety-seven leaders completed the survey, reflecting a 90 percent response rate. The survey asked leaders network questions on a range of different topics, including advice, collaboration, energy, and close relationships. For example, with respect to the advice network relation, we asked leaders to indicate "How often do you go to each administrator for advice on how to strengthen your leadership practice?" Leaders could then choose their answer on a four-point scale, ranging from 1 ("few times a year") to 4 ("daily").

Online Data Collection

In addition, this study also collected Twitter data from July 14, 2018, until March 30, 2020, from the same leaders as in the offline survey. More specifically, we tracked the profiles of all relevant leaders that were active on Twitter (65.01 percent of survey respondents) in order to visualize the network and identify influencers. This included the Tweets of the applicable accounts as well as all mentions of and replies to those accounts. We accessed Twitter's application programming interface using a dedicated server that complied with the terms and conditions for Twitter (Moukarzel et al., 2020). Overall, we then collected close to 10,000 tweets.

Social Network Analysis

In order to analyze both off- and online data, we computed the in-, out-, and overall degree centrality (Grabowicz et al., 2014). These metrics provide an indication of how often an individual has been contacted or has contacted others, respectively. We also computed individuals' betweenness centrality (Opsahl et al., 2010), which constitutes a measure detecting the influence of individual users within a network by investigating the extent to which an individual is bridging a divide between otherwise disconnected parts of the network. Generally, this type of approach is widely known and used to determine prominent roles of users (highly centrality) within a network (Burt, 2009; Lee et al., 2014). Furthermore, in order to evaluate whether online and offline networks might be overlapping and who might be fostering an exchange between these two, we combined our survey and Twitter data and determined school leaders that were part of both datasets. This resulted in a population of sixty-seven principals that could be sub-divided into two sub-populations: those principals that were part of the survey and only used Twitter to actively communicate with others from the survey (N = 47, 70 percent), and those leaders that were part of the survey and used Twitter to also communicate with others, outside their district (N = 20, 30 percent).

Semantic Analyses and Web-Scraping

In order to determine what type of information and resources were being shared online, we used semantic analyses. This approach enables us to deal with the large text corpora that are being shared and created via Twitter (Alsumait et al., 2010). More specifically, we employ latent semantic analysis (LSA) (Deerwester et al., 1990). LSA is a technique in natural language processing, in particular distributional semantics, of analyzing relationships between words. Here, for the purpose of this exploratory study, we focused on determining the most commonly hashtags, as their inclusion in Tweets has become common practice on Twitter, allowing individuals to include their contributions in a larger conversation about a certain topic, which enhances their possibility to access networks and further develop their already existing ones (Letierce et al., 2010). Furthermore, we distinguish between the collated texts directly from Tweets and the texts that are shared via the Tweets. More specifically, based on the 280 character limit for Tweets, it has become common practice to include links (e.g., to blogs or websites) in the Tweets, where the indicated information is then fully displayed and reported. Consequently, while Tweets provide a good insight in the type and nature of information that is being shared via Twitter, they do not fully capture all the underlying information that forms the basis of the Tweets. We therefore configured a web-scraper that enabled us to collect all textual elements from the links that were shared via Twitter (Mitchell, 2015; Munzert et al., 2014).

Results

Overlap between Offline and Online Networks

In order to assess the degree to which leaders were indeed able to bridge the divide between off- and online realms, we combine the two network datasets. More specifically, we combine the network data from the selected principals' Twitter handles (Figure 14.1: circular nodes), with their surveyed offline network connections (Figure 14.1: rectangular nodes), as well as their purely online Twitter network (Figure 14.1: square nodes). Figure 14.1 visualizes the results, showing sociograms for an exemplary network where we combined the Twitter data with the Survey data question of "Whom do you go to for advice?"

While Figure 14.1 indicates that online (square nodes – towards the fringe of the network) and offline (rectangular nodes – towards the centre of the network) might indeed be two different realms, it also highlights the overlap between the two, suggesting that leaders are indeed engaging in bridging activities. This perception is exemplified by the circular nodes in Figure 14.1, representing leaders that were part of both, the Twitter and the Survey data sets. Additionally, we can see leaders that are being active in both off- and online networks experience (circular nodes). This suggests that they are frequently contacted by off- and online contacts for, for example, advice or to share relevant information. In other words, offline colleagues often reach out to them for advice, and online connections regularly include them in their Tweets.

Figure 14.1 Sociograms: Bridging the divide between offline and online.

Note. Shapes—nodes that represent individual Twitter users; lines—edges that indicate relationships (e.g., Mentions, Replies) between nodes; shape of nodes—square = online Twitter data, rectangle = offline survey data ("Whom do you go to for advice"), circle = both online and offline data; layout = Fruchterman Reingold (Bastian et al., 2009).

Furthermore, we were interested in the central principals and whether there might be observable differences between them. Based on the collected data, we discovered two types of principals (Figure 14.2).

Figure 14.2a shows an exemplary principal actively using Twitter to bridge the divide between the online and offline realms. While also using Twitter as another communication channel (squares in Figure 2a) to share information and resources with colleagues that are also part of their regular offline network (circles and rectangles in Figure 14.2a). In contrast, another exemplary principal is using Twitter rather as an additional communication channel to share information and resources with members of their regular offline networks (circles and squares in Figure 14.2b).

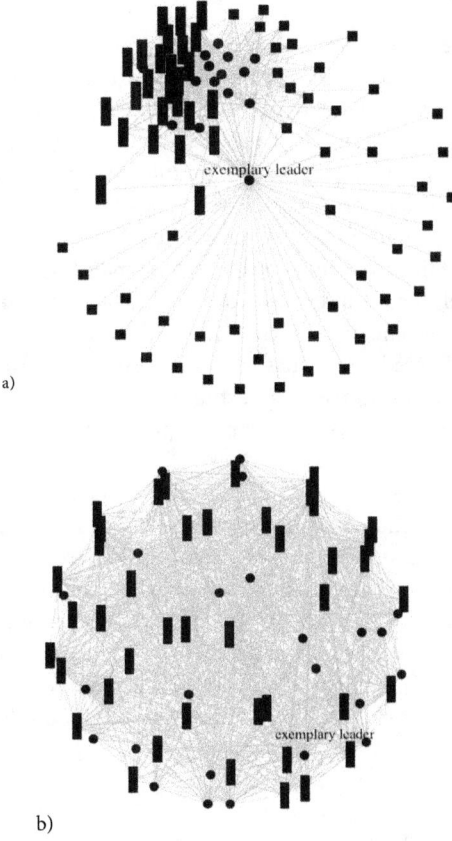

Figure 14.2 Exemplary user Combining Online and Offline Networks.

Note. Shapes—nodes that represent individual Twitter users; lines—edges that indicate relationships (e.g. Mentions, Replies) between nodes; shape of nodes—square = online Twitter data, rectangle = offline survey data ("whom do you go to for advice"), circle = both online and offline data; layout = Fruchterman Reingold (Bastian et al., 2009).

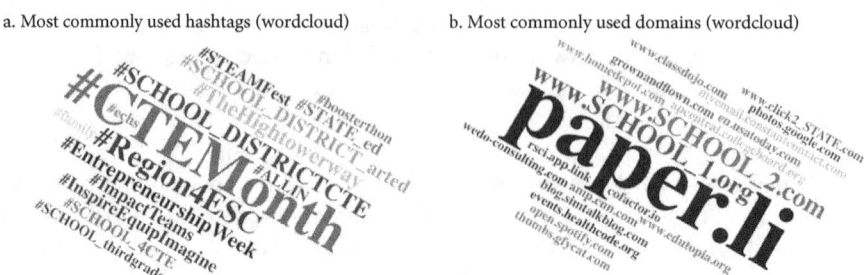

Figure 14.3 Most commonly used (a) hashtags and (b) domains (Wordcloud).

Online Data

In order to get an overview of the type of information being shared among principals and within their online networks, we then determined the most frequently used hashtags. The results are highlighted in Figure 14.3a. As can be seen, a strong focus lay on local communities (e.g., schools) and very regional and targeted activities and events. Additionally, we also discovered signs of community building in terms of contributing to a positive atmosphere and strengthening a feeling of belonging (e.g., #Region4ESC). Here, people showed appreciation for their school leaders and teachers, who strive to continuously improve their schools and education. Finally, we found a clear indication of principals not only being interested in educational innovation but also in how to effectively introduce and implement this in their immediate, practice-oriented circumstances. Highlighted by the hashtag #CTEMonth, information and resources were shared on the topic of "Career and Technical Education (CTE)" and how teachers can use different innovative ways to inform and prepare their students for their career journeys.

Using web-scraping techniques, we then also determined the most commonly used domains that were shared as part of the Twitter discussions. This allowed us to get a better picture of the underlying resources being shared (Figure 14.3b). Overall, a rather limited number of resources and links were shared (N = 58). Among the most commonly shared domains were paper.li (a content curation tool) and school-specific websites. A closer look at the underlying URLs revealed that the resources being shared predominately focused on experience-reports and suggestions, as well as detailed information on how localized communities were handling a variety of challenges.

Discussion and Implications

This chapter set out to investigate the social side of principalship and the degree to which educational leaders can potentially bridge the divide between off- and online networks. In this context, we investigated the complex network structures that emerge in leadership practices both off- and online, by combining an innovative set of methods that captured, mapped, and analyzed these interactions and specifically investigated what type of information and resources circulate in principals' social media networks.

First, we were interested in the extent to which principals are able to potentially bridge the divide between offline (face-to-face) and online (social media) networks. Here, we identified a certain degree of overlap between the offline and online networks. More specifically, we discovered a number of principals that are already actively using online communication channels not only to communicate with their regular offline networks. These principals also tap into their online networks, potentially to get access to information and resources that are not readily available in their immediate work environments, as well as to possibly share their experiences and insights on a range of topics. Moreover, following previous research, this can foster a better transfer of tacit, non-routine, or complex information (Van Waes et al., 2016), which can be instrumental in introducing educational innovation in principals' regular offline networks (e.g., Boahin & Hofman, 2012; Ketelaar et al., 2012; Prince Machado et al., 2016) by creating informal, practitioner-oriented communities among schools and the wider community (OECD, 2013). Similarly, this overlap provides preliminary support for the notion that *"boundary crossing"* (Akkerman & Bakker, 2011, p. 133) might indeed be actively pursued by principals, in order to expand their horizon and scan for new and relevant information to tackle a wide variety of new challenges (Williams, 2006).

Second, we were curious to learn more about the key influencers that actively broker between off- and online spaces. In this context, we first identified central principals that actively broker between off- and online spaces. Generally, and in line with previous research findings across different domains, we also only discovered a small minority of individuals that is gravitating around the center of their applicable networks (Cross et al., 2006). For more information on the details of this particular finding, we would like to kindly refer to previous research that has been published on this topic elsewhere (Rehm et al., 2021). Taking a closer look at these central principals, we discovered two types of relevant principals, namely (i) principals actively using Twitter to bridge the divide between the online and offline realms and (ii) principals seemingly using Twitter as an additional communication channel to share information and resources with members of their regular offline networks. Hence, while the latter type of principal already appears to have identified potential benefits and opportunities for using social media platforms in their daily work, they seemingly have not yet fully embraced the affordances of these particular social opportunity spaces. In other words, they appear to use Twitter as a collaborative memory aid (Aramo-Immonen et al., 2016) that allows different individuals to jointly contribute to a shared set of information artifacts and resources that can then be accessed and used when required (Tseng & Kuo, 2010).

Finally, using semantic analyses and web scraping, we wanted to know more about the type of information and resources being accessed and shared by principals within their online networks. Considering the most commonly used hashtags, we discovered three types of hashtags being used. One set of hashtags was focused on local communities (e.g., schools) and very regional and targeted activities and events.

A second set was targeted at community building in terms of contributing to a positive atmosphere and strengthening a feeling of belonging. The final set of hashtags dealt with parts of educational innovation and how to practically implement them in schools and districts. The first two types of hashtags support the notion that principals are using social media and the applicable social opportunity spaces are part of their community-building strategy, reaching out to relevant stakeholders (e.g., parents and other local schools) to share and exchange information and resources that are highly viable for everyday operations (OECD, 2013). The third type of hashtags seems to suggest that principals have identified Twitter, as one exemplary social opportunity space, to access information that might either not be readily available in their immediate surroundings. Additionally, once being identified they can then also share relevant information and thereby contribute to that particular part of their overall networks.

The practical implications of this are manifold. First, this study provides an innovative and unprecedented insight into the overlap between offline and online networks, who is bridging the divide between them, and what type of information might be able to flow between them. These insights can be very useful for practitioners and policymakers alike, who would like to foster the (informal) exchange of information and resources among principals and other educational leaders. Furthermore, we provide initial empirical evidence on the types of information that are actually being shared and diffused online. On the one hand, this can be considered as an indication of what types of experiences and insights principals might be interested in. On the other hand, it can also be considered as an indicator that highlights what type of information principals might be lacking in order to effectively tackle their challenges and possibly introduce educational innovation in their schools. Finally, we have been able to identify principals that seem to be successfully bridging the divide between their offline and online networks. Further zooming in on those principals and gaining a better understanding of their communication styles and strategies can provide additional valuable information not only on how to introduce new information into practice but also on how to share relevant experiences and practical insights with a larger audience.

References

Akkerman, S. F., & Bakker, A. (2011). Boundary crossing and boundary objects. *Review of Educational Research, 81*(2), 132–69. https://doi.org/10.3102/0034654311404435

Alsumait, L., Wang, P., Domeniconi, C., & Barbará, D. (2010). Embedding semantics in LDA topic models. In Berry, M. W. & Kogan, J. (Eds.), *Text Mining* (pp. 183–204). John Wiley & Sons, Ltd. https://doi.org/10.1002/9780470689646.ch10

Antheunis, M. L., Valkenburg, P. M., & Peter, J. (2012). The quality of online, offline, and mixed-mode friendships among users of a social networking site. *Cyberpsychology: Journal of Psychosocial Research on Cyberspace, 6*(3).

Aramo-Immonen, H., Kärkkäinen, H., Jussila, J. J., Joel-Edgar, S., & Huhtamäki, J. (2016). Visualizing informal learning behavior from conference participants' Twitter data with the Ostinato Model. *Computers in Human Behavior, 55*, Part A, 584–95. https://doi.org/10.1016/j.chb.2015.09.043

Bastian, M., Heymann, S., & Jacomy, M. (2009). Gephi: An open source software for exploring and manipulating networks. *Proceedings of the International AAAI Conference on Web and Social Media, 3*(1), 361–2.

Bidwell, C. E. (2001). Analyzing schools as organizations: Long-term permanence and short-term change. *Sociology of Education*, 100–14.

Boahin, P., & Hofman, W. A. (2012). Implementation of innovations in higher education: The case of competency-based training in Ghana. *Innovations in Education and Teaching International, 49*(3), 283–93.

Burt, R. S. (2009). *Structural holes: The social structure of competition*. Harvard university press.

Cho, V., & Jimerson, J. B. (2017). Managing digital identity on Twitter: The case of school administrators. *Educational Management Administration & Leadership, 45*(5), 884–900.

Chung, J. E. (2013). Social interaction in online support groups: Preference for online social interaction over offline social interaction. *Computers in Human Behavior, 29*(4), 1408–14.

Cornelissen, F., Daly, A. J., Liou, Y. H., Van Swet, J., Beijaard, D., & Bergen, T. C. M. (2015). Leveraging the relationship: Knowledge processes in school–university research networks of master's programmes. *Research Papers in Education, 30*(3), 366–92. https://doi.org/10.1080/02671522.2014.919522

Cross, R., Laseter, T., Parker, A., & Velasquez, G. (2006). Using social network analysis to improve communities of practice. *California Management Review, 49*(1), 32–60.

Cross, R., Ehrlich, K., Dawson, R., & Helferich, J. (2008). Managing collaboration: Improving team effectiveness through a network perspective. *California Management Review, 50*(4), 74–98.

Daly, A. J., Moolenaar, N. M., Bolivar, J. M., & Burke, P. (2010). Relationships in reform: The role of teachers' social networks. *Journal of Educational Administration, 48*(3), 359–91.

Daly, A. J., Liou, Y. H., Tran, N. A., Cornelissen, F., & Park, V. (2013). The rise of neurotics social networks, leadership, and efficacy in district reform. *Educational Administration Quarterly*, 0013161X13492795.

Daly, A. J., Liou, Y., Del Fresno, M., Rehm, M., & Bjorklund Jr., P. (2019). Educational leadership in the Twitterverse: Social media, social networks and the new social continuum. *Teacher College Record, 121*.

Deerwester, S., Dumais, S. T., Furnas, G. W., Landauer, T. K., & Harshman, R. (1990). Indexing by latent semantic analysis. *Journal of the American Society for Information Science, 41*(6), 391.

DeMatthews, D. E. (2018). *Community engaged leadership for social justice: A critical approach in urban schools*. Routledge.

Duguid, P. (2005). "The art of knowing": Social and tacit dimensions of knowledge and the limits of the community of practice. *The Information Society, 21*(2), 109–18.

Eraut, M. (2004). Informal learning in the workplace. *Studies in Continuing Education, 26*(2), 247–73. https://doi.org/10.1080/158037042000225245

Finsterwald, M., Wagner, P., Schober, B., Lüftenegger, M., & Spiel, C. (2013). Fostering lifelong learning—Evaluation of a teacher education program for professional teachers. *Teaching and Teacher Education, 29*(0), 144–55. https://doi.org/10.1016/j.tate.2012.08.009

Francera, S., & Bliss, J. (2011). Instructional leadership influence on collective teacher efficacy to improve student achievement. *Leadership and Policy in Schools*, *10*(3), 349–70.

Froehlich, D., Rehm, M., & Rienties, B. (2020). Reviewing mixed methods approaches using social network analysis for learning and education. In *Educational Networking* (pp. 43–75). Springer.

Froehlich, D. E., Beausaert, S., Segers, M., & Gerken, M. (2014). Learning to stay employable. *Career Development International*, *19*(5), 508–25. https://doi.org/10.1108/CDI-11-2013-0139

Grabowicz, P. A., Ramasco, J. J., Goncalves, B., & Eguiluz, V. M. (2014). Entangling mobility and interactions in social media. *Plos One*, *9*(3), 1–12. (WOS:000333352800083). https://doi.org/10.1371/journal.pone.0092196

Greenhow, C., Galvin, S. M., & Staudt Willet, K. B. (2019). What should be the role of social media in education? *Policy Insights from the Behavioral and Brain Sciences*, *6*(2), 178–85.

Heck, R. H., & Hallinger, P. (2009). Assessing the contribution of distributed leadership to school improvement and growth in math achievement. *American Educational Research Journal*, *46*(3), 659–89.

Hislop, D. (2002). Mission impossible? Communicating and sharing knowledge via information technology. *Journal of Information Technology*, *17*(3), 165–77 (WOS:000180093500005). https://doi.org/10.1080/02683960210161230

Hopkins, D. (2000). *Schooling for tomorrow: Innovation and networks*. Lisbon, Portugal: CERI/OECD.

Jehn, K. A. (1997). A qualitative analysis of conflict types and dimensions in organizational groups. *Administrative Science Quarterly*, *42*(3), 530–57.

Karimi, H., Derr, T., Torphy, K., Frank, K., & Tang, J. (2019). A roadmap for incorporating online social media in educational research. *Teachers College Record*, *121*(14), 1–24. https://www.tcrecord.org/Content.asp?ContentID=23045

Ketelaar, E., Beijaard, D., Boshuizen, H. P., & Den Brok, P. J. (2012). Teachers' positioning towards an educational innovation in the light of ownership, sense-making and agency. *Teaching and Teacher Education*, *28*(2), 273–82.

Knake, K. T., Daly, A. J., Frank, K. A., Rehm, M., & Greenhow, C. (2021). Educators meet the fifth estate: Social media in education. *The Elementary School Journal*, *122*(1), 1–7. https://doi.org/10.1086/715479

Lee, M. R., Yen, D. C., & Hsiao, C. Y. (2014). Understanding the perceived community value of Facebook users. *Computers in Human Behavior*, *35*(0), 350–8. https://doi.org/10.1016/j.chb.2014.03.018

Lefebvre, V. M., Sorenson, D., Henchion, M., & Gellynck, X. (2016). Social capital and knowledge sharing performance of learning networks. *International Journal of Information Management*, *36*(4), 570–9. https://doi.org/10.1016/j.ijinfomgt.2015.11.008

Leithwood, K., Harris, A., & Hopkins, D. (2020). Seven strong claims about successful school leadership revisited. *School Leadership & Management*, *40*(1), 5–22.

Letierce, J., Passant, A., Decker, S. & Breslin, J. G. (2010, April). *Understanding how Twitter is used to spread scientific messages*. Web Science Conf. Raleigh, NC. USA.

McPherson, M., Budge, K., & Lemon, N. (2015). New practices in doing academic development: Twitter as an informal learning space. *International Journal for Academic Development*, *20*(2), 126–36. https://doi.org/10.1080/1360144X.2015.1029485

Mitchell, R. (2015). *Web scraping with Python: Collecting data from the modern web*. O'Reilly Media, Inc.

Moukarzel, S., Rehm, M., Fresno, M. del, & Daly, A. J. (2020). Diffusing science through social networks: The case of breastfeeding communication on Twitter. *PLOS ONE.* https://doi.org/10.1371/journal.pone.0237471

Munzert, S., Rubba, C., Meißner, P., & Nyhuis, D. (2014). *Automated data collection with R: A practical guide to web scraping and text mining.* John Wiley & Sons.

OECD. (2013). *Leadership for 21st Century Learning.* Retrieved from https://www.oecd-ilibrary.org/content/publication/9789264205406-en

Opsahl, T., Agneessens, F., & Skvoretz, J. (2010). Node centrality in weighted networks: Generalizing degree and shortest paths. *Social Networks, 32*(3), 245–51. https://doi.org/10.1016/j.socnet.2010.03.006

Owen, N., Fox, A., & Bird, T. (2016). The development of a small-scale survey instrument of UK teachers to study professional use (and non-use) of and attitudes to social media. *International Journal of Research & Method in Education, 39*(2), 170–93. https://doi.org/10.1080/1743727X.2015.1041491

Owens, D. A., & Sutton, R. I. (1999). Status contests in meetings: Negotiating the informal order. In Turner, M. E. (Ed.), *Groups at Work: Advances in Theory and Research.* Mahwah, NJ: Lawrence Erlbaum and Associates.

Panahi, S., Watson, J., & Partridge, H. (2013). Towards tacit knowledge sharing over social web tools. *Journal of Knowledge Management, 17*(3), 379–397. https://doi.org/10.1108/jkm-11-2012-0364

Penuel, W. R., Riel, M., Krause, A., & Frank, K. A. (2009). Analyzing teachers' professional interactions in a school as social capital: A social network approach. *Teachers College Record, 111*(1), 124–63.

Pitts, V. M., & Spillane, J. P. (2009). Using social network methods to study school leadership. *International Journal of Research & Method in Education, 32*(2), 185–207.

Prince Machado, M. S., Tenorio Sepúlveda, G. C., & Ramirez Montoya, M. S. (2016). Educational innovation and digital competencies: The case of OER in a private Venezuelan university. *International Journal of Educational Technology in Higher Education, 13*(1), 10. https://doi.org/10.1186/s41239-016-0006-1

Rehm, M. (2016). Informelles Lernen in Sozialen Medien – Sozial-Mediale Möglichkeitsräume und die Rolle des sozialen Kapitals. Eine quantitative Vergleichsstudie von Konversationen auf Twitter. In Mayrberger, K. & Fromme, J. (Eds.), *Jahrbuch Medienpädagogik 13: Vernetzt und entgrenzt—Gestaltung von Lernumgebungen mit digitalen Medien* (Annual). Springer VS.

Rehm, M. (2018). Soziale Medien als Möglichkeitsräume für Informelles Lernen in der beruflichen Weiterentwicklung. In *Netzwerk als neues Paradigma?* (pp. 101–21). Springer.

Rehm, M. (2021). Soziale Medien als Möglichkeitsräume für Informelles Lernen: Eine (bildungswissenschaftliche) Einschätzung. In Bolten-Bühler, R., Dertinger, A., Ellinger, D., Thielsch, A., Vanvinkenroye, J., & Zender, R. (Eds.), *Schöne neue (digitale) Welt?! Tagungsband des Jungen Forums Medien und Hochschulentwicklung* 2019 (pp. 103–19).

Rehm, M., & Notten, A. (2016). Twitter as an informal learning space for teachers!? The role of social capital in Twitter conversations among teachers. *Teaching and Teacher Education, 60,* 215–23. https://doi.org/10.1016/j.tate.2016.08.015

Rehm, M., Cornelissen, F., Notten, A., Daly, A. J., & Supovitz, J. (2019). Power to the People?! Twitter discussions on (Educational) policy processes. In *Mixed Methods Approaches to Social Network Analysis for Learning and Education.* Abingdon: Routledge.

Rehm, M., Cornelissen, F., Daly, A. J., & García, M. D. F. (2020). Drinking from the Firehose: The structural and cognitive dimensions of sharing information on Twitter. *American Journal of Education*, 127(1), 77–105. https://doi.org/10.1086/711014

Rehm, M., Cornelissen, F., Notten, A., Daly, A., & Supovitz, J. (2020). Power to the People?! Twitter discussions on (Educational) policy processes. In Fröhlich, D., Rehm, M., & Rienties, B., *Mixed methods approaches to social network analysis for learning and education* (pp. 231–44). Abingdon: Routledge.

Rehm, M., Moukarzel, S., Daly, A. J., & Fresno, M. (2021). Exploring online social networks of school leaders in times of COVID-19. *British Journal of Educational Technology*. https://doi.org/10.1111/bjet.13099

Reimers, F. M., & Schleicher, A. (2020). A framework to guide an education response to the COVID-19 Pandemic of 2020. *OECD*. Retrieved April, 14, 2020.

Richter, D., Kunter, M., Klusmann, U., Lüdtke, O., & Baumert, J. (2011). Professional development across the teaching career: Teachers' uptake of formal and informal learning opportunities. *Teaching and Teacher Education*, 27(1), 116–26. https://doi.org/10.1016/j.tate.2010.07.008

Rigby, J. G. (2016). Principals' conceptions of instructional leadership and their informal social networks: An exploration of the mechanisms of the mesolevel. *American Journal of Education*, 122(3), 433–64.

Risser, H. S. (2013). Virtual induction: A novice teacher's use of Twitter to form an informal mentoring network. *Teaching and Teacher Education*, 35, 25–33 (WOS:000323024400003). https://doi.org/10.1016/j.tate.2013.05.001

Rodriguez-Gomez, D., Ion, G., Mercader, C., & López-Crespo, S. (2020). Factors promoting informal and formal learning strategies among school leaders. *Studies in Continuing Education*, 42(2), 240–55.

Rudat, A., & Buder, J. (2015). Making retweeting social: The influence of content and context information on sharing news in Twitter. *Computers in Human Behavior*, 46, 75–84. https://doi.org/10.1016/j.chb.2015.01.005

Sibona, C., & Walczak, S. (2011). Unfriending on Facebook: Friend request and online/offline behavior analysis. *2011 44th Hawaii International Conference on System Sciences*, 1–10. IEEE.

Supovitz, J., Sirinides, P., & May, H. (2010). How principals and peers influence teaching and learning. *Educational Administration Quarterly*, 46(1), 31–56.

Tang, J. H., Chen, M. C., Yang, C. Y., Chung, T. Y., & Lee, Y. A. (2016). Personality traits, interpersonal relationships, online social support, and Facebook addiction. *Telematics and Informatics*, 33(1), 102–8.

Tseng, F. C., & Kuo, F. Y. (2010). The way we share and learn: An exploratory study of the self-regulatory mechanisms in the professional online learning community. *Computers in Human Behavior*, 26(5), 1043–53 (WOS:000279138000028). https://doi.org/10.1016/j.chb.2010.03.005

Tynjälä, P. (2012). Toward a 3-P model of workplace learning: A literature review. *Vocations and Learning*, 6(1), 11–36. https://doi.org/10.1007/s12186-012-9091-z

Valli, L., Stefanski, A., & Jacobson, R. (2014). Leadership in school-community partnerships. *Procedia-Social and Behavioral Sciences*, 141, 110–14.

Van Waes, S., Moolenaar, N. M., Daly, A. J., Heldens, H. H. P. F., Donche, V., Van Petegem, P., & Van den bossche, P. (2016). The networked instructor: The quality of networks in different stages of professional development. *Teaching and Teacher Education*, 59, 295–308. https://doi.org/10.1016/j.tate.2016.05.022

Williams, D. (2006). On and off the 'Net: Scales for social capital in an online era. *Journal of Computer-Mediated Communication, 11*(2), 593–628. https://doi.org/10.1111/j.1083-6101.2006.00029.x

Yu, H., Liu, P., Huang, X., & Cao, Y. (2021). Teacher online informal learning as a means to innovative teaching during home quarantine in the COVID-19 pandemic. *Frontiers in Psychology, 12*, 2480.

Part 6

Conclusion

15

New Directions and Next Steps for Social Network Research and Design of Teachers' Professional Development: Building Critical Network Literacy

Kira J. Baker-Doyle

Since its emergence in the early 2000s, social network research on teachers' work and learning seems to have moved closer and closer to a central driving question: what are the ideal social structures for fostering teachers' social capital and learning? Early research established that social networks influence the ways that teachers learn and make sense of their work (Atteberry & Bryk, 2009; Frank et al., 2004; Penuel et al., 2009; Penuel & Riel, 2007). Next, more variables and methodological approaches were applied to research on teachers' networks, demonstrating the complexities of the social systems at play in educational reforms and in teachers' lives (Baker-Doyle & Yoon, 2010; Daly & Finnigan, 2011; Datnow, 2012; Froehlich, 2019; Liou & Daly, 2014; Moolenaar & Sleegers, 2010). Then, several scholars began to design implementation studies, moving from observation of the social network phenomena to intervention and action (de Laat et al., 2014; Farley-Ripple & Buttram, 2018; Van Waes et al., 2018). In 2018, Dr. Susan Yoon and I edited a collection of such studies and found three themes that appeared in the design of social network interventions: network inquiry, attention to the ethos of collaboration, and design of social infrastructure (Yoon & Baker-Doyle, 2018). Yet, the question of the "best" kind of network characteristics was still elusive. In this chapter, I argue that this is because we've been framing the question in the wrong way all along. It is not about working toward an ideal network structure; it is about working toward constant transformation—the dialectic process.

In this chapter I build upon recent innovations and concepts in social network research and design of teacher professional development and propose a dialectic approach to fostering teachers' social capital called Critical Network Literacy (CNL). CNL is a discourse and set of practices that educational leaders (including teachers and administrators) can adopt to cultivate continuous critical inquiry and network change with regards to learning networks in and outside of schools. It is grounded in some new and emerging ideas about social networks: that social capital is created through a dialectical process of network change, that domains of power at the institutional, disciplinary, cultural, and interpersonal influence social network formation, and, that while organic and informal, social networks will change in response to intentional social infrastructure design strategies. Here, I review scholarship about these concepts and then introduce Critical Network Literacy as an approach to harness these innovations in designing powerful, social professional development for educators. As such, the purpose of this chapter is to introduce a lens through which to examine teachers' social networks and social capital formation as well as transformative strategies to foster teacher learning and support through social capital development.

New Concepts and Innovations Social Network Research and Design

Introducing: A Dialectical Perspective on Social Capital

The divergence in analyzing social capital at different levels has created some theoretical and measurement confusions.

(Lin, 2001, p. 3)

Skeptics have therefore characterized the social capital concept as "a wonderfully elastic term," a notion that means "many things to many people" and that has taken on "a circus-tent quality."

(Adler & Kwon, 2002, p. 18)

Social capital has become extremely popular in sociology journals ... but its meaning has been contested since its inception.

(Fulkerson & Thompson, 2008, p. 536)

As is evident in the above quotations, over the years, scholars have identified several contradictions as to the nature and definition of social capital that have made the results of social network research challenging to apply to real-world contexts. One of these challenging contradictions relates to the question of ideal social network construct for development of social capital. On the one hand, scholars such as Putnam (1995) and Coleman (1990) argue that densely connected networks foster strong social capital, particularly through trust and emotional support. On the other hand, scholars such as Granovetter (1983) and Burt (2004) suggest that weak ties and structural holes foster high levels of social capital by bringing new ideas and innovation into a stale network. Scholars such as Lin (2001) and Adler & Kwon (2002) have tried their best to create multifaceted theories of social capital inclusive of these two poles, yet the essential contradiction remains: if strong ties AND weak ties both support social capital, then how can anything be ideal? However, taking a dialectical perspective on social capital resolves the issue. A Hegelian concept of dialectic processes would suggest that it is in the transformation of a network that the social capital is cultivated (McGuire, 1988). Hegel observes that contradictions are the root of change; it is in the conflict over a contradiction that stimulates the emergence of a new idea, context, or belief (Adorno,

2017). Benson (1977) noted that a dialectical perspective is essentially focused on the process of transformation that happens in the struggle between two contradictory states:

> A dialectical view is fundamentally committed to the concept of process. The social world is in a continuous state of becoming; social arrangements which seem fixed and permanent are temporary, arbitrary patterns and any observed social pattern are regarded as one among many possibilities.
>
> (Benson, 1977, p. 3)

Thus, in social capital theory, the contradiction within its definition reveals the space of emergence. A network that is extremely dense and homophilous would indeed expand its social capital by inviting new, weaker ties into the fold; the transformation of the network invites new resources and perspectives. Likewise, a network that is weakly linked and diverse could benefit from establishing stronger ties among its members; this transformation, too, promotes social capital by cultivating greater trust among members and increased flow of tacit knowledge. The benefits in both of these instances arise from network change.

Therefore, a dialectical perspective on social capital requires close attention to the current state of a network; there is no "one-size-fits-all" answer to cultivating social capital. Yet it also suggests that provoking shifts in network structures in strategic ways could help to foster new social capital. Knowledge of existing network structures and dynamics in a school or community would be required in order to design such strategic provocations.

Bringing in the Critical: Domains of Power and Social Networks

There is some precedence to dialectical perspectives on networks in organizational literature. Jean McGuire (1988) proposed that a dialectical perspective on networks could lead to a greater understanding of the complexities of social networks. She noted that a dialectical perspective of networks means that we must take a more critical understanding of networks than simply rationalizing network dynamics on the basis of resource-exchange, stating, "Dialectical analysis explicitly views network relations in terms of the larger social and political context" (McGuire, 1988, p. 112). In previous research on activist BIPOC (Black, Indigenous or Person of Color) teacher networks, my co-researchers and I observed this dynamic in action (Mawhinney et al., 2021). For example, one of the teachers that we interviewed became isolated from other colleagues at her school because of repeated microaggressions (Sue et al., 2007) directed at her, despite the opportunities she saw for potential resource-sharing and collaboration. In another case, a Black teacher was ostracized from her community because of her concerns over the lack of Black history in the school curriculum. These cases demonstrate how the informal networks in the school were influenced by domains of social power, beyond regard for access to expertise or resources.

Critical theories attempt to understand how domains of power operate in society, and seek to use this knowledge to bring about greater equity and social justice (Bohman, 2021). Patricia Hill Collins, a noted critical theorist on race and gender, introduced the

Matrix of Domination framework to describe how social power operates across four domains: institutional, cultural (hegemonic), disciplinary, and interpersonal (Collins, 2002). This framework is helpful for understanding how social power dynamics can shape network formation and social capital. In the institutional domain of power, institutions may have structural designs that enforce certain hierarchies and access to resources. In the cultural domain of power, groups or institutions may frame knowledge or values in a particular way that constrains others' identities or sense of being, such as in the example of the teacher that was ostracized due to her concerns about the curricula. In the disciplinary domain, institutions or organizations adopt management policies and rules that reinforce certain attitudes or behaviors, which in turn can influence network dynamics. Finally, interpersonal domains of power constitute both the ways people treat each other (such as the microaggressions example) and the ways that individuals see themselves.

Thus, a critical understanding of network dynamics would take into consideration the institutional, disciplinary, cultural, and interpersonal features of domains of power. Unfortunately, there are very few examples of critical approaches to social network analysis, and even fewer that attend to issues of race, class, and gender. A recent study by Hopkins et al (2022) used a "Critical Social Network analysis" (CSNA) framework built in part upon prior work from Gonzales Canche & Rios-Aguilar (2015), which looked specifically at the role of social power in school improvement efforts. While the study did show that teachers' hierarchical positions mediated their personal social network characteristics, they noted that the study had not been designed to account for race, gender, or other social identity factors that are often influenced by domains of power. Yosso (2005) also sought to bring a critical lens to social capital in her germinal work on community cultural wealth. While her work spurred much conversation on challenging deficit views about the nature and description of "wealth" of marginalized communities, her theoretical frameworks have not been widely applied to social network analysis research.

Hence, it is clear from prior research that domains of power matter, yet critical perspectives in social network research, are still in development. There is some evidence that narratives and qualitative approaches can complement quantitative approaches to social network analysis in revealing some of the invisible threads of social power that shape individuals' positioning in networks.

Critical Intentionality

In 2014, Nienke Moolenaar and colleagues introduced the concept of network intentionality. This is the idea that while some individuals work with specific intention to develop their social networks, others do so in more passive ways. Their study revealed that individuals' network intentionality also had an influence on their perceptions of their school as an "innovative" environment. Therefore, an active approach to transforming social networks changes not only the networks, but also the broader social context. Furthermore, research by Van Waes and colleagues (2015; 2018) has demonstrated that when educators have the opportunity to examine their professional advice-based social networks, they make more intentional decisions about who to ask for advice than teachers that have not had the opportunity to analyze their networks. As such, network inquiry and analysis offer the potential for greater network intentionality, and, as a consequence, greater innovation, exchange of resources, and development of social capital in a school or organization at large.

Bringing in a critical perspective adds a new dimension. A critical perspective suggests that when inequities or hegemonic constructions are revealed, attempts should be made to transform these contexts in ways that promote greater equity and access to resources. These kinds of understandings come from a combination of mapping out social networks and more personal, humanizing, storytelling (Huber & Cueva, 2012; Solórzano & Yosso, 2002). In a study on the use of a "network awareness tool" to facilitate greater teacher collaboration and social capital development, the researchers found that teachers were hesitant to enact what they learned from the tool because of existing status hierarchies in the school (de Laat et al., 2014). Although the tool supported network inquiry, underlying social power structures that had not been addressed through humanizing practices prevented network change. Thus, working with critical intentionality suggests that through network inquiry *and* humanizing work, leaders and educators can not only work to transform networks and social dynamics in their schools and communities, but do so in a way that addresses social inequities.

Critical Network Literacy: A Dialectic Approach to Intentional Network Design

Social network research, and the design of social network-based professional development, has advanced significantly since 2010, when Daly (2010) assessed the field as a small but growing area of scholarship. In this chapter, I've built upon some of the most recent conceptual work in the field and introduced some new insights that point researchers and educational leaders in the direction of a more active and critical approach to fostering social capital for teacher learning. Yet, I contend that a key barrier to moving forward in this direction is a divide between scholars and practitioners. Few educators have the language, frameworks, or understanding of social network research to engage in meaningful network inquiry, and many of the recent implementation studies are primarily led by administrators or researchers (Yoon & Baker-Doyle, 2018). To mend such a divide requires a shared discourse and set of practices in which to engage in the work. Therefore, here I propose a Critical Network Literacy approach to collectively enact transformative social network-based design of professional development.

While the term "literacy" is most often used to describe the ability to read and comprehend text, I use the more expansive definition of literacy from scholarship in multiliteracies here, which describe literacies as "multilingual and multimodal meaning making systems as a form of dynamic transformation of the social world" (Cope & Kalantzis, 2009). In addition, the term "critical literacy" is rooted in theoretical work that joins a critical perspective on social domains of power with the concept of multiliteracies (Janks, 2013; Luke & Woods, 2009; Morrell, 2012). In this way, a critical literacy of networks means that a community operates from a set of shared meanings and assumptions around social networks and criticality, and engages in work and discourse around these ideas. Prior research on professional development has demonstrated higher levels of effectiveness for programs that involve teachers in the design and development of professional development (Desimone, 2009; Garet et al., 2001). So, cultivating a shared literacy not only supports collaboration in the work, but can also shift from top-down implementation model to an effective model that supports teacher leadership and empowerment.

Key CNL Practices

While CNL requires shared understanding, it also involves shared practices. There are three practices that are central to engaging in CNL: network inquiry, humanizing work, and dialectical social infrastructure design. Elsewhere (Baker-Doyle, 2023) I have provided extensive definitions and examples of these practices. Below is a summary each:

Network inquiry are efforts, either by individuals or by organizations, to gather network data and analyze it for change implications. While historically this work has been done somewhat exclusively by scholars, there are examples (such as Van Waes et al., mentioned earlier) of practitioners learning to conduct network inquiries. In the case of CNL, educators should be at the forefront of network inquiry work.

Humanizing work are efforts to understand how the broader social contexts of organization and institutions have shaped the experiences of individuals and to bring these understandings into the design of professional development experiences, alongside information learned from network inquiry. This often involves work such as inviting testimonios (García, 2020) and counterstorytelling (Solórzano & Yosso, 2002) for those whose identities have been historically marginalized.

Dialectical social infrastructure design is the use of specific strategies that provoke change in a network in order to foster the cultivation of social capital and learning. Ranked from fostering weak/diverse ties to building strong/homophilous ties these strategies include the following: going public, use of mediational tools, teaching each other, consensus building and action planning, and shared inquiry. For example, a densely linked professional learning community may benefit from "going public" (sharing certain aspects of their work in more public spaces) in order to invite new perspectives and potential new members. Alternatively, a weakly linked online network of teachers may benefit from an opportunity to work face-to-face to do some consensus building or action-planning around future work, which would strengthen ties between members of the network. Decisions about dialectical social infrastructure design are obviously dependent on network inquiry and humanizing work, and thus all components are interconnected.

An Example of CNL Practices at Work (-in-Progress)

I am currently involved in a Community-Based Participatory Research (CBPR) project on a community education program that uses CNL practices as a means to enhance community-based social capital and program effectiveness. The organization provides educational services to early childhood families in Chicago. Prior to the research work, the organization conducted its own network inquiry, gathering data on community assets, including relationships, resources, and information in the local community. The organization held discussions among staff about the network inquiry findings and invited staff to share more personal stories that related to the findings, in hopes to generate deeper understandings of the state of the organization in terms of social capital, and what this may mean for organizational structures, curricula, and program development (humanizing work). The CPBR research builds from this network inquiry and humanizing work. Researchers are working with staff and learners to redesign, implement, and study new social infrastructures in the organization (dialectical infrastructure design). While this study is currently under way, an example of a potential outcome could be the initiation of a collective curriculum project across key community stakeholders if the social capital of the community seems to be siloed or inaccessible to some members.

Summary and Conclusions

Social network research offers a unique paradigm in which to view teacher learning and to enact innovative and impactful approaches to professional development. As I have shared here, there are exciting new developments in the field which are beginning to impact classrooms and schools. Despite these prospects, the argument for bringing the "social" into professional development is one that has been made with great frequency in academia but met with resistance on the ground in schools. I suggest that to make inroads in this area that scholars must work together with practitioners to build a greater shared understanding and literacy of networks. Furthermore, given what we have learned in the last decade of research and in the post-pandemic, post-truth era, this shared understanding must come with a critical understanding of the social domains of power. My proposal here for the elements of a Critical Network Literacy is a beginning, which I hope future scholars and educators will iterate upon.

References

Adler, P. S., & Kwon, S.-W. (2002). Social capital: Prospects for a new concept. *Academy of Management Journal, 27*(1), 17–40.

Adorno, T. W. (2017). *An introduction to dialectics.* John Wiley & Sons.

Atteberry, A., & Bryk, A. S. (2009, April 13). *The role of schools' social networks in intervention diffusion.* Paper presented at the American Educational Research Association Annual Conference (San Diego, CA).

Baker-Doyle, K. J. (2023). *Critical network literacy: Humanizing professional development for educators.* Harvard Education Press.

Baker-Doyle, K., & Yoon, S. A. (2010). In search of practitioner-based social capital: A social network analysis tool for understanding and facilitating teacher collaboration in a professional development program. *Professional Development in Education, 37*(1), 75–93.

Benson, J. K. (1977). Organizations: A dialectical view. *Administrative Science Quarterly, 22*(1), 1–21. https://doi.org/10.2307/2391741

Bohman, J. (2021). Critical theory. In Zalta, Edward N. (Ed.), *The Stanford Encyclopedia of Philosophy*, Spring 2021 Edition, https://plato.stanford.edu/archives/spr2021/entries/critical-theory/

Burt, R. S. (2004). Structural holes and good ideas. *American Journal of Sociology, 110*(2), 349–99.

Coleman, J. S. (1990). *Foundations of social theory.* The Belknap Press of Harvard University Press.

Collins, P. H. (2002). *Black feminist thought: Knowledge, consciousness, and the politics of empowerment.* Routledge.

Cope, B., & Kalantzis, M. (2009). "Multiliteracies": New literacies, new learning. *Pedagogies: An International Journal, 4*(3), 164–95.

Daly, A. J. (2010). Mapping the terrain: Social network theory and educational change. In *Social Network Theory and Educational Change* (pp. 1–16). Harvard Education Press.

Daly, A. J., & Finnigan, K. S. (2011). The ebb and flow of social network ties between district leaders under high-stakes accountability. *American Educational Research Journal, 48*(1), 39–79.

Datnow, A. (2012). Teacher agency in educational reform: Lessons from social networks research. *American Journal of Education, 119*(1), 193–201.

de Laat, M. F., Schreurs, B. & Sie, R. (2014). Utilizing informal teacher professional development networks using the network awareness tool. In Carvalho, L., & Goodyear, P. (Eds.), *The architecture of productive learning networks* (pp. 239–56). United Kingdom: Routledge.

Desimone, L. M. (2009). Improving impact studies of teachers' professional development: Toward better conceptualizations and measures. *Educational Researcher, 38*(3), 181–99.

Farley-Ripple, E. N., & Buttram, J. L. (2018). Structuring for success: Building instructional capacity through social capital at allegheny elementary. In Yoon, S. A., & Baker-Doyle, K. J. (Eds.), *Networked by design* (pp. 65–84). London, UK: Routledge.

Frank, K. A., Zhao, Y., & Borman, K. (2004). Social capital and the diffusion of innovations within organizations: The case of computer technology in schools. *Sociology of Education, 77*(April), 148–71.

Froehlich, D. E. (2019). Mapping mixed methods approaches to social network analysis in learning and education. In *Mixed methods social network analysis* (pp. 13–24). Routledge.

Fulkerson, G. M., & Thompson, G. H. (2008). The evolution of a contested concept: A meta-analysis of social capital definitions and trends (1988–2006). *Sociological Inquiry, 78*(4), 536–57.

García, J. (2020). *Testimonios of first-generation chicana faculty in counselor education: A narrative inquiry.* The University of Texas at San Antonio Press.

Garet, M. S., Porter, A. C., Desimone, L., Birman, B. F., & Yoon, K. S. (2001). What makes professional development effective? Results from a national sample of teachers. *American Educational Research Journal, 38*(4), 915–45.

González Canché, M. S., & Rios-Aguilar, C. (2015). Critical social network analysis in community colleges: Peer effects and credit attainment. *New Directions for Institutional Research, 2014*(163), 75–91.

Granovetter, M. (1983). The strength of weak ties: A network theory revisited. *Sociological Theory,* 1, 201–233.

Hopkins, M., Weddle, H., Riedy, R., Caduff, A., Matsukata, L., & Sweet, T. M. (2022). Critical social network analysis as a method for examining how power mediates improvement efforts. In Peurach, D. J., Russell, J. L., Cohen-Vogel, L., & Penuel, W.

(Eds.), *The foundational handbook on improvement research in education* (pp. 403–22). Lanham, MD: Rowman & Littlefield.

Huber, L. P., & Cueva, B. M. (2012). Chicana/Latina testimonios on effects and responses to microaggressions. *Equity & Excellence in Education, 45*(3), 392–410.

Janks, H. (2013). Critical literacy in teaching and research. Education Inquiry, 4(2), 225–242. https://doi.org/10.3402/edui.v4i2.22071

Lin, N. (2001). Building a network theory of social capital. In Lin, N., Cook, K. & Burt, R. S. (Eds.), *Social capital: Theory and research* (pp. 3–30). London and New York: Routledge.

Liou, Y.-H., & Daly, A. J. (2014). Closer to learning: Social networks, trust, and professional communities. *Journal of School Leadership, 24*(4), 753–95.

Luke, A., & Woods, A. F. (2009). Critical literacies in schools: A primer. *Voices from the Middle, 17*(2), 9–18.

Mawhinney, L., Baker-Doyle, K. J., & Rosen, S. M. (2021). "In it together": Activist teachers of color networks combating isolation. *Race Ethnicity and Education*, 1–19. https://doi.org/10.1080/13613324.2021.1997975

McGuire, J. B. (1988). A dialectical analysis of interorganizational networks. *Journal of Management, 14*(1), 109–24.

Moolenaar, N. M., & Sleegers, P. J. (2010). Social networks, trust, and innovation: The role of relationships in supporting an innovative climate in Dutch schools. In *Social Network Theory and Educational Change*. Harvard Education Press.

Moolenaar, N. M., Daly, A. J., Cornelissen, F., Liou, Y.-H., Caillier, S., Riordan, R., Wilson, K., & Cohen, N. A. (2014). Linked to innovation: Shaping an innovative climate through network intentionality and educators' social network position. *Journal of Educational Change, 15*(2), 99–123.

Morrell, E. (2012). 21st-Century literacies, critical media pedagogies, and language arts. *The Reading Teacher, 66*(4), 300–2.

Penuel, W. R., & Riel, M. (2007). The 'new' science of networks and the challenge of school change. *Phi Delta Kappan, 88*(8), 611–15.

Penuel, W., Riel, M., Krause, A., & Frank, K. (2009). Analyzing teachers' professional interactions in a school as social capital: A social network approach. *The Teachers College Record, 111*(1), 124–63.

Putnam, R. D. (1995). Bowling Alone: America's declining social capital. *Journal of Democracy, 6*, 65–78.

Solórzano, D. G., & Yosso, T. J. (2002). Critical race methodology: Counter-storytelling as an analytical framework for education research. *Qualitative Inquiry, 8*(1), 23–44.

Sue, D. W., Capodilupo, C. M., Torino, G. C., Bucceri, J. M., Holder, A., Nadal, K. L., & Esquilin, M. (2007). Racial microaggressions in everyday life: Implications for clinical practice. *American Psychologist, 62*(4), 271.

Van Waes, S., De Maeyer, S., Moolenaar, N. M., Van Petegem, P., & Van den Bossche, P. (2018). Strengthening networks: A social network intervention among higher education teachers. *Learning and Instruction, 53*, 34–49.

Van Waes, S., Van den Bossche, P., Moolenaar, N. M., De Maeyer, S., & Van Petegem, P. (2015). Know-who? Linking faculty's networks to stages of instructional development. *Higher Education, 70*(5), 807–26.

Yoon, S. A., & Baker-Doyle, K. J. (2018). *Networked by design: Interventions for teachers to develop social capital*. London, UK: Routledge.

Yosso, T. J. (2005). Whose culture has capital? A critical race theory discussion of community cultural wealth. *Race Ethnicity and Education, 8*(1), 69–91.

16

Where Are We Headed? A Relationally Focused Agenda for Research and Practice in Leadership

Yi-Hwa Liou and Alan J. Daly

In the prologue of the book we referred to the importance of "growing social roots." We argued that the book and the work of relational leadership are about growing and nurturing the social roots in order for systems to grow and thrive, and as we look back over these chapters and ahead to the future of Relational Leadership we see tremendous potential and important implication when viewing the important work of leadership from a relational lens. As is evidenced in these powerful chapters, the body of research that applies social network theory and analysis to education continues to grow, particularly in the area of educational leadership and change. The preceding chapters in this volume contain some of the latest developments in network research in this space. These rigorous studies provide detailed results and powerful insights into network theory, leadership, and educational change. They offer critical ideas and considerations on how we approach leadership, learning, and improvement in the field and offer guidance and suggest new directions for change from a relational leadership perspective. This shift toward the relational aspect of change has become increasingly important as global and local educational communities have become increasingly connected and interdependent.

In this final chapter, we leverage the knowledge and insights from these studies and focus on the meta-themes that arise from them. As one of our central aims for this volume was to suggest future directions, we also highlight promising developments in the field. In each of the four meta-themes we have identified, we describe high-leverage points where researchers or practitioners can best bring about systems change or improvement from a relational perspective. Ultimately we conclude that when we consider, plan, implement, and evaluate change from a relational social network perspective, we must (a) leverage formal and informal structures, (b) support a range of social connections, (c) catalyze social infrastructure, and (d) develop the capacity for networks to support leading, learning, and change.

Leverage Formal and Informal Structures

One of the most common threads woven throughout the chapters in this volume is the importance of attending to both the formal and informal mechanisms that exist in organizational social systems and that drive educational change. In this text, the formal social mechanisms are the organizational hierarchical structures or infrastructures—such as schools, districts, inter-school communities, reform programs or professional development events—as well as the individuals who are formally assigned as or have the title of leader. The informal social mechanisms reflect webs of social relationships that are formed or shaped by informal interactions of individuals as they go about their work, be it learning, teaching, leading, or engaging efforts toward reform. Relational leadership emerges through these webs of social interactions and holds influence in organizations.

In some ways, these relational leaders may be hidden in plain sight. Nevertheless, we still seem to focus our educational change and improvement efforts on the more formal mechanisms involved in supporting reform. Indeed, thanks in part to a long history of scholarship, we have a much deeper understanding of the value of formal mechanisms during change. However, as the work in the preceding chapters suggests, informal roles and sets of interactions may be even more influential. This work supports a more nuanced understanding of how informal social mechanisms play a critical role in change in educational systems within multiple international contexts.

The studies in this book foreground the role of relationships and investigate dynamic interactions between context and informal relations, which have the potential to support or hinder resource flows across organizational systems related to change (e.g., advice, information, knowledge, social support). As such, they are consequential to the overall understanding and impact of change efforts. When considering relational ties and change within groups of student learners, for example, the studies in Part 2 demonstrate that peer social support via friendships or wider support-seeking networks plays a significant role in change efforts at the individual level, such as social and emotional well-being (Mamas and Trautman in Chapter 3), self-efficacy and observation scores of teaching performance (Eddy and Downey in Chapter 4), or pre-service teachers' teacher identity (Bjorklund in Chapter 5). Overall, this scholarship suggests the importance of informal social relations that can be drawn upon to inform the shaping of formal change structures, such as classroom group work assignments among course peer groups or pre-service teacher cohorts, as well as school- or program-wide interventions for increasing inclusivity, collective engagement, and equitable learning.

An additional implication of this classroom-level work is the notion of relational leadership among student learners. The concept of leadership in students is not new, but in recent leadership literature it is rarely discussed as a main characteristic of effective learners. A few studies have suggested that early displays of leadership among students have a significant impact on the leadership those students exhibit later in the workplace as adults (Rothstein et al., 1990; Schneider et al., 1999, 2002). As such, understanding early leadership qualities is important as we consider the wider implications of leadership development. Nevertheless, in spite of its great potential, work in this space is still in infancy.

Most empirical research on student leadership primarily focuses on high school or typical college students and uses survey rating scales of leadership behaviors (Komives, 1994; Schneider et al., 1999, 2002). More work at the elementary school level is needed, as is work around pre-service teachers who will eventually influence countless youth and their relationships into the future. In addition, conventional survey ratings of leadership traits fail to consider the nature of leadership that is more relationally based and shaped in social interactions; consequently, a social network approach to inquiry into student leadership is well suited to examining this phenomenon. Although the studies in Part 2 were not designed to identify student leaders, this work provides much-needed network evidence to illuminate what it looks like to codify relational leaders among a group of students and how such roles may support or constrain the development of their professional and leadership identities, whole-person growth, self-efficacy, and work performance.

With respect to relational ties and change at the organizational level (e.g., school, district, or inter-school community), the studies in Parts 3 and 4 illustrate that informal social relations play a critical role in the change equation and that formal mechanisms play an important part in shaping relational networks necessary for change. The latter suggests the role of external and internal policy in creating or inhibiting opportunities for informal social interactions between individuals or schools. For instance, multiple chapters—Chapter 6 (Hopkins, Matsukata, and Sweet), Chapter 7 (Canrinus and Frøytlog), Chapter 9 (Kanavidou and Downey), and Chapter 10 (Rodway, Cann, and Sinnema)—illustrate how mechanisms such as school-wide formal professional on-the-job learning opportunities for teachers, the Norwegian policy structure for teacher collaboration, and the national policy framework for inter-school collaboration (both in England and New Zealand) challenge existing norms and routines around the work of educators; they therefore result in the restructuring of preexisting relations into a set of ties that reflect policy expectations. These studies draw on the formal mechanisms at play while pushing our thinking to see how the formal and informal interact.

The network evidence presented in these chapters documents how formal change policy can influence informal relations. These informal ties and the resulting network structures also reflect the degree of change that has been enacted and affect the success of formal change structures and mechanisms. The work in Chapter 8 (Bryant and Walker) suggests that formal structures and mechanisms (e.g., project-based team arrangement, intentional design of middle leadership in school change) are layered onto existing informal relations. For instance, the coordinating role of middle leaders is woven into a school's infrastructure design for improvement. These leadership roles are important and often overlooked. The scholarship in this space notes that preexisting networks may support or hinder the implementation of formal change efforts as well as the degree to which change is implemented. It further suggests that it is crucial to clearly understand an organization's preexisting informal relations prior to designing and enacting formal mechanisms for change.

Leadership is not simply found or manifested in formal positions or through hierarchical organization. The contributions of Rodway, Cann, and Sinnema in

Chapter 10 as well as Rodway, Liou, Daly, Pollock, and Yonezawa in Chapter 12 suggest that informal relational leadership roles in reform play a significant part in the execution of change strategies. These chapters together with several other chapters reveal that informal leaders emerge from informal networks of relationships (e.g., advice-, information-, or material-seeking [Chapters 6, 8, 12, 13, 14] and peer collaboration around teaching, learning, sharing ideas, or using data in practices [Chapters 9 and 10]) as they work jointly to promote system cohesion.

Similarly, the work in Chapter 13 by Bastón, Cramer, Daly, Hudson, Liou, Kathryn, Thompson, Umer, and Uzzo, and in Chapter 14 by Rehm, Daly, Bjorklund, Liou, and del Fresno further reveals informal leaders in a broader social sphere, such as a regional cross-sector organizational network and online networking space. These informal leaders are often sought out for advice; they may be individuals with whom many others collaborate or follow; they may broker information or resources between others. Their unique social structural position gives them advantages in disseminating, brokering, or gathering resources necessary for enacting change. This suggests that leadership is relational and embedded within and beyond individuals in formal leadership positions. Recognizing the role of informal leaders and their social landscapes is important during enactment of any change effort, as these chapters confirm. Furthermore, Trautman, Caduff, and Daly indicate in Chapter 11 that the social position of an informal leader may shift due to organizational restructuring. Thus, the role of an informal leader is not static but is instead dynamic and can flow between the agent and subject of influence.

Support a Range of Social Connections

Educational change is a human endeavor involving people doing the work of reform. In facilitating reform implementation, the relationships between and among individuals are key drivers, as they carry existing and potential resources—information, knowledge, skills, and expertise—across a network. They are necessary to implement and sustain reform. Having access to these relational resources allows individuals to develop, maintain, or enhance social capital to carry out change. Accordingly, the studies collected in this book investigate different types of relationships, each representing a unique aspect of change within a change context. These relationships can generally be divided into two (sometimes overlapping) categories: instrumental and expressive. Instrumental ties, such as information or advice seeking, tend to be information-driven and work-based; expressive ties, such as friendship or social support, are typically affect-based, as they involve the expression and perception of interpersonal affect (Umphress et al., 2003). Both are crucial to understanding individual or collective efforts toward change.

The studies described in this volume draw on both types of ties and offer insights into the complex relationships that play out in facilitating change. The studies in Part 2 demonstrate that having access to expressive type of friendship or peer support networks is critical in supporting student learning and self-concept. In Chapter 3, for example, Mamas and Trautman illustrate the importance of social and emotional support. Eddy and Downey's exploration of views of the teaching profession in Chapter 4 is complemented by Bjorklund's Chapter 5, which connects social ties to learning, teaching performance, self-efficacy, and teacher identity. The balance of these studies underscores the important role of the affective component of change.

Work-related instrumental relationships are examined in many of the studies in Parts 3, 4, and 5—all illustrate the importance of identifying and accessing work-related expertise to the success of reform. Measuring the degree of connectedness is a common approach to seeking or locating expertise in networks of schools, districts, or larger communities. We see this in Chapter 8 (Bryant and Walker), Chapter 9 (Kanavidou and Downey), Chapter 10 (Rodway and colleagues), Chapter 11 (Trautman and colleagues), Chapter 13 (Bastón and colleagues), and Chapter 14 (Rehm and colleagues). Likewise, other common approaches are brokerage (Chapter 12 by Rodway and colleagues), and depicting seeker or provider of advice (Chapter 6 by Hopkins and colleagues). From a network perspective, instrumental ties, such as advice relations, help identify sources of expertise in which knowledge resides and flows within organizations; these are consequential to organizational learning and innovation (Kilduff & Krackhardt, 2008). Accessing and leveraging such expertise to meet organizational goals is a pivotal function in change efforts.

Much of the network research on educational change privileges either instrumental or expressive ties, yet the reality is that they co-exist within the workplace and both are essential to any sustained change. In Chapter 5, Bjorklund combines two types of networks into a multiplex network relation by taking into consideration both close and advice-seeking relationships. Such multiplex ties are considered strong, influential, and enduring, as they provide individuals with multiple connection points for exchange of diverse and complex information (Reagans & McEvily, 2003). They also convey greater trust, allowing for reduced transaction costs for relational resources (Coleman, 1988). Multiplexity offers joint value to individual and organizational innovation, so attending to multiplex relations represents a promising direction in designing, enacting, and evaluating complex efforts toward change.

Another approach to considering complex ties during change is the investigation of more than one informal relation. Several chapters investigate multiple relational networks in terms of their structure, connectedness, cohesion, or change as an effort to reveal different aspects and contents of interpersonal exchange (See Chapter 8 [Bryant and Walker], Chapter 9 [Kanavidou and Downey], Chapter 12 [Rodway and colleagues], and Chapter 13 [Bastón and colleagues]). Change is a complex and complicated endeavor; exploring the nature and content of relationships and how and why they form can enrich our limited understanding of relational efforts toward change. Taken together, these studies suggest that balancing investment in expressive and instrumental relations is an important but often underutilized approach to supporting organizational change. The studies offer nuanced insights and reflect the complexities of reform efforts as well as the importance of attending to the entire person and their set of complex relations in the workplace.

Catalyze Social Infrastructure

All too often, schools, educators, and broader educational communities operate in silos that focus on individual performance at the expense of the entire educational system. Individuals often fail to understand the interdependent and interconnected nature of their work, as their efforts and focus are limited to a single classroom, grade level, subject area, region, or work unit. While this focus is important, it carries with its inattention to the wider system.

Educational organizations are knowledge-intense, complex, interdependent social entities comprising relationships that operate both within and outside their boundaries and at times even outside of awareness. Knowledge, skills, expertise, and practices—as well as attributes and beliefs—represent some of the relational resources that travel between individuals within organizations and that individuals draw upon to develop, enact, and sustain change. Change and leadership comprise a relational activity that reinforces and can challenge existing routines or deep-seated beliefs and values. Each member of an organization possesses a certain degree of change agentry—a role often not recognized or leveraged. When individuals lean into their own relational power and potential, the realization of their indispensability to the change effort becomes evident. How, then, do organizations create the awareness that Dr. Martin Luther King Jr. wrote about—that we are all operating within an "inescapable network of mutuality" (King, 1963). We are connected and interconnected in ways that are not always obvious, and better understanding of those connections unleashes the latent relational power inside of all people systems.

Creating the kind of social infrastructure that supports relational activities, as suggested by many of the studies in this volume, serves as a foundation for systemic change. Our intent is not to confuse social infrastructures (or conditions) with formal structures or mechanisms; rather, it is to highlight the supplemental role of social infrastructure in change. In general, formal organizational structures—such as positional role arrangements, workflow or job expectations, authority, communication channels, physical environment settings, or even bell schedules—are not always set up to facilitate social and relational activities, and these social relations are often not drawn upon to support formal change activities. However, the potential exists within all systems to bring the social infrastructure more to life in supporting change efforts.

Social infrastructure typically comprises assets, such as facilities, online or offline spaces, time, services, and so on, that accommodate social services in support of network building for particular organizational purposes (Coburn & Stein, 2006; Spillane & Sun, 2022). Our purpose is not to document the design of social infrastructure in each study in this volume; rather, it is to more clearly raise awareness and catalyze engagement such that systems and leaders may be better informed by evidence from social network scholarship. Network data provide insights and directions on which decisions for infrastructure design or change can be grounded.

In Chapter 3, Mamas and Trautman suggest that friendship network structures among student learners may inform school leaders in their decision-making for creating conditions to enhance inclusivity in the classroom and across the school. Eddy and Downey, in Chapter 4, demonstrate that seeking social and emotional support for pre-service teachers is a critical factor related to better teaching performance and self-efficacy; as such, teacher preparation programs should consider creating social infrastructure that facilitates peer sharing. In Bjorklund's work in Chapter 5, close friendships' peer influence is shown to be a significant factor in influencing pre-service teachers' social justice teacher identities. This has implications for teacher education programs in terms of course design, tools or frameworks, and social conditions that allow for (diverse) relationships to form.

At the school level, supportive social infrastructure—such as for teachers to engage in social activities around specific tasks for reform—can provide opportunities for accessing, sharing, or mobilizing expertise and knowledge within a school. However, all too often the educational change endeavor occurs in isolation, despite the fact that expertise may be readily available. The design of such infrastructure requires an intentional formal and informal approach that aims to make tacit expertise and knowledge visible and accessible in order to form useful connections.

In Chapter 6, Hopkins and colleagues make the case for formal/informal systems tied to social infrastructure. This suggests that schools can optimize the design of formal on-the-job learning opportunities as well as conditions that foster peer trust, allowing teachers to learn from each other's backgrounds and expertise and to collaborate at a deeper level. Canrinus and Frøytlog (Chapter 7) illustrate that Norwegian schools' social infrastructure, including "common time" and team time, is organized in a way that is formal, controlled, and supported by the school principal. While teachers are provided formal opportunities to interact, less is known about whether such mandated forms of collaboration may lead to "contrived collegiality" (Hargreaves, 1994, p. 196) or nurture informal social relationships that strengthen deeper collaboration. Focusing on the content and quality of ties during collaboration offers a better understanding of how success through Norwegian national policy is realized.

Chapter 8, by Bryant and Walker, suggests that school infrastructure design—the cascade structure of roles and responsibilities in the former—has a direct influence on how educators engage in professional development or reform-related activities. Social networks among school educators help reveal their social footprints and can further inform the (re)design of school infrastructure.

At the wider systems level, creating and sustaining social infrastructure—which facilitates school-to-district, inter-school, or inter-sector network relations—is critical to systemic change. The contributions of Kanavidou and Downey (Chapter 9) and Rodway and colleagues (Chapters 10 and 12) suggest that inter-school or inter-organizational network relations between school members (i.e., professional collaboration or exchange of advice or instructional materials), be it formal leadership roles or non-leadership roles, reflect the extent to which system-wide collaboration is achieved. For instance, Rodway and colleagues (in both chapters) illustrate a sparse network structure of inter-school or inter-district collaboration, indicating that system-wide collaborative work is limited. Often, these inter-school ties represent critical resources and social opportunity spaces where one can access knowledge and resources outside of the organization to stimulate change, innovation, and information sharing. As such, these relations provide opportunities to identify the degree of systems cohesion as well as areas in need of improvement. Interventions may be implemented together with infrastructure design to enhance organizational social capital, as suggested in Chapter 12. In Chapter 10, Rodway and colleagues also suggest that these inter-organizational ties carry a constraint in sustaining change efforts. For instance, if the ties that connect multiple schools are attached to a single individual, such as a principal, district administrator, or regional research hub, the schools may suffer if their primary source of new ideas moves on, taking those relational resources with them. This insight is also captured in the phenomenon of churn described by Trautman and colleagues in Chapter 11.

Sustaining and stabilizing social infrastructure is clearly an essential component of systemic change. In Chapter 13, Bostón and colleagues demonstrate an initiative that may sustain such social infrastructure. Specifically, they analyze the role of a regional research hub lead in bridging cross-sector resources for innovation work. The regional hub is the initiator and driver for network cohesion and change; it is, itself, an infrastructure designed to engage network members and develop long-term collaborative partnerships. Their analysis illustrates the importance of understanding network structure and evolution of inter-organizational or cross-sector collaborations in investment in infrastructure design.

The overall message of these chapters is that social ties between organizational members are critical resources for systemic change. Therefore, intentionally creating social infrastructures that facilitate interactions across schools, districts, or regions may support social ties—as cohesion between members and as bridges for resource flow and knowledge sharing. Organizational members must be intentional about shaping networks that connect to expertise within their systems as well as engage diverse resources necessary for growth and change.

Develop Capacity for Networks Supporting Leading, Learning, and Change

The success of change largely depends on the capacity of individuals within the system's network to engage in the reform. This network capacity is dynamic and multidimensional. As we describe here, it requires (a) individuals' human and social capital, (b) individuals' network intentionality and literacy, (c) a change initiation team, and (d) relevant organizational conditions and designs. We conclude this section with four critical network capacities.

Human and Social Capital

Human and social capital supplement each other in promoting change and improvement, in that individuals' knowledge and skills are likely to be accessed, shared, used, and upgraded by way of group work or social interaction. As such, investment in relational linkages between individuals and/or subgroups not only increases individuals' social capital but also enhances the capacity of schools, districts, or larger systems to leverage existing knowledge and expertise.

For instance, the studies presented in Chapters 4 and 6—by Eddy and Downey and by Hopkins and colleagues, respectively—note the importance of individual human capital to reform, such as teaching observation scores or instructional practices. They also highlight the need to create opportunities or leverage existing structures (on-the-job learning) for individuals to access or exchange resources that are necessary for improved outcomes at the individual and organizational levels. This implies not the importance of human capital *or* social capital, but rather the thoughtful and intentional intersection of the two. This is a question of placing human and social capital in the background and the foreground, rather than a singular approach. Put another way, the question is not about focusing on one or the other, but about which to foreground and which to background under what conditions.

Network Intentionality and Literacy

In addition to investment in human and social capital, capacity building around the social work of change requires individuals' intrinsic motivation for and competencies of engaging in this social work. In a network sense, such intrinsic motivation involves awareness of networks and intentions to shape individuals' networks for better outcomes. This practice is often referred to as network intentionality (Moolenaar et al., 2014) and it includes one's beliefs about the degree to which networks are important in shaping practice as well as one's intentions to access, broker, and assess network ties (resources).

Leithwood, in Chapter 2, emphasizes the critical role of intentional learning in creating individual capacity for change. In Chapter 10, Rodway and colleagues highlight the importance of educators' network intentionality to increase cross-school ties for collaboration. Both chapters suggest that systemic change is less likely to occur by solely relying on formal infrastructure design; rather, it requires awareness of both personal and system networks. When leaders in both formal and informal positions are more intentional about engaging their networks, there is greater opportunity for deep and lasting change.

An individual's intentionality about their network may aid in shaping both their personal and professional networks. However, it is important to recognize that individuals exist on a spectrum of ability and desire to leverage their networks. For networks to be acted on intentionally, an individual must have knowledge of the network, the will to engage, and the capacity to do so. Examining networks both individually and collectively is important, but equally important is a more critical approach. For example, Baker-Doyle in Chapter 15 proposes a critical network literacy approach to bringing about change and transformation for professional development that is network-informed, is teacher-led, and supports greater equity. This approach involves three interconnected practices: network inquiry, humanizing work, and dialectical social infrastructure design.

One message for those studying and enacting change on the ground in schools, districts, or larger communities is that building research–practice partnerships is fundamental to this undertaking. Researchers must work alongside practitioners in deep and trusting partnerships to build a shared, critical understanding of the complex social domain. Likewise, they must be literate about networks and leverage them to address social inequalities for better outcomes.

Change Initiation Team

Aside from orchestrating individuals' capacities for change, a team approach to leadership and reform is equally important. Individuals—and hence organizations—tend to get accustomed to the ways in which things are done in their organization. It may take extra effort and energy to break existing organizational routines and long-held assumptions. Consequently, organizations must identify, develop, and leverage a cadre of reformers in order to lead change initiatives. Leithwood thoughtfully discusses the role and function of team structure in fostering learning and innovation in Chapter 2. Based on his work, teams are more formally formed, with specified roles, tasks, and goals; as such, relationships in teams tend to be mutual, collaborative, and characterized by a commitment to teamwork. Teams can be identified in different organizational structures, such as senior leadership teams, school leadership teams (e.g., principals, middle leaders, lead teachers), teacher learning teams, and so on. Leveraging existing formal team structures and existing connections to disseminate reform-related information and resources can help promote change initiatives and diffuse knowledge and practices.

To understand the degree of diffusion of reform efforts, networks offer a practical and empirical solution. In a team approach, networks can help reveal the patterning of team structures. As evidenced in Chapter 10 (Rodway and colleagues) and Chapter 11 (Trautman and colleagues), a fragmented or sparse network in a cross-school leadership team may limit opportunities for leaders to share new ideas or collaborate with one another. This may have direct impact not only on the reform efforts of an individual school but also on the overall cohesion of reform across a district or community of learning.

The other role of networks in a team approach to change is to help identify a potential initiation team by examining network clusters or key individuals who possess critical network positions that influence resource flow. Network clusters are more or less informally shaped based on social network interactions. They therefore tend to share stronger social bonds and mutual trust. Tacit knowledge is likely to be made explicitly to those individuals within the same cluster. In Chapter 5, Bjorklund illustrates the critical role of friendship clusters in shaping pre-service teachers' social justice teacher identities.

When network clusters are less well connected with one another in their wider social system, brokers—those who connect disconnected others—can play a critical role in bridging disconnected groups. These relational brokers are movers and shakers in mobilizing resources (e.g., coordinating, filtering, connecting, blocking) and can better weave networks together. Their network position provides them a disproportionate influence over the entire social system, and this can be leveraged to increase conduits for resource flow and promotion of change efforts.

In Chapter 12, Rodway and colleagues illuminate that some teachers (including middle and senior leaders) within a community of learning in New Zealand act as brokers in bridging knowledge and teaching materials between schools. In Chapter 13, Bastón and colleagues discuss how a regional research hub lead acts as a critical broker in forming strategic collaborations among different sectors of organizations working toward innovation. At the individual level, in Chapter 14 Rehm and colleagues identify principals who actively broker resources to bridge the divide between their online and offline relational spaces. These brokers tend to be sought out by their offline network colleagues and mentioned or referred to by their online communities. All of these studies suggest that teams, clustering groups, or brokers are critical organizational features that can be leveraged to promote change. Schools, districts, or larger community systems may take advantage of these structural features and create networked improvement communities (LeMahieu et al., 2017; Russell et al., 2017) to stimulate change and evidence-informed improvement (Peurach et al., 2022).

Organizational Conditions and Designs

Network capacity for change also depends on organizational conditions and designs that promote the interconnectivity necessary for reform efforts. The development of such capacity takes a "systems thinking" perspective (Shaked & Schechter, 2020) and focuses on the interactions toward organizational development that take place between and among individuals or organizational units as a whole. Organizational conditions and designs that facilitate this joint work for better outcomes are what Leithwood (Chapter 2) called "enabling bureaucracies," a term that deserves greater attention in describing how organizations or systems learn, experiment, or adapt to new ways of operating. Typically, schools, districts, communities, and larger regions have hierarchical structures. Sustaining continued improvement requires that these structures work in ways that enable the learning and collective work of organizational members. Leithwood proposes several key conditions within both schools and districts that promote member learning and overall improvement: missions and visions, organizational cultures, participative structures, task-driven strategies and communications, and policies and resources.

In a network sense, *missions and visions* are aligned with what scholars in network and improvement science call network goals (Westaby & Parr, 2020) or problem-specific aims (LeMahieu et al., 2017; Russell et al., 2017). Having clear, accessible, and shared goals for joint work around change and improvement can engender a sense of commitment and enhance work motivation and propensity for networked practice. Supported by *organizational cultures* of trust and innovation, network members are more willing to go the extra mile in trying new ideas or approaches when they trust that members are reliable and that failure of any experiment is allowed. Across many of the studies in this book, a compelling body of evidence indicates the important role of trust in facilitating interactions, group work, or innovative reform efforts. Here, trust is understood as collegial trust (Chapter 6 by Hopkins and colleagues) or as friendship relationships (Chapter 3 by Mamas and Trautman; Chapter 4 by Eddy and Downey; Chapter 5 by Bjorklund; Chapter 9 by Kanavidou and Downey). These measures add to existing understanding of peer-to-peer or system trust. Other critical conditions or designs that support participation in joint work and communications as well as policies and resources for network capacity as suggested in this book include the following:

- **Redesigning teacher preparation programs** that explicitly focus on building (diverse) networks and peer trust as well as individual mastery experiences (Bjorklund in Chapter 5; Eddy and Downey in Chapter 4).
- **Revisiting current policy frameworks** to create more inclusive and socially responsive classrooms, schools, and communities (Mamas and Trautman in Chapter 3).
- **More effectively using on-the-job learning opportunities** to develop teachers' trust and to leverage the role of informal teacher leaders in enhancing their overall instructional practice (Hopkins and colleagues in Chapter 6).
- **Taking advantage of common time** or team time to cultivate teacher-led professional learning communities (Canrinus and Frøytlog in Chapter 7).
- **Leveraging the role of middle leaders** in developing teachers' instructional capacity for reform-related intervention (Bryan and Walker in Chapter 8).
- **Focusing on the boundary-crossing role of formal and informal school leaders** in promoting interschool collaboration, communication, and capacity building (Kanavidou and Downey in Chapter 9; Rodway and colleagues in Chapters 10 and 12).
- **Attending to leadership churn** in relation to organizational knowledge management as school districts undergo restructuring of leadership roles (Trautman and colleagues in Chapter 11).
- **Leveraging the coordinating role of regional research hubs** in promoting networking activities and strategic resource flow among diverse sectors for network innovation (Bastón and colleagues in Chapter 13).
- **Considering both online and offline networking spaces** for educational leaders to leverage their relational resources for leadership practice (Rehm and colleagues in Chapter 14).

Critical Network Capacities

We have identified several key organizational capacities for networks in support of learning, leading, and change. When designing, enacting, and evaluating change from a relational social network perspective, we believe that four critical capacities must be cultivated: (a) the capacity for network literacy, (b) the capacity for network intentionality, (c) the capacity for leveraging networks, and (d) the capacity for reflection, refinement, and renewal.

First, it is essential to cultivate the capacity for network literacy. Indeed, with respect to understanding the role of network science in change, we argue that the entire book is making this case. We live in a hyper-connected world, yet all too often we do not systematically and explicitly build the capacity for fluency in social network literacy skills. Learning this important language around the role of networks is often left to chance or assumed to be self-evident. To support individuals to succeed in social networked spaces, particularly related to educational change, we need intentional and mindful capacity building in social network literacy at all levels. Doing so may help level the playing field, increase access to consequential resources, and support important outcomes. The key lesson that is essential is knowing that relationships and networks are consequential to various levels of organizational or systems outcomes.

Second, we argue that individual and collective network intentionality is necessary. This means not just merely advocating for the importance of relationships—we refer here to awareness of networks from an individual sense (i.e., network intentionality) and collective sense (i.e., overall sense of networks that incorporates critical consciousness). Individuals must be intentional about developing, shaping, utilizing, and assessing their own networks while recognizing the complexity of social structures and attending to or addressing social inequalities that reside in their own networks or broader social systems. Moreover, we must be aware of our own comfort and skill with acting on networks as well as others with whom we collaborate.

Third, we argue for the importance of capacity for leveraging networks. When individuals are informed about network science, they are more knowledgeable about networks. They are then able to critically examine networks, interpret them, and consider how to leverage and move forward for desired outcomes. The work is about uncovering what is hidden in plain sight and then acting on that knowledge. Engaging in network inquiry is a critical course of action, whether at an individual level (e.g., brokering more, connecting to others for advice, being a source for expertise) or at the overall structural level (e.g., tending to those who are marginalized or on the periphery, those who are central or in brokerage position, or those who are of a weaker or stronger structure). This overall social structure is amenable to change—the relational leader must have the capacity to support others to engage their own networks and to leverage systems- or organizational-level social infrastructure. In addition, relational leaders need to think about the quantity *and* quality of ties, including the high-trust or strong ties necessary for change.

And finally, capacity for reflection, refinement, and renewal is essential. Networks and relationships are dynamic and require support and nurturing to be sustained. Relational leaders need the capacity to continually reflect on and refine their work around networks as well as to renew their commitment to relationships *even when* they are under enormous pressure to deliver highly technical elements of their work. This requires relational leaders, systems reformers, and key stakeholders to collectively engage in critical dialogue around network evidence and the design of social infrastructures or organizational conditions that are necessary to bring about change.

Implications for Inquiry into Relational Leadership and Educational Change

The empirical and conceptual studies presented in this book offer evidence for and ways of understanding leadership and educational change through a social network lens. Although social network theory and analysis have gained much traction in educational research, a wide range of educational change phenomena would still benefit from further inquiry. The lines of inquiry fall into three rough categories: methodological implications, capacity-driven research–practice partnerships, and critical lens considerations.

Methodological Implications

Leadership is a relational phenomenon, and it may respond differently to different organizational change initiatives (e.g., individual on-the-job learning, forming learning teams, restructuring schools or districts) and produce outcomes at different levels of organizational hierarchies. Capturing the dynamic and relational nature of leadership that occurs and flows across organizational systems will require scholars to define their units of analysis at different levels of organizations' social systems. They will have to attend to individual, dyadic, group, unit, or whole-network levels and trace the flow of leadership throughout organizations and within or across levels. Moreover, in tracing leadership footprints, researchers need to examine macro-, meso-, and micro-events of organizational social behaviors and take into consideration the effect of time on the persistence of or change in reform efforts.

Building on the empirical studies presented in this book, we offer a few methodological areas that deserve continued or new attention in research. First, we argue for a consideration of full dynamic relational models that attend to the formation, dissolution, or maintenance of ties as well as the impact of "local" dyadic, triadic, and subgroup relations, and the extent to which individuals' attitudes, beliefs, decisions, or actions are influenced by networks of peers. This will require the analysis of longitudinal data at two or more time points in order to understand the change pattern of social activities and influence. The majority of empirical studies presented in this volume demonstrate current developments in network research in education and leadership and offer examples of longitudinal data analysis at various levels of educational systems (a cohort, schools, districts, cross-school communities, or multisector regions). A few use mixed methods to gain a more holistic understanding of relational leadership. The dynamic pattern of relationships from multiple data sources remains a promising area of investigation.

Second, tracing relational leadership footprints across organizational systems will require consideration of the interplay between individuals' and organizations' formal and informal structures as well as the multilevel networks of relational activities. The former involves examining two-mode networks formed by interactions between organizational members and events, such as formal meetings, professional development activities, or informal social opportunities. Examples include (but are not limited to) educators attending team meetings, sharing membership, or joining the same social groups. These formal or informal structures serve as conduits through which individuals or groups may influence one another and shape their social networks. Such two-mode or multimode networks allow researchers not only to understand how resources are distributed or flow from one event to another, but also to leverage events with greater participation or social influence; they also allow key relational leaders to bridge information and resources between events. A better understanding of linkages between people and reform-related events is crucial to enhancing overall coherence in regard to change efforts.

The latter consideration around multilevel networks deals with the embedded nature of relational leadership—for example, relationships are nested within individuals who are embedded in local triads or subgroups that are part of the larger organizational system. As leadership flows across organizational systems, analyses that consider data collected from multiple levels of organizations are particularly useful. Results from multilevel analyses provide an integrated understanding of the social embeddedness of leadership (Alfadala et al., 2021).

Third, from a relational perspective, leadership is dynamic and occurs through interactions that are nested and exist across different organizational systems elements (i.e., people and structures). As such, researchers who attempt to capture the dimensions (depth and breadth) and dynamics of the social processes of leadership must consider where and how relationships are formed or take place as well as the nature and consequences of the relationships. This requires data from multiple sources that explain how relationships are established or dissolved, what content or resources are being accessed, shared, or utilized in the interactions, when and where the interactions take place (e.g., online social media platforms or physical in-person spaces), and what all of this means for leadership and educational reform.

Network scholars in education have embarked on a full examination of educators' social activities that stretch across their offline physical and online spaces (e.g., Hu et al., 2020; Liu et al., 2020; see also Rehm and colleagues, Chapter 14) to best understand the phenomenon of what Daly and colleagues (2019) called the new social continuum of practice. Connecting online and offline social behaviors may provide better insight into the social work of educators, such as diffusion of innovation via opinion leaders, interactions between physical and virtual learning communities, or brokerage of information and resources between social spaces. Taken together, the space, time, and data sources address the when, what, why, and how of interactions and can thus provide a more holistic picture of leadership through a network lens.

Capacity-Driven Research–Practice Partnerships

Relational leadership, as described in this book, is a concept, approach, perspective, and phenomenon for understanding social systems and how educators do their work and the consequences of both for educational change and corresponding outcomes. Our intent is not to impose another leadership style on the field, but rather to strengthen and refine the existing knowledge base on educational leadership in different contexts of change using a more socially grounded, relational approach. Motivated by the studies in this book, a critical implication of the social work of reform and improvement is the focus on connecting what is learned in network research with what can be done in practice. While each chapter addresses different issues in education, they all point toward the same direction—that is, using network evidence along with other metrices or types of data to inform change efforts.

This direction corresponds to a recent movement in applied science in education involving improvement researchers who call for improvement science to address practical needs and problems in educational settings (Peurach et al., 2022). This approach requires researchers to engage in interactive work with practitioners who are in the processes of "iterative inquiry, design, implementation, and evaluation" (Russell & Penuel, 2022, p. 5) to address identified problems or needs. Of central importance is the mutually participatory role of researchers and practitioners as well as community members and key stakeholders.

Typically, one or more initiation team or hub will need to be formed or identified to coordinate the joint work. Interactive and iterative processes allow for the teams to engage in proactive thinking and pre-planning, reflection, dialogue, action planning, strategy adjustment, and organizational arrangement. Evidence from change design, testing, and evaluation of outcomes will then be used to inform the next iterative design for change. One challenge in this applied and participatory approach to change—and an area in need of further investigation—is documentation of which data are fed back to the system. Moreover, it is important to determine how those data are managed and transformed into information necessary for change, as well as how related plans or action steps are enacted and tied to measurable outcomes that address targeted issues.

It is noteworthy that this tradition of improvement research emphasizes that the relationship between research and practice is mutual (Russell & Penuel, 2022), meaning that research can inform practice, and practice can lead to further research. Much of the improvement effort is one-way, however, focusing on how research can be translated into practice. Nevertheless, there is much to be gained through practice-informed decisions for research and related design for change. This is another promising area of investigation.

Building on this point, in order for practitioners to be capable of initiating a change agenda, they must develop individual and organizational network capacity for change. Such capacity building will require researchers to work alongside practitioners to develop network literacy (see Baker-Doyle, Chapter 15 or Baker-Doyle, 2023), increase the agency of research collaboration, and hold mutual parties accountable (Russell & Penuel, 2022). It also bears noting that several recent approaches to improvement research, such as networked improvement communities (Bryk et al., 2015; Russell et al., 2017, 2021) and research alliances (Moeller et al., 2018), have been guided by a problem-centered orientation. More strength-based models that focus on the assets and advantages of schools, districts, and larger communities are needed and can further supplement the problem-based improvement work.

Critical Lens Considerations

The deficit-thinking orientation of problem-based improvement research positions equity and justice as a particular problem that needs to be brought into the center of improvement work. While such thinking provides a clear guide and direction to shape research purposes, it may fall short in recognizing individual members, including marginalized groups and their communities, as critical elements embedded within organizations as a whole from a systems perspective. All members are equally important in the work of systems change and improvement. Individual positionality pertaining to educational issues (problems or opportunities) as well as epistemological beliefs in knowledge production is crucial and may shape approaches to research and practice.

To be more inclusive and equity- and justice-focused, researchers, practitioners, community members, and key stakeholders must engage with critical perspectives.

A critical lens encourages engagement in deep reflexivity about how to define the purposes of our work, the ongoing dialogue to form shared understanding of equity and justice, and coordination of efforts across different levels of the social and organizational systems in which we are embedded. Better understanding of how we can *transform* instead of simply *improve* the systems necessary to meet the diverse needs of learners, educators, broader communities, and stakeholders is a critical undertaking in both research and practice. It is thus imperative to develop research-practice partnerships that focus on mutual work, shared decision-making power, and capacity building for partners.

Several chapters in this book—Chapter 15 by Baker-Doyle, Chapter 5 by Bjorklund, and Chapter 3 by Mamas and Trautman—offer critical perspectives on what this may look like in practice, particularly in terms of applying a critical approach to social network analysis in classrooms and schools and among teachers or a pre-service teacher cohort. The field of critical network research is relatively new; as it continues to develop, further considerations along these lines will arise and will continue to guide our approaches to research and practice.

Conclusion

We have argued that the work of leadership and change is a deeply relational one. The collection of chapters in this book points us in a direction toward improved balance between human and social capital, formal and informal systems, and quantity and quality of social ties, as well as the rich tapestry of relations that we share with one another. We believe that the growing body of evidence in this volume and beyond is clear: relationships, in all their forms, are foundational to the work of change, regardless of the setting. Better attending to the relational aspect of leadership holds promise and more so connects to what it means to be human. We are social creatures. To think we leave that sociability at the door of the school, district, or larger system is not in keeping with our own humanity or the growing body of evidence that points us clearly in the direction we have just described.

References

Alfadala, A., Morel, R. P., & Spillane, J. P. (2021). Multilevel distributed leadership: From why to how. In Netolicky, D. M. (Ed.), *Future alternatives for educational leadership* (pp. 79–92). Routledge.

Baker-Doyle, K. J. (2023). *Critical network literacy: Humanizing professional development for educators*. Harvard Education Press.

Bryk, A. S., Gomez, L. M., Grunow, A., & LeMahieu, P. G. (2015). *Learning to improve: How America's schools can get better at getting better*. Harvard Education Press.

Coburn, C. E., & Stein, M. K. (2006). Communities of practice theory and the role of teacher professional community in policy implementation. In Honig, M. I. (Ed.), *New directions in education policy implementation: Confronting complexity* (pp. 25–46). State University of New York Press.

Coleman, J. S. (1988). Social capital in the creation of human capital. *American Journal of Sociology, 94,* S95–S120. https://doi.org/10.1086/228943

Daly, A. J., Liou, Y.-H., Del Fresno, M., Rehm, M., & Bjorklund, P., Jr. (2019). Educational leadership in the Twitterverse: Social media, social networks, and the new social continuum. *Teachers College Record, 121*(14), 1–20. https://doi.org/10.1177/016146811912101404

Hargreaves, A. (1994). *Changing teachers, changing times: Teachers' work and culture in the postmodern age.* Teachers College Press.

Hu, S., Torphy, K., Evert, K., & Lane, J. (2020). From cloud to classroom: Mathematics teachers' planning and enactment of resources accessed within virtual spaces. *Teachers College Record, 122*(6), 1–33. https://doi.org/10.1177/016146812012200606

Kilduff, M., & Krackhardt, D. (2008). *Interpersonal networks in organizations: Cognition, personality, dynamics, and culture: Structural analysis in the social sciences.* Cambridge University Press.

King, M. L. Jr. (1963). A letter from Birmingham Jail. *Ebony,* August, 23–32.

Komives, S. R. (1994). Women student leaders: Self-perceptions of empowering leadership and achieving style. *NASPA Journal, 31*(2), 102–12. https://doi.org/10.1080/00220973.1994.11072346

LeMahieu, P. G., Grunow, A., Baker, L., Nordstrum, L. E., & Gomez, L. M. (2017). Networked improvement communities: The discipline of improvement science meets the power of networks. *Quality Assurance in Education, 25*(1), 5–25. https://doi.org/10.1108/QAE-12-2016-0084

Liu, Y., Torphy, K. T., Hu, S., Tang, J., & Chen, Z. (2020). Examining the virtual diffusion of educational resources across teachers' social networks over time. *Teachers College Record, 122*(6), 1–34. https://doi.org/10.1177/016146812012200605

Moeller, E., Seeskin, A., & Nagaoka, J. (2018). *Practice-driven data: Lessons from Chicago's approach to research, data, and practice in education.* UChicago Consortium on School Research.

Moolenaar, N. M., Daly, A. J., Cornelissen, F., Liou, Y.-H., Caillier, S., Riordan, R., Wilson, K., & Cohen, N. A. (2014). Linked to innovation: Shaping an innovative climate through network intentionality and educators' social network position. *Journal of Educational Change, 15*(2), 99–123. https://doi.org/10.1007/s10833-014-9230-4

Peurach, D. J., Russell, J. L., Cohen-Vogel, L., & Penuel, W. R. (Eds.). (2022). *The foundational handbook on improvement research in education.* Rowman & Littlefield.

Reagans, R., & McEvily, B. (2003). Network structure and knowledge transfer: The effects of cohesion and range. *Administrative Science Quarterly, 48*(2), 240–67. https://doi.org/10.2307/3556658

Rothstein, H. R., Schmidt, F. L., Erwin, F. W., Owens, W. A., & Sparks, C. P. (1990). Biographical data in employment selection: Can validities be made generalizable? *Journal of Applied Psychology, 75*(2), 175–84. https://psycnet.apa.org/doi/10.1037/0021-9010.75.2.175

Russell, J. L., Bryk, A. S., Dolle, J., Gomez, L. M., LeMahieu, P., & Grunow, A. (2017). A framework for the initiation of networked improvement communities. *Teachers College Record, 119*(7), 1–36. https://doi.org/10.1177/016146811711900501

Russell, J. L., Bryk, A. S., Peurach, D. J., Sherer, D., LeMahieu, P. G., Khachatryan, E., Sherer, J. Z., & Hannan, M. (2021). *The Social Structure of Networked Improvement Communities: Cultivating the Emergence of a Scientific-Professional Learning Community.* Carnegie Foundation for the Advancement of Teaching. https://www.carnegiefoundation.org/wp-content/uploads/2021/05/The_Social_Structure_of_Networked_Improvement_Communities.pdf

Russell, J. L., & Penuel, W. R. (2022). Introducing improvement research in education. In Peurach, D. J., Russell, J. L., Cohen-Vogel, L., & Penuel, W. R. (Eds.), *The foundational handbook on improvement research in education* (pp. 1–20). Rowman & Littlefield.

Schneider, B., Ehrhart, K. H., & Ehrhart, M. G. (2002). Understanding high school student leaders, II: Peer nominations of leaders and their correlates. *The Leadership Quarterly*, *13*(3), 275–99. https://doi.org/10.1016/S1048-9843(02)00100-5

Schneider, B., Paul, M. C., White, S. S., & Holcombe, K. M. (1999). Understanding high school student leaders, I: Predicting teacher ratings of leader behavior. *The Leadership Quarterly*, *10*(4), 609–36. https://doi.org/10.1016/S1048-9843(99)00038-7

Shaked, H., & Schechter, C. (2020). Systems thinking leadership: New explorations for school improvement. *Management in Education*, *34*(3), 107–14. https://doi.org/10.1177/0892020620907327

Spillane, J. P., & Sun, J. M. (2022). The school principal and the development of social capital in primary schools: The formative years. *School Leadership & Management*, *42*(1), 4–23. https://doi.org/10.1080/13632434.2020.1832981

Umphress, E. E., Labianca, G., Brass, D. J., Kass, E., & Scholten, L. (2003). The role of instrumental and expressive social ties in employees' perceptions of organizational justice. *Organization Science*, *14*(6), 738–53. https://doi.org/10.1287/orsc.14.6.738.24865

Westaby, J. D., & Parr, A. K. (2020). Network goal analysis of social and organizational systems: Testing dynamic network theory in complex social networks. *The Journal of Applied Behavioral Science*, *56*(1), 107–29. https://doi.org/10.1177/0021886319881496

Index

across school lead role (ASL) 173, 181–2
Adler, P. S. 272
agency 195–6, 205
agent awareness 256
Ainscow, M. 153
Armstrong, P. W. 153
Asen, R. 194
attrition rates, teachers 50, 55
authentic learning activity 18–19
awareness information 256

Barber, M. 16
Barni, D. 53
Benson, J. K. 273
Berebitsky, D. 52
Berman, D. 35
betweenness centrality network 43, 213, 216, 218–20
Big Data Hubs 231, 247–8. *See also* Northeast Big Data Innovation Hub (NEBDIH)
Billett, S. 24
Bjorklund, P. 53
Bokhove, C. 59
Borgatti, S. P. 51, 56, 177
Bryant, D. A. 129–30
Buder, J. 256
Burt, R. S. 153, 272

California Math Network (CMN) 210, 216–24
California Professional Standards for Education Leaders (CPSEL) 36
capacity building 10, 128–30
   human and social capital, individuals 287–8
   leadership practices and interactions 134–5
   middle leadership 129, 144
   network intentionality and literacy 288–9

   organizational conditions and designs 290–2
   qualitative analysis 131
   research-practice partnerships 294–6
Caruso, D. R. 29
Caspersen, J. 118, 120
Chan, D. 59
Cho, V. 255
Choy, S. 24
Chrispeels, J. 59
Cochran-Smith, M. 85
Coenders, G. 58
cognitive processes 17, 25
Cohen, D. K. 127
Coleman, J. S. 53, 272
collaborative culture
   organizational 185–6
   school and system leaders 187–8
collegial collaboration 118
Collins, P. H. 273–4
CoL principal (CP) 173
Communities of Learning (CoLs) 5, 172–3. *See also* Pohutukawa CoL
   achievement challenges 173
   collaborative relationships 173
   data analysis 176–7
   ego network 174–5, 182
   leadership roles 173
   leadership team in collaboration network 180–2
   New Zealand education policies 183–4
   Pohutukawa CoL 177–80
   sample and data collection 175–6
   school and system leaders 187–8
   social network theory 174, 176
   social space 182–3
Communities of Learning-Kāhui Ako policy 172, 174–5, 182–4, 187
Community-Based Participatory Research (CBPR) project 276–7
Connor, D. J. 35

content knowledge 36–7
Coromina, L. 58
Critical Network Literacy (CNL) 271–2
  dialectical social infrastructure design 276
  humanizing work 276
  network inquiry 276
  practices at work (-in-progress) 276–7
  social network-based professional development 275–6
Critical Social Network analysis (CSNA) 274
critical theories 273–4
cross-school collaboration. *See* inter-school collaboration
curriculum implementation 5, 115, 117
  process of 120–2
  teachers' participation 119

Daly, A. J. 21–2, 52, 59, 152–4, 257, 275, 283, 294
David, L. G. 39–40
declarative knowledge 27
degree centrality network 177, 213
Demir, E. K. 54
Dhanaraj, C. 230
direct knowledge brokering 213–14, 217–19
disability and inclusive education 35
Downey, C. 59

educational change 16, 281, 284
  leadership and 3–4, 292–6
  organizational change initiatives 293–4
  policy developments 5
educational infrastructure 127. *See also* school-based educational infrastructure
  and capacity building 128–30
  for middle leadership 129–30
  mixed methods research design 131
  professional learning and 128–9
educational leadership xvi–xvii, 3–5, 54
  middle leadership 128–9
  social networks, principalship 253–4
educational policy 115–17
egocentric networks 51, 56–8
ego network (personal network) 174–5

CoL leadership team 181–2
enabling bureaucracies, professional learning 18–19, 23, 290
England
  initial teacher education in 52–3
  local school partnership in 165
  pre-service teachers in 50
  professional learning system in (*see* professional learning networks (PLNs))
English educational system 153
English learners (ELs) 96, 101
equitable learning 27–8, 35
equity and justice 295–6
Ertesvåg, S. K. 118
ESL teachers
  as leaders of professional learning 109–10
  on MLs instructional advice 105–11
ethno-racial external-internal (EI) index 8, 78–80

face-to-face networks 256
Faust, K. 51
Fenwick, T. 18
Fernandez, R. M. 223
Finnigan, K. S. 163
Flores, M. A. 50
Florian, L. 35
formal/informal leadership 6, 10, 29, 121
formal/informal social mechanisms 281–3
friendship interactions 76
friendship networks 42–5, 76, 151, 153, 156, 285
Fukuyama, F. 53
functional leadership 23

Gareis, C. R. 156
González Canché, M. S. 274
Gould, R. V. 223
Granovetter, M. 272
Grimsæth, G. 120

Hamachek, D. 73
Hargreaves, D. 153
Hatlevik, I. K. 117
Hatlevik, O. E. 117
Hegelian concept 272–3

Hermansen, H. 118–20
Holgersen, H. 120
Hooper, D. 60
Hopkins, M. 274
Hoy, A. W. 53, 59
Huang, H. 40
Hub. *See* Northeast Big Data Innovation Hub (NEBDIH)
human capital. *See* social capital
humbleness in leadership 24

Identity Theory 75
"*The Importance of Teaching*" 52
improvement research 294–5
inclusive educational system 34. *See also* relational inclusivity
indegree centrality network 213
indirect knowledge brokering 213–14, 219–20
individual social capital domain 51, 56
individual targeted learning 24–9
informal leadership 6, 10, 29
informal learning 17–18, 255–6
informal online network 256–7
initial teacher education (ITE) 50
　social network of 51–2
　in the UK 52–3
innovation network 230–1, 289–90
International Baccalaureate programs 5
International Encyclopedia of Education (Tierney et al.,) 5
inter-school collaboration 151, 282, 286–7. *See also* professional learning networks (PLNs)
　CoL leaders 180
　communities of learning 172–3
　competition 153–4, 160–3
　and leadership 163–4
　within PLN 152–3
　Pohutukawa CoL 173, 175–6, 177–80
　pre-existing collaboration relationships 232–3, 235–6
　professional practice 153
　school leaders networking and 153–4
　self-efficacy 154
　social interactions 172

Jensen, K. I. 123
Jimerson, J. B. 255

Kenis, P. N. 39
knowledge brokering 211
　data collection and analysis 214–16
　direct and indirect activity 213–14, 217–20
　hierarchical/static position 221–2
　relational foundation of 212–13
　sample data 214
　school districts 214
　social network theory and analysis 212
knowledge creation 22
knowledge mobilization (KMb) 211. *See also* knowledge brokering
knowledge sharing 115, 223
　teacher collaboration and 118–20
Kool, M. 19
Krackhardt, D. 58
Kutnick, P. 28
Kvam, E. K. 119
Kwon, S.-W. 272

latent semantic analysis (LSA) 259
leadership 2, 282–3. *See also* middle leadership; principal leadership; relational leadership
　CoL 180–2
　collaboration networks 150, 163–4
　disruptions 193
　formal/informal 6
　for relational inclusivity (*see* relational inclusivity)
　relational literacy 222–3
　social capital and 152
　in students 281–2
leadership development 129–30, 143–4, 223. *See also* capacity building
Leadership Efficacy Scale 156
leadership for professional learning (LPL) 16–17, 23–4
leadership networks
　actors 196–7
　agency 195–6
　in Bern City Unified School District 197
　data analysis 198
　data collection 197–8
　promotion, leader 198–200
　replacement of leader 200–2
　retention of leader 202–3

social network 194
social processes, study of 196
structures 194–5
learning. See also professional learning networks (PLNs)
dispositions 28–9
district and school designs 18–20
individual targeted learning 24–9
informal 17
network and team designs 21–4
skill 25–6
social process 17–18
strategic ideas, concepts, and theories 27–8
and teaching professional network 157–9
workplace 18
Learning to Teach for Social Justice-Beliefs (LTSJ-B) scale 79
Leithwood, K. 19, 290
Leonard, L. 19
leveraging networks skills 292
Liasidou, A. 35
Lin, N. 152, 272
Liou, Y.-H. 21–2, 53–4, 154
LK20 115. See also curriculum implementation

Mamas, C. 40
Mandzuk, D. 54
marginalization 37–8, 40, 46, 274, 295
Matrix of Domination framework 274
Mayer, J. D. 29
McAdam, D. 76
McGuire, J. B. 273
McPherson, M. 257
Meyer, M. 222
middle leadership 127–9, 291
cascade model 144
educational infrastructure for 129–30, 282
Midwestern schools multilingual learners 97–111
mixed methods research 8–9, 99, 121, 293
educational infrastructure 131
principal leadership 145–6
social justice teacher identity 77, 89–91
teacher collaboration 121–2
Moolenaar, N. M. 154, 274

Morud, E. B. 118–19
Muijs, D. 153, 164
multilingual learners (MLs) 96
district schools sample 99–101
English language development (ELD) instruction 101
ESL teachers 105–7
interviews, teacher 103–4
professional learning and 96–7
social network and teacher interactions 97–9
surveys, teacher 101–3
teachers' interactions and 104–9
teacher trust in 111–12
multiplex network 78, 284
multi-school networks 172, 187

network-based leadership 3–7, 21–4
network capacity for systems change
human and social capital of individuals 287–8
individuals' capacities for change 289–90
network intentionality and literacy 288–9
organizational conditions and designs 290–1
network churn 214
network inquiry 275–7, 292
network literacy/intentionality skills 4, 12, 291–2, 295. See also Critical Network Literacy (CNL)
network modeling, professional learning 103
network research 51, 56
density of network 52
direct/indirect interactions 210
education research 209–10
social capital 53–4
teacher networks 52
network theory 51. See also social network theory
New Zealand, Communities of Learning 172–3
Community of Learning-Kāhui Ako policy 182–3
educational policies 174, 182–4
Northeast Big Data Innovation Hub (NEBDIH) 231–2, 242–3
advice relationship 238, 240

collaboration 233, 237
core group of actors 243–4
go-to organization 233, 237–9
individual sectors in system 243–4
inter-organizational relationships 232–3
leadership and policies 242
network structure 235
pre-existing collaboration relationships 232–3, 235–6
social network data of 248–9
strategic planning 233, 240
survey methods and results 232–5
Norwegian Directorate for Education and Training 122
Norwegian schools
common/team time 117, 120, 286, 291
curriculum implementation 120
formal structure in 117
SNA perspective 120–3
teacher collaboration 115–17
teaching practices 118–120
null (unconditional) models, teachers' observation scores 59–61

observation scores of teachers performance 57, 60–6
Oerlemans, L. A. G. 39
Ofem, B. 51, 56
Office for Standards in Education (Ofsted) 167 n.1
offline/online networks 257–64
organizational behaviors 4, 255
organizational design
district and school designs 18–20
individual targeted learning 24–9
leadership for professional learning 23–4
learning 17–18
network and team designs 21–4
network capacity and 290–2
organizational improvement 3–4, 18
organizational learning 18–19, 116
outdegree centrality network 213
overall CoL leadership 173

Parkhe, A. 230
Paulsen, R. 76
Pohutukawa CoL 173, 175–6

collaboration within and across schools in 177–80, 182–3
educational research 188
formal roles and responsibilities 184
study designs 186–7
pre-service teachers (PSTs) 73
data collection and analysis 57–61
demographic predictors 63–6
initial teacher education 50
latent growth curve analyses 62–6
networks of 51–3
observation scores 57, 60–6
performance and development of 54–5
research design 55–6
sampling and participants in research 56–7
self-efficacy of 53, 57–8, 60–6
social capital of 54
social justice teacher identity 74–6
teacher education programs 73
principal component analysis (PCA) 156
principal leadership
boundary crossing 254–5
implications 259
offline/online data collection 258–64
research methods 257–8
semantic analyses and web-scraping 259
social media and resources 256–7
social networks in 253–6, 258–9
social processes of 254–5
professional growth 20, 54–5
professional learning communities (PLCs). *See* professional learning networks (PLNs)
professional learning/development 128
in districts and schools 18–20
dyadic-level measures 102–3
and educational infrastructure 127–9
ESL teachers as leaders of 109–10
individual-level measures 102
multilingual learners and 96
network modeling 103
social emotional dispositions 29
teacher collaboration and 118–19
professional learning networks (PLNs) 150–1, 209
case study designs 154–6
collaboration, forms of 150, 152–3
competition 153–4, 156, 160–1

learning and teaching 157–9
self-efficacy 154, 156, 160–1
social capital and 152
social networks of 151
use of data 157–61
professional practice 153
propositional knowledge 27
Putnam, R. D. 272

quadratic assignment procedure (QAP) 216
qualified teacher status (QTS) 50, 52
Qureshi, A. 54

Raaen, F. D. 118, 120
Reimers, F. M. 253
relational inclusivity 35–6
  as equity 38–9
  plurality experiences, students 37–8
  schooling 36–7
  and SNA Toolkit 44–6
  social network of 39–40
relational leadership 5–7, 39–40, 224. *See also* social networks
  and educational change (*see* educational change)
  network literacy/intentionality skills 291–2
  organizational change initiatives 293–4
  reflection, refinement, and renewal capacity 292
  research-practice partnerships 294–6
relationships
  actors 76
  and collaboration 173–4, 182–6
  and educational change 3–4
  interpersonal 22, 40
  leaders and teachers 131–3
  multiplex network and 78
  peers and social justice identities 84–6
  in social interactions 6, 194–7
  tie strength and 76
research-practice partnerships 294–6
Rios-Aguilar, C. 274
Rogoff, B. 17–18
Rokkones, K. L. 118–19
Roland, E. 118
Rudat, A. 256
Rumyantseva, N. 153

Salloum, S. J. 52
Salovey, P. 29
Schleicher, A. 253
Schmitt, N. 59
school-based educational infrastructure 127–30
  cascade model of 136–7
  Head of School and school governors 137–8
  holistic model 143
  K-12 international school 130–1
  layered infrastructure 144–5
  leaders and coordinators 138–40
  leadership practices and interactions 134–5
  middle leadership 127–30, 282
  mixed methods research 131
  principal-led structures 145–6
  program coordinators and teachers 141
  qualitative data 131
  senior leaders and teachers 142
  social network data and analysis 131–6
  subject area coordinators 140–2
school direct (SD) routes of teaching 52–3
school districts 210, 214. *See also* California Math Network (CMN)
self-efficacy 53, 57–8, 60–6, 154, 156
  collegial collaboration and 118
  cross-school collaboration 153–4, 164–5
self-improving school system 153–4
self-regulated learning 25
semantic analyses, principal leadership 259
senior leadership 127
Sharratt, L. 19
Shirrell, M. 129
Sinnema, C. 150, 153, 163–4
Skaalvik, E. M. 53
Skaalvik, S. 53
skill learning 25–6
social and emotional learning (SEL) 37
social capital 53–4
  Hegelian concept 272–3
  human and 287–8
  innovation of social network 272
  professional learning networks 152
  social power dynamics and 274

social continuum 257
social infrastructure 285–7
social justice 73–4
social justice teacher identity 74–6
  boundaries to 86–7
  ethno-racial external-internal index 79–85
  mixed-methods design 77, 89–91
  OLS regression on 82–3
  program influence on 87–9
  quantitative/qualitative data survey 77–86
  value consonance scale 79
social media 256–7
social network analysis (SNA) 40–4
  domains 51
  innovation networks 231
  middle leadership and teachers 130–6
  principal leadership 258–9
  structure of networks 52
  on teacher collaboration 115
social networks 3–4, 194
  capacity 290–2
  Communities of Learning 174, 176, 183
  concepts and innovations 272–3
  domains of power 273–4
  formal and informal structures 281–3
  individuals' network intentionality 274–5
  initiation team 289–90
  instrumental/expressive ties 283–4
  knowledge brokerage 212
  leadership through 5, 6, 253–4
  literacy 4, 288–9
  principalship 253–4, 255–6
  structure and agency 194–6
  and teacher interactions 97–9
social opportunity spaces 256
social process, learning 17
social emotional dispositions 28–9
Special Educational Needs and Disabilities (SEND) 34
  equity education 38–9
  inclusive education for 35–7
  plurality experiences 37–8
  SNA Toolkit 42–3
Spillane, J. P. 98
Stern, R. 58

Stoll, L. 19
system leadership 10, 150–66
systems change 2, 3. *See also* capacity building
  formal and informal structures 281–3
  network approach to 5, 248–9
  network capacity for 287–92
  social connections 283–4
  social infrastructure 285–7
systems thinking 184–5, 245, 290
system-wide disruptions on leadership 193. *See also* leadership networks
  agency 195–6
  social network 194
  structures 194–5

task reflexivity, organization 24
teacher collaboration 4, 9, 54, 115
  common time 117
  formal and informal 121
  and knowledge sharing 115, 118–20
  mixed methods approach 121–2
  Norwegian schools 115–17
  professionalism 120
  social network analysis on 115
  structure of school 117
  and supportive activities 118–20
  and teacher social capital 118
teacher education 19–20. *See also* initial teacher education (ITE)
teacher education programs (TEPs) 73
  social justice in 74–5
teacher identity. *See also* social justice teacher identity
  development of 50
  formation 74
  preservice teachers' (PSTs') 73
teacher networks 52
  individual factors 98
  organizational factors 98–9
  and social relationships 97
teacher professional development 119, 271
Teacher Recruitment and Retention Strategy 50
teacher self-efficacy 53. *See also* self-efficacy

teacher trust
  on growing ML population 110–11
  on ML-related advice and information 107–9
Teaching and Learning International Survey (TALIS) 117
teaching performance 54–5. *See also* observation scores of teachers performance
teams, encouraging learning 21–3, 117, 120–3
technical assistance 20
theory of networks 51
tie strength and relationships 76
Tschannen-Moran, M. 53, 59, 156
Twitter 12, 256–64

United States. *See also* multilingual learners (MLs)
  California Math Network in 96–7
  multilingual learners in 96–7
  teachers' network formation 98
university led (UL) routes of teaching 52–3

Van Waes, S. 274–5
Varga-Atkins, T. 153

Wasserman, S. 51
web-scraping, principal leadership 259
Wenger, E. 211
White Paper and the Blueprint for a Self-Improving School 153
within-school lead role (WSL) 173, 181–2
workplace learning 18. *See also* organizational design
  collaborative culture 185–6

Yosso, T. J. 274

Zeichner, K. M. 73, 86

www.ingramcontent.com/pod-product-compliance
Lightning Source LLC
Chambersburg PA
CBHW071802300426
44116CB00009B/1172